A Brief
Explanation of
The Summary of
^Abdull*a*h Al-Harariyy

The Association of Islamic Charitable Projects
Islamic Studies and Research Division

The Association of
Islamic Charitable Projects
Islamic Studies and Research Division
4431 Walnut Street, Philadelphia, PA 19104
USA
www.aicp.org

Fourth Edition

1436 H / 2015
Philadelphia, PA USA

DARUL-MASHARI^ CO

for Printing, Publishing and Distribution

Beirut - Lebanon

Address: Mazraa, Barbour, Ibn Khaldoun
Street, Ikhlas Bldg.
Tel. & Fax: 011 961 1 304 311
P.O.Box: 14-5283 Beirut - Lebanon

ISBN 978-9953-20-040-8

email: dar.nashr@gmail.com
www.dmcpublisher.com

CONTENTS

THE ESSENTIALS OF BELIEF
AND RULES OF APOSTASY

PURIFICATION AND PRAYERS
(*TAHARAH* AND *SALAH*)

ZAKAH

3

FASTING (*SIYAM*)

PILGRIMAGE (*HAJJ*)

TRANSACTIONS, MARRIAGE, AND DEALING CONTRACTS

OBLIGATIONS AND SINS

FOREWORD

Praise be to *Allah*, the Lord of the Worlds, to Him belong the endowments and proper commendations. May *Allah* increase the honor of Prophet *Muhammad, sallallahu ^alayhi wa sallam*, raise his rank, and protect his nation from what he fears for it. Thereafter;

Allah, the Exalted, praised the status of knowledge in *Surat al-Mujadalah, Ayah 11*:

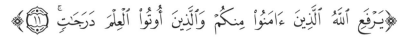

It means: [*Allah* raises the ranks of those amongst you who believed and acquired the knowledge.]

Moreover, *Allah* revealed to Prophet *Muhammad* ﷺ , *sallallahu ^alayhi wa sallam*, to praise the status of knowledge, its teachers and its students. *Ibn Majah* related that the Prophet ﷺ said: «O *Abu Dharr*, if you go and learn one verse of the *Qur'an* it will be more rewardable for you than praying one hundred *rak^ahs* of the optional prayers; and if you go and learn a chapter of knowledge, it is more rewardable for you than praying one thousand *rak^ahs* of the optional prayers.» *Al-Bukhariyy* related that the Prophet ﷺ , *sallallahu ^alayhi wa sallam*, said: «When the [Muslim] offspring of *Adam* dies, [the rewards of] his deeds stop except for three: a charity resulting in a continuing benefit, knowledge benefitting others, and a pious offspring making supplication to *Allah* for him.»

In an effort to comply with these precious principles of *Islam*, the Islamic Studies and Research Division of the Association of Islamic Charitable Projects endeavored to prepare this work. May *Allah* make it of a widespread benefit.

We humbly ask *Allah, ta^ala*, to grant us the sincere intentions, endow His mercy on us, assemble us under the banner of Prophet *Muhammad* ﷺ , *sallallahu ^alayhi wa sallam*, and make us among the winners on the Day of Judgement.

PREFACE

The Summary of ^Abdullah al-Harariyy
Ensuring the Personal Obligatory Knowledge of the Religion

As the title of the book indicates, **The Summary of ^Abdullah al-Harariyy Ensuring the Personal Obligatory Knowledge of the Religion** was authored to provide the student with the Obligatory Knowledge of the Religion--that portion of the Knowledge of the Religion which every accountable person is obligated to learn. The one who is ignorant of the Obligatory Knowledge of the Religion cannot be certain of performing any of the acts of worship--like prayers, purification, Hajj, or Zakah--in a valid manner. Moreover, one cannot be sure one is clear of committing any of the sins, e.g., the sins of the heart, hands, tongue, ear, eye, body, private parts, abdomen, foot, etc.

If one wants to truly follow the Prophet ﷺ, one has to first learn the Obligatory Knowledge of the Religion then implement it. In what pertains to the Obligatory Knowledge of the Religion, the **Summary of ^Abdullah al-Harariyy** is the most inclusive summary we have seen. The author is Shaykh ^Abdullah, the son of Muhammad, ash-Shaybiyy[1]. He was born in the city of Harar, the capital of knowledge in Ethiopia (Abyssinia or al-Habashah). He sought the Religious knowledge from many shaykhs, among whom are: Shaykh Muhammad Ibn ^Abdis-Salam, who was a very pious Shafi^iyy scholar, Shaykh Muhammad Siraj al-Jabartiyy, who was the mufti of Habashah, and Shaykh Ahmad Ibn ^Abdil Muttalib, who was the Shaykh of the Reciters of the Qur'an in Makkah.

These days, it is rare to find someone who has mastered as many different types of knowledge as Shaykh ^Abdullah has mastered. Shaykh ^Abdullah mastered the Science of Tawhid, the Science of Fiqh (Islamic Jurisprudence), the Science of Hadith, the Science of the Arabic Language and Grammar, the Science of the different Recitations of the Qur'an, the Science of the Interpretation of the

---

[1] The surname ash-Shaybiyy refers to that Shaykh ^Abdullah is from the tribe of Shaybah, a branch of Quraysh.

Qur'an, the Sciences of Calculation and Astronomy, the Science of the Fundamentals of *Fiqh*, and others. He did not only acquire many types of knowledge, but he also implemented them, and he taught them as well. He advised the people according to the laws of the Religion, ordering what is lawful and forbidding what is unlawful, while being sincerely kind and merciful to them. He was very humble in the matters of this life and detached from the worldly matters. He exerted a great deal of time, effort, and money in propagating the Religion of *Allah*.

It is our intention to explain the terms of his book without going into much detail, because the one who seeks to acquire the knowledge of the Religion should not rush to just gather a lot of information. Rather, one needs to go as slowly as is necessary for oneself to be careful and cautious in absorbing and comprehending the material. *Az-Zuhriyy*, one of the scholars among the followers of the Companions (*Tabi^un*) said:

$$ (مَنْ طَلَبَ الحَدِيثَ جُمْلَةً فَاتَهُ جُمْلَةً) $$

It means: "The one who seeks the entire knowledge of the *Hadith* all at once misses that knowledge in its entirety." By his statement, he meant that one should acquire this knowledge in steps--in a way to be sure that one absorbs and comprehends it. It is the habit of the scholars to first explain a subject or a book by defining its terms, without giving much detail or mentioning many of the exceptions, and sometimes without mentioning all the restrictions involved regarding some matters. This is to enable the student to absorb the core of the material and to understand it. The next time they explain, they may give a more in-depth explanation if they see the student has thoroughly comprehended the material, and so on. In this context, *Imam al-Bukhariyy* said that some scholars explained the term, "*rabbaniyyin*"[2] mentioned in the *Qur'an* (*Al ^Imran, 79* كُونُوا رِبّانيّين) to mean those who raise (teach) the people at first with the simple matters of the Religion, then later in more depth.

---

[2] In general *rabbaniyy* means العالم العامل i.e., a scholar who implements his knowledge.

Seeking the Knowledge of the Religion entails a great reward. At-Tirmidhiyy related that the Prophet ﷺ said:

«مَنْ خَرَجَ فِى طَلَبِ العِلْمِ فَهُوَ فِى سَبِيلِ اللَّهِ حَتَّى يَرْجِعَ»

It means: «The reward of the one who goes out seeking the Knowledge is similar to the reward of the one who fights for the sake of Allah, and this is until one returns to one's home.» Hence, the reward of the one who goes out seeking the Knowledge of the Religion is similar to the reward of the mujahid[3] for the sake of Allah. Among the different levels in Paradise, there are one hundred (100) levels specified for those who fight for the sake of Allah. Between one of these ranks and the next is a distance like the distance between the Earth and the sky. This is why Imam ash-Shafi^iyy said:

(طَلَبُ العِلْمِ أَفْضَلُ مِنْ صَلَاةِ النَّافِلَةِ)

It means: "Seeking the Knowledge of the Religion is more rewardable than performing the optional prayer."

This is also why our Shaykh ^Abdullah al-Harariyy said:

(تَعْلِيمُ النَّاسِ العِلْمَ أَفْضَلُ من تَوزِيعِ المَالِ عليهم)

It means: "Spreading the Religious Knowledge among the people is better or more important than distributing money among them." With the Knowledge of the Religion, one fights the devils among the humans and the jinn, and one can fight one's own evil inclinations. We ask Allah to facilitate for us this precious benefit.

Amin.

ءامين

---

[3] The mujahid is the one who fights for the sake of Allah.

A BRIEF BIOGRAPHY OF
SHAYKH ^ABDULLAH AL-HARARIYY
(1328 - 1429 H)

He is the great, veracious Islamic scholar of Jurisprudence (*Fiqh*), Prophetic Tradition (*Hadith*), Arabic Language, and the Fundamentals of the Religion (*Usul*), and the pious worshipper, *Shaykh Abu ^Abdir-Rahman, ^Abdullah Ibn Muhammad Ibn Yusuf Ibn ^Abdillah Ibn Jami^ al-Harariyy* by place of birth, *ash-Shaybiyy al-^Abdariyy* by lineage, *ash-Shafi^iyy* by *madh-hab*, the *Mufti* of Harar.

He was born in Harar around 1328 H/1910. He grew up in a humble house loving Islamic knowledge and its people. He memorized the *Qur'an* by heart before the age of ten. He memorized numerous books in various Islamic sciences. Then, he gave the Science of *Hadith* a great amount of attention. He memorized the six books of *Hadith* (*al-Bukhariyy, Muslim, at-Tirmidhiyy, Abu Dawud, Ibn Majah, an-Nasa'iyy*) and other books of *Hadith* with their *isnad* (names and biographies of the chains of relators). He was authorized by Islamic scholars to pass edicts (*fatwa*) and to relate *Hadith* when he was less than eighteen years old.

He went to many places in Ethiopia, Somalia, and Djibouti seeking knowledge and its people. He also lived in *Hijaz* (Saudi Arabia) for two years, then in Damascus for 10 years. Then he settled in Beirut. He visited Jerusalem (before occupation), Jordan, Egypt, Turkey, Morocco, and many European countries spreading Islamic knowledge benefitting others and defending the Religion.

His primary goal was to spread the correct belief of *Ahl-us-Sunnah wal-Jama^ah*, a task which occupied most of his time. He fought the atheists and the people of prohibited innovations to extinguish their misguidances. This did not leave much time for writing books. He left quite a few writings, however. Among them are:

1. An explanation of *Alfiyyat-us-Suyutiyy* in the Science of *Hadith*.

2. A poem in *at-Tawhid* (Islamic Belief) of about sixty lines.

3. *As-Sirat-ul-Mustaqim* in *Tawhid*.

4. *Ad-Dalil-ul-Qawim ^alas-Sirat-il-Mustaqim* in *Tawhid*.

5. *Ash-Sharh-ul-Qawim fi Halli Alfadhis-Sirat-il-Mustaqim* in *Tawhid*.

6. *Mukhtasaru ^Abdillah-il-Harariyy, al-Kafilu bi ^Ilm-id-Din-id-Daruriyy*.

7. *Bughyat-ut-Talib lima^rifat-il-^Ilm-id-Diniyy-il-Wajib*.

8. *At-Ta^aqqub-ul-Hathith ^ala man ta^ana fima sahha min-al-Hadith*.

9. *Nusrat-ut-Ta^aqqub-il-Hathith ^ala man ta^ana fima sahha min-al-Hadith*.

10. *Al-Matalibul-Wafiyyah*, explanation of *al-^Aqidat-un-Nasafiyyah*.

11. *Idhharul-^Aqidatis-Sunniyyah*, explanation of *al-^Aqidatut-Tahawiyyah*.

12. *Sharhu Alfiyyat-iz-Zubad* in the *Shafi^iyy Fiqh*.

13. *Sharhu Matni Abi Shuja^* in the *Shafi^iyy Fiqh*.

14. *Sharhu Matn-il-^Ashmawiyyah* in the *Malikiyy Fiqh*.

15. *Sharhu Mutammimat-il-'Ajurrumiyyah* in *an-Nahw*.

16. *Sharh-ul-Bayquniyyah* in the Science of *al-Hadith*.

17. *Sarih-ul-Bayan fir-raddi ^ala man Khalaf-al-Qur'an*.

18. *Al-Maqalatus-Sunniyyah fi Kashfi Dalalat Ibn Taymiyyah*.

19. *Ar-Rawa'ihuz-Zakiyyah fi Mawlidi Khayril-Bariyyah*.

20. *Al-^Aqidatul-Munjiyah*.

He took *Fiqh*, *Tawhid*, and *Nahw* (Arabic Grammar) from the righteous *Shaykh Muhammad ^Abdus-Salam al-Harariyy, Shaykh Muhammad ^Umar Jami^ al-Harariyy, Shaykh Muhammad Rashad al-Habashiyy, Shaykh Ibrahim Abil-Ghayth al-Harariyy, Shaykh Yunus al-Habashiyy*, and *Shaykh Muhammad Siraj al-Jabartiyy*. From those Islamic scholars he took many main texts, such as *Alfiyyat-uz-Zubad, at-Tanbih, al-Minhaj, Alfiyyat-ubni-Malik, al-Luma^* by *ash-Shiraziyy*, and other main texts.

He took the sciences of *Hadith* from many teachers, notably from *Hafidh Shaykh Abu Bakr Muhammad Siraj al-Jabartiyy*, the *Mufti* of *al-Habashah*, and *Shaykh ^Abdur-Rahman ^Abdullah al-Habashiyy*, and others.

10

He met with the righteous *Shaykh, Muḥaddith, Qari'* (Reciter of the *Qur'an*), *Aḥmad Ibn ^Abdil-Muṭṭalib*, the Head of the *Qari's* in *al-Masjid-ul-Ḥaram* in *Makkah* (he was appointed as the *Imam* and *Shaykh* of *al-Masjid-ul-Ḥaram* by *as-Sultan ^Abdul-Ḥamid* II, the last Muslim, Ottoman *Khalifah*). From this *Shaykh* he took the 14 ways of reciting *al-Qur'an*, as well as Science of *Ḥadith*. He also met *Shaykh, Qari', Dawud al-Jabartiyy*.

He went to *Makkah* and met its Islamic scholars, such as *Shaykh as-Sayyid ^Alawiyy al-Malikiyy* and *Shaykh Amin al-Kutubiyy*. He attended circles by *Shaykh Muḥammad al-^Arabiyy at-Tabban*. He contacted *Shaykh ^Abdul-Ghafur an-Naqshabandiyy* and took *at-Tariqah an-Naqshabandiyyah* from him.

Afterwards, he went to *Madinah* and contacted its Islamic scholars. He took *Ḥadith* from *Shaykh Muḥammad Ibn Muḥammad as-Siddiqiyy al-Bakriyy*. He stayed by and in *^Arif Ḥikmat* and *al-Maḥmudiyyah* libraries going through the manuscripts. He stayed in *Madinah* close to the Prophet's Mosque for about a year. He received permission to teach from many Islamic scholars.

He then went to Jerusalem around 1370 H/1950 and then to Damascus where its people welcomed him, especially after the death of its *Muḥaddith Badr-ud-Din al-Ḥasaniyy*. He went to Beirut, *Ḥims, Hamah, Ḥalab*, and other cities. He then lived in *Jami^-ul-Qatat*, and his fame spread in the area. Consequently, the scholars and students of the *Sham* (area including Lebanon, Syria, Palestine, and Jordan) came seeking him, and he got to know some of its scholars. They benefited from him and acknowledged his knowledge; he was called "the Successor of *Shaykh Badr-ud-Din al-Ḥasaniyy*". He was also known as "the *Muḥaddith* of the *Sham* countries". A great number of the Islamic scholars of *Sham* praised him, such as *Shaykh ^Izz-ud-Din al-Khaznawiyy, ash-Shafi^iyy, an-Naqshabandiyy* from *al-Jazirah* in the north of Syria, *Shaykh ^Abdur-Razzaq al-Ḥalabiyy*, the Director of *al-Masjidul-'Umawiyy* in Damascus, *Shaykh Abu Sulayman az-Zabibiyy, Shaykh Mulla Ramaḍan al-Butiyy, Shaykh Abul-Yusr ^Abidin*, the *Mufti* of Syria, *Shaykh ^Abdul-Karim ar-Rifa^iyy, Shaykh Naji Nur* from Jordan, *Shaykh Sa^id Ṭanatirah, Shaykh Aḥmad al-Ḥuṣariyy*, the Director of the Islamic school of *Ma^arratun-Nu^man, Shaykh ^Abdullah Siraj al-Ḥalabiyy, Shaykh Muḥammad Murad al-Ḥalabiyy, Shaykh Suhayb ar-*

Rumiyy, the Amin of Awqaf in Halab, Shaykh ^Abdul-^Aziz ^Uyunus-Sud, the Head of the Qari's of Hims, Shaykh Abus-Su^ud al-Himsiyy, Shaykh Fayiz ad-Dayr^ataniyy, the Shaykh of Damascus who knows the Seven Qira'at (ways of recitations of Qur'an), Shaykh ^Abdul-Wahhab Dibs wa Zayt of Damascus, Dr. Halawaniyy, the Shaykh of reciters in Syria, Shaykh Ahmad al-Harun of Damascus, the righteous waliyy, Shaykh Tahir al-Kayyaliyy from Hims, and others, may Allah benefit us from them.

He was also praised by Shaykh ^Uthman Siraj-ud-Din, the descendant of Shaykh ^Ala'-ud-Din, the Shaykh of an-Naqshabandiyyah in his time and they had brotherly and scholarly correspondences between them. He was praised also by Shaykh ^Abdul-Karim al-Bayyariyy, the teacher in Jami^-il-Hadrah al-Kilaniyyah in Baghdad, Shaykh Ahmad az-Zahid al-'Islambuliyy, Shaykh Mahmud al-Hanafiyy, who is one of the famous and active Turkish shaykhs, Shaykh ^Abdullah al-Ghumariyy, the Muhaddith of the Morrocan area, Shaykh Habibur-Rahman al-'A^dhamiyy, the Muhaddith of the Indian Peninsula, whom he met with many times and stayed as his guest for some time.

He took permission for at-Tariqah ar-Rifa^iyyah from Shaykh ^Abdur-Rahman as-Sibsibiyy, and Shaykh Tahir al-Kayyaliyy, and permission in at-Tariqah al-Qadiriyyah from Shaykh Ahmad al-^Irbiniyy, may Allah have mercy upon them.

He came to Beirut around 1370 H/1950, where he was the guest of the famous shaykhs, like Shaykh, Qadi Muhyid-Din al-^Ajuz and Shaykh, Mustashar Muhammad ash-Sharif and Shaykh ^Abdul-Wahhab al-Butariyy, the imam of al-Basta al-Fawqa Mosque, Shaykh Ahmad Iskandaraniyy, the Imam and Mu'adhdhin in Burj Abi Haydar Mosque and they learned and benefited from him. Then he met with Shaykh Tawfiq al-Hibriyy, may Allah have mercy on him. At his residence, he used to meet the important people in Beirut. He also met with Shaykh ^Abdur-Rahman al-Majdhub and Shaykh Muhammad al-Butariyy, the Qadi of Beirut, and they benefited from him. He met with Shaykh Mukhtar al-^Alayiliyy, may Allah have mercy upon him, the Amin of Fatwa who acknowledged his honor and breadth of his knowledge. He also prepared for his residence in Beirut to teach in different mosques. The Department of Fatwa paid the expenses of his residence during that period. In 1969, upon the request of the Director of al-'Azhar in Lebanon, he lectured in the subject of Tawhid to the students there.

Shaykh ^Abdullah al-Harariyy, may Allah have His wide mercy on him, was a very pious, humble, and worshipful Muslim. He did not care about acquiring worldly things. He had a good and pure heart. He spent his time teaching Islamic knowledge and performing dhikr (mentioning sentences glorifying Allah) at the same time. He did not waste a moment without teaching, performing dhikr, reciting, admonishing, or guiding. He was holding on to the Qur'an and Sunnah. He had a good memory and powerful and brilliant proofs. He was very critical of those who deviated from the Religion. He was wise, managing things at the right time and place. He had a high effort in bidding obedience and forbidding disobedience.

Shaykh ^Abdullah al-Harariyy died at the dawn of Tuesday on Ramadan 2, 1429 H/ September 2, 2008. May Allah have His wide mercy on him, and may He reward him greatly.

Bismillah-ir-Rahman-ir-Rahim

Explanation: *Bismillah-ir-Rahman-ir-Rahim* means 'I start with the Name of *Allah*.' *Allah* is the name of the One Whom we worship, the One attributed with Godhood, which is the power to create things (to bring things from the state of non-existence into the state of existence). *Ar-Rahman* means the One Who is merciful to the believers and the non-believers in this life, and merciful to only the believers in the Hereafter. *Ar-Rahim* means the One Who is merciful to only the believers in the Hereafter.

Introduction

Praise be to *Allah* (al-hamdu lillah), the Lord of the universe,

Explanation: The author started by praising *Allah*, thereby implementing the *hadith* of the Prophet ﷺ related by *Abu Dawud*:

$$\text{«كُلُّ أَمْرٍ ذِى بَالٍ لَا يُبْدَأُ بِحَمْدِ الله فَهُوَ أَقْطَعُ»}$$

It means: ‹‹Every religiously important matter which is not started with praising *Allah* falls short.›› The meaning of الحمد لله entails praising *Allah* for the uncountable endowments He endowed upon us.

the One Who is attributed with Life (al-Hayy),

Explanation: *Allah* is attributed with an eternal and everlasting Life which does not resemble our life. *Allah's* Life is not the combination of soul, bones, and flesh.

the One Who does not need anything (al-Qayyum),

Explanation: *Al-Qayyum* is a name of *Allah* and means the One Who does not need anything, yet everything else needs Him. The scholars also said that *al-Qayyum* means the One Whose Existence does not end.

and the One Who decreed all what happens in the universe.

Explanation: *Allah* is the One Who decreed the events of this universe. Things happen the way He willed for them to happen. The (all-inclusive) management of all the creations is an attribute of *Allah* only. *Allah* is the One Who makes everything the way it is. Some creations may have a certain management over things. However, it is a management which is commensurate with them. In *Surat an-Nazi^at, Ayah 5 Allah* said:

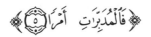

In this *ayah, Allah* attributed a proportional management to the angels. The management of *Allah* includes everything, whereas the management of the angels is restricted to what *Allah* has willed for them to manage, and it is not similar to the management of *Allah*.

The complete and perfect _salah_ and _salam_ are due to our master Muhammad, his _Al_, and his Companions.

Explanation: Invoking the _salah_ and _salam_ here means: We ask *Allah* to raise the rank of Prophet *Muhammad* and to protect his nation, his family, and his Companions from whatever harm Prophet *Muhammad* ﷺ feared for them.

This book is a summary, inclusive of most of the Obligatory Knowledge which every accountable person is obligated to know. This comprises the Obligatory Knowledge pertaining to Belief, issues from Purification (_Taharah_) up to Pilgrimage (_Hajj_), and some rules of dealings according to the school (_madhhab_) of Imam ash-Shafi^iyy. The sins of the heart and of other organs, such as the tongue, are also included.

Explanation: Every accountable person is obligated to know the aforementioned (obligatory) matters. Covered in this summary is the Obligatory Knowledge pertaining to Belief, Purification and Prayer, Zakah, Fasting, and Pilgrimage. The sins of the heart and of other parts of the body and the issue of repentance and its conditions are mentioned as well. The one who is not obligated to pay Zakah is not obligated to learn the details of paying Zakah. The same ruling applies to learning the details of Pilgrimage for the one who is neither able nor planning to perform it, and to learning the details of dealings which one is neither engaged in nor is obligated to perform.

The one who absorbs and understands the cases presented in this book eventually becomes among the People of Discrimination. One will be able to discriminate between what is good and what is bad, and between what is valid and what is invalid. What a great blessing this is!

The original book was written by the _Hadramiyy_[4] _faqih_ (scholar): ˆAbdull_ah_ Ibn _H_usayn Ibn _T_ahir.

Explanation: This book, The Summary of ˆAbdull_ah_ al-Harariyy, is a summary of another book, titled *Sullamut-Tawfiq,* written by the _Hadramiyy_ scholar, ˆAbdull_ah_ Ibn _H_usayn Ibn _T_ahir al-ˆAlawiyy. ˆAbdull_ah_ Ibn _H_usayn Ibn _T_ahir was born in 1191 AH. He acquired his knowledge from many well-known scholars. He spent some time in *Makkah* and in *al-Madinah.* He died in the year 1272 AH in Yemen.

Shaykh ˆAbdull_ah_ al-Harariyy eliminated certain parts of *Sullamut-Tawfiq* and added others. He changed still other parts--and the end result was this book, The Summary of ˆAbdull_ah_ al-Harariyy.

Many precious issues were added to the book. On the other hand, the section on Sufism[5] was omitted. Some sentences were changed in such a way that the subject would not be changed. In a few cases the author mentioned what some _Shafiˆiyy_ scholars, like al-Bul_q_iniyy, preponderated in an effort to clarify what was weak in the original book.

Explanation: This is the methodology of summarizing known to the scholars. The scholar who is summarizing another's work might change some areas, add some topics, or omit other ones. In keeping with this methodology, *Shaykh* ˆAbdull_ah_ al-Harariyy eliminated the chapters in the original book about Sufism. This by no means reflects disparaging true Sufism. Rather, it is because the basic subject of the *Summary* is to deal with the Personal Obligatory Knowledge of the Religion. The author also replaced some of the sayings that have less weight by sayings to which the scholars, like al-Bul_q_iniyy, have given more weight.

---

[4] _Hadramiyy_ refers to that this scholar is from the land of _Hadramawt_ in Yemen.

[5] Sufism is a term describing the state of the pious Muslims who perform obedience to *Allah* in compliance with the _Qur'an, Hadith,_ Ijmaˆ, and sayings of the Companions while their hearts are detached from worldly interests.

16

Al-Bulqiniyy mentioned here is *Sirajud-Din ^Umar al-Bulqiniyy* and is not either of his two sons. *Al-Bulqiniyy* attained a very high rank in many sciences such as the *Fiqh*, the *Hadith*, the interpretation of the Qur'an (*Tafsir*), and many other sciences as well. It was mentioned that he attained the rank of *mujtahid*. He lived in Egypt and died there in the year 805 AH.

Hence, one must pay due attention to this Obligatory Knowledge in order to have one's deeds accepted. The author named it:

The Summary of ^Abdullah al-Harariyy, Ensuring the Personal Obligatory Knowledge of the Religion.[6]

Explanation: There is a certain portion of the Knowledge of the Religion that every accountable person must learn. The Prophet, *sallallahu ^alayhi wa sallam*, said:

$$\text{«طَلَبُ العِلْمِ فَرِيضَةٌ عَلَى كُلّ مُسلمٍ»}$$

In this *hadith* related by *al-Bayhaqiyy*, the Prophet ﷺ told us: «Seeking the Obligatory Knowledge of the Religion is an obligation upon every Muslim.» Seeking this knowledge is an obligation on every accountable Muslim, whether male or female. This *hadith* was classified as *hasan* by *Hafidh al-Mizziyy*.

Since this book contains what is obligatory to learn of the religious knowledge, the student needs to pay due attention to it. The correct knowledge guides the person to the valid deed and the valid performance. *Imam Muslim* related from the Prophet ﷺ that he said:

$$\text{«إِنَّ الملائكَةَ لَتَضَعُ أجنحتَها لطالبِ العلمِ رِضًى بما يصنعُ»}$$

It means: «The angels lower their wings out of humbleness to the student seeking the Knowledge of the Religion, because of their delight with his deed.»

---

[6] The name of the book in Arabic is

"Mukhtasaru ^Abdillah-il-Harariyy, al-Kafilu bi ^Ilm-id-Din-id-Daruriyy."

مختصرُ عبدِ الله الهرريّ الكافلُ بعلمِ الدّينِ الضّروريّ

THE ESSENTIALS OF BELIEF

AND

RULES OF APOSTASY

Chapter 1
The Meaning of the Testification of Faith
(The Two *Shahadahs*)

It is obligatory upon all the accountable persons to embrace the Religion of *Islam*, to remain steadfast to it, and to comply with what is obligatory upon them of its rules. This means that every accountable person must be Muslim, stay Muslim, and follow the rules of *Islam*.

Explanation: It is obligatory upon the one who is accountable but not Muslim to embrace *Islam* immediately. One is accountable if one is sane, pubescent, and has received the basic message of *Islam*. Sane (^*aqil*) means not crazy. The male becomes pubescent when one of two matters occurs: he discharges his *maniyy*[7] or he becomes 15 (lunar) years old. The woman becomes pubescent by one of three matters: she discharges her *maniyy*, she becomes 15 lunar years old, or she menstruates.

One is considered as having received the message of *Islam* if one received the basic message. For example, if one heard (and understood) the Testification of Faith (No one is God except *Allah*, and *Muhammad* is the Messenger of *Allah*), one has received the basic message. To become accountable, it is not a condition that the person receives the details of the creed. Hence, if the non-Muslim was pubescent, sane, and received the basic message, it is obligatory for him/her to embrace *Islam* immediately. If one does not, and one dies in that state of blasphemy, then one deserves the everlasting torture in Hellfire.

The one who does not receive the basic message of *Islam* will not be tortured in Hellfire. This is so because *Allah* said in *Suratul-Isra'*, *Ayah* 15:

$$\text{﴿وَمَا كُنَّا مُعَذِّبِينَ حَتَّى نَبْعَثَ رَسُولًا ۝﴾}$$

It means that *Allah* will not punish (in the Hereafter) those who do not receive the basic message (the creed of *Islam*) of any prophet. Such people are not accountable.

---

[7] *Maniyy* is a term used equally for men and women. It refers to the sexual spermatic fluid of the man, and the corresponding sexual fluid of the woman.

Likewise, the person who dies before pubescence will be safe in the Hereafter, even if he worshipped a stone. Similarly, the person whose insanity continues until after pubescence and dies will be safe in the Hereafter.

To become Muslim is an easy matter: One believes in one's heart in the meanings of the Testification of Faith and utters it with one's tongue--either in Arabic or any other language (even if one knows Arabic). In English, one says:

**"I testify that no one is God except *Allah*,
and (I testify) that *Muhammad* is the Messenger of *Allah*"**

or uses other words which give the aforementioned meaning. One does not become Muslim if one does <u>not</u> <u>utter</u> the Testification of Faith--even if one holds the proper belief in one's heart.

Among what one must absolutely know, believe in, and utter immediately if one was a blasphemer is the Testification of Faith, which is: "I testify that no one is God except *Allah* and (I testify) that *Muhammad* is the Messenger of *Allah*." In the prayer, the Muslim must say the Testification of Faith in Arabic by saying:

أَشْهَدُ أَنْ لا إِلَهَ إِلا اللَّهُ وأَشْهَدُ أَنَّ مُحَمَّدًا رَسولُ اللَّهِ

*Ash-hadu alla ilaha illallah,
wa ash-hadu anna Muhammadar-Rasulullah.*

Explanation: Without delay, the blasphemer must utter the Testification of Faith to become Muslim. The Muslim must utter the Testification of Faith in the last *tashahhud* of every prayer for the validity of that prayer. The statement *sallallahu ^alayhi wa sallam* is not part of the Testification of Faith. Hence, one is not required to utter it. This statement is rewardable to say after mentioning the name of Prophet *Muhammad*. It means: May *Allah* raise the rank of Prophet *Muhammad* and protect his (Muslim) Nation from what he fears for them.

The meaning of *Ash-hadu alla ilaha illallah* is: "I know, believe, and declare that nothing is worshipped rightfully except *Allah*",

Explanation: This means that I firmly believe in my heart and declare with my tongue that nothing deserves to be worshipped except *Allah*. Some people worship things other than *Allah*. For example, some people worship Buddha. Some people worship Prophet Jesus. Some people worship idols. Some people even worship the devil. All these things are worshipped unrightfully. *Allah* is the only One Who deserves to be worshipped. As defined by *Imam Taqiyyud-Din as-Subkiyy* (d. 756 AH), who was a well-known scholar of *Fiqh*, the fundamentals of the Religion, the interpretation of the *Qur'an*, the Arabic language, and other sciences, "worship" is غَايَةُ الخُضُوع والخُشُوع, which means the ultimate submission and humbleness (to someone else). *Ar-Raghib al-Asbahaniyy*, the famous linguist, established the same definition for "worship" in his book, *Mufradatul-Qur'an*. So, worship is not simply 'to call upon one,' 'to fear one,' or 'to be hopeful of one.' Rather, calling upon, fearing, or being hopeful of something entails worship only when linked to and associated with the ultimate submitting and humbling of oneself to that thing.

Who is One (*al-Wahid*),

Explanation: *Allah* is One (*Wahid*) means *Allah* does not have a partner with Him in Godhood. 'One' here does not refer to a number. Numbers can increase or decrease, be added to or subtracted from, and can be divided. For example, to say 'one person' does not mean that this person has no partners in humanity. Rather it is mentioned in the context of a number, i.e., he is one among others. Moreover, others are similar to him in certain aspects. However, when we refer to *Allah* as 'One' it means 'the One Who does not have a partner.'

Imam Abu Hanifah (d. 150 AH), may *Allah* raise his rank, said in *al-Fiqh al-Akbar*:

(وَاللَّهُ واحدٌ لا من طريقِ العددِ ولكنْ مِن طريقٍ أَنَّه لا شريكَ لهُ)

It means: "*Allah* is One, not in the context of numbers, but in the context that He does not have any partner."

Indivisible (*al-Ahad*),

Explanation: Some scholars said *al-Ahad* has the same meaning as *al-Wahid*, i.e., there is no partner to *Allah* in His Godhood. Others said *al-Ahad* means 'the One Who is indivisible,' because He is not a body.

23

without a beginning (al-Awwal), Eternal (al-Qadim),

Explanation: Al-Awwal and al-Qadim have the same meaning, which is 'the One Whose Existence is without a beginning.' His Existence is without a beginning means His Existence was not preceded by a state of non-existence. Allah alone is the One Who is attributed with this attribute. The existence of all things other than Allah has a beginning. This matter is among the fundamentals of the Muslim's belief. Anyone who believes otherwise is not a Muslim.

Alive (al-Hayy),

Explanation: Allah is Alive and His Life is without end. Allah is attributed with an eternal and everlasting Life which does not resemble our life.

the One Whose Existence is without an end (al-Qayyum), Everlasting (ad-Da'im),

Explanation: Here al-Qayyum and ad-Da'im carry the same meaning. The Everlasting means 'the One Whose Existence does not end.' Allah is Everlasting because that which ends must have had a beginning, and therefore must be a creation, and not the Creator.

the Creator (al-Khaliq),

Explanation: The Creator means 'the One Who brings everything from the state of non-existence into the state of existence.' Nothing among the creations comes into existence except by the Creating of Allah. The slave and his actions exist by the Creating of Allah. All of us, including our doings, thoughts, and inclinations are created by Allah. The slave does not create anything. The slave does not bring anything from the state of non-existence into the state of existence. Rather, the slave only acquires his deeds. He directs his intention towards a particular deed, but Allah is the One Who creates that deed.

Likewise, causes do not create any of their results. The fire (cause) does not create burning (result). The knife (cause) does not create cutting (result). The bread (cause) does not create the feeling of satisfaction from hunger (result). Water (cause) does not create the quenching of thirst (result). The sun (cause) does not create warmth (result). Rather, these are causes followed by results and their Creator is Allah. At the point when the fire comes in contact with a certain combustible material, *Allah* creates the burning in that material. Had *Allah* not willed for that particular body to burn as a result of touching the fire, He would not have created the burning, and by consequence, it would not have burnt. This was the case with Prophet *Ibrahim* عليه السَّلام. He was put into a large, raging fire--yet he was not burned--because *Allah* did not create the attribute of burning (cause) in that fire nor did He create the burning in *Ibrahim* (result).

This case is also among the fundamentals of the creed. The one who believes that there is something or someone who shares with *Allah* the attribute of Creating (of bringing things from non-existence into existence) is not a Muslim, even if he claims so.

the Sustainer (ar-Raziq),

Explanation: The Sustainer is the One Who gives the sustenance (*rizq*) to His slaves. Sustenance (*rizq*) includes all the things which give a benefit to the person--whether from a lawful or an unlawful source.

Knowledgeable (al-ˆAlim),

Explanation: Allah is the One Who knows everything. *Allah* knows His Self, His Attributes, and His creations. *Allah* knows the things before they happen.

Powerful (al-Qadir),

Explanation: Allah is the One Who has Power over all things. He is not powerless over anything.

and the One Who does whatever He wills, i.e., whatever *Allah* willed to be shall be and whatever *Allah* did not will to be shall not be.

Explanation: This means that everything that *Allah* willed in eternity to happen must happen in the way which *Allah* knew and at the time which *Allah* willed for it to occur. That which *Allah* did not will in eternity to happen will never happen. Should an entire nation come together to inflict a harm on you that *Allah* did not will to happen to you, it will not be able to harm you. Likewise, should a nation come together to benefit you with a certain matter that *Allah* did not will in eternity for you to benefit from, it will not be able to do so. This also is among the fundamentals of the proper belief. The Prophet ﷺ, in several *hadiths* (narrated by *at-Tabariyy, Abu Dawud,* and others), explicitly mentioned that anyone who holds a creed contrary to this is not a Muslim.

No one can evade sinning except with *Allah*'s protection and no one has the ability to obey except with *Allah*'s help.

Explanation: "La *hawla wala quwwata illa billah*" لا حَوْلَ ولا قُوَّةَ إلا بالله is a statement that the Prophet ﷺ taught us to say. As *Abu Yaˆla al-Mawsiliyy* related, the Prophet ﷺ explained this statement to mean: "Without *Allah*'s protection no one can evade sinning, and without *Allah*'s help no one has the strength to obey Him."

Allah is attributed with all proper perfection

Explanation: Allah is attributed with all the perfect attributes that befit Him. Here the author specified befitting perfect attributes, because among the perfect attributes there are those which are perfect in relation to mankind, but are imperfect when attributed to *Allah*. Some examples are brilliance, intellect, nice voice, and strength of body. When attributed to a creature, these are attributes of perfection. However, they are not befitting to attribute to the Creator. This is why the author said:

and is clear of all imperfection.

Explanation: This means that *Allah* is clear of any of the attributes of the creation, such as bodily characteristics, color, shape, motion, and stillness. This is why the People of Truth, *Ahl-us-Sunnah wal-Jamaˆah*, said, "*Allah* exists without a place," because the one who exists in a place must have a limit, and everything that has a limit is in need of one who specified it with that limit. Whatever is in need certainly is not the Creator. This is why *Allah* is clear of existing in any place or any direction. We do not say *Allah* inhabits the sky. We do not say that *Allah* exists in the direction of above. We do not say that *Allah* exists in all places, or everywhere. Rather, *Allah* exists and He does not resemble other things that exist. Hence, *Allah* exists without a place.

There is absolutely nothing like Him, and He is attributed with Hearing and Sight.

Explanation: This is the meaning of Verse 11 of *Surat ash-Shura* ﴿لَيْسَ كَمِثْلِهِ شَىْءٌ ۝﴾. It means that nothing resembles *Allah* in any

26

way, just as was said by *Dhun-Nun al-Misriyy*:[8] "Whatever you imagine in your mind, *Allah* is different from it."

$$ (مَهْمَا تَصَوَّرْتَ بِبَالِكَ فَاللهُ بِخِلافِ ذلكَ) $$

Allah is clear of resembling any of the creations, tangible or otherwise. For example, *Allah* is different from the humans, angels, light, spirits, sun, and moon. *Allah* is not similar to any of the creations in any way whatsoever.

Allah exists without a beginning and everything else exists with a beginning. He is the Creator and everything else is a creation.

Explanation: *Allah* is the only One Who is eternal. Hence, *Allah* is the only One Whose Existence is without a beginning. Everything else exists with a beginning. This is the meaning of a creation, i.e., the creation is that which was not existing and then it was brought into existence. Therefore, there was a beginning to its existence. Everything other than *Allah* is a creation and is created by *Allah, tabaraka wa ta^ala*. This applies to the kind[9] and the elements, the deeds and the bodies, and the *jawhar* and the *^arads*. The *jawhar* refers to the smallest particle that cannot be further divided. The *^arad* refers to the attribute that does not exist independently.

The belief that everything other than *Allah* is a creation is among the fundamentals of the creed of the Muslims. Hence, anyone who believes that something other than *Allah* exists without a beginning is a blasphemer. Some people believe the kind of the universe is eternal (that its existence has no beginning) just like the later philosophers and *Ahmad Ibn Taymiyah* said. In his book, *Tashnif al-Masami^*, az-Zarkashiyy[10] narrated the consensus of the Muslims judging those who believe the universe is eternal to be blasphemers.

Every creation that exists, be it among entities or deeds, from the fine

---

[8] Although he is famous as *Dhun-Nun al-Misriyy*, his name was *Thawban*, the son of *Ibrahim*. Originally he was from *an-Nubah* today an area between southern Egypt and northern Sudan. He lived in Egypt, some 1200 years ago. He was among the higher ranked scholars. He was famous for being very God-fearing as well.

[9] The 'kind' is the common criterion existing in each and every element of a group which specifically characterizes that group. For example, humanity is the 'kind' of the humans.

[10] Az-Zarkashiyy is a *Shafi^iyy* scholar who lived about 700 years ago.

dust to the ^Arsh,[11] and every movement, rest, intention, and thought of the slaves is created by Allah. Hence, no one other than Allah–be it nature or cause–creates anything. Things become existent by Allah's Will, Power, and Destining, and in accordance with His eternal Knowledge,

Explanation: The nature of things means their specific normal characteristics (tabi^ah) or ^adah, as some scholars said. For example, the nature (tabi^ah) of fire is to burn. The cause (^illah) is what gives a certain result. For example, if one has a ring on one's finger and moves one's finger, the ring moves because of the movement of one's finger. So, the movement of the finger is the cause (^illah) for the movement of the ring.

Neither the laws of nature nor causes create anything in this universe. Rather, Allah is the only One Who creates. By His Power, Allah brings things into existence. Allah eternally knew about His creations and accordingly He willed for them to exist. Allah is the Creator of everything.

as mentioned in the Qur'an:

$$قال الله تعالى : ﴿وَخَلَقَ كُلَّ شَيْءٍ﴾ ﴿٢﴾$$

Surat al-Furqan, Ayah 2 means: [Allah created everything]. He brought all the creation from the state of non-existence into the state of existence. No one creates with this meaning of creating except Allah.

$$قال الله تعالى : ﴿هَلْ مِنْ خَالِقٍ غَيْرُ اللَّهِ﴾ ﴿٣﴾$$

Surat Fatir, Ayah 3 means: [No one is the Creator except Allah]. An-Nasafiyy said that if a person hit glass with a stone and broke it, then the acts of hitting and breaking and the state of being broken were created by Allah. The slave only acquires the act. Allah is the only One Who creates.

$$قال الله تعالى : ﴿لَهَا مَا كَسَبَتْ وَعَلَيْهَا مَا اكْتَسَبَتْ﴾ ﴿٢٨٦﴾$$

Surat al-Baqarah, Ayah 286 means: [Every individual self will be rewarded by Allah for the good deeds it acquired and will be accountable for the sins it committed].

---

[11] The ^Arsh is the ceiling of Paradise. It is the largest of the creations in size, having four legs. Some refer to it in English as 'the Throne.'

Explanation: The creed of the People of Truth, *Ahlus-Sunnah wal-Jama^ah*, is that the slave is a creation of *Allah*, and the doings of the slave are also creations of *Allah*. The slave does not create anything. *Allah* is the One Who creates the doings of the slave, and the slave only acquires his acts. So, if a person picks a stone from the ground, throws it at a piece of glass and breaks the glass, then breaking the glass by throwing the stone (which is the action of the slave) and the breaking of the glass (which occurs in the glass) are both created by *Allah*. Moreover, the slave's intention to throw that stone at the glass, the hand by which he threw the stone, the action of throwing, and the stone he threw are all created by *Allah*. All that happens is a creation of *Allah*. Even one's intentions, desires, inclinations, thoughts, and any changes in them are created by *Allah*.

As related by *al-Bayhaqiyy* and others, the Prophet ﷺ said:

$$\text{«إِنَّ قُلُوبَ الْعِبَادِ بَيْنَ إِصْبَعَيْنِ مِنْ أَصَابِعِ الرَّحْمٰنِ يُقَلِّبُهَا كَيْفَ يَشَاءُ»}$$

It means: «The hearts of the slaves are under the control of *Allah*. *Allah* turns them the way He willed.» Hence, the one who deviates from this belief and claims that the slaves create their own voluntary actions is belying the *Qur'an* and the *Hadith*. This is why the top scholars hold the consensus that such a person is a blasphemer. *Imam al-Maturidiyy* declared them as blasphemers. *Abu Mansur al-Baghdadiyy* said:

$$\text{(أَجْمَعَ أَصْحَابُنَا عَلَى تَكْفِيرِهِم)}$$

"The *Ash^ariyys* are in agreement that such people [those who claim people create their own actions] are blasphemers." Before them, many prominent scholars of the *Salaf*[12] declared as blasphemers those who say the slave creates his deeds. First and foremost, the Prophet ﷺ declared them as blasphemers, and the sayings of the Prophet ﷺ are sufficient.

However, saying that *Allah* is the Creator of everything, including the intentions of the slave, does not mean that the slave does not

---

[12] The *Salaf* are the Companions, their followers, and their followers who lived within the first 300 *Hijriyy* years.

have a choice. The slave has a choice; however, his choice is under the Will of *Allah*. His choice does not reach to an extent that he creates his own actions. Rather his own choice is a creation of *Allah* and is under the Will of *Allah*.

Beneficial Information: "The slave acquires his act" means that he directs his will and intention towards doing a particular deed, then *Allah* creates that deed. Although the directing of the will and the doing of the deed are created by *Allah*, still the slave is doing the directing and the deed--therefore he acquires his act. Hence, if someone runs intentionally, the fact that his intention and his running movements are created by *Allah* does not negate that he is the one running intentionally, and thus, that he is accountable for his running.

Beneficial Information: The Will of *Allah* is the attribute by which *Allah* specifies the intellectual possibilities (the creations) with their attributes.

The Speech (*Kalam*[13]) of *Allah* is without a beginning like all of His other attributes, because He, the Exalted, is unlike all the creations in the Self (*Dhat*), Attributes, and Acts.

Explanation: The Speech (*Kalam*) of *Allah* which is the attribute of His Self is eternal, i.e., it has no beginning, just like all the other attributes of *Allah*. It does not have a beginning or an ending. It is not letters which occur sequentially. The Speech of *Allah* is not similar to the speech of the creation.

The eternal Speech (*Kalam*) of *Allah* is called 'the *Qur'an*.' The term 'the *Qur'an*' can also refer to the terms revealed to Prophet *Muhammad* ﷺ and included in the Book of the *Qur'an*. These Arabic terms are created. Because these terms are expressions referring to the eternal Speech of *Allah*; they are also called 'the *Qur'an*' even though, beyond doubt, these terms are created.

To make it more clear, if someone wrote the word '*Allah*' on a chalkboard and was asked what it was he wrote, he would answer, '*Allah*.' His response does not mean those letters he wrote, i.e., the A,

---

[13] The *Kalam* of *Allah* is an attribute of the Self (*Dhat*) of *Allah* which is not created and is not a letter, sound, or language; with it, *Allah* orders, forbids, promises, and threatens.

L, L, A , and H are the Self Whom we worship (*Allah*). Rather, he means that this term is an <u>expression</u> <u>referring</u> to the Self Whom we worship--Who is *Allah*, the Self Who does not resemble anything. Likewise, the terms revealed to Prophet *Muhammad* ﷺ are expressions of the Speech of *Allah*, the attribute of His Self. Both the attribute of the Self of *Allah* and the revealed expressions are referred to as the 'Speech of *Allah*' and both are referred to as 'the *Qur'an*.'

It is not permissible for one to believe that the Speech of *Allah*, which is the attribute of His Self, the Speech which Prophet *Musa* عليه السلام heard, is a language--Arabic or otherwise. Such a belief is a misguidance, because it entails likening *Allah* to the creatures. *Allah* is absolutely unlike all the creations in His Self, in His Attributes, and in His Acts.

Allah, subhanahu wa taʿala, is greatly clear of all the unbefitting attributes that the blasphemers attribute to Him.

Explanation: *Subhanahu* means *tanzih*, i.e., we declare that *Allah* is clear of all unbefitting attributes. *Taʿala* means the same and is a re-confirmation of the same meaning. *Allah* is greatly clear of all the unbefitting attributes that the blasphemers attribute to Him.

Summing up what has been mentioned before, it is affirmed that Allah, taʿala, has thirteen attributes which were mentioned repeatedly in the Qur'an, either explicitly or implicitly. These are: Existence (al-Wujud), Oneness (al-Wahdaniyyah), Eternity (al-Qidam, i.e., al-Azaliyyah), Everlastingness (al-Baqaʾ), Non-neediness of others (al-Qiyamubin-Nafs), Power (al-Qudrah), Will (al-Iradah), Knowledge (al-ʿIlm), Hearing (as-Samʿ), Sight (al-Basar), Life (al-Hayah), Speech (al-Kalam), and Non-resemblance to the creation (al-Mukhalafatu lil-hawadith). Since these attributes were mentioned many times in the Qur'an and Hadith, the scholars said that knowing them is a personal obligation (fardʿayn).

Explanation: Among the countless attributes of *Allah*, there are some which were mentioned repeatedly in the *Qur'an*. The Prophet ﷺ concentrated on teaching these particular attributes to the people, using the terms mentioned in the *Qur'an* (*nass* نَصّ) as well as other terms carrying the same meaning (*maʿna* مَعْنَى). Accordingly, the scholars deduced that it is obligatory upon every accountable Muslim to know these particular attributes. They are thirteen (13).

Many scholars mentioned that knowing those thirteen (13)

attributes is a personal obligation. The later scholars took special care to explicitly mention this obligation, such as as-Sanusiyy (the author of The Sanusiyy Creed), al-Fudaliyy (a Malikiyy scholar), ash-Sharnubiyy (also a Malikiyy scholar), and others. Among the heads of the scholars of the Salaf who explicitly named these attributes and indicated that it was obligatory for every accountable Muslim to know them was Imam Abu Hanifah. He mentioned this in his book, Al-Fiqh Al-Akbar.

These thirteen (13) attributes are:

1. Existence (al-Wujud). Allah exists and is not similar to the other things which exist. Allah's Existence is without a beginning, without an end, and without a place. In Surat Ibrahim, 10, Allah said:

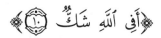

This ayah means: [The Existence of Allah is indubitable.] Allah exists without a doubt.

2. Oneness (al-Wahdaniyyah). 'Allah is One' means Allah does not have a partner with Him in Godhood. Allah said in Surat al-Ambiya', 22:

$$\text{﴿لَوْ كَانَ فِيهِمَا ءَالِهَةٌ إِلَّا ٱللَّهُ لَفَسَدَتَا ۚ ٢٢﴾}$$

This ayah means: [Had there been Gods for the heaven and Earth other than Allah, they (heaven and Earth) would have been ruined.]

3. Eternity (al-Qidam, i.e., al-Azaliyyah). Allah's Existence is without a beginning. This means His Existence was not preceded by non-existence.

4. Everlastingness (al-Baqa'). Allah's Existence does not have an end. He does not cease to exist. Allah said in Surat al-Hadid, 3:

$$\text{﴿هُوَ ٱلْأَوَّلُ وَٱلْءَاخِرُ ۖ ٣﴾}$$

This ayah means: [Allah is the One Whose Existence is without a beginning and without an end.]

5. Non-neediness of others (al-Qiyamu bin-Nafs). This means that Allah is not in need of anything, and everything else needs Him. In Surat Al ^Imran, 97, Allah said:

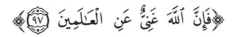

This *ayah* means: [Certainly, *Allah* does not need any of the worlds.]

6. Power (al-Qudrah). *Allah* has Power over all the creations. *Allah* is not powerless over anything, as *Allah* attributed to Himself in *Surat al-Baqarah, 109*:

$$﴿ إِنَّ ٱللَّهَ عَلَىٰ كُلِّ شَىْءٍ قَدِيرٌ ﴾$$

This *ayah* means: [*Allah* has the perfect Power over all things.]

7. Will (al-Iradah). Everything that *Allah* willed in eternity for it to exist must come into existence at the time which *Allah* willed for it to exist. Nothing will exist unless *Allah* willed for it to exist. *Surat at-Takwir, 29*:

$$﴿ وَمَا تَشَآءُونَ إِلَّآ أَن يَشَآءَ ٱللَّهُ رَبُّ ٱلْعَٰلَمِينَ ﴾$$

means: [You do not will anything except by the Will of *Allah*, the Lord of the worlds.]

8. Knowledge (al-^Ilm). *Allah* knows everything; nothing is hidden from Him, as He attributed to Himself in *Surat al-'Anfal, 75*:

$$﴿ إِنَّ ٱللَّهَ بِكُلِّ شَىْءٍ عَلِيمٌ ﴾$$

This *ayah* means: [*Allah* has the perfect Knowledge of everything.]

9. Hearing (as-Sam^). *Allah* hears all hearable things without an ear or any other instrument. No hearable thing is hidden from Him. *Allah* said in *Surat ash-Shura, 11*:

$$﴿ وَهُوَ ٱلسَّمِيعُ ٱلْبَصِيرُ ﴾$$

This *ayah* means: [*Allah* is attributed with Hearing and Sight.]

10. Sight (al-Basar). *Allah* sees all seeable things without the need of a pupil (an eye) or light. Nothing is hidden from Him. (*Surat ash-Shura, 11*).

11. Life (al-Hayah). *Allah* is attributed with an eternal and everlasting Life, which is not similar to our life. *Allah's* Life does not have a beginning or an end, and is not a combination of body and soul. *Allah* attributed Life to Himself in *Surat al-Baqarah, 255*:

$$ ﴿ٱللَّهُ لَآ إِلَٰهَ إِلَّا هُوَ ٱلۡحَىُّ ٱلۡقَيُّومُ ۝﴾ $$

This *ayah* means: [No one is God but *Allah*, the One Who is attributed with Life and is not in need of anything.]

12. Speech (al-Kalam). *Allah's* Speech (*Kalam*) is an eternal and everlasting attribute of the Self of *Allah* and is not a letter, sound, or language. *Allah* attributed Speech (*Kalam*) to Himself in *Surat an-Nisa', 164*:

$$ ﴿وَكَلَّمَ ٱللَّهُ مُوسَىٰ تَكۡلِيمًا ۝﴾ $$

It means: [*Allah* spoke to *Musa* with His Speech (*Kalam*).]

13. Non-resemblance to the creation (al-Mukhalafatu lil-hawadith). *Allah* is clear of any of the attributes of the creation, because the attributes of the creations indicate that the creatures are in need of a Creator. Had *Allah* been attributed with any of these attributes, He would have been in need of one who created Him, and *Allah* is clear of that. The proof to that *Allah* does not resemble the creations is the verse of the *Qur'an, Surat ash-Shura, 11*:

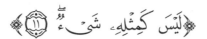

It means: [Nothing resembles *Allah* in any way whatsoever.]

Since eternity is confirmed to the Self (Dhat) of *Allah*, then His attributes are eternal, because a created attribute entails that the attributed self is created.

Explanation: This statement means that the thing which is attributed with a created attribute must itself be a created thing. It is not permissible that *Allah* would be attributed with a created attribute. Yet, some of those who liken *Allah* to the creatures say that *Allah's* Speech (*Kalam*) is letters and sounds (like our speech). Their saying is blasphemy because it entails likening *Allah* to the creatures. Some of those go even further in their absurdity and say, "*Allah's* Speech is letters and sounds like our speech; however, these letters

34

and sounds are eternal," i.e., have no beginning. Their first statement contradicts their second one! Obviously those people do not have sound mental judgement. By simple observation, one knows that letters and sounds are created. In saying the word 'bismi' one observes beyond doubt that the 'b' sound was pronounced before the 's' sound and the 's' sound was pronounced before the 'm.' What happens in succession definitely has a beginning and is a creation.

It is confirmed by the intellectual proof and by the textual proof that the Self of *Allah* is eternal, i.e., without a beginning. Since the Self of *Allah* is eternal, then it follows that the attributes of *Allah* are also eternal. In both of his books, *al-Fiqh al-Absat* and *al-Fiqh al-Akbar*, Imam *Abu Hanifah* said:

(وصِفاتُهُ غَيْرُ مُحْدَثَةٍ ولا مَخْلُوقَةٍ. ومَنْ زَعَمَ أَنَّها مُحْدَثَةٌ أَوْ مَخْلُوقَةٌ أَوْ شَكَّ أَوْ تَوَقَّفَ فَهُوَ كافِرٌ)

It means: "*Allah's* attributes are not created. Whoever claims that the attributes of *Allah* are created, or doubts it, or hesitates about whether or not they are created is a blasphemer."

The meaning of Ash-hadu anna Muhammadar-Rasulullah is: " I know, believe, and declare that Muhammad, the son of ^Abdullah, who is the son of ^Abdul-Muttalib, who is the son of Hashim, who is the son of ^Abdu-Manaf, from the tribe of Quraysh, sallallahu ^alayhi wa sallam, is the slave of Allah and His Messenger to all the humans and jinn."

Explanation: Prophet *Muhammad* ﷺ is from the clan of *Hashim*, i.e., his lineage goes back to *Hashim*, the son of ^*Abdu Manaf*. The clan of *Hashim* is a branch of the tribe of *Quraysh*, the most prestigious and honorable tribe of the Arabs. The tribe of *Quraysh* goes back in lineage to Prophet *Isma^il* عليه السَّلام, the son of Prophet *Ibrahim* عليه السَّلام. Knowing the lineage of thg Prophet back to ^*Abdu Manaf* is a communal obligation (*fard kifayah*). Prophet *Muhammad* ﷺ is the slave of *Allah* and His Messenger to all humans and *jinn*. He was not sent only to the Arabs or only to the non-Arabs, or solely to the humans. Rather, *Allah* sent him as a messenger to all the humans and *jinn*.

One must believe he was born in Makkah and sent as a Messenger therein; he immigrated to al-Madinah and was buried therein; and he was truthful in everything he told about and conveyed from Allah.

35

Explanation: Prophet *Muhammad* ﷺ was born in *Makkah* in the Year of the Elephant, the year when *Abrahah* led an army and some elephants in an (unsuccessful) attempt to destroy the *Ka^bah*.[14] He first received the Revelation in *Makkah* when he was forty (40) years old. He stayed in *Makkah* for thirteen (13) years after receiving the Revelation, then immigrated to *al-Madinah* and lived there for ten (10) years. He died and was buried in *al-Madinah* in Lady *^A'ishah's* chamber in the eleventh (11th) year after the *hijrah*. He was sixty-three (63) years old.

Knowing that Prophet *Muhammad* ﷺ was born in *Makkah* and died in *al-Madinah* is an important matter; there is a big probability for this to be among the Personal Obligatory Knowledge.

Among what the Prophet ﷺ informed us are: the torture in the grave and the enjoyment therein; the questioning of the two angels, *Munkar* and *Nakir*;

Explanation: After the person is buried, his soul which separated from his body at death, returns to his body. Two angels come to him. One angel is named *Munkar* and the other named *Nakir*. They will ask the dead person about his Lord, his Prophet, and his Religion. They have a frightening appearance. The blasphemer will be extremely frightened of them. However, the God-fearing believer does not fear them.

The people in their graves are two types. One type experience enjoyments in the grave. Their graves are widened and illuminated. These are the obedient and forgiven Muslims. The other type will be tortured in their graves, and these are also two categories. One are the blasphemers who will face the torture of the grave continually until their bodies decay. Then after their bodies decay, their souls will be taken to a place in the seventh earth called *Sijjin*, where they will be tortured until the Day of Judgment. The other category are the sinful Muslims whom *Allah* did not forgive. They will be tortured in their graves for a certain period. However, the torture will not continue for them until the Day of Judgment. Once their bodies decay, their souls are suspended between the Earth and the sky. They face their remaining torture which they deserve in the Hereafter (except those

---

[14] *Allah* destroyed *Abrahah* and his army, as described in the *Qur'an* in *Suratul-Fil*.

36

whom *Allah* forgives).

→ Believing in the torture of the grave and the enjoyments of the grave is an obligation. The one who categorically denies the torture of the grave is a blasphemer.

Resurrection (*Baˆth*);

Explanation: The Resurrection is the rising of the dead from their graves. One must believe in the Resurrection. *Allah* recreates the bodies that decayed and returns the souls to them. Then the dead will rise out of their graves. *With 1 angel as a guide & one was a witness.*

pro: don't decays pious muslims

Assembly (*Hashr*);

Explanation: After the Resurrection, the humans, animals, and *jinn* will be assembled (gathered by the angels) to one place (the changed Earth).

the Day of Judgment (*Qiyamah*);

Explanation: It is obligatory to believe in the Day of Judgment. Its length is 50,000 years of what we count. The Day of Judgment begins when the people leave their graves and lasts until those whom *Allah* willed for them to go to Paradise enter it, and those whom *Allah* willed for them to go to Hellfire enter it.

Presentation of the Deeds (*Hisab*);

Explanation: This means that on the Day of Judgment every person will be presented with one's deeds. Every person will be handed one's book in which the angels wrote what one did in this life. On that day, some will be delighted with their books and others will be sad.

Reward (*Thawab*);

Explanation: The Reward refers to the reward for the believers in the Hereafter, in return for the good things they did in this life. This reward is by both body and soul.

Punishment (*ˆAdhab*);

Explanation: The Punishment refers to the punishment that one receives in the Hereafter in return for the sins one did in this life. The Punishment is also by body and soul.

the Balance (*Mizan*);

Explanation: In the Hereafter, the deeds of the people will be weighed on a balance. The good deeds will be weighed in one pan and the bad deeds in the other. If the pan of the good deeds is heavier than the pan of the bad ones, the person is a winner. One will be saved. If the pan of the bad deeds is heavier, then one deserves punishment. On the Day of Judgment, the blasphemer will have nothing in the pan for the good deeds.

 Hellfire (*Nar*);

Explanation: Hellfire is a place where the blasphemers and part of the sinful Muslims are tortured in the Hereafter. It is a physical fire, extremely hot; it does not get extinguished and it does not come to an end. The blasphemers stay in continuous torture in Hellfire. Their torture will never lessen or stop. However, the sinful Muslims who enter Hellfire do not remain there endlessly. They eventually will be taken out and admitted into Paradise. They will not remain in Hellfire, because *Allah* does not equate between the Muslim and the blasphemer.

the Bridge (*Sirat*);

Explanation: It is obligatory to believe in the Bridge (*Sirat*). It is a bridge stretching over Hellfire to which all the humans will come. It begins at the changed Earth and ends before Paradise. Some fall into Hellfire at the very beginning of the bridge and these are the blasphemers. Some of the believers walk on the Bridge, then fall into Hellfire. The rest are saved.

the Basin (*Hawd*); .

Explanation: The basin of our Prophet ﷺ is a huge body of water. Its water comes from the water of Paradise. Every prophet has a basin from which his nation drinks. The nation of Prophet *Muhammad* ﷺ drinks from his Basin before entering Paradise. May *Allah* grant us that.

the Intercession (*Shafaˆah*);

Explanation: Intercession is defined as asking for good things of someone for others. In the Hereafter, the prophets, the pious Muslims, the angels, and the martyrs intercede for some of the sinful Muslims, and as a result, they will be forgiven by *Allah*. Prophet *Muhammad* ﷺ performs the major intercession.[15]

Paradise (*Jannah*);

Explanation: It is an obligation to believe in Paradise, which is now existing. Paradise is above the seventh sky. The ceiling of Paradise is the ^*Arsh* (Throne) and is much larger than Paradise. Paradise has many levels. Its uppermost level is called the *Firdaws* الفِرْدَوْس and the ^*Arsh* is above it.

seeing *Allah*, ta^*ala*, with the eye in the Hereafter, without *Allah* having a form or being in a place or a direction, different from the way a creation is seen;

Explanation: This is a known element of the creed of Muslims, and is a point of difference between the people of *Ahlus-Sunnah* and some deviant factions. We must believe that the believers, while in Paradise, see *Allah* with their eyes. *Allah* empowers their eyes to see Him. They will see *Allah*--not the way the creatures are seen--rather they see *Allah* without *Allah* being in a direction. They see *Allah* without having a distance between them and Him. This was explicitly stated by *Imam Abu Hanifah* in *al-Fiqh al-Akbar*, and other scholars. Seeing *Allah* is the greatest enjoyment the occupants of Paradise will experience. May *Allah* grant us this.

the dwelling forever in Paradise or Hellfire;

Explanation: It is obligatory to believe that the blasphemers will dwell forever in Hellfire, and those who enter Paradise will be there forever. This was explicitly stated in the *Qur'an* and explicitly mentioned in the *Hadith* of the Prophet ﷺ. This is a matter which is known to both the scholars and the lay Muslims.

the belief in *Allah*'s Angels,

Explanation: It is obligatory to believe in the angels, i.e., to believe that they exist. They are bodies which *Allah* created from light. They

---

[15] On the Day of Judgment, the sinful Muslims go to Prophet *Adam* عليه السَّلاَم to ask him to intercede for them to be relieved from the extreme heat of the sun. He directs them to Prophet *Nuh* عليه السَّلاَم saying, "He is your father after your father." Prophet *Nuh* عليه السَّلاَم directs them to go to Prophet *Ibrahim* عليه السَّلاَم who directs them to Prophet *Musa* عليه السَّلاَم, who directs them to Prophet ^*Isa* عليه السَّلاَم, who in turn directs them to Prophet *Muhammad* ﷺ who intercedes for them.

are not males or females. They do not eat or drink. They are never disobedient to *Allah*; they always obey His orders.

Messengers,

Explanation: We must believe in all the prophets, those of whom we know and those of whom we do not know. They were numerous. The first of them was *Adam* عليه السَّلَام. The last was our prophet, *Muhammad* ﷺ. Some of them were prophets and messengers and others were prophets but not messengers. The prophet who is a messenger is one to whom *Allah* revealed new Laws differing from the Laws of the messenger before him. The prophet who was not a messenger also received the Revelation from *Allah*, in which he was ordered to follow the Laws of the messenger before him. Both the prophets and the messengers were ordered to convey their message. Some falsely defined the prophet who is not a messenger as: "the one who received the Revelation of a new set of laws, but was not ordered to convey them to others." This is a serious error which one categorically must not adopt.

and Books,

Explanation: It is obligatory to believe in all the Revealed Books. They are one hundred and four (104). The most famous are four (4): the *Tawrah*, the *Zabur*, the *Injil*, and the *Qur'an*.[16]

and Destining (Qadar), whether the destined (qadar) is good or evil;

Explanation: The Arabic term 'qadar' can mean 'destining' and it can mean 'destined.' It is obligatory to believe that everything that happens in this universe happens according to the Will of *Allah*, by the Creating of *Allah*, and by the Destining (Qadar) of *Allah*. Destining, when used to mean the eternal attribute of *Allah*, means *Allah*'s managing things and making them occur in accordance with His eternal Will and Knowledge. In other words, it is making things the way they are.

However, destined (*qadar*) is used in the above text to mean the created thing. It refers to that which happens according to the

---

[16] Other than these four famous Books, it is narrated that fifty (50) different sheets were revealed to Prophet *Shith* عـلـيـه الـسَّـلَام, thirty (30) to Prophet *Idris* عـلـيـه الـسَّـلَام, ten (10) to Prophet *Ibrahim* عليه السَّلَام, and ten (10) other than the *Tawrah* to Prophet *Musa* عليه الـسَّلَام.

Destining (Qadar) of Allah. This is why it is divided into what is good and what is evil. It is not permissible to say about the Destining (Qadar) of Allah which is the attribute of His Self, that some is good and some other is evil. The Destining (Qadar) of Allah is good. However, as to that which happens, i.e., the created things, some of them are good and some of them are evil.

and that Muhammad, sallallahu ^alayhi wa sallam, is the last of the prophets and the best of all the children of Adam.

Explanation: Prophet Muhammad ﷺ is the last prophet Allah sent. No prophet will come after him. Although Prophet ^Isa عليه السَّلَام will descend from the sky before the Day of Judgment, he received the Revelation of Prophethood before Muhammad ﷺ, and when he descends he will rule with the Laws of Prophet Muhammad ﷺ. The last revealed prophet is Prophet Muhammad ﷺ, as was clearly stated in the Qur'an in Surat al-Ahzab, Verse 40 which specifically says that Prophet Muhammad ﷺ is the last of the prophets:

﴿مَّا كَانَ مُحَمَّدٌ أَبَآ أَحَدٍ مِّن رِّجَالِكُمْ وَلَٰكِن رَّسُولَ ٱللَّهِ وَخَاتَمَ ٱلنَّبِيِّـۧنَ ۗ ٤٠﴾

It means: [Muhammad is not the father of any of your men, rather he is the Messenger of Allah and the seal of the prophets.] Anyone who claims that a prophet will be revealed after Prophet Muhammad ﷺ is a blasphemer. For example there are some who claim that a man by the name of Ghulam Ahmad received Prophethood after Prophet Muhammad ﷺ. Ghulam Ahmad is from Qadiyan and lived about 100 years ago. He claimed Prophethood for himself, and some misguided people believed him. His followers are known as the Qadiyaniyyah. Sometimes, they refer to themselves as Ahmadiyyah. They are blasphemers for believing in the religious permissibility of some people receiving the Revelation after Prophet Muhammad ﷺ.

Moreover our Prophet, Muhammad ﷺ, is the best of all the prophets. After him in status are Prophets Ibrahim عليه السَّلَام, then Musa عليه السَّلَام, then ^Isa عليه السَّلَام, then Nuh عليه السَّلَام. May Allah raise their ranks all.

41

Moreover, it is obligatory to believe that every prophet of *Allah* must be attributed with truthfulness, trustworthiness, and intelligence.

Explanation: This means that every prophet of *Allah* is truthful. A prophet does not lie--not even one single lie--neither before Prophethood nor after Prophethood. Every one of them is trustworthy. He does not betray, neither before Prophethood nor after Prophethood. Every one of them is intelligent and able to produce the proofs to discredit the blasphemous creeds and the unlawful doings. The prophets are the most intelligent of all the creations.

Consequently, lying, dishonesty, vileness, foolishness, dullness, cowardice, and all qualities that repel people from accepting the call from them are impossible to be among their attributes.

Explanation: A prophet does not commit any vileness, such as using obscenities frequently. He does not act in a stupid manner; it is impossible that any of the prophets of *Allah* be attributed with dullness. As well, the prophets of *Allah* are clear of repulsive attributes which detract others from them--whether in their manners or in their bodies. Hence, they are clear of all diseases which disgust others. They are clear of cowardice, rather they are the bravest. They are clear of withholding the message which *Allah* ordered them to convey.

They must also be attributed with impeccability, i.e., they are protected from ever committing blasphemy, enormous sins (*kaba'ir*), and the small, abject sins before and after Prophethood.

Explanation: No prophet of *Allah* ever committed blasphemy--neither before nor after Prophethood. What some claim about Prophet *Ibrahim* عليه السَّلَام, i.e., that at one point in time he worshipped the star, then the moon, then the sun, is a total fabrication. Prophet *Ibrahim* عليه السَّلَام never worshipped other than *Allah*. The verse in the *Qur'an* some try to use to back their false statement does not have that meaning. When Prophet *Ibrahim* عليه السَّلَام said "*hadha Rabbi.!?*" ﴿هَٰذَا رَبِّي﴾ (referring to the sun, moon, and star) he was not stating his agreement with his people in worshipping those things. Rather his statement was to negate and oppose what they said. This is a form of expression in Arabic, called negative interrogative, (استفهام إنكاريّ) (i.e., a way of expressing one's strong denial of a matter by posing a question which clearly shows that the matter is ridiculous or totally unacceptable.)

42

Likewise, prophets are protected from committing enormous sins, both before and after Prophethood. Hence, when Musa عليه السَّلام killed that kafir (non-Muslim) in Egypt, it was not an enormous sin. Musa عليه السَّلام neither intended to kill that man when he hit him nor thought he would die as a result of his punch. The reason Prophet Musa عليه السَّلام regretted his action was that he fought before he was ordered by Allah to do so.

Prophets are also protected from committing small, mean sins, like stealing a morsel of bread or stealing a single grape. These are small sins, but they reflect a certain meanness. Prophets do not commit such sins both before and after Prophethood. From this, we know that the sin of Prophet Adam عليه السَّلام was not an enormous sin. Rather, it was a small sin, that did not include meanness, as was stated by Imam al-Ashˆariyy and others.

On the other hand, they may commit other small sins. However, they are immediately guided to repent before others imitate them.

Explanation: Prophets are not protected from committing a small sin which is not a mean one. However, should a prophet commit such a sin, he is immediately guided to repent of it before others follow him in doing it. As such, we know that the claim of some that Prophet Yusuf wanted to fornicate with the woman of al-ˆAziz is totally untrue. Wanting this is a mean act and is unbefitting of a prophet. The ayah 24 of Surat Yusuf:

$$\text{﴿وَلَقَدْ هَمَّتْ بِهِ وَهَمَّ بِهَا ۝﴾}$$

which some use to try to back their false statement regarding Yusuf does not mean that Prophet Yusuf wanted to fornicate with her. In reality, this verse means that the woman attempted to adulterize with Prophet Yusuf and that had he not been protected by Allah, Who would later bestow Prophethood on him, he would have attempted to fornicate. This means that he did not attempt in the first place, because Allah protected him by having eternally chosen him for the status of Prophethood. Looking lustfully at a marriageable woman is a matter the prophets do not commit, let alone committing the sin of attempting fornication.

Hence, Prophethood was not bestowed upon the brothers of *Yusuf*, who, excluding *Binyamin*, committed the mean deeds mentioned in the *Qur'an*. The *Asbat* are the descendants of *Yusuf*'s brothers who were chosen for Prophethood.

Explanation: The saying of some that the brothers of *Yusuf* (other than *Binyamin*) were given Prophethood is a false statement. *Binyamin* was the youngest of *Yusuf*'s brothers and his brother from both his father and mother. The others were *Yusuf*'s brothers from his father's side only. *Binyamin* did not participate with them in the sinful deeds they did. This is why *Binyamin* was famous to have received Prophethood.

Yusuf's brothers wanted to kill *Yusuf* unjustly. They threw him in a well. Then they sold him, claiming he was a slave, when he was truly a free man. They humiliated their father, Ya`qub, who was a prophet-- and this is blasphemy. Although later they repented of these sins, none of them received the office of Prophethood. Prophets are protected from committing such wrong doings--before Prophethood and after it. Some of the descendents of those brothers did receive Prophethood. Those descendents-- not *Yusuf*'s brothers--are the *Asbat* mentioned in the *Qur'an* (e.g., an-Nisa', 163) to be among the prophets.

Chapter 2
Types of Apostasy (*Riddah*)

It is obligatory upon every Muslim to preserve one's faith in *Islam* and to protect it against whatever invalidates, abolishes, and interrupts it, namely, apostasy (*riddah*); we seek refuge with *Allah, ta^ala*, from it.

Explanation: Every Muslim is ordered to preserve one's faith in *Islam* by protecting oneself from apostasy. Apostasy is for one to blaspheme after having been a Muslim. By this, one invalidates one's faith in *Islam*, and becomes a non-Muslim. If a Muslim apostatizes, then one is no longer a Muslim. One is a blasphemer--specifically an apostate--even if both of one's parents are Muslim.

The meaning of what *an-Nawawiyy* and others said is: "Apostasy is the most abhorrent type of blasphemy."

Explanation: The most abhorrent type of blasphemy is for one to apostatize after having been Muslim. It is the ugliest form of blasphemy in the sense that is erases all the good deeds and that it is a transition from truth to falsehood. This does not mean that every act of apostasy is the worst type of blasphemy. Denying the Existence of God (atheism) is the worst kind of blasphemy. If a Muslim apostatizes by committing atheism, then one will have committed the worst and ugliest blasphemy. If apostasy takes place by other than atheism, then this apostasy is the ugliest but not the worst blasphemy. Additionally, it means that dealing with an apostate has much stricter rules than dealing with an original blasphemer.[17] For example, it is permissible for the Muslim caliph to engage in a specific peace treaty with a group of original blasphemers. Then, once the treaty is concluded according to the rules of *Islam*, it becomes forbidden for the Muslims to kill any of those original blasphemers covered under the treaty. The apostate, however, cannot make such a peace treaty with the caliph. Moreover, it is unlawful for the caliph to ignore the apostate's case. Rather, he must order him to return to *Islam*. If, after three (3) days, the apostate does not re-embrace *Islam*, then the caliph must have him killed . Unlike the case of the original blasphemers, any marriage contract of the apostate is invalid. On the other hand,

---

[17] The original blasphemer is the one who was born and raised a blasphemer.

Muslims consider the marriage contract between original blasphemers to be valid if it was conducted in a valid manner according to them.

In this age, it has become common to speak carelessly to the extent that some people utter words which turn them out of *Islam*, without even deeming such words sinful even though they are blasphemous.

Explanation: Sadly, these words of the author realistically describe our times. Nowadays, out of negligence or extreme ignorance of the Rules of the Religion, many people identified as Muslims utter blasphemous statements. Many among them do not know that such statements are blasphemous. Some may believe that uttering those words is not even sinful. Consequently, they say them as easily as they take a sip of water, and blaspheme without realizing the very abhorrent status they reached. May *Allah* protect us from it.

This is asserted by the saying of the Prophet, *sallallahu ^alayhi wa sallam:* ⟨⟨A person may utter a statement that one thinks harmless, which results in one's falling the depth of seventy (70) years into Hellfire.⟩⟩ This falling distance of seventy (70) years leads to the bottom of Hellfire where only blasphemers will reside. This *hadith* was related by *at-Tirmidhiyy* who classified it as a *hasan*[18] *hadith*. Al-Bukhariyy and Muslim related a *hadith* with a similar meaning. This *hadith* is an evidence that it is not a condition for a person to fall into blasphemy that one must have learned the judgement of the uttered blasphemous words or that one must have liked or believed their meaning–as falsely stated in the book called *Fiqh-us-Sunnah*.

Explanation: The proof that the intentional uttering of even a single explicit blasphemous statement is blasphemy and causes one to apostatize from *Islam* -whether or not one intended to blaspheme- is the *hadith* of the Prophet ﷺ:

$$\text{«إِنَّ الْعَبْدَ لَيَتَكَلَّمُ بِالْكَلِمَةِ لَا يَرَى بِهَا بَأْسًا يَهْوِى بِهَا فِى النَّارِ سَبْعِينَ خَرِيفًا»}$$

It means: ⟨⟨A person may utter a statement that one thinks harmless, which results in one's falling the depth of seventy (70) years into

---

[18] A *hasan hadith* is one of two types of *hadiths* that can be relied upon in deducing judgments. The other type is the *sahih hadith*. A *hasan hadith* is a strong *hadith*, but its level of strength is less than that of the *sahih* one.

46

Hellfire.» This _hadith_ was related by _Imam at-Tirmidhiyy_ in his book, _Al-Jami^_.[19] At-Tirmidhiyy established this _hadith_ as having the _hasan_ classification. _Al-Bukhariyy_ and Muslim narrated the same _hadith_ with different words and established its _sahih_ classification:

$$\text{«إنّ العَبْدَ لَيَتَكَلَّمُ بِالكَلِمَةِ ما يَتَبَيَّنُ فيها يَهوى بها فى النارِ أَبعَدَ}$$
$$\text{مِمَّا بَيْنَ المشرقِ والمغربِ»}$$

This narration of the _hadith_ means: «A person may utter a statement that one thinks harmless, which results in one's falling in Hellfire a distance farther than what is between east and west.»

Both of these narrations stand as an evidence that a person blasphemes for simply uttering a statement of blasphemy, even if the person did not hold the conviction in the meaning of the statement. Simply uttering a blasphemous statement intentionally is blasphemy, even if one did not believe in what that statement means.

The one who curses _Allah_ is a blasphemer, whether or not one believes in what one says, and whether or not one feels delighted about saying it. The case is not as _Sayyid Sabiq_[20] claimed in his book, _Fiqh-us-Sunnah_. _Sayyid Sabiq_ said that for the person to be judged as a blasphemer because of a blasphemous statement that one said, it is a condition that one believes the meaning of the statement in one's heart and feels delighted about saying it. _Sayyid Sabiq_'s claim contradicts the _hadith_ of the Prophet ﷺ previously mentioned. Moreover, his claim contradicts the _Qur'an_, because _Allah_ told us in the _Qur'an_ that escaping the judgment of blasphemy because one did not feel the delight in one's heart when one uttered the statement of blasphemy is a condition only for the person who utters blasphemy under the threat of death or what leads to it if one does not do so. In _Surat an-Nahl_, Verse 106, _Allah_ said:

$$\text{﴿مَن كَفَرَ بِٱللَّهِ مِنۢ بَعْدِ إِيمَٰنِهِۦٓ إِلَّا مَنْ أُكْرِهَ وَقَلْبُهُۥ مُطْمَئِنٌّ}$$
$$\text{بِٱلْإِيمَٰنِ ﴾}$$

---

[19] Also known as _As-Sunan_.

[20] _Sayyid Sabiq_, the author of _Fiqh-us-Sunnah_, is from Egypt. He lived in Saudi Arabia for some time. He died in 1999. Despite their fame, his books contain many erroneous judgements.

This *ayah* means: [The one who blasphemes after having believed will be severely punished by *Allah*. Excluded is the one who is forced to blaspheme while one's heart is certain with faith and one is not pleased with blasphemy].

Sayyid Sabiq belied the Book of *Allah* by claiming that the case of the one who is not being threatened with death to blaspheme is the same as the one who is threatened with death to blaspheme. *Sayyid Sabiq*'s inconsistency is blatant. In order to pass his judgment on the person who unrightfully killed another person, would the judge ask him whether or not he was delighted when he killed that person? The judge would not! Would the judge ask a thief whether or not he was delighted about his thievery to pass a suitable judgment on him? The judge would not! If it is the case that the judge would not ask about one's state of heart in unrightful killing and stealing--sins which are much less than blasphemy--then it is evident that the delight in the heart is not a criterion in judging as a blasphemer the one who willfully utters a blasphemous statement.

Anger is not an excuse for one to escape the judgement of falling into blasphemy. Concerning this matter, *Imam an-Nawawiyy* said: "If a man was angry with his child or young slave and hit him severely, then another person asked him, 'How could you do this? Aren't you a Muslim?' and to that his deliberate answer was 'No,' he blasphemed." This was said by *Hanafiyy* scholars as well as others.

Explanation: The person does not escape the judgment of blasphemy for uttering a blasphemous statement because he was angry when he uttered that statement. If a person utters blasphemy intentionally, he will be judged as a blasphemer whether or not he was angry at the time he uttered the statement. A person would be excused only in such a case if his anger overwhelmed him to the point that he was no longer sane when he uttered the blasphemy. For example, if a person was so angry that he could no longer differentiate between a door and a person--and while in this state, he uttered blasphemous words without being aware of what he was saying, he would be excused from committing blasphemy. However, generally, anger does not cause a person to reach this state.

How do some people say one is excused if one utters blasphemy because one is angry? *Allah* did not exclude this case in the *Qur'an*.

48

The Prophet ﷺ did not exclude this case in the _Hadith_. Those who erroneously make anger an exceptional case are excluding what _Allah_ did not judge as an exception in the Rules revealed by Him and conveyed by the Prophet ﷺ. Such a claim implies that the basic rules revealed to the Prophet ﷺ were not complete--rather there is a need for one to change these rules--and this, in itself, is blasphemy.

In his book, _Rawdat-ut-Talibin_, _Imam an-Nawawiyy_ explicitly mentioned the case of anger. He said, 'If a man was angry with his child or young slave and hit him severely, and another person, (feeling pity for that child or slave) asked the first, 'How could you do this, aren't you a Muslim?' (implying that a Muslim should not act like that) and to that his deliberate answer was, 'No,' he blasphemed." This is a very clear statement from _Imam an-Nawawiyy_ that the person who utters a blasphemous statement (in a fit of anger) is <u>not excused</u> because of that anger. Other scholars among the _Hanafiyys, Shafi^iyys_ and _Malikiyys_ mentioned the same aforementioned rule.

An-Nawawiyy and other scholars of the four schools (madhhabs), classified apostasy into three categories: apostate beliefs, apostate actions, and apostate sayings. Each category of apostasy is divided into many subdivisions.

**Explanation:** Scholars from the four schools (_madhhabs_) classified apostasy into three categories: apostate beliefs in the heart, apostate actions committed by the various body parts, and apostate sayings uttered with the tongue. The _Shafi^iyy Imam, an-Nawawiyy,_ classified apostasy as such in his book, _al-Minhaj,_ as did the _Shafi^iyy Imam, Ibn-ul-Wardiyy,_ in his book, _al-Hawi._

Committing blasphemy of any one category, either on its own, or in conjunction with blasphemy of another category, takes the person out of _Islam_. It is not a condition that blasphemy of one category be committed in conjunction with blasphemy of another category for that judgment to hold.

1) Examples of the first category of apostasy, i.e., the apostate beliefs, are:

having the doubt in _Allah_, His Messenger, the _Qur'an_, the Day of Judgement, Paradise, Hell, Reward, or Punishment, or having the doubt in similar matters upon which there has been scholarly consensus (_Ijma^_);

Explanation: The person who doubts in *Allah*, even for a moment, becomes a blasphemer. Doubting in *Allah* means one no longer holds the unequivocal conviction that *Allah* exists. The same judgment applies if one doubts whether or not *Allah*'s existence is without a beginning, without an end, or without a place. By the same token, one should be certain that *Allah* is not like the creation in any way, and doubting it is blasphemy.

The one who doubts about the truthfulness of the Message of Prophet *Muhammad* ﷺ is a blasphemer. The person who doubts the *Qur'an* is a blasphemer. The one who doubts whether or not the Day of Judgment will occur is a blasphemer. The one who doubts whether or not the believers will be rewarded in Paradise or the blasphemers will be tortured in Hellfire is a blasphemer.

On the other hand, one needs to differentiate between the doubt that takes the person out of *Islam* and the mere involuntary thought that may come to a person whose heart remains firm on the proper belief. It is not blasphemy if a blasphemous thought merely comes to a person's mind if it does not make the person doubt in the proper belief. On the contrary, one is rewarded for hating such a thought and rejecting it.

*Ijma^* is defined as the scholarly concensus of the *mujtahids*[21] on an Islamic matter in any era. It is blasphemy to doubt the truthfulness of any matter which all Muslims (the scholar and layman alike) know the Prophet ﷺ conveyed. An example would be the weighing of the deeds in the Hereafter. It is known to the Muslim layman and scholar alike that the Prophet ﷺ informed that the person's deeds are weighed in the Hereafter. So, whoever doubts whether or not the deeds are weighed in the Hereafter is judged a blasphemer, unless he did not know that this is a matter in the Religion because he is a new Muslim.

believing the world is eternal by kind and elements or by kind only;

Explanation: It is blasphemy to believe that something other than

---

[21] *Mujtahids* refer to the top qualified scholars, such as *ash-Shafi^iyy, Malik, Ahmad Ibn Hambal, Abu Hanifah* and the like. They are the ones who are qualified to deduce Islamic judgments from the *Qur'an* and the *Hadith*. Hence, the agreement of a group of Muslims (whether laymen or non-mujtahid scholars) does not constitute *Ijma^*.

Allah is eternal. Everything other than *Allah* had a beginning to its existence. Muslim scholars judged as blasphemer the one who believes the world is eternal. Among them:

1. *al-Mutawalli* (a prominent scholar of the *Shafi^iyy* school);

2. *Qadi ^Iyad* (one of the most famous *Malikiyy* scholars; d. 544 AH);

3. *Ibnu Daqiqil-^Id* (it was said he attained the level of *mujtahid*, and was famous in teaching both the *Malikiyy* and the *Shafi^iyy* schools; d. 702 AH);

4. The famous *hafidh Ibn Hajar al-^Asqalaniyy*; and many others.

renouncing one of the attributes of *Allah, ta^ala*, known by necessity[22] He is attributed with—such as His Knowing about everything;

Explanation: There are certain attributes known among the Muslim laymen and scholars alike to be attributes of *Allah*, like Life, Power, Knowledge, Will, etc. To deny *Allah* is attributed with any of these attributes is blasphemy. For example, the one who doubts that *Allah* has Power over all things, or doubts that *Allah* is attributed with Speech (*al-Kalam*), Hearing, or Sight is a blasphemer. On the other hand, one does not blaspheme if, for example, one never thought about *Allah* being attributed with Hearing, provided one does not hold a contrary belief.

ascribing to *Allah* what is known by necessity does not befit Him—such as being a body;

Explanation: There are certain attributes which both the knowledgeable Muslim and the layman know *Allah* is clear of, i.e., attributes which are unbefitting to Him. The one who attributes to *Allah* any of these attributes is a blasphemer. For example, the person who says *Allah* is a body or has bodily attributes is attributing to *Allah* what every Muslim knows does not befit Him. Similarly blasphemes whoever says *Allah* is an illumination, or is attributed with color, because these claims entail likening *Allah* to the creations. Likewise, the one who says *Allah* is a body, but not like other bodies, is a blasphemer.

---

[22] Issues which are known by necessity are the issues that are known to the laymen and the scholars alike, without the need of any deduction.

The author of the famous _Hambaliyy_ book _al-Khisal_ related that _Imam Ahmad Ibn Hambal_ judged as a blasphemer the person who says, "_Allah_ is a body, not like other bodies." The one who says, "_Allah_ is a body" is attributing to _Allah_ an unbefitting attribute and his qualifying phrase, "not like other bodies," does not clear him of having committed blasphemy. A body by definition is something which has a format and a shape and takes up space. All these are attributes of the creation, and are not befitting to ascribe to the Creator.

legitimating what is commonly known among the Muslims to be unlawful (_haram_)-such as adultery and fornication (_zina_), sodomy (_liwat_), killing (_qatl_) a Muslim, stealing (_sariqah_), and taking the money of others unjustly (_ghasb_);

Explanation: There are certain unlawful matters which all the Muslims, scholars and laymen alike, know are unlawful. Examples are: murder, stealing, taking someone else's money by force, and similar acts. The one who claims lawful any such unlawful matters blasphemes. So, one blasphemes if one claims that it is lawful to drink wine, to eat pork, or to commit adultery or fornication. This judgment does not apply to the one who has recently embraced _Islam_ and did not yet learn the judgment of these matters. In such case, he is not judged as a blasphemer, rather he is taught what is correct.

deeming unlawful (_haram_) what is commonly known among the Muslims to be lawful (_halal_)–such as selling and marriage;

Explanation: There are matters in the Religion of _Islam_ which both the knowledgeable person and the layman know are lawful, or permissible. If a person believes or claims that any of these matters is unlawful, one blasphemes. For example, all Muslims know that marriage is lawful in _Islam_. So, the one who believes or claims that marriage is forbidden in _Islam_ blasphemes. Another example of a blasphemous belief or statement is for one to believe or claim that it is unlawful to slaughter an edible animal to eat it.

renouncing the obligation of the matters commonly known among the Muslims to be obligatory–such as the five Obligatory Prayers or one of their prostrations, _Zakah_, Fasting (_Sawm_), Pilgrimage (_Hajj_), and Ablution (_Wudu'_);

Explanation: There are certain matters in _Islam_ which both the knowledgeable Muslim and the layman know are obligatory. Praying the five Obligatory Prayers is an example of such a matter; both the Muslim scholar and the layman know that this is a daily obligation. Therefore, one blasphemes if one considers that it is no longer obligatory upon one to pray them or considers that once a person reaches a certain level of alleged 'purity', one no longer has to pray. Likewise blasphemes the one who considers paying *Zakah* is not an obligation on the wealthy people, or fasting *Ramadan* is not an obligation on the Muslims.

deeming obligatory the matters commonly known among the Muslims not to be obligatory;

Explanation: There are matters in the Religion of *Islam* which the knowledgeable Muslim and the layman alike know are not obligatory. An example of such matters is the fasting of the month of *Rajab*. Considering its fasting obligatory when one knows it is not is blasphemy.

renouncing the rewardability of what all Muslims know is religiously rewardable;

Explanation: There are matters in the Religion of *Islam* that both the knowledgeable Muslim and the layman know are rewardable, like performing the *Witr Prayer*.[23] So, the one who considers any of these matters are not rewardable blasphemes. For example, one blasphemes by believing or saying that praying the *Witr* Prayer does not involve any reward, because this entails belying the Prophet ﷺ. The same case applies to any matter which is commonly known among the Muslims to be part of the Religion. If a person knowingly considers that such a matter is not part of the Religion, he blasphemes.

Furthermore, the person blasphemes if he considers that one of the aforementioned rules is an injustice from *Allah* while knowing that it is a rule in the Religion. Such was the case of the poet, *Abul-^Ala' al-Ma^arriyy*, who dispraised marriage and slaughtering animals for food. It is also like those we see today who dispraise the fact that the Muslim man may marry four women, or those who dispraise that the

---

[23] The *Witr* Prayer is an optional prayer. One can pray the *Witr* Prayer after praying the ^Isha' Prayer until the appearance of the dawn. One prays an odd number of rak^ahs, i.e., one, three, five...etc.

woman is obligated to wear a head cover. All that is blasphemy. We accept whatever the Messenger of *Allah* ﷺ brought. Whatever disagrees with the Prophet's teachings is rejected.

intending to blaspheme in the future; intending to do any of the aforementioned;

Explanation: Intending to blaspheme in the future means one has the determination in one's heart to blaspheme sometime in the future. Such a person blasphemes immediately. So, if someone says, "I will blaspheme after one million years," one blasphemes immediately even if one does not believe that one will live that long. Also, the person who hesitates whether or not to blaspheme becomes a blasphemer immediately. Likewise, the person becomes a blasphemer immediately if one makes one's committing blasphemy contingent upon the occurrence of a certain event. The true believer is the one whose heart is firm with belief and does not want to quit being a believer at any time for any reason.

hesitating whether or not to blaspheme—but not the mere involuntary thought of it;

Explanation: There is a difference between the involuntary blasphemous thought which may come to a person whose heart remains firm on the correct belief and the hesitation which results in one's doubting that belief. Hesitating whether or not to blaspheme is blasphemy, because it means one no longer has a firm conviction in one's belief.

denying the companionship of our Master *Abu Bakr,* may *Allah* raise his rank;

Explanation: The person who believes in one's heart that *Abu Bakr* is not the Companion of the Prophet blasphemes. The scholars specified *Abu Bakr*'s companionship in this judgment, and not ^*Umar*'s or ^*Aliyy*'s because *Allah* mentioned the companionship of *Abu Bakr* in the *Qur'an*. *Ayah* 40 of *Surat at-Tawbah*:

mentions that while in the cave with *Abu Bakr* enroute to *al-Madinah,* Prophet *Muhammad* ﷺ said to his Companion, "Do not be sad. *Allah* supports us." It is known by necessity that *Abu Bakr* is the Companion mentioned in this verse. Hence, denying his companionship is belying the *Qur'an* and the consensus of the whole nation.

denying the Message of whomever is recognized by all Muslims as a messenger or a prophet;

Explanation: Denying the Prophethood of any of the prophets whom all the Muslims (scholars and laymen alike) know to be prophets is blasphemy. For example, denying that *Adam*, Noah, Moses, Jesus, and *Muhammad* were prophets is blasphemy. However, one does not blaspheme for denying the state of Prophethood of a prophet because he has never heard of his Prophethood. For example, if a person did not know that *Shith* was a prophet, and because of his ignorance said, "*Shith* was not a prophet of *Allah*," he would not be judged as a blasphemer. The scholars had different opinions as to whether *al-Khadir* was a prophet or just a highly pious Muslim. Most of the scholars hold the opinion that he was a prophet, and this is the correct saying according to the religious proofs. However, the one who claims that *al-Khadir* was a *waliyy* (a highly pious Muslim) but not a prophet does not blaspheme.

renouncing, out of stubbornness, a letter of the *Qur'an* which is known by all Muslims to be of it; adding, out of stubbornness, a letter to the *Qur'an* which is known by all Muslims not to be of it;

Explanation: If, out of stubbornness, a person insists on adding a letter or more to the text of the *Qur'an* which he knows is not part of it, he commits blasphemy. Likewise blasphemes the person who renounces even one letter of the *Qur'an* when he knows it is part of the *Qur'an*. On the other hand, the one who deletes a part of the *Qur'an*, by mistake, such as one did not memorize it properly is not judged a blasphemer. However, if one recites the *Qur'an*, before learning the proper recitation, and as a result commits a mistake, then one commits an enormous sin. *Abu Dawud* narrated from the Prophet ﷺ:

«سِتَّةٌ لَعَنْتُهُم ولَعَنَهُم اللهُ وكُلُّ نبِيٍّ مُجَابٌ» وَذَكَرَ مِنَ السِّتَّةِ
«الزَّائِدُ فى كِتَابِ اللهِ»

55

It means: «There are six people that I damned, Allah damned, and every prophet damned.» Then among the six he mentioned, «the one who adds to the Book of Allah.» This hadith applies to the person who adds to the Qur'an whether he does that knowingly or out of ignorance.

belying a messenger or ascribing an unbefitting attribute to him; making a messenger's name diminutive with the purpose of degrading him;

Explanation: Any matter which involves belying a messenger or ascribing to him an unbefitting attribute, or any attempt to degrade or humiliate a prophet is blasphemy. Examples are for a person to believe any one of the prophets was ignorant, cowardly, or untrustworthy.

believing in the possibility of the Prophethood of someone after our Prophet Muhammad, sallallahu ^alayhi wa sallam.

Explanation: Prophet Muhammad ﷺ is the last of the prophets of Allah. It is blasphemy for one to believe that it is permissible for any person to be revealed as a prophet after Prophet Muhammad ﷺ. It makes no difference whether one believes it is possible for a prophet who is a messenger to be revealed to after Prophet Muhammad ﷺ, or a prophet who is not a messenger--either case is blasphemy. For example, the Qadiyaniyys believe in the Prophethood of a man from India named Ghulam Ahmad, who lived approximately 1250 years after the Revelation of Prophet Muhammad. Some of the Qadiyaniyys believe or say about him that he was not an "independent prophet," rather he was a prophet who followed the Rules of Prophet Muhammad ﷺ. Still this is blasphemy, because they attributed prophethood to someone after Prophet Muhammad ﷺ. By that, they have belied the Qur'an, the Prophet of Allah, and all the Muslim nation (ummah). This is blasphemy. Allah said: ﴾وَخَاتَمَ ٱلنَّبِيِّـنَ ۝﴿. _Ayah 40 of Suratul-'Ahzab means: Prophet Muhammad is the last of the prophets. Prophet Muhammad said: وخُتِمَ بِي النَّبِيُّون This hadith means: «The prophets were ended with me».

2) The second category of apostasy is the apostate actions, such as prostrating to an idol, or the sun, whether or not out of worshipping them,[24] prostrating to a human out of worshipping him, like the prostration of some ignorant people to some fake sufi shaykhs out of

---

[24] Other blasphemous actions include assisting anyone to blaspheme and throwing religious materials in the trash.

worshipping them. However, if this prostration is not out of worshipping them, then it is not blasphemous. Nevertheless, it is sinful.

Explanation: The second category of apostasy is "apostasy of actions." It includes the blasphemous acts committed by the different parts of the body. An example of apostasy of actions is prostrating to an idol. The one who prostrates to an idol is judged as a blasphemer without considering one's intention in one's action. Likewise the person who prostrates to the sun, the moon, the devil, or the fire commits apostasy (of action) because all these actions are known to be done only by non-Muslims to worship other than *Allah*.

On the other hand, the case of the person who prostrates to another human is more detailed. If one's intent in one's act is to worship that human, then one is a blasphemer. However, if one prostrates to that human just to salute the latter, then it is not blasphemy. In the laws of previous Muslim nations, it was permissible for a Muslim to prostrate to another Muslim to greet him and to reflect that he is honored and held at a high status. This was the case when the angels prostrated to Prophet *Adam* عليه السلام. However, in the laws revealed to Prophet *Muhammad* ﷺ, prostrating to another Muslim became forbidden.

Another blasphemous action is knowingly throwing the Holy *Qur'an* in the garbage. Even if the person says, "My intent was not to degrade or humiliate the *Qur'an*," one is not excused, because the action itself involves degradation and humiliation. On the other hand, if the person is not aware that the book one threw in the garbage was the Book of the *Qur'an*, one does not blaspheme for doing so. This rule applies to other Islamic material as well.

The general rule governing the case of apostate actions is: "Any action which all Muslims know or agree that only a blasphemer does is blasphemy. In other words, to commit an action which all the Muslims agree that it is only committed by a blasphemer is blasphemy." An example is the case of a person who wears the religious attire specific to the blasphemers, or wears their symbol of blasphemy and mixes with them in their places of worship. This person is committing an act which is commonly known to the Muslims to be an act done only by blasphemers. Hence, the person is judged as a blasphemer for doing it.

57

3) The third category of apostasy is the apostate sayings, which are too many to be counted.

Explanation: Most of the cases pertaining to blasphemy are of this kind, as the Prophet ﷺ informed. In the *hadith* related by *at-Tabaraniyy*, the Prophet ﷺ said:

$$\text{«أَكْثَرُ خَطَايَا ابْنِ ءَادَمَ مِنْ لِسَانِهِ»}$$

This *hadith* means: «Most of the sins of the children of *Adam* are due to their tongues.»

Some examples are:

to say to a Muslim, 'O blasphemer', 'O Jew', 'O Christian', or 'O you without religion', meaning that the religion of the addressed Muslim is blasphemy, Judaism, Christianity, or not a religion. However, if one says such words to a Muslim with the purpose of only likening him to those non-Muslims in behavior, then it is not blasphemy;

Explanation: It is narrated by *al-Bukhariyy, Ibn Hibban,* and others that the Prophet ﷺ said:

$$\text{«إذا قَالَ الرَّجُلُ لأخيهِ يا كَافِرُ فَقَدْ بَاءَ بها أَحَدُهُما . فإنْ كَانَ}$$
$$\text{كما قال وإلا رَجَعَتْ عليه»}$$

It means: «If a person addresses his fellow Muslim by telling him, "You are a blasphemer," then one of the two is a blasphemer. It is either that what the addresser said is true, or the addresser himself becomes a blasphemer.» However, if by his statement, the person wanted only to liken that Muslim to the non-Muslim in his behavior, then he would not be judged as a blasphemer. This means, if he says to a Muslim, "O you non-Muslim," and by saying that he meant that his acts are so mean that they resemble the way the non-Muslim acts, then he does not blaspheme for that. However, he is not entitled to say that; saying such words to a Muslim is unlawful, even with this intention.

to mock one of the Names of *Allah*, ta^ala, His Promise, or His Threat, while knowing such matters have been attributed to Him, *subhanah*;

Explanation: Mockery is to say statements with the purpose of

58

belittling something or someone. The one who mocks *Allah*, or mocks the Promise or the Threat of *Allah* blasphemes. For example, one blasphemes if one mocks one of the Names of *Allah* while knowing this is a Name of *Allah*. If someone says he prefers to end up in Hell because he will have more fun with the sinners there, he blasphemes for mocking Paradise, a Promise of *Allah*. Similarly, mocking the Threat of *Allah* (Hellfire) is blasphemy. However, if a person mocks a matter because he is unaware that this is a Threat of *Allah*, he does not blaspheme. So, a person does not blaspheme if he does not believe that there are large scorpions in Hellfire to torture the blasphemers because he never heard of that matter. Moreover, he does not have the intention to belittle the Threat of *Allah*.

out of belittlement or stubbornness to say, 'If *Allah* ordered me with such a matter, I would not do it'; or to say: 'If the _Qiblah_ were changed to another direction I would not pray towards it'; or to say: 'If *Allah* gave me Paradise I would not enter it'.

Explanation: If one says any of the three specific aforementioned statements, or statements similar to them in content whether out of stubbornness or belittlement, one blasphemes. Stubbornness is to refuse to admit the truthfulness of something one knows is true.

to say: 'If *Allah* punished me for leaving out prayers despite my sickness, He would wrong me';

Explanation: To say, 'Allah would be unjust in punishing me for not praying because I am so sick', is blasphemy. This statement is blasphemy because it attributes injustice to *Allah*, which is an attribute of imperfection. This belies the verses of the *Qur'an*, the sayings of the Prophet ﷺ, and the judgment of the sound mind. *Allah* said:

Surat Fussilat, Verse 46 means: [Certainly, *Allah* is not unjust to His slaves.]

to say: 'Something happened without the Destining of *Allah*';

Explanation: If someone says, even about one single matter, that it occurred without *Allah* willing it to happen, he blasphemes. Every matter, whether good or evil, occurs only by the Will of *Allah*. *Allah* is not blamed for destining the evil. Rather, the slave who chooses to commit the evil is blamed for his choice.

to say: 'If prophets, angels, or all Muslims testified before me about something, I would not accept from them';

Explanation: The one who does not accept the testimony of prophets, angels, or all the Muslims is declaring them as untrustworthy; this is blasphemy. The one who says the prophets or the angels are not trustworthy blasphemes, because he is belittling them and belying the *Qur'an*. The one who claims that all Muslims are not trustworthy is attempting to destroy the credibility of our Religion, because the rules of the Religion were transmitted through them. If the unanimous testimony of all the Muslims was something rejected because it was not trustworthy, then there would not be any credibility to what we have received. This is why the person who utters such a statement is a blasphemer.

to say: 'I will not do so and so even if it is a recommended matter (*sunnah*)'—with the purpose of mockery;

Explanation: Any statement containing dispraise or mockery of the *Sunnah* of the Prophet ﷺ is blasphemy. For example, if one says, "I don't want to use the *siwak*," and means by one's statement that although one believes using the *siwak* is *Sunnah*, it is still a disgusting habit, one blasphemes. However, if one did not mean to mock the *Sunnah* of the Prophet ﷺ, rather one just meant that one did not want to use *siwak* at that point in time, then one would not blaspheme.

to say: 'If someone were a prophet, I would not believe in him';

Explanation: The one who says such a statement blasphemes, even if one knows that the person whom one named was not a prophet, because one's statement belittles the office of Prophethood.

to say: 'What is this Law (*Shar^*)?' when a scholar gives one a religious judgement—with the purpose of belittling the judgement of the Islamic Law;

Explanation: It is blasphemy to belittle any of the Laws revealed to Prophet *Muhammad* ﷺ or imply that they are not true. For example, if a person asked a religious scholar for the religious judgment of a particular case, and upon hearing the ruling he said, "What kind of Law is that?" meaning the Laws revealed to Prophet *Muhammad* ﷺ are not true, or he did not like that particular judgment, he blasphemes. However, if his statement meant that he did not believe this ruling conforms to the rules of the Religion, then his statement is not blasphemy.

to say: 'May *Allah*'s damn be upon every single religious scholar'. However, if one did not mean all of the religious scholars, but meant specific ones and there was an associating matter which indicates this meaning because one believes of their corrupt condition, then one would not blaspheme. One's words, however, are not clear of sin;

Explanation: If one generalized one's statement to include dispraise of all the religious scholars, one blasphemes because one's statement is belittling the status of Islamic knowledge. However, if it was understood from the context that one's dispraise was of a specific group of scholars, such as the scholars of one town or the scholars of one specific period, then this is not blasphemy. For example, to damn a particular group of scholars or the scholars of a certain city because they are not implementing their knowledge is not blasphemy. It is, however, sinful except if one had an acceptable religious excuse. An acceptable religious excuse would be if one said that statement to prevent those scholars from being disobedient or to warn the people against their bad status.

to say: 'I do not acknowledge *Allah*, the angels, the Prophet, the Islamic Law (*Shar^*), or *Islam*;

Explanation: To acknowledge a matter here means to recognize the existence or the truth of that matter. So, if one utters words which mean one does not acknowledge the existence of *Allah*, the angels, the Prophets, the *Qur'an*, the Islamic Laws, or *Islam*, one blasphemes.

to say: 'I do not know the judgement'—with the purpose of mocking the judgement revealed by *Allah*;

Explanation: Saying, "I don't know the Religious judgment" of a particular matter and intending by such a statement that the Religious judgment has no value, is blasphemy. On the other hand, saying, "I do not know" in the proper place is a praised matter. *Imam*

61

Muslim and *Ibn Hibban* related that when the Prophet ﷺ was asked about the best and the worst of the places, he said:

$$\text{«لا أَدْرِى، أَسْأَلُ جِبْرِيلَ»}$$

It means: "I do not know; I will ask *Jibril*." He asked *Jibril*, who said, "I do not know; I will ask my Lord." Then, it was revealed to the Prophet ﷺ that the best of all places are the mosques, and the worst of all places are the marketplaces.

to mention an *ayah* with the intention of belittling its meaning, like: to say *ayah* 34, *Surat an-Naba'* after one has filled a cup: ﴿وَكَأْسًا دِهَاقًا ۝﴾. This *ayah* refers to a cup full to the brim with the drinks of Paradise;

or to say *ayah* 20, *Surat an-Naba'* after one has emptied a drink: ﴿فَكَانَتْ سَرَابًا ۝﴾. This *ayah* refers to mountains that will vanish on the Judgement Day as if they were a mirage;

or to say *Ayah* 3, *Surat al-Mutaffifin* upon weighing or measuring:

﴿وَإِذَا كَالُوهُمْ أَوْ وَزَنُوهُمْ يُخْسِرُونَ ۝﴾. This *ayah* refers to some people cheating in measuring and weighing;

or to say *ayah* 47, *Surat al-Kahf* when seeing a crowd:

﴿وَحَشَرْنَٰهُمْ فَلَمْ نُغَادِرْ مِنْهُمْ أَحَدًا ۝﴾. This *ayah* refers to the Judgement Day when the people will be assembled without any of them being left out.

If one uses the *ayahs* of the *Qur'an* in other than their proper context, without belittling them, one does not blaspheme. However, *Shaykh Ahmad Ibn Hajar* said: "This is not far from being unlawful (*haram*).";

Explanation: It is blasphemy to recite any verse of the *Qur'an* with the purpose of belittling the terms of the verse or its meaning. For example, a person blasphemes for belittling verse 34 of *Surat an-Naba'* if he recited it while filling a cup with wine, and he was indicating that the wine he poured was actually like or better than the delicious drink promised to the people of Paradise.

However, simply reciting one of the verses of the *Qur'an* out of context without belittling it is not blasphemy. For instance, if one does not have the intention to mock verse 47 of *Surat al-Kahf* (which refers to the Judgement Day when all the people will be assembled, and none will be left out). However, one recites it when a large crowd of people enter a place, one does not blaspheme. However, *Shaykh*

Ahmad Ibn Hajar al-Haytamiyy (d. 974 AH) said that reciting the verses of the Qur'an out of context reflects a lack of due respect to the Qur'an and this is sinful.

to cuss a prophet or an angel;

Explanation: The one who cusses a prophet or an angel definitely is judged as a blasphemer.

to say words which mock the prayer, such as: to say, 'I would be a pimp if I performed prayer'; or to say, 'Nothing good has happened to me since I started praying'; or to say: 'Prayer is not proper for me' with the purpose of mockery;

Explanation: The one who says such statements with the purpose of mocking the prayers is definitely a blasphemer. If someone says, "If I pray, I will be similar to a pimp," he is belittling and mocking the prayers and therefore blasphemes. However, it is not blasphemy for the menstruating woman to say, "The prayer is not proper for me," intending by her statement that while she is menstruating she is not permitted to pray.

to say to a Muslim: 'I am your enemy and the enemy of your Prophet'; or to say to a descendent of the Prophet (*Sharif*): 'I am your enemy and the enemy of your grandfather,'meaning the Prophet, *sallallahu ^alayhi wa sallam*; or to say anything similar to those aforementioned, abhorrent, and ugly words.

Explanation: The one who belittles the Prophet ﷺ, or uses words to mock the Prophet ﷺ is by concensus a blasphemer. Moreover, whoever curses the Prophet ﷺ is a blasphemer. Judge *Abu Yusuf* (d. 182 AH) said that whoever doubts the blasphemy of a such a person is himself a blasphemer. Also, doubting that such a person (curser) deserves punishment in the Hereafter is itself blasphemy. The famous *Malikiyy* scholar, *Sahnun*, gave a similar judgement.

A large number of *faqihs*, like the *Hanafiyy faqih*, *Badr-ur-Rashid* and the *Malikiyy Qadi ^Iyad*, may *Allah*, ta^ala, have mercy upon them, enumerated many blasphemous statements which one needs to know, because whoever does not know evil is more likely to fall into it.

Explanation: *Qadi ^Iyad* (d. 544 AH) is one of the most famous *Malikiyy* scholars. He mentioned many blasphemous statements in his book, *ash-Shifa*, with the purpose of warning the Muslims against uttering such words. Other scholars from the four *madhhabs* (schools) did the same. Among them is *Badrur-Rashid*, a *Hanafiyy* scholar, who lived in the eighth century. He authored a book specifically to list many blasphemous sayings. The purpose in authoring such works was to warn the Muslims of the great danger of saying such statements. May *Allah* protect us from blasphemy.

The rule is: Any belief, action, or saying which belittles *Allah*, His Books, His Messengers, His Angels, His Rites, the well-known practices of His Religion, His Rules, His Promise, or His Threat is blasphemy. Hence, the human being must use caution with one's utmost effort to avoid blasphemy at all times.

Explanation: Any conviction, action, or saying which belittles *Allah* is blasphemy. Likewise blasphemy is to belittle the Revealed Books of *Allah*, His Messengers, or the Angels, or to belittle the Rites of *Allah* or the well-known practices of His Religion. For example, the *adhan*, Pilgrimage, mosques, the Feasts of *Fitr* and *Ad-ha*, the religious slaughtering, and prayers are all among the rites and the well-known practices of the Religion of *Islam*; anyone who belittles them blasphemes. Also, belittling the Rules of the Religion or the Promise of *Allah* or His Threat is blasphemy--whether the person did that from a conviction in his heart, or as an action of the body, or by uttering words to that effect.

The person needs to be cautious and exert the utmost effort to avoid such matters. The person who dies as a Muslim, even if he did not repent of his sins, is still hopeful for the forgiveness of *Allah*. Even if he was tortured in Hellfire, he would not remain there forever. However, the one who dies in the state of blasphemy loses in this life and in the Hereafter. Death separates the blasphemer from any enjoyment he may have had in this life and sets him on the course of everlasting torture.

One needs to preserve one's faith in *Islam* and to exert the utmost effort in avoiding blasphemy. We ask *Allah* by Prophet *Muhammad* ﷺ to protect us from blasphemy and to end our lives successfully. *Amin.*

Chapter 3
Repentance of the Apostate (*Murtadd*)

It is obligatory upon the apostate (*murtadd*) to return to *Islam* immediately by uttering the Testification of Faith and leaving off whatever caused apostasy (*riddah*).

Explanation: It is obligatory on the one who apostatized by a blasphemous belief, action, or saying to immediately clear oneself of whatever caused one's apostasy and return to *Islam* by uttering the Testification of Faith. For example, if a person apostatized as a result of a blasphemous conviction, then this person must clear himself of that blasphemous conviction, hold the correct belief, and utter the Testification of Faith to become a Muslim again.

To clear one's self from a blasphemous belief, action, or saying by uttering the Testification of Faith, it is a condition that one knows that what he did, said, or believed was blasphemy. That is, he must know that the matter committed by him actually took him out of *Islam* and rendered him a blasphemer. So, if someone intentionally uttered an explicit blasphemous word, however, he never learned and did not know afterwards that the judgment of uttering this word was blasphemy, then even if he uttered the Testification of Faith one thousand times, it would not benefit him. This means those Testifications of Faith he uttered in this case would not return him to the state of *Islam*.

In addition to knowing the judgment of blasphemy and hating it, it is conditional as well that the apostate utter the Testification of Faith to become a Muslim again. It is not enough that he just leaves the blasphemous creed, action, or saying, and believe what is correct. He must utter the Testification of Faith to clear himself of blasphemy.

Moreover, it is obligatory upon one to regret having apostatized and to intend not to return to commiting anything like it.

Explanation: It is obligatory on the one who re-entered *Islam* after having committed apostasy, to regret having apostatized in the first place. However, if one does not regret his having committed apostasy, this does not affect the validity of his return to *Islam* as long as he does not like blasphemy and does not have the intention to blaspheme in the future. So, if that apostate re-embraced *Islam*, but did not feel the remorse in his heart for his apostasy, his reentering *Islam* was valid. However, he committed a sin because he did not regret. On the other hand, uttering the Testification of Faith does not help the one who has the intention to blaspheme in the future.

If one does not quit the blasphemy by uttering the Testification of Faith, one must be ordered to do so. If one does not reembrace *Islam*, the caliph will have one killed. The caliph will rely on the testimony of two upright (^adl), male witnesses or upon the person's own admittance of committing blasphemy. This is done in compliance with the *hadith* related by al-Bukhariyy, which means: «Kill the one who leaves *Islam*.»

Explanation: If it is confirmed to the caliph that a person apostatized, either by his own admission or from two upright Muslims who testify they witnessed the blasphemy, then it becomes obligatory on the caliph to order him to re-embrace *Islam*. The caliph imprisons the apostate for three days, each day ordering him to leave out his blasphemy and return to *Islam*. If the three days pass and the person still refuses to return to *Islam*, it becomes obligatory on the caliph to have him killed. This judgment is relying upon the *hadith* of the Prophet ﷺ related by al-Bukhariyy:

$$\text{«مَنْ بَدَّلَ دِينَهُ فَاقْتُلُوهُ»}$$

It means: «Kill the one who leaves *Islam*.»

As a result of apostasy, the apostate invalidates one's Fast (Ṣawm),

Explanation: If the person apostatized while fasting during the day of *Ramadan*, one's fast is invalidated by his committing apostasy. It becomes obligatory on that person to immediately clear oneself of that blasphemy, re-embrace *Islam*, and to refrain from eating, drinking, and other invalidators of fasting for the rest of that day. The one who invalidates a day of fasting during *Ramadan*, because of committing apostasy, must make up that day immediately after the day of ^Idul-Fitr.

dry purification (tayammum),

Explanation: One's dry purification (*tayammum*) is invalidated by apostasy. So, if a person had performed dry purification, then apostatized, one needs to re-perform one's purification after one re-embraces *Islam* to perform prayers. This is not the case with one's ablution (*wudu'*), which is not invalidated by apostasy. So, if the person performed *wudu'*, then apostatized, then returned to *Islam* before any of the invalidators of *wudu'* occurred, then this *wudu'* is still valid. The dry purification is invalidated by apostasy, and not one's ablution, because the dry purification is a weaker kind of purification than ablution.

marriage before the marital consummation, and

Explanation: If two people were married, and before the first sexual intercourse took place between them, one of the two committed apostasy, then their marriage contract is invalidated. If they want to join together again in marriage, they need to conduct a new marriage contract after the one who has committed apostasy returns to *Islam*.

marriage after the marital consummation if one did not return to *Islam* within the (wife's) post-marital waiting period (ˆ*iddah*).

Explanation: The post-marital waiting period (ˆ*iddah*) is the period the woman must wait before she is allowed to get married again. The divorced woman's ˆ*iddah* is three (3) non-bleeding intervals. The pregnant woman's waiting period (ˆ*iddah*) ends when her pregnancy terminates--either by delivery, miscarriage, or otherwise.

After the marriage is consummated, i.e., the first sexual intercourse between two married people has taken place, if one of the two spouses apostatizes, the marriage contract is breached. This means that the two are no longer married. If the apostate does not return to *Islam* until after the post-marital waiting period has lapsed, then to re-marry, they need to conduct a new marriage contract. However, if the one who apostatized returns to *Islam* within the ˆ*iddah*, they do not need a new marriage contract. They are still husband and wife based on the first contract.

The marriage contract of an apostate—male or female—is not valid with a Muslim or a non-Muslim.

Explanation: An apostate cannot and does not have a valid marriage contract. If a marriage contract is conducted for him/her, it is invalid. An apostate cannot marry a Muslim or a non Muslim-- whether an original blasphemer, or an apostate like himself/herself.

67

It is unlawful (_haram_) to eat from what the apostate slaughters.

Explanation: What the apostate slaughters is Islamically forbidden to eat, even if one apostatized to embrace Christianity or Judaism. *Allah* made it lawful for us to eat the edible animals slaughtered by the Jews and the Christians. However, this pertains to the original Jews and Christians, and not to those who became Christians or Jews after having been Muslim.

The apostate does not inherit; one's wealth is not inherited.

Explanation: The apostate does not inherit one's relatives, nor do one's relatives inherit from one.

One is not prayed for, washed, shrouded, or buried in Islamic cemeteries.

Explanation: It is not lawful to perform the prayer for the apostate when he dies, because he died a blasphemer. Doing so, when one knows another died a blasphemer, is in itself blasphemy. It is not obligatory to wash the dead apostate or shroud him. It is not permissible to bury him in Islamic cemeteries, because these cemeteries were dedicated for burying the Muslims according to the rules of the *waqf*. If a non-Muslim woman pregnant from her Muslim husband died with her fetus, she would be buried in a place which is neither dedicated as a Muslim cemetery, nor as Christian or Jewish cemetery. They would direct her back towards the *Qiblah* in the grave, so that the chest of the fetus in her womb would be facing the *Qiblah*.

One's money[25] will be put in the Muslim treasury (_fay'_) when it is sound. In the absence of a sound treasury, it is permissible for a proper man to take it and spend it for Muslim interests.

Explanation: The relatives of an apostate do not inherit from him. In the presence of a sound Muslim treasury, the apostate's money is placed in the treasury to be spent for the Muslims' public benefit, or for their well-being. For example, it may be used to build a mosque or may be spent on poor Muslims. If there is no sound treasury, a proper man may take the charge of spending this money for the Muslims' public benefit as per the Islamic law.

---

[25] Money here includes currency, properties, owned crops, etc.

Chapter 4
Commanding the Obligatory (Ma ˆ ruf) and
Forbidding the Unlawful (Munkar)

Every accountable person is obligated to perform all the obligations which Allah ordained upon one. One must satisfy their integrals (rukns[26]) and their conditions (sharts[27]). Also, one must avoid their invalidators.

Explanation: It is an obligation to perform all what Allah made obligatory on us--satisfying all the integrals and conditions. It is not sufficient to perform the outward manifestation of the deed while contradicting or leaving out some of its conditions or integrals. As well, one must avoid what invalidates these obligatory deeds, or else one's case will be similar to those whom the Prophet ﷺ spoke about in his hadith related by Ibn Hibban. He said:

$$\text{«رُبَّ قَائِمٍ حَظُّهُ مِنْ قِيَامِهِ السَّهَرُ ورُبَّ صَائِمٍ حَظُّهُ مِنْ صِيَامِهِ الجُوعُ والعَطشُ»}$$

It means: «How many you may find staying up late at night praying, however, the only thing they earn is tiredness. How many you may find fasting, however, the only thing they earn from their fast is hunger and thirst.»

This hadith emphasizes the importance of learning the Obligatory Knowledge of the Religion because through this knowledge, one will learn what the obligatory matters are and how to perform them in the valid manner. One needs to learn what the integrals and conditions of these obligatory matters are. As well, one needs to learn what the invalidators of this deed are, so that one avoids them.

If one sees another person leaving out any of these obligations or performing them incorrectly, one must order him to perform them correctly,

Explanation: This means if one person sees another leaving out

---

[26] Integral (Rukn): is a part of a deed, without which the deed is invalid. For example, the opening saying of 'Allahu akbar' in prayer is an integral (rukn) of the prayer.

[27] Condition (Shart): is not part of a deed, however, without which the deed is invalid. One example is performing wudu' for prayers.

performing any obligatory matter, he must order him to perform it. Moreover, if one knows another person is performing an obligatory matter incorrectly, one must order him to perform it correctly. In doing so, one should keep in mind that some of the integrals, conditions, and invalidators of certain obligatory deeds may differ from one Islamic school (*madhhab*) to another. So, one should not rush to object to the performance (or non-performance) of another person, if the matter in question is not among the matters agreed upon by consensus, in the different schools, to be sinful.

For example, it is not a matter of consensus among the *imams* that one must wipe one's entire head in performing *wudu'*. According to the school of *Imam Malik*, it is obligatory upon one to wipe over the entire head in performing *wudu'*. However, according to *Imam ash-Shafi^iyy*, wiping over a part of the head is sufficient. So, if one following the *Malikiyy* school sees someone performing his *wudu'* by wiping over part of his head, one need not rush to object to his performance. This is unless it is known that the one making *wudu'* believes it is obligatory to wipe the entire head, however, he does not do so. In this case, the person is not performing what he himself believes is an integral of *wudu'*, and it is obligatory to order him to perform *wudu'* correctly.

and force him to do so if able.

Explanation: The obligation on one of forcing another to perform an obligation if he does not, or to force him to perform it correctly if he performs it incorrectly is a detailed matter, and will be discussed shortly.

One must denounce that incorrect performance in one's heart when one cannot force or order its change. This is the least that is required if one was unable to change the unlawful by hand or by tongue.

Explanation: If one knows an unlawful matter is happening, one must prevent that matter if one was able; and if one was unable to prevent that matter, then it is an obligation to hate it in one's heart. For example, if one knew another was committing an unlawful matter, and one knew that if one spoke to him about this matter and advised him to leave it, he would listen and correct his situation, then it would be an obligation on one to do so (i.e., to advise him in this matter, if no one else does it.) Also, if one believed the one committing the sin would not listen to one, but he would listen to another person, one might speak to this other person whom one knew would be able to influence the second one to leave out that unlawful matter. If, however, one knows that the one who was committing that unlawful matter was a person who does not listen to the proper advice, however, he can be forced (in some other way, i.e., other than verbally advising him), then one must force him to leave that unlawful matter. This is due to the _hadith_ of the Prophet ﷺ related by _al-Bukhariyy_:

«مَنْ رَأَى مِنكُمْ مُنْكَرًا فَلْيُغَيِّرْهُ بِيَدِهِ، فَإِنْ لم يَسْتَطِعْ فَبِلِسَانِهِ، فَإِنْ لم يَسْتَطِعْ فَبِقَلْبِهِ. وذلك أَضْعَفُ الإيمانِ»

It means: «If one knows of an unlawful matter, then it is an obligation on one to change that matter by one's hand. If one is not able, then one must change it by one's tongue. If one is not able, then one must denounce it in one's heart--this is the least one must do.»

Hence, if one knows of an unlawful matter, however, one is unable to change it--neither by one's hand, nor by one's tongue, then one must denounce that matter in one's heart. If one does that, one will be safe; if one does not, one is sinful.

It is conditional in using one's hand or tongue to change an unlawful matter that doing so does not lead to a situation involving a sin worse than what one is trying to change. If one believes that using one's hand or one's tongue will lead to a worse matter, it becomes forbidden for one to do so.

It is obligatory to leave out all the unlawful matters, forbid whoever commits them, and if able, force him not to commit them, or else one must reject those actions in one's own heart. The unlawful (_haram_) is what _Allah_ threatened its committer with punishment and promised its avoider with reward; the obligatory (_wajib_) is its opposite.

Explanation: The statement of the author highlights the importance of teaching the people the Obligatory Knowledge of the Religion--in particular the issues concerning the fundamentals of the belief. If it is obligatory in our Religion to order the one who drinks alcohol to quit drinking alcohol, or the one who steals to quit stealing, or the one who lies to quit lying, then it is <u>of a greater priority</u> to order the one who apostatizes to quit that blasphemy and return to Islam.

Teaching people the matters of the Religion, and in particular the matters of the creed, these days is a very great matter with a great reward. In the *hadith* narrated by *al-Bayhaqiyy*, the Prophet ﷺ said:

«مَنْ أَحْيَى سُنَّتِي عِنْدَ فَسَادِ أُمَّتِي كَانَ لَهُ أَجْرُ شَهِيدٍ»

It means: «The one who revives my methodology at a time when most of my nation commits wrong acts, has the reward of a martyr.» The reward of a martyr is Paradise without any torture. This *hadith* indicates that the one who correctly learns the matters of the creed and teaches them to the people will earn Paradise without torture, even if one committed certain sins.

Today, the factions of misguidance have become active in spreading their falsehood among the people. One must not isolate oneself and refrain from fighting their evil. This is not how the Muslims acted in previous times. During the fourth and fifth *Hijriyy* centuries, the people of misguidance became very active in spreading their misguidance. They became prominent figures in the community, i.e., rulers or close to the rulers; therefore had the power to inflict a lot of hardship on the people of *Ahlus-Sunnah*. They caused much hardships for the scholars of *Ahlus-Sunnah*. Some of those scholars even moved out of the cities to remote mountain areas to escape those hardships. Among those who stayed to confront them and fight their evil was *Abu Ishaq al-Asfarayiniyy*. He even addressed the scholars who had escaped to the mountains, telling them, "Where are you escaping to?" meaning to remind them that it was their duty to confront the people of misguidance. He said, "O you grass eaters. You escaped to the mountains and left the wolves behind preying on the Religion of Prophet *Muhammad*." He meant by his statement to dispraise them for leaving the cities to escape the tribulations and settling for eating whatever they found growing in the mountains, while they were able to confront those people of misguidance. *Abu Ishaq* dispraised them because forbidding the unlawful with the tongue, when one is able, is obligatory. May *Allah* guide us to do that and not fall short in it.

PURIFICATION AND PRAYERS

(*TAHARAH* AND *SALAH*)

Chapter 5
Times of Prayer (_Salah_)

Among the obligations is to perform five (5) prayers within the day and the night.

Explanation: It is obligatory upon every Muslim to perform five (5) prayers daily. These five prayers are the only prayers that are obligatory on every Muslim to perform. Performing these obligatory prayers is the best deed after believing correctly in _Allah_ and His Messenger. Neglecting to perform any of these obligatory prayers is an enormous sin. The one who is negligent about performing them is close to blasphemy. May _Allah_ protect us from it.

These are:

The Noon Prayer (_Dhuhr_) [four (4) rak^ahs]: Its time begins when the sun has declined westward from the middle of the sky. It remains until the length of the shadow of an object becomes equal to the length of the object itself, in addition to the length of the shadow cast by that object when the sun was at its zenith (_istiwa'_).

Explanation: Each of the five (5) obligatory prayers has a specific time in which it must be performed. It is important to know the times when each prayer time sets in and when it ends so that the person is sure to perform the prayers in their due time.

The _Dhuhr_ Prayer must be prayed during the _Dhuhr_ time. The time of _Dhuhr_ starts when the sun begins its decline from the middle of the sky towards the west. It ends when the length of the shadow of any object becomes equal to the length of that object plus the length of the shadow cast by that object at the _istiwa'_ (zenith) time.

The time of _istiwa'_ is the time at which the sun is at its highest point in the middle of the sky before it begins its decline towards the west. At this point, the shadow of any object is the shortest it will be during that day. The shadow of an object at that point in time is called its _istiwa'_ shadow.

For example, if one considers the object to be a three-foot pole which casts a shadow of one foot at the _istiwa'_ time, then the time of _Dhuhr_ starts when the sun begins its decline towards the west (the shadow starts to lengthen), and ends when the shadow of that pole becomes four feet long. This point is the end of the *Dhuhr* time and immediately afterwards, the time of the Mid-afternoon Prayer (^Asr) begins.

The Mid-afternoon Prayer (^Asr) [four (4) rak^ahs]: Its time begins after *Dhuhr* ends, and remains until sunset.

Explanation: The time of ^Asr sets in immediately after *Dhuhr* ends as described above--and remains until sunset, which is when the entire disk of the sun disappears below the western horizon. If the western horizon is blocked from view and there are high mountains in the eastern horizon, one can know that the sun has set when the reflection of the sun's rays disappears from the top of the mountains in the east. Also, if the western horizon is blocked from view but the eastern horizon is visible, one knows the sun has already set when the darkness appears in the eastern horizon. This is so because the Prophet, *sallallahu ^alayhi wa sallam*, said:

$$\text{«إِذا غَابَتِ الشَّمْسُ مِنْ ههُنا وَجَاءَ الليْلُ مِنْ ههُنا}$$
$$\text{فَقَدْ أَفْطَرَ الصَّائِمُ»}$$

It means: «When the sun sets from this side (the west) and the night starts to appear from this side (the east), then it is time for the fasting person to break his fast.» Related by *Muslim*.

The Sunset Prayer (Maghrib) [three (3) rak^ahs]: Its time begins after sunset, [i.e., when ^Asr ends] and remains until the redness disappears in the western horizon.

Explanation: The time of *Maghrib* starts immediately after the time of ^Asr ends, i.e., with the complete setting of the sun. It lasts until the redness disappears in the western horizon. One can be sure the *Maghrib* time has passed and the ^Isha' time has begun when many of the small stars are visible in the sky.

The Nightfall Prayer (^Isha') [four (4) rak^ahs]: Its time begins when the *Maghrib* time ends and remains until the true dawn (Fajr Sadiq) appears.

Explanation: The time of ^Isha' Prayer begins immediately after the *Maghrib* ends, and lasts until the appearance of the true dawn (Fajr

Sadiq). The true dawn starts as a very thin horizontal whiteness in the eastern horizon that increasingly broadens, until the sun rises. When the whiteness of the true dawn first appears, the time of ^Isha' is over, and Subh (also known as Fajr) has begun.

The Dawn Prayer (Subh) [two (2) rak^ahs]: Its time begins after ^Isha' time ends and remains until sunrise (Shuruq).

Explanation: The time of the Dawn Prayer (Subh) is from the appearance of the true dawn until the first part of the disk of the sun appears in the eastern horizon. If one's sight of the eastern horizon is blocked by mountains, for example, and one cannot see the sun rise above the horizon, then one assesses when the sun may rise above the horizon if that mountain was not there. One relies on one's assessment to conclude that the sun has risen and Subh time has ended.

These obligatory prayers must be performed in their due times by every Muslim who is pubescent, sane, and pure, i.e., other than the woman with menstrual or postpartum bleeding. Without an excuse, it is unlawful to perform these prayers ahead of their times or to delay performing them until after their times have passed.

Explanation: It is an obligation to perform the prayers in their due times. They must not be performed either before or after their due times, without a religious excuse. To do this, one must know how each prayer time sets in and how it ends. Allah said in Surat al-Ma^un, Verses 4-5:

$$﴿فَوَيۡلٞ لِّلۡمُصَلِّينَ ۝ ٱلَّذِينَ هُمۡ عَن صَلَاتِهِمۡ سَاهُونَ ۝﴾$$

In these two verses, Allah threatened with severe torture the ones who, inexcusably, delay the prayers until after their times have passed.

Although some scholars judged the one, who without a religious excuse, intentionally delays performing one's prayer until its time has passed as a blasphemer, the saying of the jumhur (majority of scholars) is that this person is an enormous sinner and is very close to committing blasphemy, but not a blasphemer. Being very close to the state of blasphemy means the person is committing one of the most enormous sins and one is under a greater danger of committing blasphemy.

HOW TO DETERMINE PRAYER TIMES

The Dawn Prayer (*Subḥ*)

The Dawn Prayer time begins immediately after the Nightfall Prayer time ends Ⓐ, i.e., with the appearance of the true dawn, which starts as a thin white light appearing on the eastren horizon. It remains until sunrise, i.e., when the disc of the sun first appears on the eastern horizon Ⓑ

The Noon Prayer (*Dhuhr*)

The time of the Noon Prayer begins when the sun has declined westward from the Zenith Ⓒ . It remains until the length of the shadow of an object becomes equal to the length of that object in addition to the length of the shadow which was cast by that object when the sun was at its zenith Ⓓ .

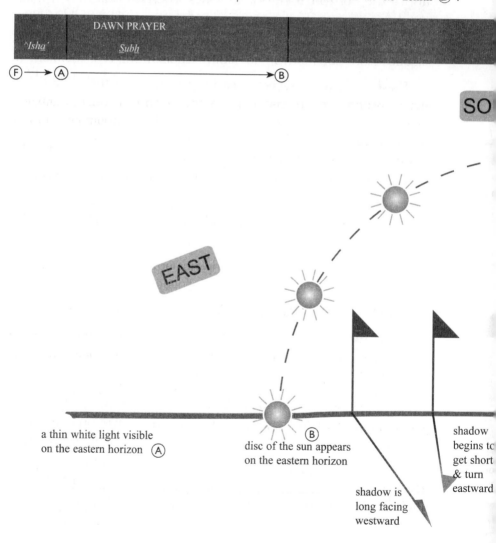

DAWN PRAYER

^*Isha'*

Subḥ

Ⓕ ⟶ Ⓐ ————————————————⟶ Ⓑ

SO

EAST

a thin white light visible on the eastern horizon Ⓐ

Ⓑ disc of the sun appears on the eastern horizon

shadow is long facing westward

shadow begins to get short & turn eastward

The Mid-afternoon Prayer begins immediately after the Noon Prayer time ends Ⓓ. It remains until sunset, i.e., until the disc of the sun sinks completely below the western horizon Ⓔ.

The Sunset Prayer begins at sunset Ⓔ. It remains until the redness in the western horizon disappears Ⓕ.

The Nightfall Prayer time begins immediately after the Sunset Prayer time ends. It remains until the appearance of the true dawn Ⓐ.

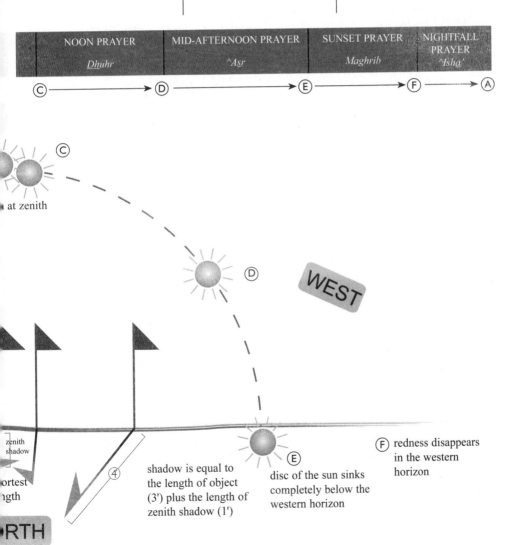

NOON PRAYER	MID-AFTERNOON PRAYER	SUNSET PRAYER	NIGHTFALL PRAYER
Dhuhr	^*Asr*	*Maghrib*	^*Isha'*

Ⓒ ———————→ Ⓓ ———————→ Ⓔ ———————→ Ⓕ ——→ Ⓐ

Ⓒ

at zenith

WEST

Ⓓ

zenith shadow

ortest gth

4'

shadow is equal to the length of object (3') plus the length of zenith shadow (1')

Ⓔ disc of the sun sinks completely below the western horizon

Ⓕ redness disappears in the western horizon

RTH

79

If a person performs the prayer before its time has set in without an excuse, his prayer is invalid. *Allah* said in *Surat an-Nisa'*, Verse 103:

$$\text{﴿ إِنَّ ٱلصَّلَوٰةَ كَانَتْ عَلَى ٱلْمُؤْمِنِينَ كِتَـٰبًا مَّوْقُوتًا ۝ ﴾}$$

It means: [Certainly, performing the prayers in their due times is an obligation on the believers.] The one who delays the prayer (without an excuse) until after its time has passed is sinful. However, the prayer is valid and is considered a make up for the missed prayer. The worse of the two cases, meaning the one that is more sinful, is the first case, i.e., to perform the prayer ahead of its time. The person is more sinful in this case because his prayer is neither considered as fulfilling the obligation in due time nor as a make up prayer. Moreover, the prayer is still due on him.

The one who combines the combinable prayers for a valid religious excuse, such as traveling, illness, or heavy rain is not sinful for doing so. These cases contain well-known details that will be discussed later.

If a prohibitive matter, such as menses, occurs after a prayer time sets in and there was time which was enough to perform that prayer, then one must make up that missed prayer. In the case of [also having] incontinence of urine, if the prohibitive matter occurs after a time which was enough to perform the prayer and its purification (*taharah*), then one must make up that missed prayer.

Explanation: If the prayer time sets in and enough time to perform the prayer lapses, however the person does not pray, then a prohibitive matter occurs which lasts until the time of that prayer is over, then once that prohibitive matter ends, the person must make up that missed prayer. So, for example, if the time of the *Dhuhr* Prayer sets in, and a time enough to perform the *Dhuhr* Prayer lapses, but before praying that *Dhuhr* Prayer, the person becomes insane, and his insanity lasts until the *Dhuhr* time is ended, then when the person becomes sane again, he must make up that missed *Dhuhr* prayer. The make up prayer is due on the person in this case because he had enough time to pray, but he did not use that time to do so.

The person inflicted with incontinence of urine or the like, who does not perform the prayer before a prohibitive matter occurs to him does not make up this prayer unless the time that lapses from the setting in of the prayer time is enough for him to perform the purification and prayer. In this context, the purification means to remove any unexempted *najasah* on his body and clothes and to perform his *wudu'* or *tayammum*.

If, on the other hand, the prohibitive matter terminates and time enough to say 'Allahu akbar' is left before the prayer time ends, then one must make up that prayer and the one before it if they are combinable. So, if the prohibitive matter terminates before sunset while there is enough time to say 'Allahu akbar', then both ^Asr and Dhuhr must be prayed. If it terminates before Fajr begins while there is time enough to say 'Allahu akbar', then both ^Isha' and Maghrib must be prayed.

Explanation: For a religious excuse, certain prayers may be combined and prayed one after the other, at the time of either one of them. These combinable prayers are Dhuhr with ^Asr, and Maghrib with ^Isha'. If the prohibitive matter (like the menses) terminates before the time of the latter of either of these two sets of combinable prayers goes out and enough time is left to say, "Allahu akbar", then this prayer must be performed along with making up the one with which it is combined. For example, if the menses terminates before the time of ^Asr is over even if by just a few moments--time enough to say, "Allahu akbar", but not enough time to perform the obligatory *ghusl* and the prayer-- then it becomes an obligation on the woman to perform the *ghusl* and pray both the ^Asr prayer and the Dhuhr prayer, because these two are prayers which are combinable for a religious excuse. However, if a woman becomes clear of her menses before Dhuhr time ends by a short time, enough to say "Allahu akbar", she is obligated to pray the Dhuhr Prayer only, and not the Subh Prayer, because Subh and Dhuhr are not prayers which are combinable for a religious excuse.

Chapter 6
Obligations of the Guardians

It is obligatory upon the guardian of the children who reached the age of mental discrimination to teach them the rules of prayer and to order them to perform it after they have completed seven (7) lunar years of age.

Explanation: This chapter deals with the obligations of the child's guardians. It is an obligation on the guardian of a child who has reached seven (7) lunar years of age to order that child to perform the prayers. If the child reaches the age of mental discrimination before he is seven (7), the guardian is not obligated to order him to pray, but he may ask the child to do so. If the child has not reached the age of mental discrimination by the time he is seven (7), the guardian waits until he becomes at that age to order him to pray. The age of mental discrimination is a stage defined as when the child understands when addressed and responds when questioned. That is, if someone asked him, 'How many times does *Ramadan* come each year?', the child would understand the question and answer. Another example, if asked, 'How many days are there in a week?', he can respond properly. The child, male or female, who can understand and respond to such questions is considered as having reached the age of mental discrimination.

The guardian must also hit them for not performing the prayer after they are ten lunar years old. The same is done in the case of fasting–if the children can bear fasting.

Explanation: It is an obligation on the guardian of the child who has reached the age of seven (7) lunar years, (usually the age of mental discrimination), to order him to pray and to fast, if he can bear fasting. However, if the child becomes ten (10) years old and does not pray or fast although he is able, his guardian must hit him for leaving out this matter in order to teach him the seriousness of his negligence and to urge him to perform these important matters. This is in accordance with the *hadith* of the Prophet, related by *Abu Dawud*:

«مُرُوا أَولادَكم بِالصَّلاةِ وَهُمْ أَبْنَاءُ سَبْعٍ، وَاضْرِبُوهُمْ عَلَيْهَا وَهُمْ أَبْنَاءُ عَشْرٍ. وَفَرِّقُوا بَيْنَهُمْ فِى المَضَاجِعِ.»

It means: «Order your children with prayer when they reach seven (7) lunar years of age, and hit them for leaving it out when they reach ten (10); and separate them in their sleeping places.» To separate them in their sleeping places means to let each one sleep under a separate cover such that they are not touching skin to skin. It is prohibited to let them sleep while their unlawful nakedness (^awrah) is uncovered under one covering in such a way that they can touch these parts skin to skin. In this case, it is an obligation to separate them. If their unlawful nakedness (^awrah) is covered while they sleep, having separate covers is recommended (sunnah).

In the case when hitting the child for leaving out prayers or fasting is an obligation, it is a condition that the hitting is commensurate with the offense, i.e., it must be harsh enough to show the child the enormity of one neglecting prayers and fasting. However, it must not be so severe as to break his bones, poke out his eye, or otherwise harm him severely.

Moreover, the guardian must teach the children of the basic beliefs and rules, what is obligatory and what is unlawful, the rewardability of the toothstick (siwak), and congregational prayers (jama^ah).

Explanation: It is an obligation upon the guardian to teach the children certain matters of the Religion. He must teach the child the necessary matters of the Religion that the child will need to know after pubescence, those matters which both the knowledgeable and the lay person knows. Among the matters related to the creed that the guardian must teach the child are:

* That *Allah* exists and that He does not have a partner;

* That *Allah* is Eternal and Everlasting and does not resemble the creation;

* That among the uncountable Attributes of *Allah*, there are 13 attributes of *Allah* that every accountable Muslim must know;

* That Prophet *Muhammad* is the Messenger of *Allah* and that he is the last of all the messengers;

* That Prophet *Muhammad* was born in *Makkah* and immigrated to *al-Madinah*;

* That *Allah* sent many messengers, the first of whom was *Adam*;

* That *Allah* revealed Books to His messengers;

* That *Allah* created the angels;

* That humans and *jinn* will die and then they will be brought back to life after which they will be judged for their deeds;

* That *Allah* prepared an abode for enjoyment called Paradise, and an abode for torture called Hellfire; and

* Other similar matters among the essentials of the belief.

Also the guardian must teach the child other matters of the Religion commonly known to the scholar and layman alike, like:

* Stealing and lying are forbidden;

* Adultery and sodomy are forbidden;

* Gossip and talebearing are forbidden;

* Hitting a Muslim unjustly is forbidden;

* Performing the congregational prayer is very rewardable;

* Using the *siwak* is *sunnah*; and

* Similar matters among the commonly known matters of the Religion.

Furthermore, the father must take his non-pubescent son(s) to the Friday Prayer (*Jumu^ah*). Many parents are negligent of teaching their children these matters. They neither themselves teach their children nor do they provide someone else to teach them. Rather, such parents only take care to feed, clothe, and provide shelter for their children, not much more than what they do for the animal they may own.

It is obligatory on the Muslim rulers to order the killing of the person who does not pray out of laziness, if one does not repent. However, this person is still deemed a Muslim. It is obligatory on every Muslim to order one's family and everyone else one is able to order with prayers if they do not pray.

Explanation: If the caliph learns of someone who does not pray out of laziness, he orders him to perform that prayer. Should the person refuse, the caliph must order this person's execution. If the prayer is a combinable one, the caliph waits until the time of the later of the combinable prayers goes out. If the person still does not pray by that time, the caliph will have him killed. If the prayer is not a combinable one, then the caliph will grant him until the time of that particular prayer is over. Hence, if the caliph orders one to pray the _Subh_ Prayer, and this person does not do so by sunrise, the caliph orders his execution. If the caliph learns of one who did not pray the _Dhuhr_ Prayer, he grants him until sunset to do so. If the sun sets and he still insists not to pray, the caliph will have him executed.

The one executed for refusing to perform the prayer is treated as a Muslim, i.e., he is washed, shrouded, prayed for, and buried in the Muslim cemetery. This is unless one refused to pray because he denounced or belittled the prayers or believed that the prayers were not obligatory. In this case, he is executed because he is an apostate, and is treated as one treats the dead apostate.

It is a communal obligation (_fard kifayah_) on the Muslim, if able to order one's family to perform the prayers as well as anyone else who neglects prayers. One's family here refers to one's wife, children, and the like. A communal obligation is the obligation, which if done by some members of the community, relieves the rest from performing it. However, if neglected, then every member who was able to do it is sinful.

Chapter 7
Ablution (*Wudu'*)

Ablution (*Wudu'*) is one of the conditions of the prayer.

Explanation: Ablution is a condition for the validity of the prayer. Prayers are invalid without purification. Ablution effects purification.

Integrals of Ablution:

The integrals of ablution are six (6):

Explanation: There are six matters a person must satisfy for one's *wudu'* to be valid. All the other matters ordered in the Religion to perform during *wudu'* are *sunnah*.

1. According to *Imam ash-Shafi^iyy*, to have the intention of purification (*taharah*) for prayer—or any equivalent intention—when the water first touches the face. However, according to *Imam Malik*, it is enough if the intention precedes washing the face by a short time;

Explanation: The first integral of *wudu'* is the intention; one must have the intention in one's heart to perform the purification for the prayers. For instance, one establishes in one's heart, I intend to perform *wudu'*, or I now intend to perform the obligations of *wudu'*, or the required purification for praying, or the like. The intention is in the heart. It is not sufficient for one to merely utter the words without having the intention in one's heart. According to the school of *Imam ash-Shafi^iyy*, may *Allah* raise his rank, one must have the intention when the water first touches the face. However, according to *Imam Malik*, it is sufficient if one's intention for purification preceded washing the face by a short time.

2. To wash the whole face, from the normal hairline to the chin and from one ear to the other including the hair and skin, but not the inner part of the man's thick beard;

Explanation: One has to wash the entire face when performing *wudu'*. The boundary of the face vertically is from the normal hairline to the chin, and horizontally from ear to ear.

One must wash all the skin and hair within these boundaries except the inner part of the man's thick beard and *^aridan*. The *^aridan* is the hair--other than the sideburns--growing on the

86

jawbone (beneath the lower end of the ear) and is considered part of the beard. If the hair of the beard is thin, then one must wash the hair and skin underneath it. If one considers a string stretched from the normal hairline at the middle of the face to the pinna of the ear, then the hair below the string must be washed along with the face. As to the hair on the other side, it is considered part of the head and one is not required to wash it with the face.

3. To wash the hands and the forearms up to and including the elbows and what is on them;

Explanation: One must then wash the entire area from the the tips of the fingers up to and including the elbows. If one leaves out washing the elbows, one's *wudu'* is invalid. It is better (*sunnah*) to start at the tips of the fingers and finish at the elbows.

4. To wet wipe the head or part of it—even if it is only one hair—within the boundary of the head;

Explanation: The obligation is to wet wipe at least a part of the hair of the head or part of the skin of the head. The vertical boundaries of the head are from the point of the normal hairline to the occiput. If one washes even just part of a hair, which, as it normally falls, is contained within the boundaries of the head, it will be sufficient to fulfill this integral.

5. To wash the feet, including the ankles, or else to wet wipe the footgear (*khuff*) when the conditions of the footgear are fulfilled;

Explanation: The fifth obligation of *wudu'* is to wash one's feet and ankles. If one leaves out washing the ankles, one's *wudu'* is invalid. One can instead wet wipe the footgear (*khuff*) when the conditions of the footgear (*khuff*) are fulfilled. Some of the conditions to consider shoes a valid footgear (*khuff*) are for the shoes to:

1. Be pure (*tahir*);

2. Cover the feet including the ankles;

3. Withstand walking back and forth in errands of the traveller at loading and unloading without them being torn apart;

4. Be worn when one is in the state of complete purity (*taharah*.)

More details about this matter are mentioned in the more comprehensive books of the Religion.

6. To observe the aforementioned order.

Explanation: One must observe the proper order of washing/ wiping the body parts for one's *wudu'* to be valid. So, one must start with the intention of purification when the water first touches the face, then wash the entire face, then wash the hands and forearms, up to and including the elbows, then wet wipe the head, then wash the feet with the ankles. If one does not observe this aforementioned order, one's *wudu'* is invalid. *Allah* mentioned this order in the *Qur'an* in *Suratul-Ma'idah, Ayah* 6. *Allah* said:

$$\text{﴿يَـٰٓأَيُّهَا ٱلَّذِينَ ءَامَنُوٓاْ إِذَا قُمۡتُمۡ إِلَى ٱلصَّلَوٰةِ فَٱغۡسِلُواْ وُجُوهَكُمۡ وَأَيۡدِيَكُمۡ إِلَى ٱلۡمَرَافِقِ وَٱمۡسَحُواْ بِرُءُوسِكُمۡ وَأَرۡجُلَكُمۡ إِلَى ٱلۡكَعۡبَيۡنِۚ ۝﴾}$$

It means: [O you who believed, if you stand up to perform prayers, then wash your faces and your hands up to (and including) the elbows, and wet wipe your heads and wash your feet with the ankles.]

Invalidators of Ablution:

Ablution is invalidated by:

1. **The emission of anything from the eliminatory outlets, except *maniyy*;**

2. **Touching the penis, vagina, or anus of a human with the inside part of the bare hand;**

3. **Touching of the male the skin of the marriageable female when both have attained to an age at which they are normally desired;**

4. **Losing sanity or consciousness, except if one is sleeping with one's buttocks firmly seated.**

Explanation: The invalidators of ablution are only these four matters that are mentioned above.

1. The first is the emission of any material other than the *maniyy* from the eliminatory outlets, whether usual or unusual. By itself, the emission of the *maniyy* does not invalidate one's *wudu'*. However, it makes the purificatory bath (*ghusl*) obligatory.

2. Touching the penis, vagina, or anus of the human with the inside part of the bare hand invalidates one's *wudu'*. The inside part of the hand is defined as the area of the hand which does not show when one places one's hands together, palm to palm with fingers spread, and applying a slight pressure. Touching the penis, vagina, or anus with the back of the hand does not invalidate one's *wudu'*. Likewise touching these areas with a barrier between the hand and the organ does not invalidate one's *wudu'*.

3. Touching the skin of the marriageable woman who attained to an age at which she is normally desired means touching, skin on skin, a person of the opposite sex to whom one is allowed to be married. This is with the condition that both the toucher and the touched have reached an age when normally they would be desired, even if they did not yet reach the age of puberty.

Although touching the skin of one's wife invalidates one's *wudu'* (and hers), touching the skin of the woman whom one cannot marry in any case does not invalidate the *wudu'* of either. For example, if the man touches his mother, daughter, sister, aunt, mother-in-law, or the like, neither the man nor the woman's *wudu'* is invalidated. Similarly, by touching the skin of her uncle, her father-in-law, or her son by wet-nursing, the woman does not invalidate her *wudu'*. Although it is forbidden, touching the tooth, hair, or nail of a marriageable woman does not invalidate one's *wudu'*.

4. If one becomes insane, even for one moment, one's *wudu'* is invalidated. As well, every kind of loss of consciousness invalidates one's *wudu'*-even sleeping-unless the person falls asleep with his buttocks firmly seated, in such a way that it is certain one does not pass gas, and one wakes up in the same position in which one sleeps-whether sitting legs crossed on the ground or stretched out or on a chair or the like.

Chapter 8
Cleaning Oneself after Defecation and Urination (*Istinja'*)

Istinja' is obligatory after the emission of any wet material from the eliminatory outlets, except *maniyy*. *Istinja'* is performed with water by rinsing the soiled area until it becomes pure, or else by wiping the soiled area three times or more until the area is clean (although a trace that can only be removed with water may be left), with an uprooting, pure, solid, and unrespectable material such as a stone or paper. *Istinja'* may be performed in this way even if water is present, provided the wet *najas*-filth (*najasah*) is not displaced or has not dried before cleaning it, or else water must be used.

Explanation: Performing *istinja'* (or cleaning one's eliminatory outlet) after the emission of any wet material other than the *maniyy* is obligatory for the validity of the prayers. The *maniyy* is an exception because it is pure (*tahir*). One is not obligated to perform *istinja'* from what exits dry, without wetness.

It is valid to perform *istinja'* with a stone (or its equivalent), with water, or with both stone and water. In using a stone or its equivalent only, one must wipe the outlet at least three times, until the place is clean. If the outlet is cleaned by only two wipes, one still has to wipe one more time, to make three wipes. If three wipes are not enough to clean the area, one continues wiping until the spot is clean.

The equivalent of a stone is any material that is:

1. **uprooting** (hence, one cannot use a smooth material like glass or bamboo);

2. **pure** (hence, one cannot use the dry stools of an animal);

3. **solid** (hence, one cannot use something like sand);

4. **dry** (hence, wet tissue cannot be used);

5. **religiously unrespectable** (hence, one may not use something religiously respectable, like a paper containing religious information, or the cover torn from a *Mus-haf*, or the food consumed mostly by humans, or food both equally humans and animals eat. However, it is permissible to use food known to be mainly food for animals only).

When using a stone or its equivalent to perform *istinja'*, it is enough that the physical *najasah* is removed-even though its trace may be left. The trace meant here is that which can be removed only with water or with small pieces of baked clay.

If the *najasah* was spread from its place of exit, one cannot use the stone exclusively to perform *istinja'*; one must use water with or without using the stone. For example, if the urine spreads from the place it exits, past the head of the penis for the man or spread to the mouth of the vagina of the woman (i.e., the place where the penis enters), one must also use water. As well, if the defecation spreads beyond the area where the buttocks meet when standing, then using the stone alone to perform *istinja'* is not sufficient. Moreover, if the urine or defecation dries before removing it, then using the stone alone is not sufficient.

It is also valid to only use water to perform *istinja'*, and if one has the choice of using only water or a stone, then using water is better. To perform *istinja'* using water, one pours the water on the exit while rubbing the exit with one's hand until the place is clean from the physical *najasah* and its trace. The *Sunnah* is to use one's left hand to rub the exit.

The best way to perform *istinja'* is to use the stone (or the like) first (to remove the physical presence of the *najasah*), then to follow with water (to remove the traces).

Chapter 9
The Purificatory Bath (*Ghusl*)

Among the conditions of prayer is purification from the state of major ritual impurity (*hadath akbar*) by performing the purificatory bath (*ghusl*). Dry purification (*tayammum*) is performed when one cannot perform ghusl.

Explanation: Purification is a condition for the validity of prayers. Just as the one who is in the state of minor ritual impurity (*hadath asghar*) must clear oneself of that state for the prayers by performing *wudu'* or the dry purification (*tayammum*) when unable to use water, the one who is in a state of major ritual impurity must clear oneself of that state for the validity of the prayer.

To purify oneself from the major ritual impurity (*hadath akbar*) one performs the purificatory bath (*ghusl*). When one cannot perform the purificatory bath, one instead performs the dry purification (*tayammum*) using soil to enable one to pray (although performing tayammum does not purify one from the state of major ritual impurity).

One is required to perform the purificatory bath after any of these five (5) matters occurs:

1. The emission of *maniyy*;
2. Sexual intercourse;
3. Termination of menses (*hayd*);
4. Termination of postpartum bleeding (*nifas*);
5. Childbirth.

Explanation: The occurrence of any one of these five matters causes the person to be in a state of major ritual impurity and obligates the person to purify oneself from that state for the validity of one's prayer. The occurrence of other than these five matters does not make the purificatory bath (*ghusl*) an obligation on one.

Washing the dead Muslim is not a matter pertaining to purifying him from the state of major ritual impurity. Moreover, performing this ghusl is not an obligation on the dead person himself, because he is no longer accountable. Rather, this *ghusl* is performed for him out of honoring him. Performing the *ghusl* for the dead Muslim is a collective obligation on the Muslim community.

1. The emission of *maniyy*: The exiting of one's own *maniyy* renders the purificatory bath (*ghusl*) obligatory. One can judge the fluid that exits from oneself as *maniyy* if one observes that the fluid has any one of the following signs:

a. it exits with a sense of pleasure;

b. it exits in spurts;

c. when dry, it smells like egg white and when wet, it smells like dough or the male spadix of the palm tree.

By these signs, one may differentiate between *maniyy* and other fluids. Observing any one of these signs is enough to judge the material as *maniyy*. Hence, it is not necessary that all the signs be present to judge the fluid as *maniyy*.

If a woman has performed a purificatory bath after a sexual intercourse with her husband and afterwards has a discharge of *maniyy* from her vagina which she knows is her husband's *maniyy* only (because she knows during the intercourse her own *maniyy* did not discharge) she does not reperform a *ghusl* for the discharge of that *maniyy* (because it is not her own, nor is it mixed-hers and his). Rather she performs *istinja'* and *wudu'* only.

2. Sexual intercourse: Sexual intercourse, or the entrance of the head of the penis into the vagina, renders the *ghusl* an obligation on both the man and the woman, even if *maniyy* was not emitted during the intercourse. Also, sodomy renders the *ghusl* an obligation on both parties involved in that act--whether male or female.

These two matters, i.e., the emission of *maniyy* and sexual intercourse are matters common between the man and the woman, i.e., if either of these matters occurs to the man or the woman, then the *ghusl* becomes an obligation on them. There are three matters specific to the woman that cause her to be in a state of major ritual impurity and require, once they terminate, a purificatory bath (*ghusl*) to clear herself of this state. They are:

3. menses (*hayd*);

4. postpartum bleeding (*nifas*);

5. childbirth.

The purificatory bath (*ghusl*) becomes an obligation on the woman when her menses or postpartum bleeding terminates. That is, when the blood of the menses stops (terminating the menses) or the blood that exits after delivery stops (terminating the postpartum bleeding period--even from a caesarean birth), then it becomes obligatory on the woman to perform the purificatory bath (*ghusl*) in order for her to pray.

The menses is defined as the usual blood that exits from the womb of the woman, neither as a result of an illness, nor as a result of childbirth. The minimum time of the menses is the duration of a day and a night, i.e., twenty-four (24) hours of bleeding. So, if the duration of the bleeding adds up to less than twenty-four (24) hours, it is not considered blood of the menses. The maximum period is fifteen (15) days. So, bleeding which continues past fifteen (15) days is not considered blood of the menses.

The postpartum blood is the blood that comes out of the woman after delivery, because of delivery. It may last for only a moment. The maximum bleeding period after delivery is sixty (60) days. Bleeding after that time is not considered a postpartum bleeding, i.e., the blood of *nifas*. Also, if the woman bleeds while giving birth, it is not considered the blood of *nifas*.

Giving birth renders *ghusl* obligatory on the woman, whether or not she delivered at term or before, and whether or not she delivered a live or dead child. If the woman delivers and does not bleed afterwards, she still must perform *ghusl* for the prayers. Since the child originally developed from the combination of the *maniyy*s of the man and the woman, its exit is similar to the exit of *maniyy*, which requires *ghusl*.

Integrals of the Purificatory Bath

The integrals of the purificatory bath are two (2):

1. **To have the intention to clear oneself of the state of major ritual impurity (_hadath akbar_), or a similar intention;**

2. **To wash the whole body with water, including the skin and the hair, even if the hair is thick.**

Explanation: The integrals of the purificatory bath are two matters; matters other than these two are not obligatory. The first of the two integrals of the purificatory bath is the intention. The intention is established in the heart. One establishes the intention in one's heart to clear oneself of the major ritual impurity when the water first touches one's body. If one establishes the intention before pouring the water on one's body, without having it when the water came in contact with one's body, this washing is not valid. Note, however, that this is not a case of consensus. Rather, according to _Imam Malik_, for example, if one makes the proper intention shortly before starting to pour the water, one's _ghusl_ is still valid.

A valid intention is to establish in one's heart, I now perform the _ghusl_ to purify myself from the major ritual impurity (_hadath akbar_), or to establish in one's heart the intention to perform the obligatory _ghusl_, or what is similar to these intentions.

The second integral is to wash once the whole body, including the skin and the hair, with purifying water. One needs to let the water reach to the skin under the hair, even if the hair was thick. Washing three times is a recommended matter (_sunnah_). Any tangible _najasah_ on the body must be removed from the contaminated part of the body first for the lifting of the major ritual impurity from that part to be valid.

Chapter 10
Conditions of Purification (*Taharah*)

The conditions for one's purification (*taharah*) to be valid are:

1. To be Muslim;

Explanation: The *taharah* performed by a blasphemer is not valid.

2. To be at the age of mental discrimination (*mumayyiz*);

Explanation: The purification is invalid from an insane person or one who has not yet reached the age of mental discrimination.

3. To remove anything that prevents water from reaching the part to be washed;

Explanation: This condition for a valid purification entails removing any kind of a physical barrier that prevents the water from reaching the part of the body to be washed or wiped. The barrier must be removed so that the water can reach the part underneath it. Nail polish, for example, is a barrier which prevents the water from reaching the fingernail, and must be removed before performing *wudu'* or *ghusl*.

4. To let the water flow on the part to be washed;

Explanation: One condition of a valid purification is for the water to flow on the part to be washed. One may use one's hand to spread the running water over the part to be washed. However, simply wetting one's hand and wiping it over the part to be washed does not meet the condition of flowing (running) water and is invalid.

5. To use purifying water;

Explanation: One must use purifying water--water that is both pure in itself and effects purification. Water that is pure and purifying is water that retains its original state, as it was created. There are several factors that affect the water's attribute of being purifying and/ or pure. For water to remain pure and purifying, four conditions must be met.

i.e., the water that has not changed by being mixed with a pure (*tahir*) material, such as milk or ink, from which the water can be easily shielded. If the water changes because of its mixing with some material in such a way that it is not called water anymore, then using this water for purification is not valid.

Explanation: Water loses its quality of effecting purification when it changes considerably due to its mixing with another pure material resulting in a mixture that one no longer calls absolute water. So, for example, if water is mixed with milk, ink, or the like, and the resulting mixture is so changed in color, taste, or odor such that when one looks at the resulting mixture one does not call it water, then it can no longer be used for purification. The judgment of that mixture is that it is pure, but cannot be used to effect purification. However, if the change in the water in this case was only slight, it remains purifying water, i.e., it retains its attribute of effecting purification.

If water acquires the taste or smell of a pure material that does not dissolve in it, the water remains pure and purifying. For example, if one puts a stick of sandalwood in the water, the sandalwood does not dissolve, but the water acquires its nice smell. The judgment of this water does not change because of acquiring that smell, since the sandalwood did not dissolve in it, i.e., the water retains its purifying quality.

If, however, the water changes because of its mixing with materials which are in its original place or its pathway or the like, and from which this water cannot be easily shielded, then this does not affect the purifying property of this water.

Explanation: The pure material which mixes with water causing a significant change in that water does not cause the water to lose its purifying quality (as long as it will still be called water) if one cannot easily shield the water from that material, i.e., if there is a hardship involved in shielding the water from that material. So, for example, water the taste, color, or odor of which changed significantly to the taste or odor of sulfur because it mixed with sulfur present in its pathway or in its collecting places, remains pure and purifying because it is difficult to shield the water from the sulfur contained in the ground.

If the water is plenty (two (2) or more *qullahs*[28]), it must not have changed even slightly, because of its contact with a *najas*-filth.

---

[28] Two *qullahs* are approximately 500 *Baghdadiyy ritls* (pounds). According to the strongest saying, this is the amount of water which fills a round hole in the ground one cubit in diameter and two and one-half cubits in depth. This translates into approximately 191 liters, i.e., 51 gallons or 204 quarts.

Explanation: If the plentiful water changes even slightly from contacting a *najas*-filthy material, then this water becomes *najas*-filthy. If the amount of water is large enough (two (2) *qullahs* or more), the *najasah* that falls into it does not render the water itself *najas*-filthy-- unless the water is changed (even slightly) by that *najasah*.

The proof of this judgment is the saying of the Prophet, *sallallahu ˆalayhi wa sallam*, narrated by the four *hafidhs*,[29]

$$ \text{«إذا بَلَغَ المَاءُ قُلَّتَيْنِ لم يَحْمِلِ الخَبَثَ»} $$

It means: «If the water becomes two (2) *qullahs* (plenty), then it does not become *najas*-filthy.» That is, the plentiful water does not become *najas*-filthy simply by contacting a *najasah*, unless as a result of that contact, the taste, color, or odor of that water changes.

If the water is less than two (2) *qullahs*, an unexempted *najas*-filth must not have contacted it, even if it does not change the water.

Explanation: For the little water (defined as less than two (2) *qullahs*), to remain pure and purifying, it is a condition that no unexempted *najas*-filth has come into contact with it. If *najas*-filth comes into contact with an amount of water less than two (2) *qullahs*, then the water becomes *najas*-filthy--whether or not that *najas*-filth changed any of the attributes of the water.

An exempted *najas*-filth is like the dead small insects that do not bleed if cut open. So, if a fly, for example, falls into a small amount of water and dies there, it does not make that water *najas*-filthy. Other liquids are like water in this particular judgment.

Moreover, the water must not have been used already in clearing someone of a ritual impurity (*hadath*), and it must not have been used to remove a *najas*-filth.

Explanation: Water that was previously used to clear a ritual impurity loses its attribute of purifying. It remains pure (*tahir*), but is no longer purifying (*mutahhir*) water. So, the little water used to perform the integrals of *wudu'* or *ghusl* remains pure but is not purifying.

---

[29] The four *Hafidhs* are: at-Tirmidhiyy, Abu Dawud, an-Nasa'iyy, and Ibn Majah.

If the water poured on a *najas*-filthy place purifies it without the water being changed, the water remains pure. However, it is no longer purifying. In this case, the place is affected by the water, i.e., the place becomes _tahir_. However, if that water is changed by that *najas*-filthy place, it becomes *najas*-filthy. In this case, the water is affected by the *najasah*.

If the little water removed the *najasah* in one wash, and the *najasah* neither remained a separate, distinguishable entity, nor did it change the water in color, taste, odor, or weight, then that water used to remove the *najasah* remains pure, but is no longer purifying. It is "used" water.

Consider the case of one having a drop of wine on one's hand and pouring water to clear it. If the *najasah* was removed with this one wash without the water being changed by the wine, and the wine did not remain a separate entity, distinguishable from the water, then the water used, even if little, is pure, but no longer purifying.

If it was a cat hair instead of a drop of wine and one removed it by pouring water, then this little water, containing the cat hair as a separate entity, becomes *najas*-filthy itself for being in contact with a *najasah*--even though the cat hair did not change any of the attributes of the water.

Moreover, if the little water poured on the *najasah* to remove it did not completely remove the *najasah* in one pour, then the water used in this first pour is judged as *najas*-filthy water.

Chapter 11
Dry Purification (*Tayammum*)

To be in a state of *taharah*, one uses water to perform *wudu'* and *ghusl*. However, one may need to perform *taharah*, yet not find water, or may have water but will be harmed if one uses it. In these cases, the person performs dry purification (*tayammum*), as the author said:

If one needs to pray, but one is in the state of ritual impurity (*hadath*), and one cannot find water or will be harmed upon using it, one performs dry purification (*tayammum*).

Explanation: From the author's saying "one performs *tayammum* if one cannot find water" it is understood that if one performs dry purification (*tayammum*) because one does not have water, one's *tayammum* is invalid, unless one first has sought the water. So, one must first seek the water--then, if one does not find it, one performs the dry purification. Also, one performs *tayammum* instead of using water to perform *taharah* if using water harms one. So, if using water to perform *taharah* will cause one's death, or damage an organ, or lengthen the recovery time from an illness, or cause a disfigurement in any of one's apparent body parts, like the hands or the face, then one performs *tayammum*--even if one has water.

There is a specific procedure that is applied for one to be considered as one who did not find water. For example, the traveler who cannot find water is the person who neither has water with him, nor do his companions have water with them, or they have water which they want to sell to him at a higher price than the norm, or he has just enough water to keep him alive so that he does not die of thirst, or he has just enough to keep his animal alive. If this person is in a land where he is certain there is no water within the distance of half a *farsakh* (3000 cubits, approximately 1.4 km), he may perform *tayammum*. If he knows that there is water close to him (i.e., 1/2 a *farsakh* or less), it is an obligation on him to fetch the water.

If the person is in an unfamiliar land, i.e., he does not know whether or not there is water nearby, he must seek the water. To seek the water means for a person to physically look for the water, either by walking in the four directions for a distance that if he shouted for help, his companions would hear him, (about 300 cubits in each direction), or, if he was in a flat land and can see as far as that distance, he would look in each direction for the water. If he does either of these and does not find water, he is considered as one who sought the water and did not find it. Hence, he can perform *tayammum*.

Tayammum is performed after the time of the prayer per se sets in

Explanation: The person who wants to perform *tayammum* for a prayer must do so after the time of that prayer has begun. So if a person makes *tayammum* before the time of _Dhuhr_ sets in to perform the _Dhuhr_ Prayer, his *tayammum* is not valid. He must perform the *tayammum* for the _Dhuhr_ Prayer after the sun declines from the center of the sky towards the west.

and after the unexempted *najas*-filth is removed.

Explanation: If able, one must remove any unexempted *najas*-filth on one's body before performing *tayammum*. If one had an unexempted *najas*-filth on one's body and had only a small amount of water--sufficient either to remove the unexempted *najas*-filth or to perform *wudu'*, one should use the water to remove the *najas*-filth, and then, if one did not have enough water left to perform *wudu'*, one would perform *tayammum*. If one had an unexempted *najas*-filth on one's body and had no water at all, then one must attempt to lighten this *najas*-filth in some way before performing *tayammum*. If one was unable, one would perform the *tayammum* with the *najas*-filth still on oneself.

Tayammum is performed by using unmixed soil, which is purifying and dusty.

Explanation: *Tayammum* is valid only when performed using the dusty soil, i.e., soil that contains fine dust. Hence, it is not valid to make *tayammum* using a rock. Also, it is not valid to use the beach sand as soil, because these sand particles do not contain fine dust particles. It is also not valid to use the dust particles that gather on the house furniture, for example, to perform *tayammum*, unless that dust was the fine dust of soil.

It is invalid to use a *najas*-filthy soil to perform *tayammum* or soil mixed with another pure (_tahir_) material, such as ashes. As well, it is invalid to reuse the soil which was previously used in performing *tayammum*. For example, if one were to collect the soil which had fallen from the face after using it to wipe the face, one cannot reuse that to wipe one's arms or to perform a separate *tayammum*.

One strikes the soil with the inside part of the hands, then makes and maintains the intention of making the obligatory prayer permissible to do while transferring the dust of the soil from the ground until it is wiped on part of the face. One wipes the entire face and then strikes the soil a second time to wipe the hands and forearms.

Explanation: Performing *tayammum* involves transferring the soil (while maintaining the intention during the transfer) and wiping the specific body parts. One strikes the soil with the inner side of one's hands with the fingers spread. Then one lifts one's hands up to begin transferring the soil to wipe one's face. During the entire time of transferring the soil, from when one first lifts one's hands from the first strike of the soil, until one wipes the first part of one's face, one must hold the intention of performing *tayammum*. Hence, if one's intention was interrupted between the time of the beginning of the transfer until the wiping of the first part of the face, the intention is invalid and by consequence, the *tayammum* is invalid. However, holding the intention for the entire duration of the transfer is a case of difference in opinion; some scholars, like *Imam Malik*, said if the intention was interrupted in the process of transfer, it would not affect the validity of the *tayammum*.

With the fine soil-dust from the first strike, one wipes the whole face, the boundaries of which were previously defined. (It is not a condition that the soil reaches to the skin under the beard of the man, even if it was thin, because this involves a hardship.) Then one strikes the soil a second time to transfer (its dust) to wipe the forearms and elbows. One wipes the entire forearm, up to and including the elbow--that same area washed in *wudu'*--using the soil on the inner side of the left hand to wipe the right arm, and the soil on the inner part of the right hand to wipe the left arm.

It is invalid to wipe both the face and the hands with just one strike of the soil. It is invalid to use one *tayammum* to pray two obligatory prayers. Each obligatory prayer needs a separate *tayammum*--even if that obligatory prayer was a make-up. One may pray as many optional prayers as one wants with one *tayammum*.

Chapter 12
Prohibitions While in the State of Ritual Impurity (*Hadath*)

There are certain deeds one is prohibited to do while in a state of ritual impurity. To be able to perform them, one must first clear oneself of this state.

The person who invalidated one's *wudu'* is prohibited to perform prayer, circumambulate the *Ka^bah*, and to carry or touch the Book of the *Qur'an* (*Mus-haf*). However, the child who has reached the age of mental discrimination (*mumayyiz*) and is studying in the Book of the *Qur'an* is allowed to carry it and touch it without *wudu'*.

Explanation: The person who invalidates his *wudu'* is in a state of minor ritual impurity and while in that state it is unlawful for him to pray, perform *tawaf*, or touch or carry the Book of the *Qur'an*. Praying without *wudu'* is invalid and sinful. Similarly, *taharah* is needed for *tawaf* (circumambulating the *Ka^bah*). The one who loses his *wudu'* is not allowed to perform *tawaf* until he reperforms his *wudu'*. The one who does not have his *wudu'* is not allowed to touch, pick up, or carry the Book of the *Qur'an*--even with a barrier. He is not allowed to touch the words, the margin, or the cover of the Book of the *Qur'an*, unless there was a necessity.

The child who has reached the age of mental discrimination may touch the Book of the *Qur'an* without having *wudu'* for the purpose of studying in it. For instance, the child who does not have his *wudu'* may carry the *Qur'an* to his teacher to teach him or may hold it to study in it. The child has this facility because enforcing the issue of *wudu'* on the child each time he wants to study in the *Qur'an* may be a hardship on him, which may discourage him from wanting to study in it. This facility is for the child to study in the *Qur'an*. Hence, one may not ask the child who has reached the age of mental discrimination and who does not have his *wudu'* to carry the *Qur'an* for one's own purpose. Examples are to bring it to someone else to read or to move it from one place to another so one could dust under it.

It is unlawful for the person who emitted *maniyy* or had sexual intercourse (*junub*) to do the aforementioned, and also to recite the *Qur'an*, and stay in a mosque.

Explanation: The person who is in the state of major ritual impurity because he emitted *maniyy* is prohibited from the same three deeds (mentioned above prohibited for the person in the state of minor ritual impurity). Furthermore, certain other matters are prohibited for him. These are reciting the *Qur'an* and staying in the mosque. It is not permissible for the *junub* to recite the *Qur'an* out loud, i.e., so that one could hear oneself, although it is permissible to read it silently by moving one's lips and tongue in doing so. It is permissible for one to recite the words in one's heart or to read them with one's eyes, as long as one does not produce any sound or touch the Book of the *Qur'an* while in this state.

Likewise, it is prohibited for the *junub* to stay in the mosque, or to go back and forth inside the mosque. However, one is allowed to pass through the mosque, that is, to enter from one door and leave through the other. If one has had a sexual intercourse without emitting *maniyy*, a *ghusl* is required, and the same aforementioned rules of the *junub* apply to one.

It is unlawful for the menstruating and postpartum-bleeding women to do all the aforementioned actions, to fast before the cessation of bleeding, and to allow the husband or the master to enjoy the area between their navels and knees before they have performed their purificatory bath (*ghusl*). Some scholars said that anything other than sexual intercourse is allowed, however.

Explanation: The menstruating women and the women in their postpartum bleeding period are prohibited from performing the five matters mentioned before, as well as two more matters: fasting before the cessation of bleeding, and allowing the husband to enjoy the area between their navel and knees before they have performed the purificatory bath (*ghusl*). So, they are prohibited from performing prayer, *tawaf*, touching and holding the *Qur'an*, reciting the *Qur'an*, and staying in the mosque. As well, these women are prohibited to fast before the cessation of bleeding. However, they may make the intention to fast and begin fasting after the cessation of bleeding, and before performing the *ghusl*. That is, these women do not have to perform the *ghusl* (to clear themselves of the state of major ritual impurity) to intend to fast for the next day, or to begin fasting.

The menstruating women and the women in their postpartum

bleeding period are also prohibited from allowing the husband to enjoy the area between their navel and knees without a barrier, before performing the obligatory *ghusl*, even if the blood stops. Sexual intercourse is prohibited before the obligatory *ghusl*. If the woman wore something that covered the area between her navel and knees, then she would not be prohibited from allowing her husband to enjoy that area--above the barrier. The same judgment holds for the unmarried slave woman with regards to her master.

A less-famous saying in the school of *Imam ash-Shafi^iyy* states that before performing the obligatory *ghusl* enjoying what is between the wife's navel and her knees is permissible, even without a barrier; only sexual intercourse is prohibited.

Chapter 13
Removing *Najas*-Filth

Among the conditions of prayer is to be clear of *najas*-filth in one's body, clothes, place of prayer, and what one carries in prayer, such as a bottle carried in one's pocket.

Explanation: Being clear of unexempted *najas*-filth in one's body, clothing, place of prayer, and what one carries is a condition of prayer. One's place of prayer means any place that the body touches in prayer. So, if one touches a *najāsah* placed anywhere while praying, the prayer is invalid. For example, if one stands on a *najāsah*, or while in *sujūd*, puts one's hands, forehead, knees, or other parts of one's body on a *najāsah*, then one's prayer is invalidated. However, the exempted *najas*-filth does not affect the validity of the prayer. An exempted *najas*-filth is such as the blood or pus of one's own wound. These are overlooked *najāsahs*, meaning they do not affect the validity of one's prayer, even if the blood or pus contaminated one's body or clothes.

If a *najas*-filth contacts one or what one carries, one's prayer is invalidated unless the *najas*-filth is thrown away immediately, or it is an exempted *najas*-filth, such as the blood of one's wound.

Explanation: If, during the prayer, an unexempted *najas*-filth comes into contact with one's body or clothing or what one carries, one's prayer will be immediately invalidated unless one throws the *najas*-filth, moist or dry, away immediately, without one carrying it (or doing what is like carrying it). Removing a *najas*-filth with one's sleeve is similar to carrying it. However, if the *najas*-filth, moist or dry, fell on what one was wearing, and one shook it off, or shrugged out of that clothing immediately, the prayer would not be invalidated. In the case of moist *najas*-filth, using a stick to scrape it off the contaminated area of the clothing invalidates the prayer. The moist *najas*-filth itself must be rid of (without carrying) immediately along with the contaminated area or clothing. An example is to throw the contaminated cloak off one's shoulder.

Using purifying water to remove the *najas*-filth and its properties, i.e., the taste, color, and odor, is the only way to clean an area contaminated with an unexempted *najas*-filth.

106

Explanation: To remove a *najas*-filth present as a physical entity, one must use purifying water to remove both the physical entity of that *najas*-filth as well as its properties, i.e., its color, taste, and odor. A place is not purified by removing the entity and its properties with soil, or by exposing it to the sun until its properties disappear. To purify the place contaminated with a discernible *najas*-filth, one must wash it with purifying water until the physical entity of that *najas*-filth and its properties are removed. As long as the odor of the *najas*-filth is detectable, it is dealt with as discernible *najas*-filth (*najasah ^ayniyyah*), even though one may not be able to see the *najas*-filth.

The *najas*-filth which does not have any discernible characteristics (*najasah hukmiyyah*) is the *najas*-filth the color, taste, and odor of which cannot be detected. The place contaminated with such a *najas*-filth is purified by pouring water on it.

Explanation: If a wet *najas*-filth comes into contact with a particular spot, then the entity of that *najas*-filth as well as its color, taste, and odor disappear without using water to remove it, then the judgment of the location contacted by the *najas*-filth is that it is *najas*-filthy. To purify this location, it is enough to run water over it once.

The *najas*-filth of a dog [or a pig] is removed by washing the *najas*-filthy area seven times, one of which is mixed with purifying soil. The washes which remove the physical presence of the *najas*-filth are deemed one wash, even if they were numerous.

Explanation: One wash is not sufficient to purify the place contaminated with the *najas*-filth of a dog or a pig. Seven washes are required, one of which must be mixed with pure soil. To clean the *najas*-filth from a dog or pig, one must first pour water on that location until the physical entity is removed. This is considered one wash-- even if one needed to pour fifty (50) times to remove the entity and its properties. Still needed are six (6) more washes. One of those seven (7) washes must be mixed with soil so that it forms a suspension (i.e., the water would be colored by the soil). It is preferable to use this suspension for the first wash.

All the parts of a dog or a pig are *najas*-filthy (*najasah kalbiyyah* or *khinziriyyah*), including their skin, hair, saliva, excrement, or other. So, if a dog licks something, or touches it with its wet nose, or if a person pets a dog with his wet hand, then the contaminated place must be washed in this way to purify it.

107

In the case of using little water for removing the *najas*-filth, i.e., less than two (2) *qullahs*, it is required to pour the water on the *najas*-filth. [However, putting a *najas*-filth in an amount of water which is two (2) *qullahs* or more will not make the water *najas*-filthy unless it changes it.]

Explanation: If one is using little water (less than two (2) *qullahs*) to remove a *najas*-filth, it is conditional that the water runs over the location to affect it, i.e., to purify it. Putting this *najas*-filth into that little water itself instead of pouring the water over it does not remove the *najas*-filth, rather it causes the water to become *najas*-filthy. For example, if a person had a *najas*-filth on his shirt, and put the shirt into a little water, then removed it, even though the *najas*-filth and its properties might no longer be present, that shirt was not purified. Rather, all the parts of the shirt that were immersed in the water became *najas*-filthy, as well as all of the water. This is so because the *najas*-filth was placed into the water rather than running the water over the *najas*-filth. However, when the water is plenty (two (2) *qullahs* or more), putting a *najas*-filth into it does not affect it, as long as the water is not changed by that *najasah*.

Chapter 14
Additional Conditions of Prayer

The following matters are conditions that must be met for one's prayer to be valid.

Among the conditions of prayer are:

1. To direct one's chest towards the Qiblah;

Explanation: One of the conditions is to direct one's chest towards the Qiblah, that is, one must face the Ka^bah. The one who sees the Ka^bah faces it. The one who cannot see the Ka^bah, but can see another who sees the Ka^bah, follows the direction pointed by the latter. One makes *ijtihad* (i.e., endeavors to find out the direction of the Qiblah in relation to one's present location) when one can neither see the Ka^bah oneself nor follow another who can see the Ka^bah. If one neglects to make the proper effort to determine the direction of the Ka^bah, one's prayer is not valid.

2. The setting in of the prayer time;

Explanation: Performing a prayer before its time sets in is invalid. Beginning a prayer without knowing whether or not the time of the prayer came in invalidates that prayer. This means if one initiates one's prayer without first determining (for certain or most likely) by a religiously valid method that the prayer time actually has set in, then one's prayer is invalid--even if it is done within the time.

3. To be Muslim;

Explanation: Praying is an act of worship, and any worship is not valid (or accepted) if done by a blasphemer. Worship is only valid after one believes correctly in *Allah*, the only One Who deserves to be worshipped, and His Messenger.

4. To be at the age of mental discrimination (*mumayyiz*), i.e., the age at which the child understands when addressed and answers when asked;

Explanation: Prayer is not valid from the one who is not at the age of mental discrimination. Hence, one should not order the child who did not reach the age of mental discrimination to pray, because his prayer is invalid. Instead, one may tell that child to observe how others pray.

5. To deem the obligatory prayer an obligation;

Explanation: To know that the prayer per se is obligatory is a condition for the validity of that prayer. For example, if someone who had embraced *Islam* recently (and did not know that Muslims were obligated to pray five (5) obligatory prayers) saw Muslims praying *Dhuhr* Prayer and joined them in that prayer without knowing of its obligation, his prayer would be invalid[30].

The one who is raised among Muslims and doubts that the five (5) obligatory prayers are obligatory, or denies the obligation of one of them blasphemes.

6. Not to deem any of the integrals of the prayer recommended (*sunnah*[31]);

Explanation: If one believes any integral of the prayer is a recommended matter rather than a matter necessary for its validity, one's prayer is invalid--even if one performs that integral. For example, if one believed that the final *tashahhud* was a recommended matter and not an integral, one's prayer would be invalid, even if one recited that *tashahhud* in the prayer.

7. To cover the whole body of the free woman with the exception of her face and hands, i.e., to conceal the skin and hair and their colors; to cover the area between the navel and the knees of the male and of the female slave from all sides except from underneath.

Explanation: Covering the unlawful nakedness (ˆawrah) is a condition for the validity of the prayer. For prayer, the unlawful nakedness of the free woman is her entire body with the exception of her hands and face. Hence, when in prayers, she has to cover all of her body except for her hands and face. This means she has to conceal the color of her skin and hair--despite the appearance of the shape of the ˆawrah. If she prays wearing what conceals the color of the skin and hair, but reveals the shape of her ˆawrah, then her prayer is valid-- however it is *makruh* (disliked).

---

[30] This prayer that he prayed is not considered a *Sunnah* prayer for him, because it is invalid.

[31] Recommended (*Sunnah*) means it is rewardable if done with the proper intention, but if it is not done at all, one is not sinful.

110

The unlawful nakedness for the man is the area between his navel and knees--and excludes both the navel and the knees. The man must cover this area during prayer. The unlawful nakedness of the slave woman for prayers is the same as the man's. That is, if the slave woman performs her prayers while covering only the area between her navel and knees, her prayer is valid. This does not mean that she may go out walking on the streets covering this area only.

One must cover the ˆawrah from all directions, except from underneath. So, if one prays while covering the ˆawrah from all directions except from underneath such that the ˆawrah will be apparent only if one looks from underneath, the prayer is valid. For example, if a man wraps an *izar* around himself, from his navel to mid-calf, however by looking from underneath one is able to see his thigh, this does not affect the validity of his prayers.

Note: The free woman needs to take care that her ˆawrah does not become apparent during the different moves of the prayer. If she is covering with one piece of cloth, reaching from her head to the ground and when she is making *rukuˆ*, for example, her ankles become exposed, then her prayer is invalid. If she is covering with two or more pieces of cloth, a top part reaching to the waist and a skirt to the floor, and the top part is flowing (or baggy) and is not tucked into the skirt, she needs to make sure that when she moves to the different positions, her ˆawrah would not be exposed to one looking from underneath. For example, when she bends for *rukuˆ*, if the top covering falls away from her body in such a way that one looking from underneath would be able to see her uncovered stomach, neck, or arms, then her prayer is invalidated. If she is wearing a skirt which reaches to her mid-calf and knee socks underneath in such a way that her upper thigh, for example, would be exposed to one looking from underneath, this is not sufficient.

On the other hand, if a free woman covering her ˆawrah from all directions prays on an elevated platform such that her ˆawrah can be seen by one looking up from a lower level, her prayer is still valid.

Chapter 15
Invalidators of Prayer

Prayer is invalidated by:

1. **Uttering two letters or any letter which carries a meaning, unless one forgets and few words are said;**

Explanation: Among the invalidators of the prayer is for one to speak words people usually converse with one another. This excludes making *dhikr* in remembering *Allah*, which does not invalidate the prayer. If a person intentionally utters two letters, even if these letters do not have a meaning, or if he utters just one letter that has a meaning, while remembering that he is in prayer, this invalidates his prayer. There are some words in Arabic that have a meaning and are composed of just one letter. For example, the letter *fa* (ف) pronounced with a *kasrah*, (i.e., *fi* ف) means "keep your word or promise". If a person utters this letter intentionally, during his prayer, while remembering he is praying, his prayer is invalidated.

This judgment applies to the one who is aware that speaking in prayer (other than the words spoken for prayer) is a forbidden matter. It does not invalidate the person's prayer if he speaks a little while praying because he forgets that he is praying.

2. **Performing many moves, which according to some scholars are as many as what would last for the duration of one *rak^ah*. According to other scholars three consecutive moves invalidate the prayer. The first saying, however, has a stronger evidence;**

Explanation: Among the invalidators of prayer is for one to make many moves during the prayer that are other than the actions of the prayer. Some scholars said moving three consecutive moves or moving three body parts at once invalidates the prayer. Other scholars said the moves that invalidate the prayer are those that last for a period of time which is equal to the duration of one *rak^ah*. This saying has a stronger evidence.

3. **Performing an excessive move;**

Explanation: If one performs one excessive move while in prayer, one's prayer is invalidated. For example, if one jumped or punched a person, one's prayer would be invalidated.

4. Adding an extra integral of action;

Explanation: If one performs an extra integral of action while remembering this is an extra action, one's prayer is invalidated. For example, if one started one's prayer, recited the *Fatihah*, performed the *ruku^*, straightened for the *i^tidal*, and, while remembering, performed an additional *ruku^*, one's prayer would be invalidated.

5. Performing one move with the purpose of playing;

Explanation: Moving, even slightly, while praying with the purpose of playing invalidates the prayer, because the intention of playing conflicts with the intention of praying.

6. Eating and drinking, except if one forgets and it is little;

Explanation: If a person eats or drinks while remembering he is praying, his prayer is invalidated. His prayer is invalidated, even if he eats or drinks a very little amount, like, if he intentionally swallows the food stuck between his teeth.

7. Intending to interrupt the prayer;

Explanation: Having the intention to interrupt the prayer invalidates it. For example, if one says to oneself, "I now interrupt my prayer", then one's prayer is invalidated immediately upon the intention.

8. Making an intention to interrupt the prayer contingent on the occurrence of an incident;

Explanation: If a person makes the interruption of his prayer contingent upon the happening of a certain matter, then his prayer is invalidated immediately upon his intention. For example, if a person decides that he will interrupt his prayer to answer the door should the doorbell ring, then his prayer is invalidated immediately--whether or not the doorbell rings.

9. Hesitating about interrupting the prayer;

Explanation: As well, if one hesitated or wavered in that matter, like if he was praying and hesitated thinking to himself, "If a thief comes in now while I am praying, should I interrupt my prayer or not?", then his prayer would be invalidated.

10. **Completing an integral while the doubt persists about whether or not one established the intention to perform prayer during the opening saying of *Allahu akbar* (*taharrum*), or doubting for a long time about this intention.**

Explanation: If a person doubts whether or not he established his intention to perform the prayer during the opening *takbir* (saying *Allahu akbar*), and this doubt lasts for the duration of an integral, his prayer is invalidated. For example, if a person doubts about his intention while reciting the verses in the *Fatihah*, then goes to *ruku^* while he is still in doubt, once he reaches the *ruku^* with the doubt still in his heart, his prayer will be invalidated.

Similarly, if a person doubted about his intention for a long time, even if he did not complete an integral, then this would invalidate his prayer. For instance, if a person was reciting a *surah* after the *Fatihah*, before performing *ruku^*, and while reading this *surah*, he doubted about his intention, if this doubt lasted for a long time during that recitation, this would invalidate his prayer.

If one doubted about the intention, but cleared oneself of that doubt quickly, that is, before the termination of the integral, one's prayer would not be invalidated.

Chapter 16
Conditions for the Rewardability of Prayer

In addition to what has been mentioned, prayer is rewardable by *Allah, subhanahu wa taʿala,* **if the following conditions are satisfied:**

Explanation: This chapter deals with the conditions that must be met for the prayer to be rewardable. These conditions do not affect the validity of the prayer.

1. One performs the prayer for the sake of *Allah* only;

Explanation: Among the conditions for one's prayer to be rewardable is for one to perform the prayers with sincerity, that is, for the sake of *Allah* only. For a person to be sincere in one's worship means to establish in one's heart that one is performing this worship (prayer, in this case) out of obedience to *Allah*, seeking the reward from *Allah*, out of glorifying *Allah,* or the like. The prayer of the one who performs it seeking the recognition of the people or the like is valid, but not rewardable. Moreover, this insincerity is an enormous sin.

2. One's food, clothing, and place of prayer are lawful;

Explanation: If any of these matters was unlawful one's prayer would be valid, but not rewardable. For one's prayer to be rewardable, the food one has in one's stomach while one is praying, the clothes one is wearing while one is praying, and the place where one is praying must be lawful. If any of these is unlawful for one to use or consume, like if the food one has in one's stomach is *najas*-filthy, (like wine or pork), then one's prayer is not rewardable.

3. One's heart has (reverently) feared *Allah* for at least a moment during the prayer.

Explanation: For the prayer to be rewardable, one has to have the fear of *Allah* in one's heart for at least a moment during that prayer. One must establish in one's heart, for at least a moment during that prayer, the fear of *Allah* in glorifying and submitting to Him.[32] If one has this fear--even for a moment--during the prayer, it is sufficient. However, the more one humbles oneself to *Allah*, fears *Allah*, and submits to Him, the more reward one earns.

---

[32] Once, the Prophet was with ʿAʾishah at night and said to her, O ʿAʾishah, let me pray to *Allah*. Then he took some water, made *wudu'*, and started to pray. He cried until his beard and the soil below him were soaked with his tears. His crying was a reflection and result of his *khushuʿ*. It was not the fear of losing in the Hereafter, because the prophets know that they are not losers in the Hereafter. Rather, it was out of the deep feeling of the greatness of *Allah* and the submission to Him.

One's prayer is valid but not rewardable if these three conditions are not met.

Explanation: If the integrals of one's prayer are fulfilled and the invalidators are avoided, but the three above mentioned conditions are not fulfilled, one's prayer is valid. However, one is not rewarded for that prayer.

Chapter 17
Integrals of Prayer

The integrals (*rukns*) of prayer are seventeen (17):

Explanation: There are seventeen (17) matters that one must perform in prayer. If these are not performed, the prayer is not valid. These are the integrals (*rukns*) of the prayer. They are seventeen (17) when counting the *tuma'ninah* as a distinct or separate integral (*rukn*) each time it is required.

1. **To have the intention in the heart of performing the prayer, to specify the prayer which is performed for a particular reason or time, and of its obligation when obligatory;**

Explanation: The first integral of the prayer is the intention. The place of the intention is the heart. Hence, it is not sufficient for one to only utter the intention by the tongue without establishing it in one's heart at the beginning of the prayer. The time of establishing the intention is during the *takbir* of *ihram*, i.e., when saying the opening *Allahu akbar*.

If the prayer was an obligatory one, one should specify its obligation in one's intention. If it was a prayer that must be performed in a specific time, one has to specify that time in one's intention. For example, the *Dhuhr* prayer has a specific time in which it must be performed. Hence, one must specify in one's intention that one is performing the *Dhuhr* prayer in particular and not performing an unspecified prayer at that time. Likewise in performing the *^Id* prayer, one has to specify in one's intention that one is now praying the *^Id* prayer and not an unspecified prayer.

If the prayer is performed for a particular reason, then one has to specify the reason. For example, the prayer of the eclipse is performed when an eclipse of the sun or the moon occurs. So one must establish in one's intention that one is praying the prayer of the eclipse, because it is performed for that reason.

Examples of valid intentions are:

* If one wants to pray the *Subh* prayer (the obligatory prayer with a specific time) one establishes in one's heart: I now intend to pray the obligatory *Subh*, or what is similar to this intention.

* If one wants to pray the prayer of ^Id (a prayer for a specific reason), one establishes in one's heart, I now intend to pray the prayer of ^Id, or what is similar to it.

* If one wants to pray an optional prayer that does not involve a specific time or reason (nafl mutlaq), it is sufficient just to establish the intention of praying, like I now pray.

2. **To say 'Allahu akbar' loud enough to hear oneself, as is required in every verbal integral;**

Explanation: The second integral is to say "*Allahu akbar*," which is the opening *takbir*. One must say it at least loud enough to hear oneself. It is required that every verbal integral to be uttered at least as loud as one can hear oneself.

3. **To stand (qiyam) for the obligatory prayer, when able;**

Explanation: Standing up straight (*qiyam*) when one is able is one of the integrals of the prayer, that is, to stand on one's feet with one's back straight. The one who is unable to stand prays while sitting, facing the Ka^bah. If one was unable to sit, then one would pray while lying down, either on one's right or one's left side (preferably right, if able), while facing the Qiblah. If one was unable, one would pray while lying on one's back, with one's feet pointing towards the Qiblah with something under one's head (if able) to lift one's face towards the Qiblah.

4. **To recite the Fatihah[33], including the basmalah بسم الله الرحمٰن الرَّحيم، and doubling the letters that must be doubled, in order and succession without lengthy interruption, articulating its letters properly,**

Explanation: The fourth integral of prayer is reciting the *Fatihah* (the opening chapter of the Qur'an). For the validity of the recitation of the *Fatihah*, one must recite the *basmalah* ("bismillahir-Rahmanir-Rahim, بسم الله الرحمٰن الرَّحيم) because it is the first verse of the *Fatihah*.

---

[33]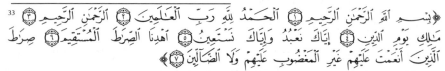

Bismillahir-Rahmanir-Rahim. Al-hamdu lillahi Rabbil-^alamin. Ar-Rahmanir-Rahim. Maliki Yawmid-Din. Iyyaka na^budu wa iyyaka nasta^in. Ihdinas-Siratal-Mustaqim. Siratal-ladhina an^amta ^alayhim, ghayril-maghdubi ^alayhim wa lad-dallin.

118

One must take care to properly pronounce the words of the *Fatihah*, including reciting the verses in order and in succession without lengthy interruption between the verses or between the words of a verse. For the validity of the recitation of the *Fatihah*, one must articulate its letters properly, meaning one must pronounce the letters from their original exits and one must double the letters that must be doubled in pronunciation. If one cannot pronounce the letter perfectly, one's recitation is valid as long as one pronounces the letter from its proper exit. However, if one was negligent of that, one's recitation would be invalid. For example, if one pronounces the letter *ta* [ط] as a *ta* [ت] or pronounces the *dhal* [ذ] as a *zay* [ز] (like to say *al-lazina* [الَّزِينَ] instead of *al-ladhina* [الَّذِينَ]), the recitation is invalid and the prayer is invalid, unless it is a slip of the tongue and the person goes back and corrects one's recitation.

and avoiding the error which breaches the meaning, such as saying أَنْعَمْتُ (*an^amtu*) instead of أَنْعَمْتَ (*an^amta*). It is prohibited to commit an error which does not breach the meaning, but it does not invalidate the prayer;

Explanation: Making an error in reciting the *Fatihah* is unlawful, even if one committed that mistake because one was negligent in learning the proper recitation of the *Fatihah*. Making an error in recitation which changes the meaning, like to say "*an^amtu*" (which refers to the person reciting) instead of saying "*an^amta*" (referring to *Allah*), is unlawful and invalidates the prayer. This is so unless it is a slip of the tongue, and one corrects the mistake.

The error, which does not change the meaning, is unlawful. However, it does not invalidate the prayer unless it was done intentionally. For example, if one was ignorant and thought the proper pronunciation was *al-hamdulillahu* instead of *al-hamdulillahi*, then one's prayer would not be invalidated. However, if one knew that this was the wrong recitation, and yet recited it as such on purpose, one's prayer would be invalidated, because one was taking the performance of the prayer as an occasion to play, and the intention of playing invalidates the intention of praying.

5. **To bow until one's palms can reach one's knees (*ruku^*);**

Explanation: The fifth integral is for one to perform *ruku^*, that is, to bow until one's palms can reach one's knees, without the latter being bent. It is not a condition to actually place one's palms on the knees, however, it is a *sunnah*. Saying "*subhana Rabbiyal-^Adhim*" (three times) in the position of *ruku^* is also *sunnah*.

6. To remain motionless in *ruku^* for the duration of saying 'subhan Allah' (tuma'ninah);

Explanation: The sixth integral is *tuma'ninah* which is for all one's body to remain motionless at least for the time it takes to say "*subhan Allah*".

7. To straighten up after *ruku^* (i^tidal);

Explanation: *I^tidal* means to go back to the position prior to the *ruku^*. Saying "*sami^Allahu liman hamidah*" while straightening the back up from the *ruku^* is a *sunnah*.

8. To remain motionless in *i^tidal* for the duration of saying 'subhan Allah';

Explanation: After straightening (to reach the position one had before *ruku^*) one must remain motionless (*tuma'ninah*) for the duration of saying *subhan Allah*.

9. To prostrate (perform *sujud*) twice by putting all or part of one's uncovered forehead on one's praying ground while applying a slight pressure, with one's lower body (buttocks) higher than one's upper part, and putting part of one's knees, the inside of one's hands and the bottom of one's toes on the ground. A non-*Shafi^iyy* scholar said that the prayer is valid even if the head was higher in *sujud* than the buttocks;

Explanation: The ninth integral of prayer is prostration (*sujud*) and it is performed twice in every *rak^ah* (cycle). Among the conditions of prostration is for one's uncovered forehead to come in contact with one's place of *sujud*. So, if one's hair (or scarf) came in-between the forehead and the place of *sujud*, preventing all the skin of the forehead from touching the place of *sujud*, the prostration is not valid. One must let the weight of one's head rest on the place of *sujud*. The lower body must be elevated higher than the upper body, i.e., one's hips need to be higher than one's shoulders. Some *Shafi^iyys* said the prostration is still valid if one's lower body and upper body are at the same level. In the school of *Imam Ahmad*, it does not matter which part of the body is higher, as long as this position is still classified as a prostration.

10. To have _tuma'ninah_ in prostration (_sujud_);

Explanation: One performs _tuma'ninah_ (as explained before) in the prostration.

11. To sit between the two prostrations;

Explanation: One raises one's head off the ground to a sitting position.

12. To have _tuma'ninah_ in this sitting;

Explanation: After performing the first prostration, one sits up motionless for a period of time long enough to say "_subhan Allah_", then performs another prostration. Intentionally leaving out sitting between the two prostrations invalidates one's prayer.

13. To sit for saying the last _tashahhud_, the _Salah ^alan-Nabiyy_, and the closing _salam_;

Explanation: Sitting to perform the _tashahhud_, the _Salah ^alan-Nabiyy_, and the closing _salam_ at the end of the prayer is an integral of the prayer. It is invalid to perform the _tashahhud_ or the _Salah ^alan-Nabiyy_ while standing. Moreover, intentionally saying _as-salamu ^alaykum_ while standing invalidates the prayer.

14. To say the last _tashahhud_; (one version of which is:)

التَّحِيَّاتُ المُبَارَكَاتُ، الصَّلَوَاتُ الطَّيِّبَاتُ لله . السَّلامُ عَلَيْكَ أَيُّهَا النَّبِئُ وَرَحْمَةُ الله وَبَرَكاتُهُ . السَّلامُ عَلَيْنَا وَعَلَى عِبَادِ الله الصَّالِحِينَ . أَشْهَدُ أَنْ لا إله إلا الله وَأَشْهَدُ أَنَّ مُحَمَّدًا رَسُولُ الله .

Explanation: The fourteenth integral is to say the last _tashahhud_ in the final sitting, i.e., in the sitting after the second prostration of the last _rak^ah_. There are several _sahih_ narrations from the Prophet, _sallallahu ^alayhi wa sallam_, pertaining to the recitation of the last _tashahhud_.

A famous narration (mentioned in the text above) is narrated from the route of _Ibn ^Abbas_ from the Prophet, _sallallahu ^alayhi wa sallam_:

121

《*At-tahiyyat-ul-mubarakat-us-salawat-ut-tayyibatu lillah. As-salamu ^alayka ayyuha-n-nabiyyu wa rahmatullahi wa barakatuh. As-salamu ^alayna wa ^ala ^ibadillah is-salihin. Ash-hadu alla ilaha illallah wa ash-hadu anna Muhammadar rasulullah.*》

The minimum *tashahhud* is:

التَّحِيَّاتُ لله . سَلامٌ عَلَيْكَ أَيُّها النَّبِيُّ وَرَحْمَةُ الله وَبَرَكاتُهُ . سَلامٌ عَلَيْنَا وَعَلَى عِبادِ الله الصَّالِحِينَ . أَشْهَدُ أَنْ لا إِلَه إِلا اللَّهُ وَأَنَّ مُحَمَّدًا رَسُولُ اللَّهِ .

Explanation: The shortest among the narrations of the *tashahhud* is:

《*At-tahiyyatu lillah. Salamun ^alayka ayyuha-n-nabiyyu warahmatullahi wabarakatuh. Salamun ^alayna wa ^ala ^ibadillah is-salihin. Ash-hadu alla ilaha illallah wa anna Muhammadar rasulullah.*》

Reciting any of the *sahih* narrations of the *tashahhud* for the prayer is valid.

15. To say the *Salah* ^alan-Nabiyy, sallallahu ^alayhi wa sallam. The minimum is اللهُمَّ صلّ على محمَّد *Allahumma salli* ^*ala Muhammad*.

Explanation: According to the school of *Imam ash-Shafi^iyy*, to say the *Salah* ^alan-Nabiyy after the last *tashahhud* is an integral. An example of what would be sufficient is:

اللهُمَّ صَلّ عَلَى مُحَمَّدٍ

i.e., "*Allahumma salli ^ala Muhammad*". If one said, "*Sallallahu ^ala Muhammad*" this would be sufficient. Likewise, saying "*Sallallahu ^ala rasulillah*" is also sufficient, as is saying "*Sallallahu ^alan-Nabiyy*". However, saying "*Sallallahu ^ala Ahmad*" is insufficient.

16. To say the closing *salam*. The minimum is: السَّلامُ عَلَيْكُم *As-salamu* ^*alaykum*:

Explanation: One must be careful in pronouncing the closing *salam* to say "*as-salamu ^alaykum*" and not just "*salamu ^alaykum*". The obligation is to say the first *salam*. The second one is *sunnah*. It is not an obligation to say "*wa rahmatullah*", but it is better to do so.

17. To observe the order.

Explanation: The order of the integrals is as mentioned:

1. To stand (if able), say, "*Allahu akbar*", and establish the intention for that prayer while saying "*Allahu akbar*";

2. To recite the *Fatihah*;

3. To perform *ruku˄*, and establish the *tuma'ninah* in it;

4. To go back to the position before *ruku˄*, having *tuma'ninah* in it;

5. To prostrate twice with the *tuma'ninah* in each prostration, and to sit (with *tuma'ninah*) between the two prostrations;

6. To sit in the last *rak˄ah* after the second prostration and recite the *tashahhud*, then make *Salah ˄alan-Nabiyy*, then say the closing *salam*.

To intentionally perform the integrals of prayer out of order invalidates the prayer. An example is if one intentionally prostrates before one's *ruku˄*.

Explanation: The prayer is invalidated when its integrals of action are performed out of the prescribed order. Likewise, to intentionally say the closing *salam* before its proper place invalidates the prayer. By consensus, the person who prostrates before the *ruku˄* intentionally invalidates his prayer because he is playing while praying and this invalidates the prayer.

If one forgets (to perform) an integral, one must return to perform it unless one has reached that same integral or what is after it in the next or subsequent *rak˄ah*. In such a case, what was performed in-between is canceled. An example is if one does not remember leaving out *ruku˄* except after having performed the *ruku˄* or prostration of the subsequent *rak˄ah*. In such a case what is between the missing *ruku˄* and the performed *ruku˄* is canceled, and what is after this performed *ruku˄* is the continuation of the *rak˄ah*.

Explanation: There are two different ways to correct the mistake if a person unintentionally breached the order of the integrals of prayer, depending on how far he continued from the place he had breached the order, until the time he realized his mistake.

Case 1.

If the person remembers that he has skipped an integral before reaching the same integral in the next *rak^ah*, he immediately goes back to the integral he missed, performs it, and continues in the correct order from there. An example is if he finished reciting the *Fatihah*, and instead of performing *ruku^*, he went directly to *sujud*, then while in the first or second *sujud*, he remembered that he had left out the *ruku^* before it. Here, he would immediately stand up, then go down to *ruku^*, then straighten up, then go to *sujud*, then continue the *rak^ah* in order from there.

Case 2.

If the person remembers that he skipped an integral when (or after) he reaches the same integral of the next *rak^ah*, he continues the order from where he is, but he considers that he is continuing the actions of the previous *rak^ah*, and disregards all what he did in-between. For example, if a person did not remember that he had left out the *ruku^* until he reached the *ruku^* of the next *rak^ah*, he would assume that he was presently continuing the previous *rak^ah*, and considers all what he did between the *ruku^* that he forgot and the *ruku^* of the following *rak^ah* as if it did not occur. It is the same judgment if he remembered in the *ruku^* of the third *rak^ah* that he forgot to perform *ruku^* in the first *rak^ah*, i.e., he considers that he is currently continuing the actions of the second *rak^ah*, and disregards the extra actions he performed (between the *ruku^* which he forgot to do and the *ruku^* which he did in the next *rak^ah*.) Then he continues to do the remaining parts of the prayer.

Chapter 18
The Congregational Prayer (Jamaˆah)
and the Friday Prayer (Jumuˆah)

The Congregational Prayer (Jamaˆah) is a communal obligation (fard kifayah) upon the free, residing, pubescent, and unexcused males.

Explanation: To pray each of the five prayers in congregation is a communal obligation. To do it in the Friday Prayer is a personal obligation. *Allah* specified a great reward for the prayers prayed in congregation. The *hadith* of the Prophet ﷺ narrated by *Muslim*:

$$\text{«مَنْ صَلَّى العِشَاءَ فِى جَمَاعَةٍ كَانَ كَمَنْ قَامَ نِصْفَ اللَّيلِ وَمَنْ صَلَّى الصُّبْحَ فِى جَمَاعَةٍ فَكَأَنَّمَا قَامَ اللَّيلَ كُلَّهُ».}$$

means: «The reward of the one praying ˆIsha' in congregation is like the reward of praying half of the night (i.e., optional prayers) and the reward of the one praying *Subh* in congregation after having prayed ˆIsha' in congregation, is like the reward of praying the entire night (i.e., optional prayers).» The *hadith* of the Prophet ﷺ narrated by al-Bukhariyy:

$$\text{«صَلاةُ الجَمَاعَةِ تَعْدِلُ صَلاةَ الفَذِّ بِخَمْسٍ وعِشْرِينَ دَرَجَةً».}$$

means: «The reward of the prayer in congregation is equivalent to twenty-five (25) times the reward of praying alone.»

The congregational prayer is a communal obligation upon the free, residing, pubescent, unexcused males. It is not an obligation on the females, the slaves, those who are traveling, or the non-pubescent children. However, it is an obligation on the guardian (waliyy) of the boy who attained the age of mental discrimination to order the boy to perform the congregational and the Friday Prayers. Unexcused males are those who do not have an Islamically acceptable excuse for missing congregational or Friday Prayer. Examples of what makes one excused from this obligation are to fear for one's safety from an enemy in the place where the congregational prayer is being held, and to fear being robbed along the way, and to need to protect one's belongings from thieves, or the like. The author did not mention sanity among the conditions in this issue because it is an apparent matter. Hence, the one who is insane is not obligated with the congregational prayer or the Friday Prayer (or any prayer).

In the Friday Prayer (*Jumuˆah*), to pray in congregation (*jamaˆah*) is a personal obligation (*fard ˆayn*) upon the free, pubescent, and unexcused male inhabitants if they are forty (40) in number and living in buildings, not in tents.

Explanation: The Friday Prayer is a personal obligation on those upon whom the congregational prayer is a communal obligation, i.e., the free, residing, pubescent and unexcused males, if they were forty (40) in number. If they were less than forty (40), it is not obligatory on them to pray the Friday Prayer and is invalid from them to do so. Rather, they must pray the *Dhuhr* Prayer.

If the people of a community were living in tents and not in buildings, then praying the Friday Prayer would not be an obligation on them even if there were among them forty (40) free, inhabitants, pubescent, unexcused males. However, if in a community forty (40) free, inhabitants, pubescent and unexcused males live in buildings, then it is an obligation on them to pray the Friday Prayer.

The Friday Prayer is also obligatory upon the men who intend to stay in the town of *Jumuˆah* for four whole days, excluding the day of entry and the day of exit,

Explanation: If a person who is not an inhabitant of the town where the Friday Prayer will be held enters that town and intends to stay there for four or more days other than the day of entry and the day of exit, he is obligated to pray the Friday Prayer. Although he is obligated to pray the Friday Prayer, he is not counted as one of the forty (40) needed for establishing the obligation of conducting the Friday Prayer in the community.

The day of entry ends at the beginning of the dawn. The day of exit ends at sunset. If a person enters a town on Monday any time between dawn and sunset, then Monday is his day of entry. So if his intention is to stay in that town Tuesday, Wednesday, Thursday, and day-time Friday, then to leave after sunset on Friday, it is obligatory on him to pray the Friday Prayer with the forty (40) men. However, if his intention was to leave during the daytime on Friday (that is, before sunset), then he is not obligated to pray the Friday Prayer with them because he did not stay for four (4) days. Monday was the day of entry and Friday was the day of exit, because he left before sunset. So, excluding the day of entry and the day of exit, he is staying only three (3) days: Tuesday, Wednesday, and Thursday. Hence, he is not obligated to pray the Friday Prayer with them.

and upon those who reside out of the town, but can hear the resounding call of a person who is standing at its edge closest to them.

Explanation: Living outside the boundaries of the town means there is an interruption of buildings between one's house and the last buildings in the town. If a person living outside the boundaries of the town could recognize that he was hearing the *adhan*, should a person who has a strong voice call the *adhan* loudly from the edge of the town closest to his house, then it would be an obligation on him to pray the Friday Prayer with the people of the town. It is not a condition that he is able to distinguish each word of the *adhan*, but rather that he is able to recognize that what he hears is the *adhan*.

Note: It is not a condition that the Friday Prayer be held in a mosque.

Conditions of the Friday Prayer (*Jumuˆah*)

The conditions of the Friday Prayer are:

Explanation: The previous sections addressed the conditions that, if met, make it an obligation to hold the Friday Prayer in a community and the conditions that make praying the Friday Prayer an obligation on one. Now the author mentions the conditions for the validity of the Friday Prayer.

1. **The setting in of *Dhuhr* Prayer time;**

Explanation: It is invalid to hold the Friday Prayer before the time of *Dhuhr* comes in, or after it goes out. If one misses the Friday Prayer (2 *rakˆahs*), one makes it up as the *Dhuhr* Prayer (4 *rakˆahs*).

2. **The aforementioned forty inhabitants must hear the two speeches (*khutbahs*) during the time of *Dhuhr* Prayer and before praying the *Jumuˆah* Prayer;**

Explanation: It is a condition that two speeches be performed before the Friday Prayer, and that both speeches be delivered during

127

the _Dhuhr_ time. Moreover, the forty (40) inhabitants must hear the (integrals of the) two speeches. This means that at least forty (40) among those who, if present, make it required that a _Jumuˆah_ be held, must be present to hear the integrals of the two speeches.

3. **The _Jumuˆah_ Prayer must be performed in congregation by the aforementioned forty inhabitants;**

Explanation: The Friday Prayer is invalid unless it is performed in congregation; praying it by oneself is invalid.

4. **Another _Jumuˆah_ Prayer must not be performed simultaneously with it (or preceding it) in the same town. If the opening _Allahu akbar_ (_tahrimah_) of one prayer preceded that of another, the former would be valid and the latter would be invalid. This is true if the people were able to meet in one place. However, if it was hard for them to meet in one place, then both _Jumuˆah_ prayers would be valid, the former and the latter.**

Explanation: Among the conditions of the validity of the Friday Prayer is that another Friday Prayer must not be performed simultaneously in the same town unless there was an excuse for it. An excuse would be like if it was hard for the people who want to pray to all meet in one place. If the meeting of all in one place constituted a hardship for them, and there was a need for two _Jumuˆahs_ to be held, then both Friday Prayers would be valid. However, if all this did not involve a hardship, and there was no other excuse, and two Friday Prayers were held in the same town at the same time, meaning both _imams_ pronounced the last letter (r) of the opening _Allahu akbar_ of the prayer at the same time, then both Friday Prayers would be invalid. As well, both would be invalid if it could not be known which was the former (started before the other) and which was the latter (started after the other). However, if this could be known, then the former would be valid and the latter invalid.

Some of the _Shafiˆiyy_ scholars said that two _Jumuˆahs_ are not to be held in the same town, in any case. According to those, even if it is a hardship for the people to gather in one place, only one _Jumuˆah_ must be performed and all those obligated to perform it in the town must attend. According to them, if two (2) or more _Jumuˆahs_ were held in the same town, only the former one would be valid and the latter one(s) invalid.

Note: During the time of the Prophet ﷺ, and until the year 204 AH, during the caliphate of one of the ^Abbasiyy caliphs named al-Mu^tadid billah, Muslims used to conduct only one Friday Prayer in every village, town, or city. Al-Mu^tadid billah was the first one to conduct a second Jumu^ah Prayer. He did so because he was afraid he would be killed if he went to the mosque to pray the Jumu^ah Prayer. When this happened, the scholars had different opinions. Some said, "For an excuse, it is permissible to hold a second Jumu^ah." Others said, "There are no excuses which make conducting a second Jumu^ah permissible and valid."

Integrals of the Two Speeches (Khutbahs)

The speaker must observe the following integrals of the two speeches:

Explanation: The two speeches before the Friday Prayer would be valid only if these five integrals were satisfied. The first is:

1. To say al-hamdu lillah in both speeches;

Explanation: The first integral is to praise Allah, in Arabic, in both speeches, and to do so one must utter the term "al-hamd" الحَمْد. It is not sufficient to say 'ash-shukrulillah' الشكر لله, nor is it sufficient to say, 'al-hamdu lir-Rahman' الحمد للرحمن --one must utter the term 'al-hamd' الحَمْد (or one of its derivatives) and the term Allah, like to say "al-hamdu lillah", "ahmadullah," أَحْمَدُ اللهَ or the like.

2. To perform the Salah ^alan-Nabiyy, sallallahu ^alayhi wa sallam, in both speeches;

Explanation: In both speeches, one must say, صَلَّى الله عليه وسَلَّم "sallallahu ^alayhi wa sallam", after saying the Prophet's name; "As-Salatu ^alan-Nabiyy; الصلاة على النبيّ "Allahumma salli wa sallim ^ala Sayyidina Muhammad," or the like.

3. To command the audience to be God-fearing (to have taqwa) in both speeches;

Explanation: Commanding the audience to be God-fearing is the main aim of the two speeches. It is insufficient just to urge the people to leave out the worldly matters. It is a must that the speaker orders the audience to perform the obligations and/or forbid what is unlawful. Saying اتقوا اللهَ ittaqullah, which means: "Be obedient to

Allah," is sufficient to satisfy this integral.

Note: One must perform each of the three aforementioned integrals in both of the two speeches.

4. To recite a complete *ayah* which has a sought meaning in either of the two speeches;

Explanation: The fourth integral is to recite, in either of the two speeches, a complete *ayah* that has a sought meaning, i.e., either it gives a religious judgment or it tells a story (from which a wisdom can be deduced). It is not sufficient to recite part of an *ayah* or an *ayah* which does not have a sought meaning. It is not sufficient, for example, to recite *Ayah* 21 of *Surat al-Muddaththir*:

to satisfy this integral because this *ayah*, (which means, 'then he thought') does not have a complete sought meaning. That is, standing alone, this *ayah* neither gives a judgment nor tells a story with wisdom even though considered in context, it gives a sublime meaning. The person giving the speech would look for an *ayah* that has a complete meaning or an *ayah* that in itself gives a judgment, a preaching meaning, news, or the like. It is better to recite this *ayah* in the first speech.

5. To say a supplication (*duˆa'*) for the believers in the second speech.

Explanation: The fifth integral is to say a supplication for the believers (or at least for forty (40) men among those who attended the *Jumuˆah*) in the second speech. One might say: اللهُمَّ اغْفِرْ لِلْمُؤْمِنِينَ (*Allahummaghfir lil-mu'minin*) which means: "O *Allah* forgive the believers." It is not a condition to specify both the male and female believers in the supplication. However, it is *sunnah* to do so.

Conditions of the Two Speeches

The conditions[34] of the two speeches are:

1. Purification from both states of ritual impurity and from *najas*-filth on the body, place, clothes, and what is carried by the speaker;

---

[34] The conditions are those things that must be fulfilled for the validity of the worship, but they are not parts of that worship.

Explanation: The speech-giver (kha*tib*) (the one who is delivering the speech for the Friday Prayer) must be clear of both the major and the minor ritual impurities. He must also be clear of any unexempted *najas*-filth on his body, clothes, and anything he carries. As well, for the validity of his speech, the place where he stands must be clear of any unexempted *najas*-filth. Hence, having an unexempted *najas*-filth on his body or clothes, or on something he has in his pocket invalidates his speech. As well, if he stood on an unexempted *najas*-filth to deliver his speech, his speech would not be valid.

2. To cover the unlawful nakedness (ˆawrah);

Explanation: Delivering the speech while uncovering one's unlawful nakedness, or part of it, invalidates the speech.

3. To stand up;

Explanation: The speech-giver must deliver the two speeches while standing, unless he has an excuse. One may, because of a valid excuse, deliver the khu*t*bah while sitting. However, it is better for him to appoint another who is able to stand to give the speech.

4. To sit between the two speeches;

Explanation: The speech-giver (kha*tib*) must sit between the two speeches, or else his speeches are invalid. After finishing the first speech, he sits down for a short time, at least as long as saying "*subhanallah*" سُبْحانَ الله takes, then he stands up to deliver the second speech.

5. To observe the succession without lengthy interruption between the integrals of the two speeches, and between the two speeches and the prayer;

Explanation: The speech-giver (kha*tib*) has to perform the two speeches in succession, meaning to give both speeches without the interruption between them being long and unrelated to them. So, for example, if the speaker started delivering the speech, satisfied part of the integrals, then went out to the market to do an errand, then came back to continue, his speech would not be valid.

However, if he said, "*al-hamdulillah*", then he said the *Salah* ˆalan-Nabiyy, then he took some time to warn the people--advising them not to be attached to this world--before ordering them to be God-

131

fearing, this does not invalidate the speech because this separation between the integrals of the speech pertains to that speech.

Likewise, there should not be a long separation between the speeches and performing the Jumuˆah Prayer, i.e., with something unrelated to either the speeches or the prayer.

Note: The saying of our Master ˆUmar, "O Sariyah watch the mountain, watch the mountain", occurred during his speech of the Jumuˆah Prayer. Yet, it was not a long enough separation to invalidate the speech.

6. To say the integrals of the two speeches in Arabic.

Explanation: Another condition for the validity of the speeches is to say the integrals in Arabic, even if all those who were present were non-Arabic speakers. If no one among them knows enough Arabic to say the integrals, and there is not enough time for one of them to learn, then the speech-giver gives the speech in his own language with the exclusion of the ayah, because it is not permissible to recite an ayah in other than Arabic and it is not enough to just give the meaning of the ayah (in any language).

Note: It is forbidden for the person obligated to pray the Jumuˆah to buy, sell, or do other transactions after the second adhan instead of coming to the Jumuˆah. This is unless he has an excuse for not attending it, like if he himself was traveling, and he sold to someone else such as a traveler or a woman. In such a case one is not sinful.

Following the Imam in the Prayer

Everyone who follows an imam while performing the prayer–the Jumuˆah Prayer or other prayers–must fulfill the following obligations:

Explanation: This chapter deals with those matters that make one's followership of an imam in prayer either valid or invalid. Hence, if one is following an imam in prayer, whether the Friday (Jumuˆah) Prayer or another prayer, one must satisfy certain conditions for one's followership to be valid.

1. **The follower (ma'mum) must not be ahead of one's imam in the standing position or in saying the opening Allahu akbar. The prayer of the follower is invalid if one says one's opening Allahu akbar during that of the imam. Simultaneity with the imam in other parts of the prayer is disliked (makruh), with the exception of saying: "Amin";**

Explanation: Among the conditions is for the follower not to be in front of one's *imam*, i.e., not to stand in front of one's *imam*. For the one who is standing, the criterion to determine one's position in relation to one's *imam* is by the heels of the feet. So, if the follower's heels are in front of (closer to the direction of the Qiblah than) those of the *imam*, then the follower's followership and hence, prayer, is invalid.

Likewise, the follower must not say the opening "*Allahu akbar*" before the person whom one intends to take as *imam*. Similarly, it is invalid to say the opening "*Allahu akbar*" simultaneously with the *imam*. Rather, one must wait until the *imam* finishes saying the entire *takbir* (saying 'Allahu akbar'), then one starts.

Performing the other parts of the prayer simultaneously with the *imam* is disliked with the exception of saying *Amin*. Saying *Amin* simultaneously with the *imam* is *sunnah*.

2. The follower is prohibited to precede the *imam* by one integral of action.

Explanation: It is unlawful (*haram*), and among the enormous sins, for the follower (*ma'mum*) to end an entire integral of action before one's *imam* begins that action. For instance, if while the *imam* is reciting the *Fatihah*, the follower completes reciting the *Fatihah*, bows to perform *ruku^*, then lifts up from *ruku^* to return to the standing position (and one's *imam* is still reciting the *Fatihah*), then by this, the follower has ended an entire integral of action before one's *imam* started it. This is unlawful and is an enormous sin. Al-Bukhariyy, Muslim, the *Sunan's* authors,[35] and others related the *hadith* of the Prophet, *sallallahu ^alayhi wa sallam*:

$$ أَلَا يَخْشَى الَّذِى يَرْفَعُ رَأْسَهُ قَبْلَ الإِمَامِ أَنْ يُحَوِّلَ اللَّهُ رَأْسَهُ رَأْسَ حِمَارٍ؟ $$

It means: «Is not the person who lifts his head before his *imam* afraid that *Allah* may change his head into a donkey's head?»

To be ahead of the *imam* by part of an integral is disliked, but not a sin.

---

[35] The *Sunan's* authors here refer to *Abu Dawud*, *at-Tirmidhiyy*, *an-Nasa'iyy*, and *Ibn Majah*.

One's prayer is invalidated by inexcusably preceding the *imam* by two consecutive integrals of action, which are both long or one is long and the other is short.

Explanation: It is unlawful for the follower (*ma'mum*) to end one integral of action before his *imam* starts it; however, doing so does not invalidate the prayer. However, if the follower precedes his *imam* by two consecutive integrals of action without an excuse, his prayer is invalidated. For example, if, while the *imam* is reciting the *Fatihah*, the *ma'mum* performs the *ruku^*, rises for the *i^tidal*, and starts descending to go down to the *sujud* (while the *imam* is still reading the *Fatihah*), then the follower has preceded his *imam* by two consecutive integrals of actions. This invalidates his prayer.

One's prayer would not be invalidated although one preceded one's *imam* by two consecutive integrals of action if one did so for an excuse like if one forgot that one was following an *imam*.

Similarly, the *ma'mum* invalidates one's prayer if one lags behind the *imam* by two consecutive integrals of action without an excuse,

Explanation: Lagging behind one's *imam* by two consecutive integrals of action with no excuse invalidates one's prayer. For example, if the *imam* and the follower both finish reciting the *Fatihah*, and the *imam* continues to perform the *ruku^*, rises for the *i^tidal*, and goes to perform *sujud* while the follower stays in the standing position for no excuse, then the prayer of the follower is invalidated.

It is not forbidden (or sinful) for the follower to lag behind his *imam* by only one integral of action, and doing so does not invalidate the prayer.

and by more than three long integrals of action despite an excuse. If the *ma'mum* stays behind to finish the *Fatihah* and during this time the *imam* has finished his *ruku^* and two prostrations, and has sat for the *tashahhud* or stood up for another *rak^ah*, then the *ma'mum* must have the intention in the heart of following the *imam* and be in unison with him. In addition to this, the *ma'mum* must perform a *rak^ah* after the closing *salam* of the *imam*. However, if the *ma'mum* finishes reciting the *Fatihah* before the *imam* has sat for the *tashahhud* or stood up for another *rak^ah*, then the *ma'mum* follows one's own order until one catches up with the *imam*.

Explanation: As previously mentioned, the prayer of the *ma'mum* is invalidated if one, without an excuse, lags behind one's *imam* by two integrals of action. However, if the follower has an excuse for lagging behind, such as if one recites the Fatihah slower than one's imam, then one's prayer is not invalidated unless one lags behind the imam by more than three long integrals of action. For example, if the imam recites the Fatihah quickly, and while the ma'mum, who is a slow reciter, is still reciting the Fatihah, the imam performs ruku^, rises to i^tidal, goes down to perform the first sujud, performs it, sits, then performs the second sujud, then rises from the second sujud to sit down for the tashahhud or to go up for another rak^ah, then the ma'mum must be in unison with one's imam. That is, depending on the position of the imam, either one sits to recite the tashahhud with the imam or keeps standing, but continues reciting the Fatihah intending to follow the imam if the imam stands to do so. If in this case, the follower does not interrupt one's own order to be in unison with one's imam, one's prayer is invalidated. This is due to one's imam being ahead of one by more than three long integrals of action, even though the follower lags behind for an excuse.

Note: The three long integrals of action here are:

1. the ruku^ (the i^tidal is short and is not counted);
2. the first sujud (sitting between the two prostrations is a short integral of action);
3. the second sujud.

Then, after the imam says one's closing salam, the ma'mum stands to perform the rak^ah which one interrupted. However, if one finishes reciting the Fatihah before the imam has engaged in the tashahhud or stood up for another rak^ah, then the follower follows one's own order until one catches up with one's imam.

3. The follower must know the movements of one's imam;

Explanation: Among the conditions for the ma'mum to follow the imam in a valid manner is that the ma'mum knows the movements (integrals of action) of one's imam. One would be certain about the movements of one's imam when one sees the imam. Although the one who cannot see the imam cannot be completely certain of the imam's movements, one can rely on the voice of the imam or the one who conveys the movements of the imam by saying loud the conveying statements to know his movements. Also, if one sees the one who sees the imam one's followership will be valid. However, if the ma'mum has no means of knowing the movements of one's imam, it is

135

invalid for one to follow him. An example would be if one prayed behind an *imam* in complete darkness without hearing the *imam's* voice or the voice of someone conveying from the *imam* and without seeing him or seeing someone who sees him. Such a congregational prayer would be invalidated once the *imam* rises from the *ruku^* before the follower becomes aware of one's *imam's* integrals of action.

4. The follower must be with one's *imam* in a mosque (*masjid*), or else within 300 cubits;

Explanation: It is a condition for one to follow an *imam* in a valid manner that both the *imam* and the *ma'mum* are together in one place. Both are considered as being together in one place if they were in a mosque regardless of the distance between them. If they were not in a mosque, then it is a condition that the distance separating the *ma'mum* from the *imam* (or from the last line of people praying behind the *imam*) not exceed 300 cubits. However, if many people were following one *imam* and they were standing in consecutive lines without a great distance between any of the lines, then the followership is still valid regardless of the distance between the farthest line and the *imam*.

5. [In other than a mosque,] there should be no barrier between the *imam* and the follower that prevents the follower from reaching the *imam*;

Explanation: In other than a mosque, it is invalid for one to follow an *imam* in the presence of a barrier that separates one from the *imam*. In other words, due to the barrier, one cannot reach the *imam* or one may reach him only by deviating from the *Qiblah*. A barrier is something that is usually placed to separate two places, like a door, wall, or window. Hence, following an *imam* from behind a closed door is invalid because a closed door is a barrier that prevents the *ma'mum* from reaching the *imam*. Following an *imam* from behind a high, open window is not valid, even if one could see the *imam*, because a high window-although open-is a barrier that prevents the *ma'mum* from normally reaching the *imam*. The congregational prayer is valid although the *imam* and *ma'mum* are separated by fire or a small river, because in the norm these are not considered barriers used to separate two places.

6. **The format of the follower's prayer must agree with the format of the *imam*'s prayer. For example, it is invalid for the performer of the daily obligatory prayer to follow the performer of the Funeral Prayer (*Salatul-Janazah*);**

Explanation: It is a condition for the validity of the congregational prayer that the format of the *ma'mum*'s prayer agree with the format of the *imam*'s prayer even if the number of *rak^ahs* and the intentions of each are different. Hence, it is valid for the one praying the *Dhuhr* Prayer to follow the one praying the ^*Asr* Prayer, the *Subh* Prayer, or a *sunnah* prayer (although such a congregational prayer is disliked). However, for example, it is invalid for the one who is praying the *Dhuhr* Prayer to follow an *imam* who is praying the Funeral Prayer because the formats of these two prayers differ greatly. Unlike the *Dhuhr* Prayer, the Funeral Prayer does not include bowing or prostration.

7. **The follower must not disagree enormously with one's *imam* in a recommended act (*sunnah*) by doing it, like the sitting for the first *tashahhud*, or by leaving it out, like the *sujud* of *sahw*;**

Explanation: The *ma'mum* needs to follow the *imam* in the *sunnah* that he performs. If the *imam* does not sit for the first *tashahhud* (a *sunnah* act) the *ma'mum* should follow him in that action. The *ma'mum* invalidates one's prayer if one's *imam* omits the sitting for the first *tashahhud* and the *ma'mum* intentionally sits to perform this *sunnah* act, while remembering that one is following an *imam*, and knowing this is forbidden. One's prayer is invalidated because one disagreed enormously in an obvious action to perform a *sunnah* that the *imam* left out. In this case one left out following the *imam* (which is an obligation on one) to perform a *sunnah* (which is not an obligation on one).

On the other hand, if the *imam* sits for the first *tashahhud* (a *sunnah* act) the *ma'mum* should do the same. However, although it is an enormous disagreement, the prayer of the *ma'mum* is not invalidated if one intentionally left out sitting for the first *tashahhud* while one's *imam* sat for it because the *ma'mum* left out following the *imam* in this *sunnah* action to perform an integral of action.

Disagreeing with one's *imam* in a *sunnah* which does not constitute an enormous disagreement does not affect the validity of one's prayer. An example of such a *sunnah* action is the brief sitting after the second *sujud*, before standing up to perform the next *rak^ah*. It is permissible for the *ma'mum* to perform this *sunnah* matter whether or not the *imam* does it because this is a slight disagreement in action.

8. **In the *Jumu^ah* Prayer, the follower must have the intention to follow the *imam* while saying the opening *Allahu akbar*, and in other prayers, before following the *imam* (in his moves) and without a long waiting for him.**[36]

Explanation: One of the conditions for the prayer of the *ma'mum* to be valid is that one must have the intention of following the *imam* (i.e., praying in congregation with him). One may establish the intention to follow the *imam* while or after saying the opening *takbir*, as long as one establishes this intention before following the *imam* in his moves and there is no long waiting for him. Hence, if the *imam* starts praying and a little while later a person stands behind him and starts praying without having the intention of following the *imam*, one's prayer will be valid as far as one does not wait for the *imam* to bow so that one may do the same, or wait for the *imam* to prostrate so that one does the same. If later this person wants to join the *imam* and become his follower, it will be sufficient for one to have the proper intention. However, one must not be standing ahead of the *imam*.

However, for certain prayers it is a condition for one to establish the intention to follow the *imam* during the opening *takbir*. These prayers are the *Jumu^ah* Prayer, the repeated prayer, and the combined prayer due to rain (prayed at the time of the earlier of the two prayers), because these prayers are valid only when performed in congregation.

Also, the one who makes a *nadhr* (vow) to perform a prayer in congregation must establish one's intention to do so during the opening *takbir* of this prayer.

---

[36] If the *ma'mum* was performing the *Jumu^ah* Prayer without having the intention to follow the *imam* within the opening *Allahu akbar*, one's prayer would be invalid. In other than the *Jumu^ah* Prayer, if the *ma'mum* mimics the moves of the *imam* after a long wait without any intention of praying in congregation with him, one's prayer is invalidated. However, if one waits for the *imam* without mimicking him, or one's mimicking is unintentionally coincidental, or one's mimicking is intentional without a long wait, the follower's prayer is not invalidated.

In the *Jumu^ah* Prayer and the repeated prayer, it is obligatory upon the *imam* to intend to lead the prayer, but this is recommended (*sunnah*) in other prayers.

Explanation: For both the *Jumu^ah* Prayer and the repeated prayer, the *imam* must have the intention of being the *imam* because these two are valid only when performed in congregation. In the congregational prayer other than these, it is not an obligation on the *imam* to have the intention to be the *imam*. Rather it is *sunnah* for him to do so. However, if he leaves out the intention of being an *imam*, he does not get the reward for the congregational prayer. However, those who are following him with the intention of congregational prayer get the reward for it.

The repeated prayer is the prayer that one reperforms in congregation after having prayed it in congregation or alone.

Explanation: If a person performed any of the five (5) obligatory prayers (alone or in a congregation) and later found another *jama^ah* performing that same prayer, it would be *sunnah* for him to repeat his prayer with them to gain the reward. As well, it would be *sunnah* for one to repeat one's prayer with another to enable the other to earn the reward of praying in congregation.

Chapter 19
The Funeral (Janazah)

This chapter deals with preparing dead people for burial and burying them.

Washing, shrouding, praying for, and burying the dead Muslim is a communal obligation (fard kifayah) if one was born alive.

Explanation: It is a communal obligation on the Muslim community to prepare the dead Muslim for burial and to bury him if he was born alive (even if he lived only for a moment). It is a communal obligation to wash, shroud, perform the Funeral Prayer for, and bury him when he dies. If a Muslim died, and no one washed, shrouded, performed the Funeral Prayer for, or buried him, then all those who were aware of his death and neglected performing these matters would be sinful.

Shrouding and burial are obligatory for a member of the People of the Book who is a subject of the Islamic State (Dhimmiyy[37]).

Explanation: It is an obligation on the Muslims to take care of shrouding and burying the dead *Dhimmiyy* if his own people did not take care of these matters. If the *Dhimmiyy* did not leave behind (or have any) money to prepare him for shrouding and burial, the money to do so would be taken from the Muslim treasury. The blasphemer is not buried in Muslim cemeteries and the Funeral Prayer is not performed for him. Moreover, performing the Funeral Prayer for the blasphemer is blasphemy.[38]

Moreover, washing, shrouding, and burial are obligatory for a stillborn Muslim. The Funeral Prayer is not performed for a *Dhimmiyy* or the stillborn Muslim.

Explanation: The obligation concerning a stillborn Muslim is to wash, shroud, and bury him. The Funeral Prayer is not performed for him. However, if it was an undeveloped fetus, the human features of

---

[37] The *Dhimmiyy* is the blasphemer (Christian, Jew, or Majus) who pays *jizyah* to the caliph. The *jizyah* is an amount of money the *Dhimmiyy*s pay each year to the Muslim treasury in return for guaranteeing their safety and protection of their property.

[38] Praying for the blasphemer is blasphemy, because one asks *Allah* to forgive the dead person. *Allah* does not forgive those who die with the sin of blasphemy.

which could not be recognized yet, it is only recommended to wrap and bury it. It is not an obligation to do so.

Whoever dies as a result of fighting the blasphemers will be shrouded in one's battle clothes. If the battle clothes are not enough, more material will be added. One will be buried, but not washed; and the Funeral Prayer will not be performed for one.

Explanation: The Muslim who is killed in the battlefield or dies as a result of fighting the blasphemers in the battlefield, even if the Muslims killed him by mistake, is considered as a battlefield martyr. The clothes the martyr was wearing when he died are left on him as his shroud (or part of it) even if they are covered with blood. This is to maintain the traces of martyrdom on him. If his clothing was not enough (to cover his whole body) more material would be added. The martyr is not washed for burial because *Allah* purified him with the state of martyrdom. The Prophet ﷺ said:

$$«السَّيْفُ مَحَّاءُ الخَطَايا»$$

This *hadith* means: «The sword erases sins». This implies that all the sins of the one who dies as a martyr in the battlefield will be forgiven.

The martyr must be buried, but the Funeral Prayer is not performed for him because *Allah* promised him mercy. Hence, he does not need the supplications for mercy from the Muslims who pray for him. It was reported in the *hadith* that when the God-fearing Muslim dies, he does not wish to return to this life again. However, the martyr would wish to come back to this life so that he could be killed again as a martyr because of the great enjoyments and mercy that *Allah* endows upon him after he dies.

Washing the dead Muslim is done out of the obligation and not to purify him from the state of impurity, because the body of the human does not become *najas*-filthy at death.

Washing and Shrouding the Dead

The minimum obligatory washing of the dead is to remove the *najas*-filth and to use purifying water to wash the dead's whole skin and hair, even if the hair was thick.

Explanation: In performing the obligatory washing of the dead Muslim one must first remove any *najas*-filth on the body by pouring water over that place to purify it. To complete the minimum obligation of washing, it is enough to pour water over the entire skin and hair once. The intention is not a condition for that washing. Therefore, it is valid if a blasphemer performs this washing. It is better to use cold, salty water for washing the dead.

It is not permissible for the washer[39] to expose the ^*awrah* of the dead person, nor to touch the dead's ^*awrah* with one's bare hand. It is also not permissible to turn the body of the dead Muslim in a degrading manner, like to throw him on his face, or leave him face-down while washing his back.

The minimum obligatory shroud is that which covers the whole body. Three wraps are used for the person who died leaving an inheritance exceeding one's debts, provided one did not leave a will advising against the three wraps.

Explanation: The minimum obligatory shroud is that which covers the entire body. Any material or cloth that was permissible for the person to wear while alive is permissible to use as his shroud, unless it was considered degrading for the dead person, like a material made from jute.

If the dead person left an inheritance exceeding his debts, then three wraps must be used to shroud him. However, if the dead person left a will asking that he be wrapped by one wrap rather than three wraps, then it is not obligatory to shroud him with three wraps. The obligation is a shroud that covers the whole body.

---

[39] The washer should be of the same gender as the dead Muslim, i.e., men would wash the dead man and women would wash the dead woman. It is permissible for the husband to wash his dead wife or vice-versa. If there is no one other than a marriageable person to take care of the dead, then he is not washed. Instead, *tayammum* is performed for him.

The Funeral Prayer (Salatul-Janazah)

The minimum obligatory prayer for the dead is:

Explanation: The obligation of performing the Funeral Prayer may be fulfilled by performing the least of what *Allah* made obligatory upon the Muslims in this matter. It also has a more complete form. The minimum required to perform the Funeral Prayer is:

1. **To intend to perform the obligatory Funeral Prayer for that dead person in particular, as one is saying the opening 'Allahu akbar'.**

Explanation: One must have the intention in one's heart of performing the Obligatory Funeral Prayer for that dead person while saying the opening *takbir*. One must specify the dead person. For example one could name him in one's heart, intend "the dead person who is laid before me ", or "the dead person for whom the *imam* is praying ", or the like.

2. **To say *Allahu akbar* while standing, if one is able; then**

Explanation: Standing while performing the prayer is an obligation if one was able. If one was not able, one would sit.

3. **To recite the *Fatihah*; then**

Explanation: One may delay reciting the *Fatihah* until after the second, third, or fourth *takbir*. However, one has to recite the *Fatihah* before saying the closing *salam*. It is better to recite the *Fatihah* after the opening *takbir*.

4. **To say *Allahu akbar*; then**

Explanation: This is the second *takbir*.

5. **To say *Allahumma salli ˆala Muhammad*; then**

Explanation: One says, *Allahu akbar* a second time, then after it says, *Allahumma salli ˆala Muhammad*. Making *salah* on the Prophet must be after saying the second *takbir*.

6. **To say *Allahu akbar*; then**

Explanation: This is the third *takbir*.

7. **To supplicate *Allah* to forgive and have mercy on that dead Muslim; then**

Explanation: One says a third *takbir*, then supplicates *Allah* to forgive and have mercy on that dead Muslim. One's *du^a'* must include asking *Allah* for matters concerning the Hereafter for that dead Muslim.

8. To say *Allahu akbar;* then

Explanation: This is the fourth and last *takbir*.

9. To say the closing *salam*.

Explanation: After supplicating *Allah* to forgive the dead Muslim, one says, "*Allahu akbar*" for the fourth time, then one says the closing *salam*. The most complete form for the Funeral Prayer is that after saying the fourth "*Allahu akbar,*" one makes *du^a'* for that dead Muslim even if it takes a long time. Then one says the closing *salam*.

The one who performs the Funeral Prayer must satisfy the conditions and avoid the invalidators of prayer.

Explanation: The one performing the Funeral Prayer must satisfy the conditions of prayers, like to have one's *wudu'*, to face the *Qiblah*, to be clear of *najas*-filth, and the like. One must also avoid any of the invalidators of the prayer.

Burial of the Dead

The minimum obligatory burial of the dead requires a hole dug in the ground which prevents the smell from rising and protects the body of the dead person from wild animals. It is recommended (*sunnah*) to dig the grave as deep as a man's height with his arms extended overhead and to widen it. The chest of the dead must be directed towards the Qiblah. It is unlawful (*haram*) to bury the dead in a mausoleum.

Explanation: The minimum obligation to be fulfilled in burying the dead is to bury him in the ground in a hole at least deep enough to prevent his smell from being apparent either to people or to wild animals who may dig him up and eat him. What is better is to widen the grave to the extent that the one burying the dead person and his assistant can maneuver in it and to have it as deep as a man's height with his arms extended overhead.

It is an obligation to direct the chest of the dead Muslim towards the Qiblah. It is unlawful to bury the dead in a mausoleum because it is degrading to that Muslim. It is also forbidden to bury two people in one grave without a need, that is, before the body of the first decays in the soil.

It is also forbidden to open up or excavate the grave of the Muslim without a need, that is, before his body decays.

145

Zakah

Chapter 20
Items Subject to *Zakah*

It is obligatory for one to pay *Zakah* for having:

1. **Camels, cattle, sheep, and goats;**

2. **Dates, raisins, and staple crops consumed by choice;**

3. **Gold, silver, golden and silver ores, and golden and silver treasure-troves (*rikaz*);**

4. **Trade articles;**

5. ***Fitr*.**

Explanation: This chapter deals with the rules of *Zakah*. *Zakah* is one of the most important matters in *Islam*. It was mentioned in the *hadith* of the Prophet ﷺ that *Zakah* is one of the five matters on which *Islam* is based.

Ibn Hibban narrated from the Prophet, *sallallahu ^alayhi wa sallam*,

$$\text{«لَعَنَ اللّٰهُ ءَاكِلَ الرِبَا وَمُوكِلَهُ وَمَانِعَ الزَّكَاةِ»}$$

It means: "*Allah* damns the one who consumes the usurious gains (*riba*), the one who gives them, and the one who does not pay *Zakah*." The one who abstains from paying the obligatory *Zakah* commits an enormous sin.

Zakah is obligatory only in the matters mentioned in the text. All other owned items are not subject to *Zakah*. Hence, there is no *Zakah* on the house rented out or owned land or cars kept for other than trading. Similarly, fruits and vegetables, like apples, pears, tomatoes, and zucchini are excluded. Animals, such as horses and poultry, are not subject to *Zakah*. Factory machinery used to produce certain products are excluded from *Zakah*. There is no *Zakah* on employee wages, doctor fees, or earnings from other than trading. According to the schools of *Imam ash-Shafi^iyy* and *Imam Malik*, may *Allah* raise their ranks, paper money is excluded from *Zakah*, if it is not of trading. However, according to *Abu Hanifah*, paper and metallic money (coins) which are used as currency are subject to *Zakah*. In this matter, following the school of *Abu Hanifah* puts one on the safer side.

However, whoever does not follow it is not blameworthy in the Hereafter.

Camels are subject to *Zakah*, regardless of their kind. Cattles are subject to *Zakah* including all kinds of cows and water buffalos (*jamus*). Finally, sheep and goats are also subject to *Zakah* .

Dates are subject to *Zakah*. The owner of the palm trees waits until the dates are dry before paying *Zakah*. Similarly, the owner of grape vines waits until the grapes turn into raisins before paying the due *Zakah*. As to the rest of the fruits, there is no *Zakah* on them in their own right.

Additionally, staple crops are subject to *Zakah*. These include grains that provide sustenance to the body, like wheat, barley, corn, rice, lentils, and chickpeas. Crops used for the sustenance of the body at times of necessity such as famine, but which are not used for sustenance at other times are not subject to *Zakah*. An example is the bitter crop of colocynth.[40] People do not choose to eat this crop in normal situations. Athough consumed for sustenance in the case of necessity, no *Zakah* is due on it.

Gold and silver in all forms are subject to *Zakah*, including currency, jewelry, ores, or treasure troves. However, permissible gold and silver jewelry worn by females are not subject to *Zakah*, according to some scholars. In this regard, *Imam ash-Shafi^iyy* held two opinions: one, *Zakah* is due on them, and the other, it is not.

Trade articles are also subject to *Zakah*. Trade articles are articles purchased to be sold for profit, with the purpose of purchasing other articles, to be sold for profit, and so on.

The aforementioned items are the ones subject to *Zakah*; all other items are not. Moreover, there is one kind of *Zakah* which is paid per person, but is not due on what one owns: *Zakah* of *Fitr*.

---

[40] Colocynth, called in Arabic *handhal*, is a tendril-bearing Old World vine bearing yellowish, green-mottled fruits the size of small lemons.

Chapter 21
Zakah on Animals

The first quotum (*nisab*) of camels is five (5).

Explanation: If one owns less than five (5) camels, no *Zakah* is due on them. Once one owns five camels, the quotum is satisfied, and such camels are subject to *Zakah*. The *nisab*s for camels are the following amounts: 5, 10, 15, 20, 25, 36, 46, 61, 76, 91, 121. Beyond these, the value of due *Zakah* is contingent upon the sum of multiples of forty and fifty that comprises the number of owned camels. Hence, one does not pay any additional amount as *Zakah* until the subsequent quotum is reached.

The first quotum of cattle is thirty (30).

Explanation: The first *nisab* is thirty (30). One's cattle is not subject to *Zakah* when one owns less than thirty cows. The next *nisab* is forty. After that, one pays *Zakah* depending on how many thirties and forties one has.

The first quotum of sheep and goats is forty (40).

Explanation: There is no *Zakah* on sheep and goats that are less than forty (40). This includes the different kinds of sheep and goats. The subsequent quota are 121, 201, and 400. Then, one pays for each hundred. Hence, the due *Zakah* on 800 sheep/goats, is eight (8) sheep/goats.[41]

No *Zakah* is due before having that first quotum. Once the quotum is established, a lunar year must lapse on it.

Explanation: If one's camels, cattle, sheep, or goats do not reach their respective first quotum, they are not subject to *Zakah*. Then for one's animals to be subject to *Zakah*, a full lunar year (*hawl*) must have passed on owning that respective quotum. Hence, if one sells the flock, even one day before the lapse of one lunar year, one does not have to pay *Zakah*.

---

[41] One pays four sheep/goats for the first four quotas, in addition to four sheep/goats for the remaining 400 owned sheep/goats, one for each hundred. This adds up to eight sheep/goats.

The animals must have been grazed by the owner or any person authorized by him in a pasture not owned by anyone;

Explanation: If the flock is out grazing on its own without the owner or someone authorzied by him grazing it, those animals are not subject to *Zakah*, even if they are thousands. Similarly, if the owner buys the feed for the flock, the flock is not subject to *Zakah*. The sole purchase of water for the flock does not exempt it from *Zakah* .

and they must not be working animals. Animals which are put to work, like plowing animals, are not subject to *Zakah*.

Explanation: No *Zakah* is due on working animals. Hence, a camel used to transport goods or water is not subject to *Zakah* because it is a working animal. Similarly, bulls put to work in plowing one's own fields or hired out to other people for a certain sum of money, and water buffalos used to get water out of the well are not subject to *Zakah* because they are working animals.

The obligatory *Zakah* for the first quotum of camels is a female sheep which lost its baby teeth.

Explanation: The *Zakah* for the first quotum of camels [i.e., 5 camels] is a female sheep that has dropped its two upper front baby teeth, or one which has attained one lunar year of age. One can pay instead a two-year old goat. The due *Zakah* in this case must be either sheep or goats, whether male or female. Paying *Zakah*, in other than these two kinds of animals is invalid. Although more valuable, paying in cows or camels is invalid. Similarly, paying the monetary value of these animals rather than the animals themselves is invalid.

The obligatory *Zakah* for the first quotum of sheep or goats is a female sheep which lost its baby teeth or a two-year old female goat.

Explanation: The due *Zakah* for the first quotum of sheep (40 sheep or goats) is the same as that of camels, namely one female sheep or one female goat, of the same aforementioned criteria. Male sheep or goats are valid only if females were not found. The second quotum is 121 sheep or goats. The due *Zakah* is two (2) sheep or goats. The third quotum is 201 and the due *Zakah* is three (3) sheep or goats. The fourth quotum is 400 and the due *Zakah* is four (4) sheep or goats. After that, for each additional hundred the due *Zakah* is one sheep or goat.

The obligatory Zak̲ah for the first quotum of cattle is a one-year old bull.

Explanation: The obligatory Zak̲ah for the first quotum of cattle (30) is to pay a one-year old bullock (or female cow). The second quotum is forty (40) cows. The due Zak̲ah is a two-year old cow. After that, for each additional 30 cows, a one-year old bullock is due, and in each additional 40, a two-year old cow is due.

If one's animals exceed that first quotum, then more Zak̲ah is due. It is one's obligation to learn the amount of Zak̲ah which Allah has ordained one to pay on these animals.

Explanation: If one's animals exceed the first quotum, one is obligated to learn about the amount of Zak̲ah that Allah made obligatory on one to pay, and to act accordingly, i.e., to pay the due Zak̲ah.

Hence, when one's camels become ten (10), the due Zak̲ah is two (2) female sheep having the same aforementioned criteria. When they become fifteen (15), three female sheep are due. When they become twenty (20), four (4) female sheep are due. When they become 25, a one-year old female camel is due. No additional Zak̲ah is due until they become thirty six (36) when the Zak̲ah due is a two-year old female camel. For forty six (46) camels, a three-year old female camel is due. When they become sixty one (61), a four-year old female camel is due. When they become 76, two (2) two-year old female camels are due. When they become 91, two (2) three-year old female camels are due. When they become 121, three (3) two-year old female camels are due. If the number of camels exceeds 121, then one (1) two-year old female camel is due in each forty (40) and one (1) three-year old female camel is due in each fifty (50). Please see the following chart:

ZAK*A*H TABLE FOR ANIMALS

Camels	5 – 24	For every 5 camels: (a) A one-year old (male or female) sheep or one which has lost its front teeth, or (b) A two-year old female goat
	25 - 35	a) A one-year old female camel, or if unavailable b) A two-year old male camel
	36 – 45	A two-year old female camel
	46 – 60	A three-year old female camel
	61 – 75	A four-year old female camel
	76 – 90	Two two-year old female camels
	91 – 120	Two three-year old female camels
	121 – 129	Three two-year old female camels
	130 – 139	A three-year old female camel and Two two-year old female camels
	140 & more	For every 40 camels, a two-year old female camel For every 50 camels, a three-year old female camel Example: 180 camels = (2 x 40 + 2 x 50) camels
Cattle	Every 30	(a) A one-year bullock, or (b) A one-year old cow
	Every 40	(a) A two-year old cow, or (b) Two one-year old bullocks
Sheep and Goats	40 – 120	(a) A one-year old (female) sheep or one which has lost its front teeth, or (b) A two-year old female goat
	121 – 200	Two of either (a) or (b)
	201 – 399	Three of either (a) or (b)
	400	Four of either (a) or (b)
	500 & more	For every 100, one more animal of (a) or (b)

Chapter 22
Zakah on Dates, Raisins, and Staple Crops

The first quotum of dates, raisins, and staple crops is five (5) wasqs which are equivalent to three-hundred (300) saˆs, according to the saˆ of the Prophet ﷺ, sallallahu ˆalayhi wa sallam, the measure of which is kept in al-Hijaz.

Explanation: Saˆ in Arabic means a certain container used as a measurment tool. To determine the saˆ meant by the Prophet ﷺ in calculating the due Zakah, Imams Malik and ash-Shafiˆiyy depended on the particular volume considered to be one saˆ by the people of Madinah at their time, because they took it from their parents who learned it from their parents who were the Companions of the Prophet ﷺ and who in turn learned it from the Prophet.[42] One saˆ equals four mudds, and the mudd is the fill of a joined pair of average-sized, cupped hands.

On the other hand, a wasq is a known volume measurement which equals 60 saˆs. The first quotum (5 wasqs) is equal to 300 saˆs (1200 mudds). The one who has less than 5 wasqs of dates, raisins, or staple crops does not have to pay Zakah on them.

Crops of the same type harvested in the same year are to be combined to check if a quotum is reached.

Explanation: It is obligatory to combine the harvest of the same kind of crops in the same year to determine whether or not the quotum is reached. For example, if one plants two types of wheat which mature at diferent times during the same year, one must combine the harvest of both in determining the yield. If each type harvested separately measures less than the quotum, but by combining them the quotum is reached, then Zakah is due.

Similarly, if one owns two kinds of palm trees, and one of them ripens before the other in a way that the latter produces its pollen before harvesting the first, then if the two types are harvested in the same year, the two harvested amounts must be added together to check whether or not Zakah is due on them.

---

[42] Even today in Madinah, one can purchase a one-saˆ container or a one-mudd container.

Crops of different types are not required to be combined, like barley with wheat.

Explanation: If one harvests in one year two different types of crops, like barley and wheat, and each one was less than a quotum, but when combined together they form a quotum, then *Zakah* is not due on either one of them. This is so because the quotum of each of the different types is considered on its own.

Zakah is due upon:

1. **The ripeness of the fruits, i.e., when they are ready to be eaten; hence, no Zakah is due on unripe grapes or dates; and**

2. **The hardening of the seeds of the crops.**

Explanation: *Zakah* is not due on one's fruits (dates/grapes) before they reach the stage at which they are usually sought for consumption, or on the grain before the seeds harden. Hence, if one harvests the dates before they reach the *rutab*[43] stage, or grapes before they ripen, no *Zakah* is due on them. Similarly, if one harvests wheat or other staple crops before the seeds harden, no *Zakah* is due on them.

Zakah becomes due on all one's harvest as soon as one grape/date reaches the edible stage, when people usually seek to eat the grapes/dates. At this stage, one holds off selling the grapes/dates or giving them away until all are dry to the point at which they are normally preserved. Hence, when one grape/date ripens, one waits until all the grapes/dates ripen, and turn into raisins/*rutab*, then one calculates and pays the due *Zakah*.

N.B. Although the due *Zakah* is calculated based on the dry dates/raisins produced, if the field owner wishes to sell the harvest prior to reaching this stage, he can get an expert to project the amount of the dry harvest of the existing fruits, then pay the respective *Zakah*.

The due Zakah is one-tenth of the harvest if one did not irrigate at an expense, and half of that if one irrigated at an expense. Proportionate Zakah is due upon what exceeds a quotom.

---

[43] *Rutab* is the stage when dates have a specific moisture content, i.e., juice comes out of them when squeezed.

Explanation: The proportion of one's harvest subject to *Zakah* depends on how one irrigated the crops. If the fruits or grains were irrigated without an expense to the owner, for example, by rain, flood waters, or via canals, the due *Zakah* is one-tenth (1/10) of the yield. If the crops were irrigated at an expense to the owner, like buying water, or using animals to transport the water to the crops, then the due *Zakah* is one-twentieth (1/20) of the yield. Judge Ibn Kajj said: Had the owner bought the water, he would have payed 1/20 of the yield. The usurper has to pay the owner the value of the water that he took unrightfully from him. Hence, the due *Zakah* on crops irrigated with usurped water is one-twentieth (1/20) of the yield.

The same proportion of the harvest (1/10 or 1/20) is due as *Zakah* on whatever exceeds the (first) quotum.

No *Zakah* is due on what is less than a quotum. However, one can volunteer to pay on what is less than a quotum.

Explanation: There is no *Zakah* due on one's harvest if it is less than the quotum (less than 300 *sa*ˆs). One may give part of the crops in charity, but not with the intention of paying the obligatory *Zakah*. However, according to the school of *Imam Abu Hanifah*, one must pay *Zakah* on the crops even if they were less than a quotum.

Chapter 23
Zakah on Gold and Silver, Golden and Silver Ores, and Golden and Silver Treasure-Troves (Rikaz)

The quotum of gold is twenty (20) Dinars and the quotum of silver is two-hundred (200) Dirhams.

Explanation: The quotum of gold is twenty (20) Islamic *mithqals*, i.e., twenty *dinars*. No *Zakah* is due on what is less than twenty *dinars* of pure gold. A *mithqal* is a unit of weight measure. It is equivalent to the weight of seventy-two (72) average-sized, unpeeled barley grains, with their stalks cut off. The particular kind of barley used to determine the weight is the type of barley which was grown in the area of *Hijaz* at the time of the Prophet ﷺ and known to the people there. Twenty (20) *dinars* of pure gold (1440 barley grains) are (84.875 grams) about 85 grams of pure (24-karat) gold, 97 grams of 21-karat gold, and 114 grams of 18-karat gold.

The quotum of silver is two hundred *dirhams*. No *Zakah* is due on one's silver if it totals to less than 200 *dirhams* of pure silver. One *dirham* is the unit of weight measure equivalent to the weight of fifty and two-fifth (50 2/5) average-sized, unpeeled barley grains (of the same type as above) after their husks have been cut off. Two hundred *dirhams* (10080 barley grains) of silver are (594.124 grams) approximately 594 grams of pure silver.

After a lunar year has passed on the gold and silver, the due Zakah is one-fortieth of those amounts, and proportionate Zakah is due upon what exceeds the quotum.

Explanation: The *Zakah* due on the quotum of gold or silver is one fortieth (1/40) of the amount. Whatever exceeds the quotum is also subject to the same *Zakah*. *Zakah* becomes obligatory on the quotum of gold and silver once the person has owned them for one lunar year.

When gold and silver are extracted from the place where they were originally formed, one-fortieth is the due Zakah. When gold or silver is found as a treasure-trove (rikaz), one-fifth is due. In these two cases, Zakah must be paid immediately.

Explanation: The due *Zakah* on the quotum of gold and silver which are mined is one fortieth (1/40) of the total amount. One does not wait until one has owned them for one year. Rather, one pays the due *Zakah* immediately after cleaning them from the soil and other impurities.

If the mined gold/silver does not constitute a quotum alone but if added to what one owns it reaches this quotum, *Zakah* is due on them. Similarly, if one owns trade items that are valued with the respective (gold or silver) metal and the sum (with the mined metals) reaches the quotum, then the *Zakah* is due.

Note: if one rents a piece of land and finds gold or silver buried in it, one is not allowed to take it for oneself because one does not own this land.

The due *Zakah* on the gold and silver found as a treasure-trove which becomes under one's ownership is 1/5 of the total amount. The treasure-trove becomes under one's ownership if one finds it in a land unowned by a particular person and it was buried before the Prophet ﷺ received the Revelation.

However, if the treasure-trove is found in a land owned by another person, or was buried during or after the time of the Prophet ﷺ it does not become under one's ownership. Its judgment is the same as the *luqatah* (the lost and found article), and no *Zakah* is due. In this case, one must advertise about it for an entire year. If its owner is still not known after the year passes, one may hold it until its owner is known, or spend from it with the intention of paying its value to the owner once he appears.

Verses 34 and 35 of *Suratut-Tawbah* state:

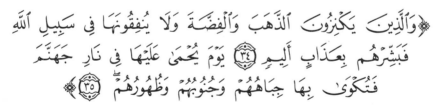

They mean: "Those who hoard up gold and silver and do not pay their *Zakah* (after it is due) give them (O *Muhammad*) tidings of a painful doom in the Hereafter. On that day, those items are heated, then their foreheads, sides, and backs are burned with those items." It is mentioned in the *hadith* that on the Day of Judgement, the gold or silver upon which *Zakah* was not paid will be turned into a large snake that will eat up the hand of the owner. *Al-Bukhariyy* narrated from the route of *Abu Hurayrah* that the Messenger of *Allah* ﷺ said:

عَنْ أَبِى هُرَيْرَةَ رَضِىَ اللَّهُ عَنْهُ قَالَ: قَالَ رَسُولُ اللَّهِ ﷺ: مَنْ ءَاتَاهُ اللَّهُ مَالاً فَلَمْ يُؤَدِّ زَكَاتَهُ مُثِّلَ لَهُ مَالُهُ يَوْمَ الْقِيَامَةِ شُجَاعًا أَقْرَعَ لَهُ زَبِيبَتَانِ، يُطَوَّقُهُ يَوْمَ الْقِيَامَةِ ثُمَّ يَأْخُذُ بِلِهْزِمَتَيْهِ يَعْنِى بِشِدْقَيْهِ ثُمَّ يَقُولُ أَنَا مَالُكَ أَنَا كَنْزُكَ. ثُمَّ تَلَا: ﴿وَلَا يَحْسَبَنَّ الَّذِينَ يَبْخَلُونَ بِمَا ءَاتَاهُمُ اللَّهُ مِن فَضْلِهِ هُوَ خَيْرًا لَّهُم بَلْ هُوَ شَرٌّ لَّهُمْ سَيُطَوَّقُونَ مَا بَخِلُواْ بِهِ يَوْمَ الْقِيَامَةِ﴾ الآيَةَ.

It means: "Anyone whom *Allah* has given wealth and does not pay its due *Zakah*, on the Day of Resurrection his wealth will be made like a baldheaded poisonous male snake with two black spots over the eyes (or poisonous glands in its mouth). The snake will encircle his neck and bite his cheeks and say, 'I am your wealth, I am your money from which you abstained to pay the due *Zakah*." Then the Prophet ﷺ recited verse 180 of *Surat Al ^Imran*.

Chapter 24
Zakah on Trade Articles

The quotum of trade articles is the quotum of the gold or silver with which they were bought, and *Zakah* is due at the end of the lunar year. The due *Zakah* is one-fortieth of the market value of these trade articles.

Explanation: Trade articles are those articles one purchases with the intent of trading with them, that is those articles which one purchases with the intent of selling to generate money, then to purchase other articles to sell in turn to generate money, and so on. If, for example, one buys articles for trade at the beginning of *Muharram*, and continues trading until the following *Muharram*, one needs to assess whether or not *Zakah* is due. To do so, one assesses the value of one's stock of trade articles (in gold or silver) in addition to the money that was generated from trading during that year and which one still intends to use for trade. If the sum equals the quotum, then *Zakah* is due.

If one's intention of trading changes before the lapse of the lunar year, i.e., if one no more has the intention to trade with those articles, then no *Zakah* is due on them. Later, if one starts trading again, a new year is established without any regard to the previous period of trading. Similarly, if one sells all the trade articles during the year for less than the quotum, the year is interrupted and no *Zakah* is due until then. If one buys again with that golden or silver currency articles to trade with them, a new trading year is established from that time on.

If one begins trading by buying the trade articles with silver, then one evaluates whether or not they reached the quotum of silver (200 *dirhams*). If one begins trading by buying them with gold, then one evaluates whether or not they reached the quotum of gold (20 *dinars*). If one buys the trade articles with other than gold or silver, then one evaluates them according to whichever of gold or silver is the most common circulated currency in the region. If the region no more uses gold or silver currency, then one evaluates with the lastly used gold or silver currency.

The trade articles are evaluated according to the price that would be given if they were sold all at once. If it reaches the quotum, one pays *Zakah* 1/40 of the sum. The due *Zakah* paid on the trade articles evaluated in gold must be paid in gold, and the *Zakah* paid on the trade articles evaluated in silver must be paid in silver.

Regarding the quotum and the due *Zakah* when the conditions of mixing have been satisfied, the mixed money of two or more persons is the same as that of one person.

Explanation: Those whose livestock, crops, or trade articles are mixed (i.e., they satisfy the religious conditions of mixing), pay *Zakah* as if the livestock, crops, or trade articles belong to one person. For example, the cattle of the two parties must drink from one place, be gathered in one place before they are taken to the grazing area, go to the pasture on the same route, graze in one place, drink from the same water, be sheltered at night in one place, and be milked in one place. Similarly, in the case of the mixed plants, the people in charge of plowing the soil, transferring the pollen, harvesting, and carrying and protecting the harvest need to be the same people for both parties. Moreover, the two yields must be stored in the same place.

In the case of mixing the plants, it is a condition that the mixing remains until the fruits and the crops ripen, and, in the case of the golden or silver currency or livestock, that it remains for one lunar year. Those two people who have such a mixing pay *Zakah* as if their mixed belongings are owned by one person.

Chapter 25
Zakah of *Fitr*

The *Zakah* of *Fitr* is due on every Muslim who is alive for a part of *Ramadan* and a part of *Shawwal*.

Explanation: *Zakat-ul-Fitr* is due for every Muslim who is living before the sunset of the last day of *Ramadan* and is still alive after the sun sets completely on that day.[44]

The due *Zakah* for each is a *sa*ˆ of the most common staple food of that region. It is an obligation upon the Muslim to pay the due *Zakah* for oneself and one's Muslim dependants on the Day of the Feast of *Fitr* (ˆId-ul-Fitr) if one has enough money to meet one's debts, clothing, lodging, and sustenance, and the sustenance of those whom one must support for the Day of the Feast of *Fitr* and the night after it.

Explanation: The *Zakah* of *Fitr* due on one Muslim is one *sa*ˆ, that is, four *mudd*s of the most common staple crops of that region. The Muslim must pay it for oneself and for every Muslim whom one is obligated to support. For example, the man pays for his non-pubescent children, wife, Muslim slave, and poor parents. The unmarried pubescent woman pays it for herself and her Muslim slave. The wife pays it for her Muslim slave whom the husband is not obligated to provide for her. Among the pubescent dependants are one's handicapped or insane children who are unable to support themselves.

Moreover, for the *Zakah* of *Fitr* to be due on one, it is a condition that one has what exceeds one's debt -even if it is not due yet- and what is enough to provide for one's self and dependants the proper clothing, lodging, and sustenance for the Day of ˆId and the night after it. Consequently, if one does not have what exceeds the aforementioned matters, one is not obligated to pay the *Zakah* of *Fitr*.

If one's baby is born or one gets married after the sunset of the last day of *Ramadan*, then no *Zakah* of *Fitr* is due for this baby or wife that year. Similarly, no *Zakah* of *Fitr* is due if one becomes solvent or

---

[44] If one doubts whether one's child was born before or after the sunset of the last day of *Ramadan*, one is not obligated to pay *Zakat-ul-Fitr*.

embraces *Islam* after that sunset. Moreover, one's pubscent children, whether male or female, are not among those whom one is obligated to support. Thus, one is not obligated to pay the *Zakah* of *Fitr* for them. However, if they authorize one to pay it on their behalf, one may do so.

One must pay the *Zakah* of *Fitr* before the sun sets on the Day of ^*Idul-Fitr*. It is best to pay it on the Day of *Fitr* before the ^*Id* prayer. It is permissible to pay it at any time during *Ramadan*.

Note that there are five times to pay the *Fitr Zakah*:

1. Time when it is permissible: The whole month of *Ramadan*.

2. Time when it is obligatory: After the sunset of the last day of *Ramadan* until before the sunset of the Day of ^*Id*.

3. The best time: Before the ^*Id* prayer, except if one delays paying it to wait for a deserving relative.

4. Time when it is disliked: After the ^*Id* prayer until the sun sets.

5. Time when it is prohibited: After the sunset of the Day of ^*Id*.

In general, it is prohibited to delay paying any type of *Zakah* until after its due time if one can reach one's money, the deserving people are present, the palm fruits are dried, the grains are separated from the hay, the mined gold or silver is separated from the impurities, and there is no important religious or worldy matter that delays the owner from paying *Zakah*.

Therefore, it is sinful to delay paying *Zakah* after its due time while one is able and has no excuse. One has to pay the due amount of *Zakah*, even if one's money was lost due to fire, robbery, or otherwise.

When one delegates another to pay one's own *Zakah*, it is one's own responsibility to ensure that the delegate is trustworthy and knowledgeable of distributing *Zakah*.

Chapter 26
Recipients of Zakah

For all types of Zakah, the intention is obligatory upon setting one's Zakah aside.

Explanation: To pay Zakah in a valid manner, one must establish the intention in the heart that the money, which one is setting aside is the Zakah due on one. The intention is also valid at the time of giving Zakah to its deserving recipients. An example of such an intention is: "This is the Zakah due on my money", or "This is the Zakah of Fitr of myself". If part of this money is given as charity to a poor person it cannot be considered a part of the obligatory Zakah, since the intention of paying the obligatory Zakah was not established in the heart at that point in time.

Zakah must be paid to the eight categories of Muslims deserving of Zakah, who are in the town where the money is present. They are:

1. **The poor who earn less than half of their basic needs (al-fuqara');**

2. **The poor who earn half or more, but not all of their basic needs (al-masakin);**

3. **The Zakah workers who are assigned by the caliph (al-ʿamiluna ʿalayha);**

4. **The new converts to Islam whose hearts are to be reconciled (al-mu'allafatu qulubuhum);**

5. **The slaves who are short in satisfying their contract for purchasing their freedom from their owners (ar-riqab);**

6. **Those who are unable to pay their debts (al-gharimun);**

7. **The volunteer fighters (fi sabilillah). This does not include any other charitable project.**

8. **The travellers who do not have enough to enable them to reach their destination (ibn-us-sabil).**

Explanation: Zakah can be paid only to the eight (8) categories of people specified in the Qur'an in ayah 60 of Suratut-Tawbah, known as ayatus-sadaqat. Allah said:

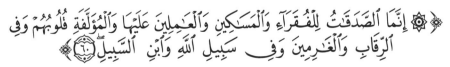

165

The eight categories are:

1. *Al-Fuqara'*: The poor people who earn less than half of their own basic needs and those of their dependants. They themselves have no one obligated to support them. Basic needs include essential food, clothing, and shelter.

2. *Al-Masakin*: The poor people who earn at least half but less than all their basic needs.

3. *Al-^Amiluna ^alayha*: The *Zakah* workers whom the caliph assigns to collect *Zakah* without a paid salary. Included are *Zakah* collectors, bookkeepers, distributers, guards, and talliers. Those people are paid from *Zakah* even if they are rich. If *Zakah* is paid directly to those who deserve it without the need for the *Zakah* workers, the latter do not deserve a share from *Zakah*.

4. *Al-Mu'allafatu qulubuhum*: The new converts to *Islam* who need help in integrating into the Muslim community, because they are still not used to the Muslims. These people are given from *Zakah*, even if they are rich. This type also includes those who embrace *Islam* and have a high social status among their people. If such people are given from *Zakah*, other people with similar status are encouraged to embrace *Islam*. Included are Muslims who inhabit the areas bordering the land of enemies and help in fighting them. Similarly, *Zakah* is paid to those who, upon the orders of the caliph, fight the ones who abstain from paying *Zakah*.

5. *Ar-Riqab*: The slaves who agreed with their owners to work and pay a certain amount of money to purchase their own freedom. If they fall short in paying that money to their owners, they are given from the money of *Zakah* to help them purchase their freedom.

6. *Al-Gharimun*: Those who are unable to pay their debts. Similarly included are those who borrow money, whether rich or poor, to prevent a tribulation. If a tribulation between two parties is about to occur as a result of not knowing the killer of a person, then an individual borrows money and gives it to the relatives of the killed person to prevent this tribulation, in this case if this individual does not pay this debt back, he is helped to pay it back from the *Zakah* money. Similarily, *Zakah* is paid to those who borrow money to build a mosque, provide for a guest, liberate a Muslim prisoner, or

similar purposes that have general benefits for the society. This is true when they do not have enough currency to pay the due debt. Consequently, they are helped for that purpose even if they are not poor and own holdings other than currency that exceed the value of the debt.

7. *Fi sabilillah*: The volunteer fighters who are fighting for the sake of *Allah* and who are not given salaries for their service. Even if they are rich, those volunteer fighters are given from the *Zakah* money to assist their preparation for fighting. This is the meaning of *fi sabilillah* in the verse (by consensus, as related by *Ibn Hazm* and others). It does not refer to any charitable project, because the Prophet ﷺ said:

$$\text{«وليس فيها حقٌّ لِغَنِيّ ولا لِقَوِيّ مُكتسِبٍ»}$$

It means: "There is no right in *Zakah* for the one who is rich or for the one who is healthy and able to find a job". This *hadith* was related by *Abu Dawud* and *al-Bayhaqiyy*.

Hence, it is not permissible to give *Zakah* to the solvent or sane who is able to work. Not a single *mujtahid* said that it is permissible to pay *Zakah* for any charitable matter. Moreover, *Ibn Hazm* cited the consensus that it is not permissible to pay *Zakah* directly to build mosques, for example. Had it been permissible to pay *Zakah* for any good act, the Prophet ﷺ would not have said:

$$\text{«تُؤخَذُ مِن أغنيائِهم وتُرَدُّ على فُقَرائِهم»}$$

It means: "*Zakah* is taken from the solvent Muslims to be spent on their poor." (*al-Bukhariyy*). Good acts may be done to the wealthy and poor. However, *Zakah* can be paid only to the poor.

8. *Ibn-us-sabil*: The traveller who does not have enough money to enable him to reach his final destination. For example, if the traveler loses his money, he is given enough from the money of *Zakah* to help him reach his destination and return to his hometown. This is the judgment, even if he has enough money in his hometown.

Additionally, for one to deserve *Zakah*, one has to be a Muslim and free.

One has to pay Zakah to at least three of each of these eight categories. However, in the case of Zakah workers, it is valid to give Zakah to one or two of them when there are no other workers. Some scholars said it is sufficient to pay one's whole Zakah to one of them. If one does not find all the eight types in one's town, then one pays Zakah to any of the types one finds therein. The famous saying is that it is not permissible to pay Zakah in other than the town where the money is present. However, Imam al-Bukhariyy was among the mujtahids who said that it is permissible to transfer Zakah to other regions.

Note: If a brilliant person is involved in his Islamic studies to the extent that he is unable to support himself, and moreover, if it is expected of this person to attain the level of mufti by knowing the different judgements for all the cases according to the school that he is studying, the scholars said that if working to earn living prevents him from reaching this level of knowledge, then it is permissible to give him from Zakah to enable him to reach that level of knowledge.

It is not permissible to pay Zakah to any member of the Hashim or al-Muttalib clan, or to their freed slaves. Thus, it is forbidden for those slaves to take Zakah just as it is for the original members of the Hashim and al-Muttalib clans. Hashim and al-Muttalib were brothers, the sons of ^Abdu Manaf. It is forbidden for the one who is among their offspring to take Zakah.

The offspring of the other brothers of Hashim, i.e., ^Abdu Shams and Nawfal do not have the same judgment as the offspring of al-Muttalib in the issue of Zakah because the Prophet ﷺ said:

$$\text{«إِنَّمَا بَنُو الْمُطَّلِبِ وبَنُو هَاشِمٍ شَيْءٌ وَاحِدٌ».}$$

It means: "We (Hashim's clan) and the Muttalib clan are like one clan". (al-Bukhariyy)

It is neither permissible nor valid to pay Zakah to other than those eight types of people specifically mentioned.

Explanation: It is invalid to pay Zakah to other than the aforementioned eight categories. If one pays one's money as Zakah to build a mosque, a hospital, a wall around a cemetery, or an Islamic school, this payment is not considered a valid Zakah. The one who pays such an invalid *Zakah* is still accountable in the Hereafter for not having paid *Zakah* in a valid manner. Moreover, he is sinful for doing an invalid act of worship. His act is invalid just like the act of the person who prays without *wudu'*. One needs to be very careful where to spend one's *Zakah* money.

A Parable: In one of the villages of Harar in Ethiopia, a group of poor people came to take grains of *Zakah* from the farmers of that area. The farmers said: "Today, we will harvest and clean the grains, then tomorrow we will give you of it." In their hearts, they had no intention of giving any of their grain. Before the break of the following day, the earth opened up and swallowed all the grains. Had they been sincere in giving *Zakah*, such adversity would not have befallen them. *Allah* blesses the money of those who pay *Zakah*. This is certified by the *hadith* narrated by *Muslim*:

عَنْ أَبِى هُرَيْرَةَ عَنِ النَّبِيِّ ﷺ قَالَ: «بَيْنَا رَجُلٌ بِفَلاةٍ مِنَ الأَرْضِ، فَسَمِعَ صَوْتًا فِى سَحَابَةٍ: اسْقِ حَدِيقَةَ فُلانٍ. فَتَنَحَّى ذَلِكَ السَّحَابُ. فَأَفْرَغَ مَاءَهُ فِى حَرَّةٍ. فَإِذَا شَرْجَةٌ مِنْ تِلْكَ الشِّرَاجِ قَدِ اسْتَوْعَبَتْ ذَلِكَ الْمَاءَ كُلَّهُ. فَتَتَبَّعَ الْمَاءَ. فَإِذَا رَجُلٌ قَائِمٌ فِى حَدِيقَتِهِ يُحَوِّلُ الْمَاءَ بِمِسْحَاتِهِ. فَقَالَ لَهُ: يَا عَبْدَ اللهِ مَا اسْمُكَ؟ قَالَ: فُلانٌ، لِلاسْمِ الَّذِى سَمِعَ فِى السَّحَابَةِ. فَقَالَ لَهُ: يَا عَبْدَ اللهِ لِمَ تَسْأَلُنِى عَنِ اسْمِى؟ فَقَالَ: إِنِّى سَمِعْتُ صَوْتًا فِى السَّحَابِ الَّذِى هَذَا مَاؤُهُ يَقُولُ: اسْقِ حَدِيقَةَ فُلانٍ، لاسْمِكَ. فَمَا تَصْنَعُ فِيهَا؟ قَالَ: أَمَّا إِذْ قُلْتَ هَذَا، فَإِنِّى أَنْظُرُ إِلَى مَا يَخْرُجُ مِنْهَا، فَأَتَصَدَّقُ بِثُلْثِهِ، وَءَاكُلُ أَنَا وَعِيَالِى ثُلُثًا، وَأَرُدُّ فِيهَا ثُلُثَهُ».

It tells about a man who paid one third of his harvest as charity, one third to his family, and one third to maintain his land. Then, the man saw a cloud and heard [an angel's] voice saying: "Irrigate the land of so and so." The cloud dropped rain on the land of that man but not on any other land around it.

FASTING

(_SI_Y_A_M)

Chapter 27
Who Must Fast

Every accountable Muslim is obligated to fast the month of *Ramadan*. The fast of a menstruating or a postpartum-bleeding woman is not valid; however, they have to make up the missed days.

Explanation: This is a chapter that deals with the rules of fasting. Fasting *Ramadan* is one of the five most important matters of *Islam*. As in the *hadith* of the Prophet ﷺ

«بُنِيَ الإِسلامُ على خمسٍ : شهادةِ أن لا إله إلا اللَّهُ وأنَّ محمَّدًا رسولُ اللَّهِ، وإقام الصَّلاةِ، وإيتاءِ الزَّكاةِ، وحَجّ البيتِ، وصَومِ رَمَضانَ . »

in which the Prophet told us that *Islam* was based on five issues, one of which is fasting during the month of *Ramadan*. (al-Bukhariyy, Muslim)

Ramadan is the best month of the year. It is obligatory on every accountable Muslim to fast *Ramadan*. A blasphemer is not ordered to fast *Ramadan* during this life. However, in the Hereafter, he is accountable for not fasting the month of *Ramadan*. The fast of a menstruating or postpartum-bleeding woman is not valid. Although they are not obligated to eat, drink, or to do what otherwise invalidates the fast, it is unlawful for them to abstain from these with the intention of fasting. Hence, if they abstain from drinking or eating but not with the intention of fasting, they are not sinful. However, they have to make up the days they miss. Similarly, the one who is unable to fast during *Ramadan* because of sickness or a similar excuse has to make up the missed days. However, whoever does not fast *Ramadan* because of old age or because of an illness from which one does not hope to recover, one does not have to make up the missed days.[45]

One is obligated to fast *Ramadan* when one of two matters occurs: either by sighting the crescent of *Ramadan*, or by completing 30 days of *Sha^ban*. Hence, if an upright (^adl) Muslim male testified that he saw the crescent of *Ramadan* after the sunset of the 29th day of *Sha^ban*, then the following day is the first day of *Ramadan*.

---

[45] However, this person is required to fulfill an expiation (*fidyah*), which comprises paying to the poor Muslims for every missed day of *Ramadan* a *mudd* of the most common staple food in the region. One has to pay the expiation day by day, or else whenever able to do so.

However, if the crescent is not sighted after the sunset of the 29th day of Sha^ban, then the following day is the 30th of Sha^ban and the day after that will be the first day of Ramadan.

Even if fasting is not tedious, it is permissible for the traveller of a shortening (qasr) distance not to fast.

Explanation: If one was travelling a shortening distance (two marhalahs), then one does not have to fast. Each marhalah is 8 farsakhs; each farsakh is 3 (Islamic) miles; and each (Islamic) mile is 6,000 cubits. Hence, the two marhalahs equal 48 (Islamic) miles which are approximately equal to 130 km or 80 customary miles.

Hence, if one is travelling for this distance or more during the month of Ramadan, one is entitled not to fast, even if fasting is not tedious, as long as one's travel is not sinful and one leaves one's hometown before the dawn (fajr) breaks in.

Breaking the fast is permissible for the sick person, the pregnant woman, and the nursing woman who cannot bear the hardship of fasting. However, they are obligated to make up the missed days.

Explanation: It is permissible for the person with severe sickness not to fast during Ramadan, as such a person encounters a hardship similar to the hardship that allows the person to make tayammum instead of using water for wudu'.[46] Fasting is not an obligation if it harms one, such as if it prolongs one's illness, or results in one's death or in impairing an organ, or the like.

Also the pregnant woman and the nursing woman who cannot bear the hardship of fasting, are allowed not to fast, whether they fear for themselves, or for their babies, or for themselves and their babies. When the pregnant woman fears that fasting may result in the miscarriage of the baby and the nursing woman fears having insufficient milk for the baby, they are allowed not to fast. However, they need to make up the missed days. If they break their fast out of fear for the baby only, then they need also to pay an expiation besides making up the missed days. The expiation per missed day is a mudd of the most common staple food of the region.

---

[46] If a sick person feels such a hardship from fasting while working and is in need of working, he makes the firm intention at night to fast the following day. If during the day one cannot bear fasting one may break the fast. The person in need of working is the person who does not have the basic needs for oneself and the people one is obligated to support.

Chapter 28
Integrals of Fasting

It is obligatory:

1. Each night to make a specific intention to fast the following day;

Explanation: For the validity of the obligatory fasting, it is a condition that the person establishes a specific intention each night preceding the day of fasting. *Imam Ahmad* and others narrated that the Messenger of *Allah* ﷺ said:

$$\text{«مَنْ لَمْ يُبَيِّتِ الصِّيامَ قَبْلَ الفَجْرِ فلا صِيامَ له»}$$

It means: "The fasting of a person is not accepted if one does not have the intention before dawn to fast the following day." Islamically, night begins at sunset and terminates at dawn (*fajr*). When establishing the intention of fasting, one has to specify the type of fasting, i.e., whether it is for the obligation of *Ramadan*, a vow (*nadhr*), an expiation or the like; even though one does not have to specify the reason for the expiation. If the person does not establish the specific intention during the night and attempts to fast the following day, one's fasting will be invalid.[47] As to the optional fasting, it is valid for one to fast if one estalishes the intention before the time of *Dhuhr* starts.

Eating the *sahur* meal at night to fast the following day is considered an establishment of a valid intention. Hence, leaving out the intention, or forgetting about the intention rarely happens during *Ramadan*.

The intention is not valid if after *fajr*, one doubts whether or not one has had the intention to fast in one's heart before *fajr*, or while one is making the intention one doubts whether or not *fajr* has already broken in. However, if after having had the firm intention one doubts whether it was done before *fajr*, one's fast is valid. Also valid is the intention if after sunset one doubts whether the intention for the day one has just fasted took place before or after *fajr*. However, the intention is not valid if established at the exact same time *fajr* comes in.

---

[47] If out of her habit, a menstruating woman expects her menses to stop before dawn, then she makes the intention to fast the following day and sleeps before the blood stops. If when she wakes up in the morning, she finds that the blood has stopped, then her intention is valid.

2. To abstain from sexual intercourse,

Explanation: For the validity of fasting during *Ramadan*, one has to abstain from sexual intercourse during the day. Hence, if one performs sexual intercourse during the day of fasting, this invalidates one's fast, unless one forgets about fasting, or one is unaware that this is unlawful (because one is a new Muslim). In such a case, one's fasting is not invalidated.

masturbation,

Explanation: Masturbating during the day of *Ramadan* invalidates one's fasting. Similarly, one invalidates one's fasting by ejaculating as a result of intentional kissing or touching without a barrier, while knowing that it is prohibited, whether or not one wanted to ejaculate.

inducing vomit,

Explanation: Inserting one's fingers or anything else inside the mouth until one throws up invalidates one's fasting. However, unintentional vomiting does not invalidate one's fasting, as long as one does not swallow the vomit or one's *najas*-filthy saliva.

apostasy,

Explanation: Anyone who apostatizes invalidates one's fast. This is regardless of whether the apostasy is a result of apostate convictions, actions, or sayings. Such a person must immediately return to *Islam* and must abstain during the rest of the day from all the invalidators of fasting. Then one must make up this day immediately after the ^*Id*.

and inserting any substance into the head or the body cavity through an open inlet. However, swallowing one's pure (*tahir*) saliva while in the mouth is permissible

Explanation: If the person inserts any tangible substance into one's head or into one's body cavity through an open inlet, one's fast is invalidated. However, when one's saliva is not mixed with another substance, one's swallowing it while still inside the mouth does not invalidate the fast. The exit of the Arabic letter *ha'* ح (middle of throat) is considered within the body cavity, and what is above the exit of the letter *ha'* ح is not considered within the body cavity. Hence, swallowing the phlegm coming up out of the body cavity (above the exit of the Arabic letter _ha'_ ح) into the mouth invalidates one's fast. The nostrils, anus, and mouth are examples of open inlets. The top scholars of _Islam_ have a difference in opinion whether or not the ear is an open inlet. The eye is not an open inlet. Hence, using eyedrops, even if tasted does not invalidate the fasting. Similarly, one's fasting is not invalidated as a result of hypodermic, intravenous, and intramuscular injections.

Having enema, using vaginal douche, and smoking invalidate the fast. Inhaling incense, flour, or road dust does not invalidate one's fasting even if one opens one's mouth on purpose.

Swallowing one's own contaminated saliva by blood from the gum invalidates the fasting. However, there are two sayings about the validity of the fast if one does not swallow this saliva but after a while this saliva is no more contaminated with blood, then one swallows it without rinsing the mouth. According to one the fast is invalidated; according to the other it is not.

The fast is not invalidated if saliva is swallowed after its taste changes, due to a long time of silence, without it being mixed with anything. Fasting is not invalidated if during _wudu'_ water is swallowed involuntarily while inserting it into the mouth or nose without forcing it deep into them. Eating and drinking while forgetting about fasting does not invalidate the fast.

Asthmatic medicine inhaled through the mouth or nose invalidates the fasting. Whoever wakes up after _fajr_ and swallows one's saliva, then discovers that it was contaminated with blood invalidates the fast. One refrains from eating the rest of the day. One is not sinful, but one has to make it up after _Ramadan_.

It is _sunnah_ (recommended) to break one's fast immediately after one is sure that _maghrib_ is in, and to delay the _sahur_ meal until the end of the night before _fajr_. It is _sunnah_ (recommended) to break the fast by eating moist dates; if unavailable dry dates; if unavailable by drinking water.

One's fasting is valid as long as one does not become insane, even if it were for a moment, and if one does not lose consciousness the whole day [,i.e., from dawn until sunset].

Explanation: Losing one's sanity, even for a moment, during fasting invalidates one's fasting. Also, fasting is invalidated by losing consciousness the entire day. Hence, if a person loses consciousness a few hours during the day, but not the entire day, one's fasting is not invalidated. On the other hand, sleeping throughout the entire day does not render the fasting invalid.

Chapter 29
Days on which Fasting is Unlawful

It is invalid to fast the day of the Feast of *Fitr* (^*Id-ul-Fitr*), the day of the Feast of *Ad-ha* (^*Id-ul-Ad-ha*), and the three (*Tashriq*) days after the day of *Ad-ha*.

Explanation: It is invalid and unlawful to fast the day of the feast of *Fitr* or *Ad-ha*. Similarly, it is sinful and invalid to fast the three days that follow the Day of *Ad-ha*.

It is also invalid to fast the last half of *Sha^ban* and the Day of Doubt, except if one joins the fasting of these days with those before them. The same rule holds for make-up fasting (*qada'*), vow fulfillment (*nadhr*), or habitual rewardable practice (*wird*).

Explanation: It is *sunnah* to fast the 15th of *Sha^ban*. Whoever fasts the 15th of *Sha^ban* is permitted to fast the day after it. It is invalid for one to fast the last half of *Sha^ban*, unless one joins that fasting with what was before it. That is, if one fasts the 15th of *Sha^ban*, one is allowed to fast the second half of *Sha^ban*. On the other hand, if one fasts the 11th, 12th, 13th, and 14th, but not the 15th, one may not fast without an excuse the 16th, 17th, or the days that follow up to the end of the month. Examples of some excuses are if one fasts the second half of *Sha^ban* for a make up, even if one does not join them with days before them. Similarly, if one fasts such days to fulfill a vow (*nadhr*), such as vowing to fast every Monday, then one can fast all the Mondays of *Sha^ban*, even in the second half of *Sha^ban*. The same rule holds if, for example, one has the habit or the practice (*wird*) of fasting Mondays and Thursdays. In this case, one is allowed to continue fasting Mondays and Thursdays during the second half of *Sha^ban*.

Fasting the Day of Doubt is also prohibited. It is not permissible for one to fast this day because ^*Ammar* the son of *Yasir* (a famous Companion) said that the one who fasts the Day of Doubt disobeys the Messenger of *Allah*. The Day of Doubt is the day that follows the 29th of *Sha^ban*, if after the sunset of the 29th of *Sha^ban*, unreliable people, such as committers of enormous sins and children, claim to have sighted the new moon of *Ramadan*. The following day is considered the 30th of Sha^ban, and it is called the Day of Doubt. It is prohibited to fast such a day as a precautionary act. Al-Bukhariyy and Muslim narrated that the Prophet ﷺ said:

«لا تَقَدَّمُوا رمضانَ بيوم أو يومين . صُومُوا لرؤيتِه وأفطرُوا لرؤيتِه . فإن غُمَّ عليكم فأكمِلوا عِدَّة شعبانَ ثلاثين يوما»

It means: "Do not fast a day or two before Ramadan starts. Fast when you see the crescent (of Ramadan) and break your fast when you see the crescent (of Shawwal). If the crescent was not seen due to clouds or the like, then finish the thirty days of Sha^ban."

In validating the beginning of Ramadan, the Muslim judge relies on the saying of an upright Muslim man who avoids committing enormous sins, does not insist on committing small sins, and adheres to the behavior and the manners of his peers. For instance, although not sinful, such a person does not play chess frequently, fly pigeons around, or occupy his time by telling non-beneficial funny stories.

If an upright Muslim male testifies that he has seen the crescent, then the people of that town and all the towns around it, in which the sun rises and sets at the same time, fast the next day. However, according to Abu Hanifah, once the start of Ramadan is confirmed in one place, then all Muslim countries who hear about it fast too. However, if astronomers say that the crescent will appear on a certain day, Muslims do not rely on that to determine the beginning of Ramadan. In the well known Hanafiyy book called al-Mi^raj, it is said that one cannot rely on what the astronomers and the people who calculate the lunar cycle say for fasting Ramadan. One cannot determine the start of the month of Ramadan based on calculations. This is against the Religion because of the saying of the Prophet ﷺ :

نحنُ أُمَّةٌ أُمِّيَّةٌ لا نَكتُبُ ولا نَحسُبُ . الشَّهرُ هكذا وهكذا .

It means: "We are a nation that does not depend on calculations to see when the month starts and ends. Sometimes the month is thirty days and sometimes it is twenty nine." This hadith was narrated by al-Bukhariyy. A similar ruling is mentioned in the books of the Malikiyy scholars like the commentary of ad-Dasuqiyy on the explanation of the Summary of *Khalil*, the *Hambaliyy* books, like the book *Kashshaful-Qina^*, and the *Shafi^iyy* books, like the explanation of *Rawdut-Talib*.

Invalidating the fasting of one day of *Ramadan* by engaging in sexual intercourse without an excuse is sinful. One must make it up immediately, and one must fulfill an expiation of *dhihar*. The expiation of *dhihar* is to free a Muslim slave; if one is unable, one fasts two consecutive lunar months; and if one is unable, one feeds sixty poor Muslims. To feed sixty poor Muslims means to give every one of them a *mudd* of the most common staple food in that town.

Explanation: If one engages in sexual intercourse to break one's fast due to a religious excuse, such as travelling, one is not sinful. However, one is sinful to invalidate the fast of any day of *Ramadan* by engaging in sexual intercourse without an excuse. Moreover, the man -not the woman- fulfills an expiation of *dhihar*, which is:

1. To free a Muslim slave who is clear of any physical defects which impede his handiwork.

2. If unable, to fast two consecutive months. If one leaves out fasting one day, even for an excuse, one has to repeat fasting the two months from the beginning.

3. If unable, to feed sixty (60) poor Muslims, each a *mudd* of the most common staple food in one's town, such as wheat or rice.

Although the expiation is due on the man, the woman is not allowed, without excuse, to enable her husband to have sexual intercourse with her during the day of fasting. An excuse is forgetting about fasting.

The expiation is due only when a full day is invalidated. Hence, if he becomes insane or dies before sunset he does not have to pay the expiation. The expiation multiplies with the days invalidated by sexual intercourse.

The violater who forgets about fasting and does not know the ruling -such as a new Muslim- or is forced to copulate does not invalidate the fast and is not required to pay an expiation. Moreover, the expiation is not due on the person who breaks the fast of a day other than *Ramadan*, even if it was an obligatory fast.

It is sinful for the traveller or sick to copulate, for other than the intention of employing travelling or sickness as a facility to break the fast. However, no expiation of *dhihar* is due.

Note: Some scholars, like *Imam Malik*, said that every person who breaks the fast during *Ramadan* without an excuse is sinful. Moreover, one has to make up that day, and has to pay an expiation of *dhihar*.

Important Remarks:

Before breaking the fast, one has to make sure that the sun has set. One cannot rely on the *adhan* of untrustworthy persons whether live, recorded, or broadcast. Some untrustworthy people have called or broadcast the *adhan* earlier than sunset. Hence, one has to be careful.

Gossip does not invalidate the fast. *Imam Ahmad* said: "Had gossip invalidated the fast, not a single day of fasting would have counted for us." However, the alleged *hadith*: "five things invalidate the fast: kissing, gossiping, talebearing, lustful looking, and lying", is not a *sahih hadith*.

Committing any of the following sins against a Muslim takes away the reward of fasting: Cursing, slandering, backbiting, talebearing, and testifying falsely. It is narrated by *al-Bukhariyy* that whoever does not leave out testifying falsely and lying, then his fast is not rewarded.

It is *sunnah* for the person who is fasting to say upon breaking the fast:

«اللَّهُمَّ لَكَ صُمْتُ وعَلَى رِزْقِكَ أَفْطَرْتُ» .

«ذَهَبَ الظَّمَأُ وابْتَلَّتِ العُرُوقُ وثَبَتَ الأَجْرُ إن شاءَ الله» .

These two supplications mean: "O *Allah*, I have fasted for your sake and I break my fast with the sustenance You provided." "My thirst is gone, my veins are moist, and by the Will of *Allah*, I will be rewarded for my fasting." Both were narrated by *Abu Dawud*.

When breaking the fast at someone else's place, it is *sunnah* to make *du^a'* for that person by saying:

«أَفْطَرَ عِندَكُمُ الصَّائِمونَ، وأَكَلَ طعامَكمُ الأَبْرارُ،
وصلَّتْ عليكُمُ الملائِكةُ».

It means: "May *Allah* grant you the reward of giving a meal to a fasting person to break the fast, may the pious people eat at your house, and may the angels make *du^a'* for you."

Ramadan is the month of cleansing oneself and purifying one's soul. It is not a month for living luxuriously, as many people do. In Ethiopia, to train themselves to be satisfied with little, many Muslims spend all *Ramadan* breaking their fast on eating fried corn and drinking coffee. Having a variety of food in one meal is *tana^^um* (eating luxuriously) and is *makruh* (disliked), except if there is a need to do so.

Pilgrimage

(*Hajj*)

Chapter 30
Who Must Perform Pilgrimage

Performing *Hajj* and ^*Umrah* once in a lifetime is obligatory

Explanation: In the *Hadith* narrated by *al-Bukhariyy* and *Muslim*, the Prophet, *sallallahu ^alayhi wa sallam*, said:

روى البخاريُّ ومسلم أن رسولَ ﷺ قال: «العُمْرةُ إلى العُمْرةِ كَفَّارَةٌ لما بَينهُما. والحَجُّ المَبرورُ ليس له جزاءٌ إلا الجنةِ».

It means: "Performing ^*Umrah* erases the sins done after the previous ^*Umrah* and there is no reward for the acceptable *Hajj* except Paradise." Performing *Hajj* involves one going to the Ka^bah to perform specific known actions. ^*Umrah* is also performed by one going to the Ka^bah to perform specific known actions. *Imam ash-Shafi^iyy* said that it is obligatory on the free Muslim who is able, to perform ^*Umrah* at least once in a lifetime. Others, like *Imam Malik*, considered ^*Umrah* as optional (*sunnah*). As to *Hajj*, there is no difference in opinion with regards to the one who is able. All scholars hold the consensus that it is obligatory on the one who is able. Hence, it is blasphemous to claim that *Hajj* is not obligatory on the Muslim who is able. However, they hold different opinions as to whether one must perform it immediatley or one may delay doing it for some time. *Imam Malik* said that one who is able has to perform *Hajj* immediately, that is, one has to go to *Hajj* in the same year. *Imam ash-Shafi^iyy* said that one is entitled to delay it as long as one performs it before death.

As the Prophet said (in the *hadith* related by *al-Bukhariyy* and others), *Hajj* is one of the five most important matters upon which *Islam* is built. *Hajj* has a special merit: If one performs it in an acceptable manner, one becomes clear of all one's sins, just as if one was newly born to one's mother.

For *Hajj* to be acceptable, one's intention has to be for the sake of *Allah*, the money used for pilgrimage has to be *halal* (Islamically lawful), and one must avoid committing enormous sins and sexual intercourse during *Hajj*. On the other hand, committing small sins

187

during Pilgrimage does not make it unaccepted, i.e., it does not prevent the pilgrim from getting the reward of *Hajj*. When the Prophet, *sallallahu ^alayhi wa sallam*, was performing *Hajj* a beautiful woman from the tribe of *Khath^am* asked him about certain matters. His cousin *al-Fadl* looked at her lustfully. The Prophet, *sallallahu ^alayhi wa sallam*, turned his cousin's face to the other side. The Prophet did not tell him that he had lost the reward of his Pilgrimage by looking lustfully at that woman. This *hadith* is narrated by *al-Bukhariyy* and *at-Tirmidhiyy*.

upon the Muslim who is free, accountable, and can afford to reach Makkah and return to one's homeplace. This includes that one has in excess of one's debts, appropriate lodging and clothing, and what one is obligated to spend on those whom one must support from the time of one's departure until one's return.

Explanation: *Hajj* has conditions that pertain to rendering a person obligated to perform *Hajj*, and conditions that pertain to its validity.

The conditions that make one obligated to perform *Hajj* are:

1. *Islam*: Hence, the blasphemer is not ordered to perform *Hajj* in this life, although he will be punished in the Hereafter for leaving it out.

2. Pubescence: Hence, the one who is not pubescent is not obligated to perform *Hajj*, even if one was rich.

3. Sanity: Hence, the one who is insane is not obligated to perform *Hajj*.

4. Ability: It means that one can afford to reach *Makkah* and return to one's homeplace. It includes that one has more than what one needs to pay for one's debts, appropriate lodging and clothing, and what one is obligated to spend on those whom one must support from one's departure until one's return. This includes helping one's father to get married if one's father needs it.

This obligation applies if one feels safe for one's self and belongings. However, if one knows that one may be killed or robbed on the way to *Hajj*, then one is not obligated to go to *Hajj*.

If one has the financial ability for the trip, but is severely sick and cannot ride to travel to *Makkah* to perform *Hajj*, one may hire someone to perform it on one's behalf. This is the case of whoever resides at least a two-day walking distance from *Makkah*. Those who live closer exert a bigger effort to perform *Hajj* on their own.

Hiring someone to perform Pilgrimage on one's behalf is achieved in either of two ways: One hires another to perform *Hajj* himself, or one hires another to have *Hajj* performed, whether by doing it himself or appointing someone else to do it. In the second case, the fee has to be delivered in the session when the contract takes place. It is not permissible to delay it even until one moment after they separate from the session. It is permissible for someone to volunteer to perform *Hajj* on another's behalf at no cost.

There is another kind of ability, unrelated to one's physical ability. This is the woman finding a *mahram* (unmarriagable man) to accompany her to *Hajj*. If she cannot find such a *mahram*, because she does not have one, or because he is not willing to go with her despite her paying him the usual fee, or because she does not have enough money to pay him that amount, then she may go with three trustworthy women if she can find them. If such three were not available, then with two of them; if not, then one is enough. If she does not find even one, then she is allowed to go alone. On the other hand, she is not allowed to travel alone to visit the grave of the Prophet, because this is not an obligation. More so, she is not allowed to travel alone for tourism or the like because the Prophet ﷺ said in the *hadith* narrated by *Abu Dawud*:

$$ \text{«لا تُسافِرُ المرأةُ بَرِيدًا إلا ومعها مَحْرَمٌ»} $$

It means: «A woman is not allowed to travel the distance of half a day without the company of an unmarriagable male (*mahram*).»

5. Freedom: Hence, the slave is not obligated to go to *Hajj*.

There is only one condition for the validity of *Hajj*: One has to be a Muslim. Hence, it is valid to take a little child for Pilgrimage. To be able to perform the acts of *Hajj* by himself, the child has to be in the state of mental discrimination (*mumayyiz*) and has to take his guardian's permission. However, when the child is not in the state of mental discrimination, the guardian makes the intention on his behalf.

For example, the guardian says in his heart: I now make my child in the state of Pilgrimage. Hence, the guardian accompanies the child to the different locations of _Hajj_, such as the Ka^bah and ^Arafah, to do the acts that the child cannot do by himself.

If one makes a vow to perform _Hajj_, for one's vow to be fulfilled one needs to perform _Hajj_ while one is in the state of _Islam_ and is accountable. Thus, if one performs _Hajj_ before getting pubescent, one's vow is not fulfilled yet and one needs to perform _Hajj_ after becoming accountable if one is able.

There are two conditions that have to be satisfied for one's obligatory _Hajj_ to have been performed without the obligation of reperforming it during one's lifetime: Accountability and complete freedom.

Chapter 31
Integrals of Pilgrimage

The integrals (*rukn*s) of _Hajj_ are six (6):

Explanation: _Hajj_ involves integrals (*rukn*s), requisites (*wajib*s), and recommended matters (*sunnah*s). The integrals of _Hajj_ are defined as those parts of _Hajj_ which, if left out, cannot be compensated for by slaughtering. Rather, one's _Hajj_ will not be valid if all these integrals are not performed.

The requisites (*wajib*s) are parts of _Hajj_ which are sinful for one to leave out, but leaving them out does not invalidate _Hajj_. However, slaughtering is required to compensate for leaving them out.

As to the recommended matters (*sunnah*s), they are the rewardable non-obligatory doings of _Hajj_ which if left out, one is not sinful and one's _Hajj_ is not invalidated.

Hence, concerning the rules of _Hajj_, there is a difference between the *rukn* and *wajib*. This difference does not exist with other issues, like the rules of Purification, Prayer, and Za_kah_. Concerning those rules, an integral (*rukn*), an obligation (*fard*), and a requisite (*wajib*) all have the same meaning.

There are six (6) integrals of _Hajj_, i.e., the parts which if left out render one's _Hajj_ invalid. One cannot compensate for leaving them out by slaughtering.

1. **To have the intention to be in the state of Pilgrimage (*Ihram*), i.e., to say in one's heart: "I now enter into the actions of _Hajj_ (or ˆ*Umrah*)";**

Explanation: The first of the integrals is to have the intention to be in the state of Pilgrimage (*Ihram*). This does not mean to wear the clothes of _Hajj_, rather it means to have the proper intention. An example of a valid intention is for one to say in one's heart, "I now commence the actions of _Hajj_", or "I now intend to become in the state of Pilgrimage". In the same way, one intends ˆ*Umrah* instead of _Hajj_.

Planning to go to *Makkah* to perform _Hajj_ or ˆ*Umrah* is not considered an intention of *Ihram*. On the other hand, one may intend *Ihram* without specifying _Hajj_ or ˆ*Umrah*. However, before starting the actions, one has to specify doing either or both simultaneously.

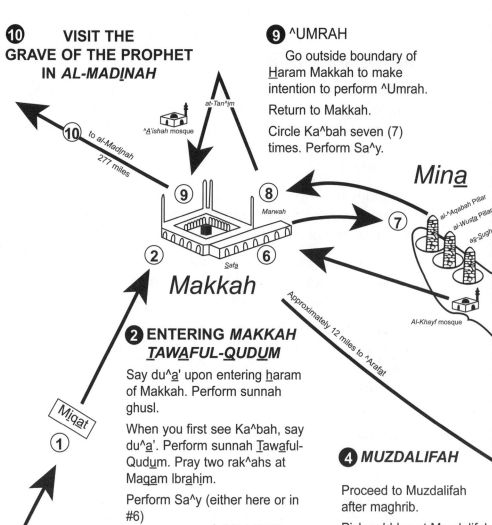

❿ VISIT THE GRAVE OF THE PROPHET IN *AL-MADINAH*

❾ ^UMRAH

Go outside boundary of Haram Makkah to make intention to perform ^Umrah.

Return to Makkah.

Circle Ka^bah seven (7) times. Perform Sa^y.

at-Tan^im

^A'ishah mosque

❿ to al-Madinah 277 miles

⑨

⑧

Marwah

Mina

al-^Aqabah Pillar
al-Wusta Pillar
as-Sughr

②

⑥

⑦

Safa

Makkah

Al-Khayf mosque

Approximately 12 miles to ^Arafat

Miqat

①

Start

❷ ENTERING *MAKKAH TAWAFUL-QUDUM*

Say du^a' upon entering haram of Makkah. Perform sunnah ghusl.

When you first see Ka^bah, say du^a'. Perform sunnah Tawaful-Qudum. Pray two rak^ahs at Maqam Ibrahim.

Perform Sa^y (either here or in #6)

❶ INTENTION FOR *IHRAM*

Perform sunnah ghusl, perfume body

Dress in proper clothes for ihram

Pray two rak^ahs sunnah for ihram

Before crossing miqat,

establish intention

Refrain from prohibitions of ihram
Recite talbiyah, make du^a'

^ARAFAT

❸ Perform sunnah ghusl

Go to ^Arafat after zawal of 9th of Dhul Hijjah and stay until after maghrib.

Combine Dhuhr and ^Asr prayers and perform them together at the time of Dhuhr

Repeat often words glorifying Allah

Ask Allah for forgiveness, make du^a', recite Qur'an

❹ *MUZDALIFAH*

Proceed to Muzdalifah after maghrib.

Pick pebbles at Muzdalifah (either 49 or 70).

Stay the night at Muzdalifah and go at dawn to Mina,

OR Proceed to Mina after the middle of the night.

192

The _Hajj_ Journey

8 _TAW**A**FUL-WAD**A**^_

Perform farewell ṯawaf after finishing actions of Ḥajj.

**Ḥajj completed

---

7 **STAYING AT _MIN**A**_ AND THROWING PEBBLES**

Return to Minā the evening after the ^Id and spend the night there.

Throw seven (7) pebbles at each of the 3 jamrah stations the next day (1st Tashriq day) before sunset, making sure they land in the basin.

Similarly, throw pebbles the 2nd and 3rd Tashriq days. One may forego throwing on the 3rd day if one leaves before sunset on the 2nd day.

INTEGRAL
(underlined and bolded type)

The matter which must be performed for the Hajj to be valid which cannot be replaced by slaughtering.

REQUISITE
(bolded type)

An obligatory action of Ḥajj, which If not done, the Ḥajj is still valid, but the person is sinful and an expiation is required.

---

④

Muzdalifah

---

6 _TAW**A**FUL-IF**A**DAH_

Perform tawaf after the middle of the night preceding the ^Id day.

Pray two sunnah rak^ahs.

Perform Sa^y (either here or in #2)

**(FINAL TAḤALLUL) All Iḥram's prohibitions lifted.

---

5 _MIN**A**_

Throw the first seven (7) pebbles at jamratul- ^Aqabah.
Slaughter an animal in Minā and distribute the meat to the poor in Makkah.

Shave head or trim hair.
**(1ST TAḤALLUL) All iḥram's prohibitions lifted, except for sexual intercourse.

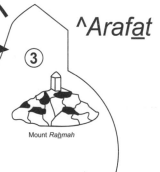

^_Arafat_

③

Mount _Raḥmah_

Namirah mosque

This intention must be established during the months of _Hajj_, which are _Shawwal_, _Dhul-Qa^dah_, and _Dhul-Hijjah_, i.e., the first ten (10) days of _Dhul-Hijjah_.

If the person makes the intention during the months of _Hajj_ while one is wearing regular habitual clothes, one's intention is valid, but one is sinful for not wearing the proper clothing.

If the person makes the intention before the months of _Hajj_, i.e., if before the month of _Shawwal_, one makes the intention of becoming in the state of _Hajj_, one's intention for _Hajj_ is not valid. However, by doing so one becomes automatically involved in _^Umrah_, i.e., one becomes in the state of _^Umrah_ and has to perform it.

Before having the intention of Pilgrimage, it is _sunnah_ for both males and females to make _ghusl_ and to wear perfume on their bodies, but not on their clothes. _Abu Dawud_ narrated that the wives of the Prophet ﷺ did it without the objection of the Prophet ﷺ. On the other hand, it is sinful for the pilgrim to wear perfume after making the intention.

2. **To be present at _^Arafah_ sometime between the start of _Dhuhr_ on the 9th of _Dhul-Hijjah_ and the dawn (_fajr_) of the following _^Id_ day.**

Explanation: The second integral of _Hajj_ is to be present at _^Arafah_ or _^Arafat_. The time for doing it is tight. This is why the Prophet ﷺ said:

$$\text{«الحَجُّ عَرَفَة»}$$

It means: "The one who misses being at _^Arafah_ in the designated time misses _Hajj_."

The designated time to be at _^Arafah_ starts at the beginning of the _Dhuhr_ time on the 9th of _Dhul-Hijjah_ and ends at the dawn of the following day. Hence, one needs to be within the boundaries of _^Arafah_ during that time. It is better for one to join between the day and the night, that is, to be present there before the sunset of the ninth day of _Dhul-Hijjah_ (_Dhuhr_ time) until after the sunset.

It is recommended (_sunnah_) for the pilgrims to be in the state of ritual purity (_taharah_) during their time of stay in _^Arafah_. Moreover, it is _sunnah_ to keep one's heart away from the worldy matters, concentrating on obeying God, to face the _Qiblah_, and to say a lot of *tahlil, tasbih, takbir, salatu ^alan-nabiyy, istighfar*, supplication, and recitation of the *Qur'an*, especially *Suratul-Hashr*.

3. To circumambulate the *Ka^bah* (*tawaf*);

Explanation: The third integral is to go around the *Ka^bah* (*tawaf*). It is valid only after the midnight of the *^Id's* eve.[48] One circles the perimeter of the *Ka^bah* seven times with one's left shoulder to the *Ka^bah*, starting at the Black Stone and directing oneself towards the *Hijr*. This means that upon making *tawaf*, one's entire body must be outside the *Ka^bah*, without any part of one's body over the *Hijr* or the *Shadharwan*.[49]

A proper intention is required when one circumambulates the *Ka^bah* for other than performing Pilgrimage.

Moreover, there are seven rounds around the *Ka^bah*, no more or less, just as no more or less *rak^ahs* are accepted in the prayer. When one doubts about the number of rounds, one takes the lower number and performs what adds up to seven. When one doubts whether one finished five or six rounds, one considers oneself to have done five and adds two more rounds.

It is a condition for circumambulating the *Ka^bah* to be inside the *Haram* Mosque even if it takes place on its roof, while one is higher than the *Ka^bah*.

It is recommended (*sunnah*) to walk while making *tawaf* although it is permissible to make it while riding an animal, for example. Similarly, it is recommended to make *tawaf* with bare feet although it is permissible to make it while wearing slippers or sandals as long as they are pure and clean and do not dirty the mosque. Also, it is *sunnah* to make one's steps short and to touch the Black Stone, kiss it without making a sound, and put one's forehead on it. However, such a matter is not recommended for the female except at the time when no marriageable men are thereat. Additionally, it is *sunnah* for men to walk faster in the first three rounds, and to pass the *rida'* from under the right arm and to put it on the left shoulder. It is *sunnah* also not to

---

[48] Islamically, the night starts with sunset and ends with the break of dawn. Hence, midnight refers to the midpoint between sunset and dawn (*fajr*) . It does not mean 12 o'clock at night necessarily.

[49] The *Shadharwan* is part of the *Ka^bah* at its bottom all around. It rises about one cubit above the ground (see the figure at the end of the chapter).

separate between the rounds of _tawaf_ with a long time. Taking a long break between rounds to rest, drink, or eat is permissible.

After completing _tawaf_ it is _sunnah_ to pray two _rak^ahs_, and the best place for it is behind _Maqam Ibrahim_. This _sunnah_ occurs by praying the two _rak^ahs_ at any place within the mosque or even within the borders of the _haram_ of _Makkah_. It is disliked to leave out doing those two _rak^ahs_. On the other hand, this _sunnah_ is fulfilled if instead of those two _rak^ahs_ one prays any obligatory or optional prayer after completing _tawaf_. However, the reward in this case is less.

Note: The wisdom of making _tawaf_ is to show one's adherance to the obedience of _Allah_, as if one is saying, wherever I am and whichever way I turn, I will adhere to the orders of _Allah_.

4. **To walk between the mounts of _as-Safa_ and _al-Marwah_, seven times from one border line to the other (sa^y);**

Explanation: Walking (_Sa^y_) between the mounts of _Safa_ and _Marwah_ is among the integrals of _Hajj_. Both _Safa_ and _Marwah_ are small mountains. Originally a valley existed between them. However, nowadays, the valley is filled with soil and stones to make walking between these two mountains easier for the pilgrims.

After completing _tawaf_, one must walk between these two mounts seven times, starting at _Safa_, and ending with _Marwah_. Going to _Marwah_ is considered one round, and returning to _Safa_ is a second round. There are marks at the beginning of _Safa_ and the beginning of _Marwah_; so one has to walk at least between these two marks. Purification (_Taharah_) is not a condition for the validity of _sa^y_. Similarly, it is not a condition for one's presence at _^Arafah_. However, it is a condition for the validity of circling the _Ka^bah_ (_tawaf_).

Stopping _sa^y_ to rest, eat, or drink then resuming from the place where one stopped is valid.

Adding intentionally one or more rounds on top of the seven rounds in this walking is prohibited. However, if one doubts whether the rounds are seven or less one goes according to the lower number. It is _sunnah_ for men to walk fast between the two green marks in that area.

5. **Cutting the hair by shaving (_halq_) or trimming (_taqsir_);**

Explanation: Among the integrals of *Hajj* is for the pilgrim to shave the head or trim it. This happens by shaving at least three hairs, or by burning or trimming them, or the like. It is better for the man to shave his entire hair as the Prophet ﷺ did. However, for the woman, it is forbidden to shave her head without a necessity. Rather, she trims her hair. It is better for her to trim from all sides.

Its time starts, like *tawaf*, by the midnight of ^*Id*. Removing any hair of the body before that is *haram* (sinful). It is recommended (*sunnah*) for the shaving or trimming to be done during the day of ^*Id* and its better to do it after the sun rises and before *tawaf* and *sa^y*. It is also *sunnah* to start with the right front part of the head, to face the *Qiblah*, and to make *takbir* after finishing it.

6. Observing the order in most of the integrals.

Explanation: Observing the order is one of the integrals of *Hajj*. One must establish the intention to be in the state of Pilgrimage before performing any other integral. One must delay performing *tawaf* around the *Ka^bah*, and shaving or trimming the hair until after being at ^*Arafat*. *Sa^y* between *Safa* and *Marwah* is valid only if it done after (any optional or obligatory) circling of the *Ka^bah*.

All of these are also integrals of ^Umrah except to be present at ^Arafah.

Explanation: The integrals of ^*Umrah* are five:

1. Holding the intention of being in the state of Pilgrimage,

2. Making *tawaf*,

3. Making *sa^y* between *Safa* and *Marwah*,

4. Trimming or shaving the hair,

5. Observing the order.

Observing the order in the case of ^*Umrah* is a must with regards to all the integrals. Hence, one must start with the intention of being in a state of *Ihram*, then make *tawaf*, then make *sa^y*, and at the end shave or trim one's hair.

These integrals have requisites (*fards*) and conditions (*sharts*) that must be observed.

Explanation: Every one of these integrals has conditions for it to be valid. To give an example of that the author said:

Among the conditions of *tawaf* is to circumambulate the *Ka^bah* seven times starting at the Black Stone and back to it, while keeping one's left shoulder towards the *Ka^bah* without facing or turning one's back to it; to cover the unlawful nakedness (*^awrah*); and to be pure.

Explanation: One circles the *Ka^bah* seven (7) times starting at the Black Stone. If one's left shoulder is turned away from the *Ka^bah*, one must return to that spot or continue moving forward but add one more round. As in the prayer, covering the *^awrah* and having *taharah* are two other conditions for *tawaf*.

Chapter 32
What is Unlawful During Pilgrimage

It is unlawful for the one who has intended to enter into the actions of Pilgrimage (_Hajj_ or ^_Umrah_):

Explanation: This chapter deals with what becomes unlawful to do during the state of Pilgrimage. There are eight matters that the pilgrim is prohibited to do:

1. To wear perfumes;

Explanation: The first prohibition is wearing perfumes by the person who is in the state of Pilgrimage, _Hajj_ or ^_Umrah_, even if the person is not able to smell. However, it is recommended (*sunnah*) to wear perfumes before and for entering the state of _Hajj_ or ^_Umrah_. Imam ash-Shafi^iyy said that this was a *sunnah* for both men and women, because Lady ^A'ishah said that the Prophet's wives used to wear musk for _Ihram_ (making the intention of _Hajj_). The Prophet ﷺ saw the musk running down their foreheads, but did not forbid them to do it. This *hadith* also stands as a proof that women are allowed to go out of their houses wearing perfumes, if they do not intend by that to seduce men. However, if the woman intends by wearing perfume to seduce men, then it is forbidden for her to do it. If she goes out wearing perfume without having this intention, then it is disliked and not sinful. As mentioned earlier, it is *sunnah* for her to wear perfume for making _Ihram_ of Pilgrimage.

Perfume in this context means what is usually sought by people for its smell, like musk and rose (oil). Substances, like apples and henna, which are usually sought as food or medicine and have a good smell, are not considered perfume. If the pilgrim needs to use perfume for medical reasons, he is allowed to do it. However, he has to pay an expiation. If the perfume was mixed with other medical substances in a way that its color, smell, and taste do not appear any more, it is permissible for the pilgrim to use the mixture and consume it with no due expiation.

It is not permissible for the pilgrim to consume rose water even if it is mixed with food as long as its fragrance is still apparent.

It is not sinful for the pilgrim to carry the ˆ*ud* (fragrant wood) or touch the dry musk, because people do not seek their fragrance in this manner. Carrying the musk or amber in the pilgrim's clothes or in the case of a woman in her jewelry box and putting them in one's nose or eye is prohibited. Moreover, an expiation is due. However, if the pilgrim carries the musk or the like in a tied piece of material, one is not sinful even if one smells the musk because there is a barrier.

Sitting intentionally on a perfumed place, stepping intentionally on perfume, and using scented soap are prohibited. Moreover, an expiation is due.

It is not sinful and no expiation is due upon the one who uses perfume while forgetting about one's *Ihram*, the one who is forced by another person to wear perfume while one is ignorant about the prohibition of doing so, or the one who does not know that the substance one is using is perfume.

The pilgrim may wash the hair and body with unscented soap, although it is better not to do it. Similarly, it is permissible for the pilgrim to put decorative *kuhl* in the eyes like *ithmid* (antimony) or black *kuhl*. However, it is disliked to do so except for an excuse, like to treat an eye illness.

2. To anoint the head or beard with oil, melted grease, or melted honey wax;

Explanation: The second prohibited matter is for one to anoint the head or beard with any kind of ointment. It is not a condition that the prohibited ointment be a perfume. This includes oil, melted grease, melted honey wax, melted blubber,[50] melted tallow,[51] and similar materials that are called *duhn* in the Arabic language.

However, when in the state of *Ihram*, one is entitled to rub one's body hair with oil. Forbidden is anointing the hairs of the head and beard. If one is bald, one is allowed to anoint one's head. Similarly, when one cannot grow a beard, one is allowed to anoint the area of the beard with oil or similar substance.

---

[50] Blubber is the thick layer of fat between the skin and the muscle layers of whales and other marine mammals, from which an oil is obtained.

[51] Tallow is the hard fat obtained from parts of the bodies of cattle, sheep, or horses, and used in foodstuffs or to make candles, leather dressing, soap, and lubricants.

3. **To remove or cut fingernails, toenails, and hair;**

Explanation: It is forbidden for the one who is in the state of *Ihram* to remove one's fingernails or toenails or to remove any hair (except at the proper time) whether by burning it, pulling it off, or cutting it. However, if a part of one's fingernail is broken and harm is inflicted if it remains as is, then one is allowed to remove it. In such a case, one is not sinful and no expiation (*fidyah*) is due. The same ruling holds if one's hair falls off without one's own action.

4. **To perform sexual intercourse or its inviting actions;**

Explanation: The fourth prohibited matter is to perform sexual intercourse or any of its inviting actions. Hence, even if the woman is not in the state of *Ihram*, she must not allow her husband, who is in the state of *Ihram*, to have any sexual advances or intercourse with her. Examples of the inviting actions (sexual advances) are a lustful look, touch, or kiss. The pilgrim who does any of the aforementioned forbidden matters is sinful, and, with the exception of lustful look, is obligated to slaughter a specific animal as an expiation. In the case of sexual intercourse, one is obligated to make up this invalidated *Hajj* in the following year (without delay, as explained at the end of this chapter).

Note that some scholars say that if a woman makes the intention of the optional Pilgrimage without her husband's permission, then it is permissible for him to have sexual intercourse with her to break her state of *Ihram*. He is not entitled to do that in the case of the obligatory *Hajj* or ^*Umrah*. However, some other scholars said that even in the obligatory *Hajj* or ^*Umrah* she needs to take his permission. If she does not, he is entitled to have sexual intercourse with her to break her state of *Ihram*.

5. **To conduct marriage;**

Explanation: This is the fifth prohibition. It is not permissible for the pilgrim to conduct marriage or authorize someone to do it on one's behalf. Such a marriage is invalid regardless of who is in the state of *Ihram*, the groom or the woman's guardian. The Prophet ﷺ prohibited the pilgrim to conduct a marriage contract for oneself or for others, as narrated by *Imam Muslim*.

6. **To hunt any Islamically edible, wild animal;**

Explanation: The sixth prohibition is for the pilgrim to hunt any Islamically edible, wild land animal, such as a deer, or an ostrich. One is allowed to kill any animal which is naturally harmful. In fact, such an action is recommended. Examples are killing rats, snakes, and their similars. The pilgrim is not forbidden to kill a sea animal or an inedible animal, even if it is a wild one, except for what the Prophet ﷺ prohibited us to kill. In one *hadith*, the Prophet ﷺ prohibited us to kill four creatures: (the *Sulaymaniyy* large, red) ants, honey bees, hoopoe birds, and *surad* (a specific bird with a big head that hunts smaller birds). Killing honey bees is prohibited except for protecting oneself from their harm after their attack.

The pilgrim is also prohibited to destroy and take the eggs of an Islamically edible, wild animal. Similarly, one is prohibited to take its milk, feathers, or hair.

As an expiation, the pilgrim who kills an Islamically edible, wild animal has to pay to the poor people of *al-Haram* (vicinity of *Makkah*) an animal among camels, cattle, sheep, or goats which is closest in shape to the killed animal. Hence, if one kills an ostrich, one pays a camel, because the camel is more similar in form to it than the other aforementioned animals. The one who kills a hyena pays a sheep. Similarly, the expiation of killing a deer is a goat.

If the killed animal does not have a clear similarity to any one of these types: camel, cattle, sheep or goat, then the person goes back to what the Prophet ﷺ said about this case. If there is no *hadith* about it, then the person goes back to what the Companions said. If they did not mention this case, then one goes back to the scholars who are allowed to make *ijtihad*. For example, the pilgrim who kills a pigeon has to pay a sheep. This is an example of an animal which does not have a clear similarity to any one of these types: camel, cattle, sheep, or goat. However, this was the practice of the Companions.

It is permissible, but disliked, for the pilgrim to kill lice. If a louse is killed, it is recommended to pay charity, even if it is one bite of food.

It is neither *sunnah* nor disliked to kill an animal which harms and benefits, such as the leopard. As for the animal that has no apparent benefit and does not harm, like the crab, it is disliked to kill it.

It is prohibted to eat frogs, snails, and the small animals that live in

202

and out of the water.

7. In the case of a man: to cover the head or wear clothes that are sewn, felted, or the like, to surround the body;

Explanation: The seventh prohibition is for the man who is in the state of *Ihram* to cover part or all of his head with anything that is considered by the norm a headgear (e.g., a *qalansuwah*). Hence, it is not forbidden for one to place his own hand over his head, nor to put a thin thread on top of his head because both the hand and the thin thread are not considered by the norm as head covers. Also, the male pilgrim is forbidden to wear clothes that are meant to surround the body, either via sewing or felting. Rather, he covers his body by using a wrap around it, such as an *izar* (which is not sewn to surround the body). However, it permissible for him to wear a belt or tie a rope to hold his *izar* up and to keep his money.

Felting[52] refers to compressing wool until it becomes compact (because of pressing). Once he becomes in the state of *Ihram*, the male pilgrim is forbidden to wear a material that surrounds his body via felting. Hence, wearing a felted or sewn shirt or a *qamis*, whether long or short, is prohibited.

It is permissible for a male pilgrim to wear a ring and to wrap the turban around his waist without tying it. Also, it is permissible for him to put his shoes in a bag with a handle and carry it on his shoulders or in the same way of carrying the sword.

It is not permissible for the male pilgrim to wear what surronds his body by snaps or safety pin. It is not permissible for him also to put the towel on his head to dry his head in a way that the towel is considered to cover his head. It is permissible for him to hold its edge and use it to dry his head without covering it. However, it is not permissible for him to cover his head with a blanket or the like when he sleeps.

Both *al-Bukhariyy* and *Muslim* narrated that the Prophet ﷺ prohibited the pilgrim to wear a *qamis*, a turban, burnous (hooded cloak), and shoes. Exempted is the one who does not find slippers to wear. Then he wears shoes cutting them from below the ankles.

---

[52] Felting is the practice or process of making felt, which is a fabric of matted, compressed animal fibers, such as wool or fur, sometimes mixed with vegetable or synthetic fibers.

8. In the case of a woman: to cover the face and to wear gloves.

Explanation: It is forbidden for a woman in the state of *Ihram* to cover her face with a material that touches her face. However, such a woman is permitted to wear her veil as long as she prevents it from touching her face, similar to what the wives of the Prophet ﷺ used to do.

If the cover touches her face unintentionally, she has to remove it immediately. If she ignores to do that, she is sinful and an expiation is due on her, provided she knows that it is not permissible for the female pilgrim to cover her face. If she is ignorant of it, she is not sinful and the expiation is not due on her.

Similarly, it is forbidden for the woman in *Ihram* to wear gloves, even one. However, it is not forbidden for her to cover her hands with her long sleeves or with a cloth tied around her hands. The prohibition for the woman during the state of *Ihram* to cover her face in that manner tells us that the face of the woman is not an unlawful nakedness (^awrah), and that she is allowed to be in public while her face is uncovered.

Some people say that it is forbidden for the woman to go out uncovering her face. This is a nonsensical exaggeration. They deem as obligatory a matter that *Allah* did not make obligatory. In refutation, we say: It is confirmed that a beautiful, young woman came to the Prophet ﷺ during *Hajj* to ask him about a case pertaining to Pilgrimage. Her face was uncovered. *Al-Fadl*, the cousin of the Prophet, looked lustfully at the woman and she looked lustfully back at him. The Prophet turned the face of his cousin to the other side, without telling her to cover her face. This is a *Sahih hadith* related by al-Bukhariyy. Consequently, had the face of the woman been an ^awrah as some people claim, or had it been obligatory on the beautiful woman to cover her face, the Prophet would have ordered that woman to cover her face.

Some -out of their ignorance- said this incident took place before the verse of the *hijab* was revealed making it obligatory on the woman to cover. This is totally untrue, because this incident occurred during the last *Hajj* the Prophet ﷺ performed; and this was about five years after the revelation of the verse of the *hijab*.

Some other people say that this case is specific to *Hajj*. They mean that the Prophet did not order that woman to cover her face because it is prohibited for the woman to cover her face during *Hajj*. Their statement is invalid because the Prophet could have ordered the woman to cover her face using an object which prevents the cover from touching her face, just as he ordered his wives to do. The Prophet ﷺ had ordered his wives to cover their faces in that manner, because it was an obligation on them in particular to cover their faces always before marriageable men. Being in the state of *Ihram* did not prevent them from covering their faces in the aforementioned explained manner. So, had it been an obligation upon the woman to cover her face before marriageable men, the Prophet ﷺ would have ordered the aforementioned woman to cover her face even if she was in *Hajj*, in the same way his wives used to do. Since women -other than the wives of the Prophet- are not obligated to cover their faces when they go out, the Prophet ﷺ did not do it.

Qadi ^Iyad (a famous *Malikiyy* scholar) said that by consensus the woman is allowed to uncover her face, and it is an obligation on the men to lower their gazes (that is, to abstain from looking in a forbidden way).

Similarly, the *Shafi^iyy* scholar *Ibn Hajar al-Haytamiyy* relayed the consensus upon this case. He mentioned it in his commentary on *an-Nawawiyy*'s book *al-Idah*. In the same book, he also relayed the ruling that it is disliked for women to wear tight clothes that cover their unlawful nakedness. However, it is not sinful as long as the clothes cover their ^awrah. The Eygptian *Malikiyy* mufti *Muhammad ^Illaysh* mentioned it in his explanation of *Khalil*'s Summary. The same judgement is also mentioned in the explanation of the *Malikiyy* scholar *al-Hattab* and in other *Shafi^iyy* and *Hambaliyy* books. Some late *Hanafiyys* said that neither men nor women are permitted to wear tight clothes that show the contours of the body parts. Their saying is not supported by any proper proof from the *Qur'an, Sunnah, or the sayings of Imam Abu Hanifah* or his *mujtahid* students.

Note that it is not permissible for the female pilgrim to put a mask that covers her mouth and nose. However, it is permissible for the male pilgrim to wear it. It is not prohibited for the female pilgrim to put her hand in her pocket to take money out. Similarly, it is not

205

prohibited for her to put her hand on her face. However, it is prohibited for her to cover her face with the towel when she dries it. However, she may take the edge of the towel with her hand and dry her face with it. Similarly, it is prohibited for her to cover her face with a blanket or the like when she sleeps.

It is not permissible for her to wrap a wide piece of material around her forehead or to cover her face with her dress when she wears it. If she does that intentionally, an expiation is due on her. She should hold her dress from its edges when she wears it until it passes her face without covering it in the prohibited way.

The one who does any of these unlawful matters has sinned. An expiation (*fidyah*) is obligatory for committing these matters [with the exception of conducting marriage and looking lustfully].

Explanation: The expiation is to slaughter a sheep, to give three sa^s to six poor people, or to fast three days. One has the choice between these three matters. As to the expiation of hunting an Islamically edible, wild animal one pays what is similar in form among the camels, cattle, sheep and goats. Then one has the choice between slaughtering it and distributing it to the poor people in the vicinity of *al-Haram*, or to feed them wheat equivalent in value to that animal. As a third choice, one evaluates this food, and for every *mudd*, one fasts one day.

For example, the pilgrim who kills an ostrich, either slaughters a camel and distributes that to the poor people in the vicinity of the *Haram*, or if unable assesses the value of that camel in terms of wheat, and distributes that equivalent amount to the poor people, or else fasts a day for every *mudd* of that quantity. Hence, if the value of the camel to be slaughtered is 2 000 *mudds*, one fasts 2 000 (consecutive or discontinuous) days.

Moreover, in the case of sexual intercourse, one's *Hajj* is invalidated, and one is obligated to complete this invalidated *Hajj* and re-perform it immediately, i.e., the one who invalidates one's *Hajj* by performing sexual intercourse continues with *Hajj*, does not interrupt it, then makes it up in the coming year [if one is able].

Explanation: The first *tahallul* occurs when the pilgrim does two out of three things: performing the obligatory *tawaf*, trimming or shaving the hair, and throwing the pebbles at Jamratul-ˆaqabah. The pilgrim who performs sexual intercourse before the first tahallul, invalidates one's Hajj. Although one's Hajj is invalidated, still one has to continue with it and, if able, make it up immediately in the following year. Moreover, one has to pay an expiation (kaffarah). The kaffarah is a camel. If one cannot find one, then one pays a cow, or else one pays seven (7) sheep. If unable to find sheep, one assesses the value of the camel in wheat and distributes the assessed quantity to the poor people in the vicinity of al-Haram, and if not able to do so, then one fasts one day for each mudd of that quantity.

However, if one had the sexual intercourse after the first but before the second tahallul, one's Hajj is not invalidated. However, one is sinful, and has to pay an expiation identical to that of committing the inviting actions of sexual intercourse, namely, a sheep, three saˆs to six poor people, or fast three days.

After the first tahallul, all the eight prohibited matters become permissible, except for those pertaining to women, that is, conducting marriage, performing sexual intercourse, and committing the inviting actions for sexual intercourse. These three matters remain prohibited until finishing one's Hajj.

The kaffarah (expiation) is due on the pilgrim each time Hajj is invalidated by sexual intercourse. This means if one invalidates one's Hajj by sexual intercourse the first year, one has to make it up and pay the expiation. If in the following year while making it up one invalidates it again by sexual intercourse, a new expiation is also due. Moreover, one has to make it up. Hence, if this process was repeated ten times, one has to pay ten expiations and one still has to make up Hajj (once).

Chapter 33
Requisites of Pilgrimage

It is a requisite (*wajib*) for the one who has intended to enter into the actions of Pilgrimage (*Hajj* or *^Umrah*):

Explanation: After mentioning the integrals of *Hajj*, the author started talking about the requisites (*wajibs*) of Pilgrimage. A requisite (*wajib*) in this context is an obligatory action that, when left out, can be compensated by slaughtering. Leaving it out does not invalidate *Hajj*. However, one is sinful.

1. **To have the intention of *Ihram* before crossing the site prescribed for it (*miqat*). The *miqat* is the place which the Messenger of *Allah* specified as the starting site of the intention of *Ihram*, such as the land called *Dhul-Hulayfah*, for the people of *al-Madinah* and those who take the same route to *Makkah*;**

Explanation: Among those obligations is that the person must have the intention of *Ihram* before crossing the *miqat*. The *miqat*s are specific places that the Prophet ﷺ designated for the people not to cross without having the intention of *Ihram* (when coming to Pilgrimage).

The *miqat* of the inhabitants of *Madinah* and the pilgrims who pass by this holy city in their way to *Makkah* is *Dhul-Hulayfah*. Today it is also known as *Abar ^Aliyy*.

The *miqat* of the pilgrims coming from *Sham*, Egypt, and the rest of North Africa is *al-Juhfah*, or *Rabigh*.

The *miqat* of Yemen's people is Yalamlam.

The *miqat* for the people of Iraq is called *Dhatu ^Irq*.

The *miqat* of the people of *Najd* and those who go by their route is *Qarnuth-Tha^alib*.

Hence, the one who makes the intention of entering into the actions of *Hajj* after crossing the *miqat* is sinful and has to pay the expiation. On the other hand, if one returns to the *miqat* before one is involved in any of the acts of *Hajj*, no expiation is due. If after one crosses the *miqat* with the intention, for example, to visit a friend or a relative in *Makkah*, one changes the intention to make Pilgrimage, one's *miqat* becomes one's spot. One does not have to go back to the *miqat* which one crossed.

Whoever lives in *Makkah* makes the intention of *Hajj* while in *Makkah*. As for the ^*Umrah*, although valid, it is not permissible for the resident of *Makkah* to make the intention from within *Makkah*. Rather one has to go outside the borders of the *Haram*, make the intention of ^*Umrah* thereat, then proceed with the acts of ^*Umrah*. The best places for it are *al-Ji^ranah*, then *at-Tan^im*, then *al-Hudybiyyah*. If one makes the intention of ^*Umrah* from within *Makkah* an expiation is due, unless one goes outside the borders of *Makkah* before getting involved in any of the acts of ^*Umrah*.

Note: There is a specific time to make the intention of *Hajj* which are (the months of) *Shawwal*, *Dhul-Qa^dah* and the first ten days of *Dhul-Hijjah* ending with the dawn of the ^*Id* day. Making the intention of *Hajj* in other than this time is not valid. One becomes automatically in the state of *Ihram* for ^*Umrah*.

As for the ^*Umrah*, one may make its intention at any time of the year, unless one is still involved in another ^*Umrah*, i.e., before finishing it. Similarly, one cannot make the intention of ^*Umrah* if one is already involved in *Hajj* and did not yet finish it by leaving *Mina* properly.

2. To stay at night in *Muzdalifah*

Explanation: This means that one has to be present -standing, sitting, or sleeping- in *Muzdalifah* after midnight of the ^*Id*'s eve, even for a moment. People with certain excuses, such as those who provide water to the pilgrims and shepherds who are taking care of the flock are not obligated to stay at night in *Muzdalifah*. According to a second saying, staying in *Muzdalifah* is a recommended matter, but not a requisite. Accordingly, one is not sinful and does not have to pay the expiation for avoiding it.

and *Mina* during *Hajj*. This is according to one saying of *ash-Shafi^iyy*. However, according to another saying of *ash-Shafi^iyy* neither is a requisite;

Explanation: The pilgrim is obligated to spend in *Mina* most of the eve of each day of *Tashriq*. That is, one spends in *Mina* most of the eve of the first day of *Tashriq* and most of the eve of the second day of

Tashriq, if one leaves Mina before the sunset of the second day. If one does not, one has to stay most of the eve of the third day in Mina. Like in the case of staying in Muzdalifah, the excused people are not obligated to stay in Mina during the aforementioned days. This staying at night in Mina is a recommended matter (sunnah) and not a requisite according to another saying of Imam ash-Shafi^iyy. Based on this second saying, one is not sinful and is not required to pay the expiation for avoiding it.

3. **To throw pebbles at the station of Jamrat-ul-^Aqabah on the Day of the Feast of Ad-ha (^Id-ul-'Ad-ha);**

Explanation: Among the requisites of Hajj is to throw seven pebbles at Jamarat-ul-^Aqabah on the Day of ^Id. This is the closest among the three stations of throwing the pebbles (jamrahs) to Makkah. The time for throwing the pebbles starts after midnight of the ^Id's eve and extends until the sunset of the last day of Tashriq.

4. **To throw pebbles at the three stations of jamrahs during the days of Tashriq;**

Explanation: One is obligated to throw pebbles at the three stations every day of Tashriq (those are the days that the pilgrim has to spend the eve of which in Mina). At each station, one throws seven (7) pebbles. The pilgrim starts with the one which is closest to the Khayf mosque (farthest from Makkah), then moves on to the middle one, and then to the closest one to Makkah (Jamrat-ul-^Aqabah). The pilgrim must on one's own throw the pebbles one by one. Throwing all the pebbles at once is counted as throwing one pebble.

It is narrated that the Devil appeared to Prophet Ibrahim عليه السلام to dissuade him from obeying Allah. Prophet Ibrahim عليه السلام responded by throwing pebbles at him to humiliate him. The followers of Prophet Muhammad ﷺ are ordered to throw the pebbles at the same locations where the Devil appeared to Prophet Ibrahim to show that one must not follow the Devil and to follow the Sunnah of Prophet Ibrahim in disobeying the Devil and humiliating him. As if the one who throws the pebbles says to the Devil: "If you appear to me like you appeared to Prophet Ibrahim, I will throw the pebbles at you and humiliate you just like Prophet Ibrahim did." Those locations are not where the Devil lives or stays as some ignorant people think.

For the validity of throwing the pebbles, the following conditions must be satisfied:

1. One starts throwing at the station closest to the *Khayf* mosque, then the middle one, then ends at the ^*Aqabah*. This order is followed on every day of *Tashriq*.

2. One has to throw pebbles (stones), even if precious like ruby.

3. The act has to be considered throwing. Hence, placing pebbles at the different stations is invalid.

4. While able, one has to throw the pebbles with the hand, not with the foot or an instrument.

5. One's intention must be for ritual throwing. Hence, throwing for practice is not valid.

6. One's intention must be aimed at hitting the designated stations (*jamrahs*). Therefore, throwing pebbles at snakes is invalid. If pebbles hit the proper station then roll out of it, or enroute hit a person or an animal then fall inside the proper station, the throwing is valid.

If one doubts whether or not the pebble went inside the station one discounts it and throws another one making sure that it goes inside the station.

As long as one is able to throw the pebbles without any fear on one's safety, one is not permitted to authorize another to throw them on one's behalf. The authorized person must throw the pebbles for oneself before throwing them on behalf of the excused person. This means that one throws the pebbles at the first station for oneself then throws them on behalf of the authorizing person. Then one moves to the second station and throws for oneself then for the authorizing person. Then one moves to the third station and throws for oneself then on behalf of the authorizing person.

Leaving out throwing all the pebbles requires one expiation only.

It is *sunnah* to throw the pebbles after the sun rises as high as a spear and to say *Allahu akbar* after throwing each pebble.

5. **To perform the farewell circumambulation before leaving *Makkah* (*tawaf-ul-wada*^) according to a saying in the school (*madhhab*) of ash-Shafi^*iyy.**

Explanation: After the pilgrim leaves *Mina*, whether on the

211

second day of *Tashriq* before sunset, or on the third day of *Tashriq*, one has to perform *tawaf-ul-wada^* (circle the *Ka^bah* seven times) before travelling a shortening distance, or returning to one's own hometown. According to another saying within the school, this *tawaf* is a recommended matter (*sunnah*), not a requisite.

In summary, there are five matters that are requisites (*wajibs*) in *Hajj*. If one leaves out any of them, one's *Hajj* is not invalidated. However, one has to pay the expiation. As the author said:

The one who does not fulfill these five (5) matters does not invalidate one's _Hajj_, although one is sinful and must fulfill an expiation (*fidyah*). This is different from the one who does not perform an integral. If one leaves out an integral of _Hajj_, then one's _Hajj_ is not valid. Slaughtering an animal will not compensate for it.

Explanation: The one who leaves out one of the requisites (*wajibs*) of *Hajj* has to pay the expiation (*fidyah*), i.e., to slaughter a sheep. If one is unable, one fasts ten (10) days, three (3) days at *Hajj* and seven (7) upon returning home.

It is unlawful for one, whether or not one is in a state of _Ihram_, to hunt the animals of _Makkah_ and _al-Madinah_, or to cut or pick their plants. If this is done in _Makkah_, then the obligation of fulfilling the expiation (*fidyah*) is added. There is no expiation (*fidyah*) due for hunting the animals or cutting the plants in _al-Madinah_, i.e., the area between Mount ^Ayr and Mount Thawr.

Explanation: Among the rules that are specific to both *Harams* of *Makkah* and *Madinah*, is that one is neither allowed to cut down their trees or pick their plants nor to hunt their animals. The one who hunts in *Madinah* or picks or cuts the plants of *Madinah* is sinful, but is not obligated to pay an expiation. The valley of *Wajj*, in *Ta'if*, has the same judgments as *Madinah* as was narrated from the Prophet ﷺ.

As to *Makkah*, the one who hunts its animals or cuts or picks its plants is sinful. Moreover, one has to pay the expiation. The expiation is to slaughter an animal that resembles the hunted animal among camels, cattle, sheep, or goat. One slaughters it within the borders of *Makkah*'s *Haram*, and distributes it to the poor people there, whether or not they are residents of *Makkah*. It is not valid to give it to those beyond *Makkah*'s *Haram*.

As for *Makkah*'s plants, if one cuts a large tree, one pays a camel. If one cuts a small tree, about one-seventh of what is considered a large one, one pays a sheep. For smaller plants, one pays its value.

Beneficial Note: Whoever wants to make Pilgrimage and fears that something may prevent him from it, let him say in the intention: "I now intend to be in the state of *Hajj*. If anything, such as an enemy, prevents me from performing it, I go out of the state of *Ihram* thereat." In such a case, one exits the state of *Ihram* by shaving the head or trimming the hair and slaughtering. If one is unable to slaughter, one distributes the common staple food having the same value of the animal that one is unable to slaughter. If one is unable to distribute the staple food, then one fasts a number of days equal to the number of *mudd*s of that food.

The pilgrim who misses being at ˆ*Arafah* at the proper time goes out of the state of *Ihram* for *Hajj* by doing the actions of ˆ*Umrah* and slaughtering. One is obligated to make up this missed *Hajj*.

Note: It is recommended (*sunnah*) for the pilgrim to drink from *Zamzam* water until full while facing the *Qiblah*. Moreover, it is recommended to say:

اللَّهُمَّ إِنَّهُ بَلَغَنِى أَنَّ نَبِيَّكَ قَالَ: «ماءُ زَمْزَمَ لِمَا شُرِبَ لَهُ». وإِنّى أَشْرَبُه مُسْتَشْفِيًا بِهِ. فَاشْفِنِى وَاغْفِرْ لِى. اللهمَّ إِنّى أَسْأَلُكَ عِلْمًا نافِعًا ورِزْقًا واسِعًا وشِفاءً مِن كُلّ داءٍ.

It means: "O *Allah*, it reached me that your Prophet ﷺ said: 'Zamzam water is useful for whatever purpose it is drunk.' I now drink it seeking cure by it. So, O *Allah*, cure me and forgive me. O *Allah*, I ask you beneficial knowledge, wide sustenance, and cure from all afflictions." Similar supplications can be made also.

213

Visiting the Grave of the Prophet ﷺ

It is suitable to end the chapters of *Hajj* by addressing the rewardability of visiting the grave of the Messenger of *Allah* ﷺ.

Visiting his grave is by consensus a *sunnah*; some of the scholars even said it is an obligation (*wajib*). This is due to several religious proofs. One of them is the *hadith*:

$$\text{مَنْ زَارَ قَبْرِى وَجَبَتْ لَهُ شَفَاعَتِى}$$

It means: "The one who visits my grave has earned my intercession." This *hadith* is narrated by *ad-Daraqutniyy* and classified as "*hasan* for other than itself" (*hasan lighayrih*).

The false claim of *Ibn Taymiyah* that it is forbidden for one to travel with the purpose of visiting the grave of the Prophet, is a matter that does not comply with the rules of the Religion. *Ibn Taymiyah* misinterpreted the *hadith* of the Prophet ﷺ, narrated by *al-Bukhariyy*:

$$\text{«لا تُشَدُّ الرّحَالُ إلاَّ إلى ثلاثةِ مَساجِدَ: المَسجِدِ الحَرامِ،}$$
$$\text{والمَسجِدِ الأَقْصَى، وَمَسجِدِى هذَا»}$$

Due to his ill understanding of this *hadith*, *Ibn Taymiyah* claimed that it means that one is not allowed to travel except to those three mosques: The *Haram* Mosque (in *Makkah*), the *Aqsa* Mosque (in Jerusalem), and the Prophet's Mosque (in *Madinah*). Based on that, he ruled that it is forbidden for one to travel to visit the grave of the Prophet ﷺ. *Ibn Taymiyah*'s claim breached the consensus of all the scholars who preceded him.

The correct meaning of the *hadith* is: "One ought not travel to a mosque with the purpose of praying in it, except if one was travelling to one of these three mosques: The *Haram* Mosque (in *Makkah*), the *Aqsa* Mosque (in Jerusalem), and the Prophet's Mosque (in *Madinah*)." This is so because the reward of praying is multiplied in these three mosques compared to the reward of praying in other mosques. This is a merit specific for those three mosques and not for any other mosque.

What sheds clear light on the meaning of the *hadith* is another narration of the same *hadith* that explains the aforementioned one. *Imam Ahmad* narrated that the Prophet ﷺ explicitly said:

«لا يَنبَغِي لِلْمَطِيِّ أَن تُعْمَلَ إِلَى مَسْجِدٍ تُبْتَغَى فِيهِ الصَّلاةُ غَيرِ المَسجِدِ الحَرامِ وَالمَسجِدِ الأَقْصَى وَمَسجِدِي» .

It means: "One should not drive the animals in travelling towards a mosque with the purpose of praying in it, with the exception of the three mosques, The *Haram* Mosque (in *Makkah*), the *Aqsa* Mosque (in Jerusalem), and the Prophet's Mosque (in *Madinah*). This narration is very explicit in clarifying the meaning of the aforementioned *hadith*, and it is in compliance with the consensus of the nation, contrary to the false claim of *Ibn Taymiyah*.

Moreover the Prophet, *sallallahu ^alayhi wa sallam*, said:

«لَيَهْبِطَنَّ عِيسَى ابنُ مَريمَ حَكَمًا مُقْسِطًا، ولَيَسلُكَنَّ فَجًّا حَاجًّا أو مُعتَمِرًا، وَلَيَأتِيَنَّ قَبرِي حتَّى يُسَلِّمَ عَلَيَّ، وَلأَرُدَّنَّ عليه» ، ورواه ابن عساكر بلفظ: «وَلَيَسلُكَنَّ فَجَّ الرَّوْحَاءِ» .

It means: "Prophet *^Isa* (Jesus) shall come down from the (second) heaven to Earth and rule Earth justly. Moreover, he will take a route between two mountains to make *Hajj* or *^Umrah* and come to my grave. He will say: *As-Salamu ^alaykum* to me and I will respond to him." This *hadith* is narrrated by *al-Hakim* and Ibn *^Asakir*. Al-Hakim, *hafidh adh-Dhahabiyy*, and others classified it as a *sahih hadith*. This *hadith* proves that traveling to visit the grave of the Prophet, *sallallahu ^alayhi wa sallam*, is not sinful. On the contrary, this is what Prophet *^Isa* will do. By this, it is very clear that no weight should be given to the deviated claim of *Ibn Taymiyah*.

Note: When one gets into the Prophet's Mosque, one makes two optional *rak^ahs* to salute the Mosque. Then, one stands politely facing the grave of the Prophet about four (4) cubits away from the wall, lowering one's gaze and filling one's heart with love and respect for the Prophet ﷺ. Then, one says with a medium voice: *As-Salamu ^alayka ya Rasulallah; as-salamu ^alayka ya Nabiyyallah*, and the like.

215

Then, one makes *as-salah* ^*alan-Nabiyy*. Afterwards, one goes about one cubit to the right and says *as-salamu* ^*alayka ya Aba Bakrinis-Siddiq*, then one more cubit to the right and says *as-salamu* ^*alayka ya* ^*Umaral-Faruq*. Then one goes to where one first stood and makes *du*^*a'* asking *Allah* by the Prophet ﷺ. One faces the *Qiblah* and makes *du*^*a'* for oneself and for whomever one wishes. If anyone requested of one to convey one's *salam* to the Prophet ﷺ, one says: O Prophet of *Allah*, so and so gives you *salam*.

The Honorable Ka^bah
(The Qiblah of Muslims)

1. The Black Stone
2. The Door of the Ka^bah
3. The Mizab (Spout)
4. Ash-Shadharwan
5. The Hijr of Isma^il
6. The Multazam
7. Maqam Ibrahim
8. Ar-Ruknul-Yamaniyy
9. Ar-Ruknul-Yamaniyy
10. Ar-Ruknush-Shamiyy
11. Ar-Ruknush-Shamiyy
12. The Cover of the Ka^bah

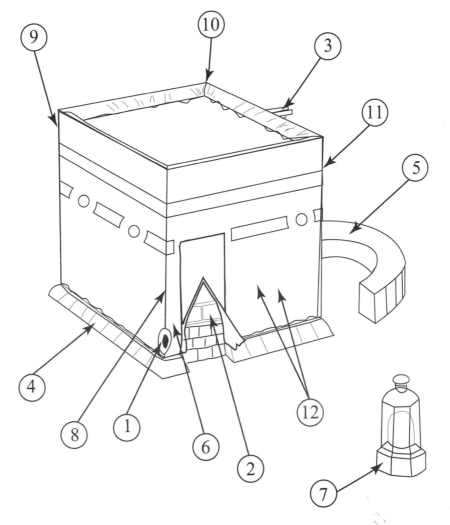

TRANSACTIONS, MARRIAGE, AND DEALING CONTRACTS

Chapter 34
Knowledge Before Action

Allah commanded us with matters, and we must comply with what He commanded. Hence, every accountable Muslim has the obligation not to engage in anything until one knows what Allah ordained as lawful or unlawful about it. Allah made the selling (bay^) lawful and the usurious gain (riba) unlawful. Only the selling which satisfies the proper integrals and conditions is lawful, and not any selling per se.

Explanation: One has to obey the Creator by following His orders and refraining from what He prohibited, because Allah deserves to be obeyed, regardless of whether or not one knows the wisdom. Hence, we have to be obedient to Allah by fulfilling the obligations and refraining from the prohibitions in all the aspects of our lives, whether or not we perceive the wisdom behind what Allah ordered us to do. This is a test for the slaves. The obedient ones who rush to obey Allah in every thing become known and those who do not also become known.

In the Arabic language, "bay^" refers to exchanging one matter for another. Religiously, it refers to the exchanging of an article for another of certain value with specific conditions. In verse 275, Suratul-Baqarah, Allah said:

$$ ﴿وَأَحَلَّ ٱللَّهُ ٱلْبَيْعَ وَحَرَّمَ ٱلرِّبَوٰاْ ۝﴾ $$

It means: «Allah made al-bay^ (the selling that complies with the religious rules) lawful and the usurious gain unlawful.» The lawful selling is restricted to a specific selling, namely, one that satisfies the conditions and integrals stated in the religious texts.

Among the conditions of the valid selling is for both the money and the article to be pure (tahir) and for the sold article to be present (unless it falls under the contract of salam, the rules of which are clarified in more advanced religious books). Thus, it is invalid to sell an apartment that is not built yet, because the sold article in this case does not exist yet.

Hence, one must learn the aforementioned if one wants to sell or buy or else one will consume the usurious gain (riba), whether or not one wants to do so.

221

The Messenger of *Allah, sallallahu ^alayhi wa sallam,* said: «The truthful tradesperson shall be assembled on the Resurrection Day with the prophets, the highly-ranked righteous Muslims (*siddiqs*), and martyrs.» This is because of what this person faces, when struggling with oneself and one's desires, in subduing one's self to conduct contracts according to the Islamic law. The threat of *Allah* to punish those who violate His Laws is known.

Explanation: Since the permissible selling is the one that satisfies the conditions and integrals stated in the laws of the religion, one has to learn these conditions and integrals before engaging in such transactions. If one neglects that, then one may commit sins, whether or not one wants to do so. Due to the great importance of this matter, our master ^Umar, may *Allah* raise his rank, used to pass in the market place and test the knowledge of the traders therein. If he found someone with insufficient knowledge to transact in the market place he would pull him out of the market place and tell him to learn. ^Umar used to say: "Let the one who did not learn how to buy and sell not transact in our market place."

The person who acquires the knowledge of these rules and implements them, trading in an honest way and avoiding the forbidden transactions, will be assembled on the Resurrection Day with the prophets, the highly-ranked Muslims, and the martyrs. This is the meaning of the *hadith,* mentioned above in the text, narrated by *at-Tirmidhiyy.* This *hadith* carries the good tidings for the honest trader that he will be saved on the Day of Judgment. On the other hand, it implies that the untrustworthy cheating trader deserves the punishment in the Hereafter. Among the prohibited actions upon buying or selling are cheating and swearing falsely.

Among the remaining contracts are:

Explanation: One must also observe the conditions and integrals of other remaining contracts. The one who wants to engage in any of these contracts must, before the engagement, learn enough of their religious rules, conditions, and integrals. Among such contracts are:

Renting articles and hiring people's services (*ijarah*),

Explanation: *Ijarah* is giving the ownership of a permissible benefit for a certain payment or fee. Hence, one cannot rent something in which there is no benefit. Similarly, one is not entitled to hire someone for a service that has no benefit. Consequently, the singers do not own the money they receive for their singing. In this context, singing is not considered religiously of hirable benefit.

Hiring is engaging the services of someone for a fee. Payment is received either for completing a specified job or for spending a certain time carrying out a task. For instance, one hires the services of a worker to plow one's field, by defining the area of the land to be plowed for a certain sum of money. In this case, no limitation is placed on the amount of time needed for the task. The other way is to hire the worker on a rate basis, such as some dollars per hour, week, or month. In this case, the owner of the field does not specify for the worker which part of the field to be finished hourly, weekly, or monthly. If the owner specifies in the contract the two matters: the time to finish the job and the amount of work that has to be done during that time, this invalidates the contract. An example of an invalid hiring contract is for the owner of the field to say to the worker: I now hire you to plow these two acres of my field in three days for $500.00.

trading with another person's money for profit sharing (qirad),

Explanation: Qirad is for one to give a person a certain amount of money authorizing him to trade with it on one's behalf, provided they shared the profit between them proportionately. For the validity of this contract, the used money must be either gold or silver. Hence, authorizing a person to trade with one's own paper or copper money and sharing equally the profits is invalid. This is the Judgment in the Shafi^iyy school and several other schools. However, according to some top scholars (mujtahids) among the salaf, such a contract is permissible.

putting up a collateral (rahn),

Explanation: Putting up a collateral means to put an entity that has a monetary value against a debt. When the borrower cannot pay the debt, the lender may use the collateral to collect the debt. Hence, once the owner of something places it as a collateral against a debt, one is no longer entitled to sell that entity or to give it away until one pays the debt. Nevertheless, one can use that entity for one's own benefits or lend it to others.

commissioning a person to act on one's behalf (_wakalah_),

Explanation: _Wakalah_ is commissioning a person to carry out a task (by proxy). The _wakalah_ cannot be an absolute, general authorization; the authority given must be specific in one or more aspects. Hence, it is invalid for one to authorize another person by telling him, 'I authorize you to manage all my affairs.' However, it is valid to say to him, 'I authorize you to sell my belongings.'

entrusting a person with property for safekeeping (_wadiˆah_),

Explanation: _Wadiˆah_ is what one deposits with another for safekeeping. The _wadiˆah_ must have a religiously recognized benefit. Hence, one cannot put a forbidden musical instrument with someone for safekeeping.

lending an article for use (ˆ_ariyyah_),

Explanation: ˆ_Ariyyah_ refers to an article lent to another person permitting him to use and benefit from it for free, as long as the physical borrowed article is not consumed totally through usage. It is permissible for the borrower to assign someone to help him get the benefit from the borrowed article. If someone borrows a car, one is permitted to assign a person to drive it for the borrower's benefit.

partnership (_sharikah_),

Explanation: The partnership between two or more people is a contract that establishes the right for two or more partners in an article, without specifying the part of the article that each person owns. For instance, if three people enter into partnership of owning a piece of land, each one of them has ownership in that land. However, it is not specified, for example, that the first one has the northwestern corner of that land, the second one has the southeastern corner, and the third the rest. Rather, all three have the ownership of that land in a collective way, without specifying the ownership of any partner in the land.

According to _Imam ash-Shafiˆiyy_, the correct partnership constitutes mixing two or more amounts of money (belongings) owned by two or more people in a manner that the original ownership is no longer identifiable. These amounts have to be of the same kind, i.e., gold mixed with gold, silver with silver, wheat with wheat, barley with barley, etc., measured by volume or weight, and with well specified characteristics.

So, if one wants to enter into partnership with another person to purchase a house, each one of them brings a certain amount of golden *dinars*, for example. Then, they mix the two amounts, and purchase the house with the mixed money. Each one of them has a share in this house equivalent to the share of his money in the mixture. Similarly, people can enter into partnership by mixing two or more amounts of wheat, barley, currency, or the like, as long as the mixture is composed of quantities that are from the same kind and well determined by measure and characteristic.

Other kinds of partnership that are not based on the mixing of two or more amounts of money are not valid. For example, it is an invalid partnership for the owner of a car to authorize another person to drive his car around as a taxi, with the condition of sharing the generated money proportionately. This contract is based on contributing money from one side and labor from the other. It is not based on mixing two capitals of the same kind, which are well defined in measure and characteristics.

and tending (watering, weeding, etc.) grape vines or palm trees for a part of the crop (*musaqah*).

Explanation: The *musaqah* is a contract established between the owner of an orchard and someone to tend the trees for a specific share of the fruits. Tending includes watering, weeding, picking the fruits and other pertinent work. In the *Shafi^iyy* school, this contract is valid only if it is about grape vines or palm trees. It is not valid concerning other types of trees, like apples and oranges.

On the other hand, the *muzara^ah* is invalid. It is a contract in which the landlord provides the seeds for the other party who tends them for a proprotion of the crop. However, the *muzara^ah* becomes valid if it is made a subcontract of a valid contract of *musaqah*. In this case, the contract is valid as long as it is difficult to water the grape vines or palm trees separately from the other plants.

One must also observe their conditions and integrals.

Explanation: One must observe the conditions and integrals of each transaction one conducts. To be able to do so, one needs to learn enough about it before being involved in it.

Chapter 35
Marriage Contract

One must be exceptionally cautious in verifying the conditions and integrals of the marriage contract for fear of what will result if any of these are not satisfied.

Explanation: Knowing the rules of the marriage contract is more important than knowing the rules of many other contracts. The one who does not learn the rules of marriage may think an invalid marriage contract to be a valid one, which consequently generates much harm. For example, sexual intercourse becomes adultery or fornication, and the resulting children are unlawful. Hence, the marriage contract deserves more attention.

Protecting the lineage (*nasab*) is one of the five general rules that were revealed to all the messengers. Abstaining from having prohibited sexual relations (which may result in having unlawful children) is the way to protect the lineage. These five general rules are:

1. Preserving life

2. Preserving property

3. Preserving sanity

4. Preserving lineage

5. Preserving honor (^*ird*).

There are conditions and integrals for the validity of the marriage contract. The integrals are five: a guardian (*waliyy*), two witnesses, a groom, a bride, and the contract statement. According to the school of *Imam ash-Shafi^iyy*, a woman cannot give herself in marriage. Her guardian (*waliyy*) does it. Moreover, the marriage is invalid without the presence of two upright (^*adl*) Muslim male witnesses. A statement must be uttered that establishes the contract instantaneously. In the presence of the two witnesses, the *waliyy* may say to the man, 'I now give you my daughter in marriage', or 'I now marry you my daughter', or a similar statement. The man responds by saying, 'I now accept marrying her' or any similar statement signifying his accepting to marry the woman.

It is a condition that the marriage contract is not limited to a certain period of time. So, if the *waliyy* tells the man, 'I now give you my daughter in marriage for a year', this invalidates the contract. However, if the man intends to end the marriage after a year, but he does not establish it as part of the contract, the contract is valid.

Once the valid marriage contract is conducted, a *mahr* is involved, whether or not it was mentioned during the contract. However, it is a *sunnah* to mention it. A "*mahr*" is something that the husband is obligated to give to the wife. If it was specified in the contract (i.e., uttered within the marriage contract), then the mentioned amount should be confirmed as her *mahr*. However, if it was not mentioned during the contract, then she should be entitled a *mahr* equivalent to what is paid usually to her female paternal relatives, and if not applicable other female relatives and peers, taking in consideration her age, beauty, education, etc.

It is also important to learn the rules of divorce. Many people divorce their wives, without knowing that they have done it. As a result of their ignorance, they continue to live with them in a forbidden manner.

Divorce is of two kinds: Explicit and implicit.

The explicit divorce is achieved through an explicit statement of divorce that has the sole meaning of establishing divorce. Examples are when the man tells his wife, 'I now divorce you', or if he is asked, 'do you establish divorcing your wife now?' and, to this, he answers "yes". In this case, there is no need to check one's intention.

The implicit divorce is achieved through an implicit statement with the intention of divorcing. An implicit statement of divorce bears the meaning of divorce as well as other meanings. If the intention is not of divorce, divorce is not materialized. Examples of implicit divorce statements are, when a man says to his wife, 'Start observing your ^*iddah* (post-marital waiting period)', or 'cover your ^*awrah* in my presence', or 'you are on your own', or to say after a quarrel, '*salamun ^alayki*' (I wish you safety, a statement habitually said when one departs from another person). In such instances, only if the person intends to establish the divorce, do those cases constitute cases of divorce.

Moreover, if a man divorces his wife once or twice, then he is entitled to take her back within her ˆiddah without needing a new marriage contract. However, if the ˆiddah expires, a new marriage contract is needed for them to live together. However, after a man divorces his wife three times, they cannot join again together in marriage unless-after the expiration of her divorce ˆiddah-firstly, she consummates her marriage to another man, and secondly, her divorce or widow ˆiddah from the second man expires. Statements of divorce ensue in three divorces when all (three) are uttered at once (at the same moment), unless the second and third divorce statements are uttered to emphasize the first one, then one divorce is in effect. Similarly, if the three divorce statements are uttered separately at one or more occasions, then three divorces are in effect.

The Honorable *Qur'an* referred to this by the saying of *Allah* in *Surat at-Tahrim*, ayah 6:

﴿ يَٰٓأَيُّهَا ٱلَّذِينَ ءَامَنُوا۟ قُوٓا۟ أَنفُسَكُمْ وَأَهْلِيكُمْ نَارًا وَقُودُهَا ٱلنَّاسُ وَٱلْحِجَارَةُ ۖ ﴿٦﴾ ﴾

It means: [O you, who believed, protect yourselves and your families from Hellfire which is fueled by people and stones.] ˆAta' Ibn Abi Rabah, may *Allah* raise his rank, said: "To learn how to perform the prayer and fasting, how to sell and buy, and how to marry and divorce."

Explanation: This verse entails that the one who neglects acquiring the Obligatory Knowledge of the Religion, and neglects teaching that knowledge to his family, then he has lead himself and his family to destruction. Such a person has not protected himself and his family from Hellfire. Explaining this verse, *Imam* ˆAliyy said, "Teach yourselves and your families, what is good." The *Tabiˆiyy Imam* ˆAta' Ibn Abi Rabah gave a similar statement which is mentioned in the text. He became among the most prominent followers of the Companions. He took his knowledge from ˆAbdullah Ibn Masˆud, Ibn ˆAbbas and other knowledgeable Companions of the Prophet ﷺ. He was the teacher of *Imam Abu Hanifah*. The father of ˆAta' was a slave, from Africa either Nubia or Abyssinia.

Chapter 36
Usurious Gain (*Riba*)

It is unlawful (*haram*) to do, consume, take, write down, or be a witness to usurious gain (*riba*). *Riba* comprises the following:

1. Selling gold for silver, silver for gold, gold for gold, or silver for silver—whether coined or not, made into jewelry, the ore itself, or otherwise—with the condition of postponing the payment;

2. Selling the aforementioned items with the buyer or seller leaving one another before exchanging the payments;

3. Selling gold for gold or silver for silver with inequality in weight;

4. In the case of selling foods for other foods, it is not lawful to sell one type of food for another, such as wheat for barley, except with two (2) conditions: the buyer and seller must not postpone the payment and must not leave one another before exchanging payments. In the case of similar types of food, such as wheat for wheat, one must fulfill the aforementioned two conditions along with equality in measurement.

Explanation: This chapter deals with forbidden transactions. The author started by mentioning the usurious gain (*riba*). The most common type of *riba* is what is known as *ribal-qard*, i.e., the usurious gain established by a loan. The definition of this type is summarized in the *hadith* of the Prophet ﷺ, related by *al-Bayhaqiyy* and others:

«كُلُّ قَرْضٍ جَرَّ مَنْفَعَةً فَهُوَ رِبا»

It means: «Every lending contract that generates (by its terms) a benefit (for the lender only or him and the borrower) is a case of *riba*». Examples of it are:

1. Lending money to a person with the condition that if he does not pay it back on a specific date, he adds a certain increment to the due amount.

2. Lending money to another person with the condition that he pays it back at a specific time with an additional increment.

3. Lending money to another person with the condition that the lender uses the borrower's house free of charge until he pays him

229

back the money. In such a case, the terms of the lending contract generate a benefit to the lender. What sums up the other cases of usurious gain (riba) is the hadith of the Prophet ﷺ related by *Muslim* and others:

«الذَّهَبُ بالذَّهَبِ والفِضَّةُ بالفِضَّةِ والبُرُّ بالبُرِّ والشَّعِيرُ بالشَّعِيرِ والمِلحُ بالمِلحِ والتَّمرُ بالتَّمرِ رِبا إلا مِثلاً بِمِثل يَدًا بِيدٍ سَوَاءً بِسَواءٍ . فإذا اختلفتْ هذه الأصنافُ فبيعوا كيف شئتم إذا كان يدًا بيدٍ».

It means: «Selling gold for gold, silver for silver, wheat for wheat, barley for barley, salt for salt, and dates for dates, is a case of *riba*, unless equal quantities of the same kind are exchanged and mutual delivery of the goods in the same session is made. However, if the exchanged types are different, then sell the way you want, along with delivering the goods in the same session.»

This means if one wants to sell gold for gold, for instance, then the pure amounts of gold on both sides must be equal. Even if the gold of one of the two parties was made into golden jewelry, and the other's was a block of gold, the equity between the pure quantities of gold on both sides must be observed.

Moreover, the buyer and seller must exchange the goods in the same session of transaction, without including a condition of postponement in payment, even for a moment. Hence, if the buyer tells the seller, "I now buy this pound of gold that you have for this pound of gold that I have, with the condition that I deliver my gold to you in half an hour," the contract is forbidden and invalid. It is a case of *riba* which is specifically called *riban-nasa'*.

The same judgment applies (i.e., it is *riba*) if the seller tells the buyer, "I now sell you this pound of gold that I have for this pound of gold that you have", without any condition of postponement, but one of them leaves the session before exchanging the merchandise. This type of *riba* is called *ribal-yad*.

Due to the inequality of the pure amount of gold on both sides, it is an invalid transaction if the seller says, "I now sell you this pound and half of gold made into jewelry, for that pound of coined gold that you have." This kind of riba (when the exchanged goods are unequal) is called ribal-fadl.

The same judgment holds when one sells silver for silver and food for food. Hence, when one sells gold for silver or vice versa, then equality in the quantities is not a condition. However, exchanging the merchandise within the session and avoiding the postponement of the payment are still considered conditions for the validity of the contract. The same judgment holds if one sells one kind of food for another kind of food.

However, when selling food for gold or silver (like selling barley for silver), none of the three conditions is required. Hence, one can sell 100 lbs of wheat for 2 dirhams (of silver), with payment postponed for a month.

The equivalence is determined either by weight or by volume. The weight is the reference of equity for every item that was measured by weight at the time of the Prophet ﷺ. Likewise volume is the reference of equity for each kind that was measured by volume at the Prophet's era. This is why we determine the equity in the case of gold and silver, for example, based on weight and, in the case of wheat and barley, based on volume.

Chapter 37
Some Rules of Selling (Bay^)

It is unlawful (haram) to sell:

1. What one has not received;

Explanation: Among the prohibited types of selling is for one to sell what one has not received yet. This includes all kinds of items, food and otherwise. To receive the item that can be handed in (like books, pens, and the like), it is enough that the buyer takes it physically with his hand from the seller. If the item is portable (like a car or a closet), it is enough for receiving it to transport it to a spot that does not belong to the seller. Receiving the item that is not portable (like the real estate) takes place when the seller removes any barrier that prevents the buyer from possessing and fully controlling the item. In the case of a house, the buyer receives it when the seller empties it from his belongings and delivers the key to the buyer.

2. Meat in exchange for living animals;

Explanation: As related by *at-Tirmidhiyy* from the Messenger of Allah, it is prohibited to sell meat for a living animal, whether or not the meat and the living animal are of the same kind.

3. One debt for another debt.

Explanation: Selling a debt for another debt is a forbidden matter. This involves several scenarios. For instance, if ^Amr owes Zayd a debt, it is forbidden for Zayd to sell a third person what ^Amr owes him for a certain amount of money postponed for a day, two days, or a month. Al-Bayhaqiyy, al-Hakim, and others narrated that the Prophet ﷺ explicitly mentioned the prohibition of such a transaction.

$$\text{«نَهَى رسولُ الله ﷺ عن بيع الكالِئ بالكالِئ»}$$

Moreover, *Imam Ahmad* relayed the consensus (ijma^) on this judgment.

4. What one does not own or is not authorized to sell;

Explanation: This kind of selling is called in Arabic *bay^ul-fuduliyy*. It means for the person to sell something that he does not own, or he is not properly authorized to sell. Such a selling is not valid. On the other hand, the guardian of an orphan is entitled to manage the orphan's finances in the most profitable way for the orphan.

5. **What one did not see. According to a saying of ash-Shafiˆiyy, if the merchandise was described, then this selling would be allowed;**

Explanation: If the buyer or the seller does not see the merchandise at the moment of the contract, and has not seen it before, then the contract itself is invalid. An example of this is to buy or to sell what is inside a sealed box without knowing what it contains.

Most of the *mujtahids* (top scholars) say that buying what one did not see is permissible, provided that the buyer can revoke that sale after seeing it.

According to one saying (of *Imam ash-Shafiˆiyy*) if the merchandise is clearly described to the buyer, the contract is valid. "Clearly described" in this context means that once the buyer sees it, he knows that this is the item that was described to him.

6. **What cannot be delivered;**

Explanation: It is unlawful for one to sell that which one cannot deliver to the buyer. However, if the buyer is able to receive the merchandise without a great expense, then the contract is valid. For instance, if someone's house was taken away from him by force, and he sells it to a person who can force the occupiers out of it (without a big expense or effort), in this case, the sale is valid.

Moreover, selling the unborn animal babies (i.e., while they are still inside their mother's womb) is invalid. Similarly, it is invalid to sell milk while it is still in the udders, fish while they are still in the sea, birds while they are still flying in the sky, and camels that have escaped and cannot be retrieved.

7. **What has no benefit;**

Explanation: It is not valid to buy or sell any item that has no physical or religious benefit. For instance, there is no physical benefit in eating burnt bread. Therefore, selling it is invalid. Additionally, despite their monetary value, crosses do not have a religiously recognized benefit. Consequently, selling them is unlawful and invalid.

Similarly, it is forbidden to sell the prohibited musical instruments and the little insects, such as ants. However, if the insect has a religiously recognized benefit, such as the leech, it is valid to sell and buy it.

8. What is not owned by one, such as the free person and unowned land;

Explanation: It is forbidden for one to sell what cannot be lawfully owned. Hence, it is not permissible to sell a free person. Similarly, it is unlawful to sell rivers, oceans, or their beaches. Moreover, it is not permissible to sell the unowned land. However, one may own such a land by reviving it in the religiously proper way. Thereafter, one may sell it.

9. The unknown;

Explanation: Among the conditions for the validity of selling is that the merchandise and its price are known. An example of an invalid transaction is when the seller says, "I sell you one of these two cars of mine," without specifying which one he means (even if the two cars are alike). Another example is to say, "I now sell you 10 boxes of my merchandise," without specifying the boxes (even if all his merchandise is similar). A third example is for one to say: "I now sell you this horse for $2000 or $2500 depending on the market price."

10. The *najas*- filthy materials, such as blood;

Explanation: Selling *najas*-filthy materials is invalid. Examples are blood, urine, dogs, pigs, and meat that was not slaughtered properly.

11. Every intoxicant;

Explanation: Selling any substance that changes the mind causing intoxication and ecstasy is forbidden. The judgment applies whether it was made out of barley, grapes, dates, honey, or other materials.

12. Unlawful articles, such as the *tumbur* (a musical instrument which resembles the lute);

Explanation: Among the forbidden sellings is selling any unlawful article, like selling a die (*nard*) or any musical instrument that is forbidden, such as the flute, lute, and *kubah* (a drum that is narrow in its middle). Although buying the dice is forbidden, the selling transaction is valid if the dice can be used as stones for chess.

13. The lawful (halal) and pure article to the person whom one knows will disobey Allah with it, like selling grapes to the one who will make wine out of them and a weapon to the one who will assault people with it;

Explanation: It is forbidden for one to sell the lawful, pure article to another person knowing that the second one will disobey Allah with it. This is so because it involves helping another person to commit a sin. In the Qur'an (al-Ma'idah, 2), Allah forbade us to assist others in sinning:

$$﴿وَلَا تَعَاوَنُوا۟ عَلَى ٱلْإِثْمِ وَٱلْعُدْوَٰنِ ۚ ٢﴾$$

It means: [Do not help one another in committing sins]. Hence, it is forbidden for one to sell grapes to another person whom one knows will make wine out of them, or to sell a weapon to someone that one knows will assault people unrightfully with it. Similarly, selling wood to someone whom one knows will make forbidden musical instruments out of it is forbidden. At-Tabaraniyy narrated in his book al-Mu^jamul-awsat from the Prophet ﷺ:

$$«مَنْ حَبَسَ العِنَبَ حتى يَبيعَهُ مِمَّنْ يَتَّخِذُهُ خَمْرًا فَقَد تَقَحَّمَ النَّارَ على بَصيرَةٍ»$$

It means: "Whoever holds grapes to sell them to the one who will make wine out of them is stepping knowingly into Hellfire." Hafidh Ibn Hajar mentioned it in "Bulugh al-Maram" and said its chain of narration was hasan.

14. Intoxicating substances;

Explanation: It is forbidden to sell intoxicating substances, whether the buyer wants to use them as a drink or for other usage. Hence, it is forbidden to purchase alcohol to use it as a fuel. Such a sale is invalid. This is due to the hadith of the Prophet ﷺ which al-Bukhariyy and Muslim related:

$$«إنَّ اللَّهَ وَرَسُولَهُ حَرَّمَ بَيعَ الخَمرِ والمَيتةِ ولَحمِ الخنزيرِ والأَصنامِ»$$

It means: «Allah and His Messenger made it forbidden to sell alcohol, the animal that was not killed properly (maytah), the pig, and the idols». A person asked the Prophet ﷺ about selling the tallow of *maytah* to apply it to the ships and to use it as fuel for the lanterns (i.e., not to eat it). The Prophet ﷺ replied by reaffirming that such a transaction is still forbidden. It stands as a proof that selling ethyl alcohol, whether for drinking or otherwise, is forbidden.

15. The defective article without showing its defects.

Explanation: If the seller knows of a defect that an article has, and of which the buyer does not know, it is obligatory on him, upon selling it, to tell the buyer about it. If he conceals that defect, the sale is valid, but he is sinful. However, the buyer is entitled to revoke the sale, as soon as he knows about the defect.

The selling by and to the non-accountable is invalid. So, the selling by and to the insane and non-pubescent is invalid. According to the school (*madhhab*) of Imam Ahmad, the selling by and to the child who attained the age of mental discrimination (*mumayyiz*) is allowed.

Explanation: It is invalid for an insane person to sell, or to buy. Similarly, it is invalid for the non-pubescent boy or girl to buy any thing from the store, even with the permission of one's parent. This is the judgment according to the *Shafi^iyy* school. However, according to the school of *Imam Ahmad*, it is permitted for the child who attained the age of mental discrimination to buy, if permitted by the guardian.

According to some scholars, it is also invalid to sell anything without the exchange of appropriate verbal statements from both parties. According to others, the mutual consent of both parties is enough.

Explanation: Imam ash-Shafi^iyy established that for the selling contract to be valid, a verbal format must be performed by both parties. For instance, the buyer says, "I now buy this thing from you for such an amount of money," and the seller says, "I now accept" or "I now sell it to you for the amount you mentioned".

Some other top scholars said that the mutual consent of both parties is enough. The exchange, which is normally considered by the people as a selling transaction, is accepted as valid, even if it does not involve verbal statements (as long as the other conditions of validity are satisfied).

* Useful information:

It is invalid to divide the inheritance of a deceased person or to sell it until one's debts and will have been fulfilled. Something may be sold, however, to pay off a debt or fulfill the will. The compensation paid to a hired person to perform *Hajj* and ^*Umrah* on behalf of the deceased must be taken out if *Hajj* and ^*Umrah* were obligatory on one. The inheritance is like a collateral held for that purpose. This is similar to the case of a slave who stole an amount of one-sixth of a *Dirham* (*Daniq*); selling him is invalid until what is due on him has been paid, or the creditor gives permission to sell him.

Explanation: Before distributing the inheritance of a deceased person, one checks if he has debts on him. After isolating what is needed to prepare the dead for burial, the rest of the inheritance is used to pay off the debts of the deceased person. Moreover, the heirs check if the deceased performed *Hajj* and ^*Umrah* (if they were obligatory upon him). If not, they put aside a part of the inheritance enough to meet the expenses of performing the obligatory *Hajj* and ^*Umrah* on behalf of the deceased. If the money he left is in excess of his debts, then the heirs consider if he left any valid will behind. If he did, then the money in excess is used to fulfill the will. The remaining money is distributed among the heirs.

It is permissible to sell a part of the inheritance items with the purpose of settling the debts and the like. Before taking care of the aforementioned matters, the inheritance is like a collateral held for these matters. Before taking care of those matters, the heirs are not entitled to distribute the inheritance or to sell it. This is similar to the case of the slave who steals money, even one *daniq* (one sixth of a *dirham*). Selling this slave is unlawful and invalid until the amount due on him is paid, or the creditor gives permission to sell him.

After establishing the price, it is unlawful (*haram*) for one to weaken the desire of the buyer or the seller with the purpose of selling to the buyer or buying from the seller.

Explanation: If two people agree to establish a transaction by agreeing on the price and merchandise, then it is unlawful for a third person, who knows of the agreement, to interfere by saying to the seller, "Don't sell it; I will buy it from you for a higher price", or telling the buyer, "Don't buy it, I will sell you the same item for less", or "I will sell you a better item for the same price". *Al-Bukhariyy* and *Muslim* narrated from the Prophet ﷺ that he explicitly forbade it:

$$\text{«ولا يَسُومُ على سَوْمِ أَخِيهِ»}$$

It is more sinful if this act is done after the contract has been conducted and during the period of choice of canceling the sale.

Explanation: After establishing the contract with the agreement on a period of choice entitled by either or both of the seller and buyer, it is more sinful for a third person to interfere by offering more money to the seller to back off this sale, or offering the buyer a lower price to revoke the sale. However, if the person affected by such interference gives the permission, then it is allowed.

It is unlawful (*haram*) to buy food when it is expensive and needed in order to hoard it and sell it for a higher price.

Explanation: This is the forbidden hoarding (*ihtikar*). Imam *Muslim* narrated that the Prophet ﷺ said:

$$\text{«مَنِ احْتَكَرَ فَهُوَ خَاطِئٌ»}$$

It means: «Whoever performs the prohibited hoarding is sinful». Thus, it is forbidden to buy the staple food when it is expensive and the people are in need of it, with the purpose of hoarding and saving it to sell it later for a higher price. Some of the *Shafi^iyy* scholars said that the aforementioned judgment applies to every article the people at large need, such as clothes and gasoline. Other scholars restricted the judgment to staple food (wheat, barley, corn, etc.).

It is unlawful (*haram*) to bid a higher price for an article in order to deceive another person.

Explanation: This act is called in Arabic *najsh*. The Prophet ﷺ prohibited it as *al-Bukhariyy* and *Muslim* related from him. It constitutes someone bidding a higher price for an article in order to deceive a second bidder that this article deserves that higher price. An example is when the auctioneer agrees with a person to bid a higher price each time someone else bids a certain price, not intending to buy the item, rather with the intention of deceiving other participants about the item's price. It is also forbidden to lie in praising the merchandise.

238

It is unlawful (_haram_) to separate the female slave from her child before the child is at the age of mental discrimination (_tamyiz_).

Explanation: It is not permissible for the owner of a female slave and her child to separate the mother from her child, either by selling or by giving either of them away, as long as the child has not reached the age of mental discrimination yet. As narrated by _at-Tirmidhiyy_, _Ahmad_, and _al-Hakim_, the Prophet ﷺ said:

«مَنْ فَرَّقَ بَيْنَ والِدَةٍ وَوَلَدِهَا فَرَّقَ اللَّهُ بَيْنَهُ وبَيْنَ أَحِبَّتِهِ يومَ القِيَامَةِ»

It means, «Whoever separates a mother from her child, Allah will separate him from his beloved ones on the Day of Judgment».

It is unlawful (_haram_) to cheat, betray, or lie in measuring articles by volume, weight, arm length, or count.

Explanation: Cheating is forbidden in selling. _Imam Muslim_ narrated that the Prophet ﷺ said,

«مَنْ غَشَّنَا فَلَيْسَ مِنَّا»

It means: «Whoever cheats us is not adhering to our way.» This means that he is not among the pious Muslims. In fact it is an enormous sin to betray while measuring by volume, weight, arm length, or count. An example is if the seller gives the buyer nine eggs making him think that he sold him ten.

Allah said in the _Qur'an_:

﴿وَيْلٌ لِّلْمُطَفِّفِينَ ۝﴾

In this first verse of _Surat-ul-Mutaffifin_, _Allah_ threatened the cheaters in measuring by volume with a severe torture in the Hereafter. The verse talks about those who have two measures of volume; when they purchase they use the correct measure, and when they sell they use the incorrect one to gain from the difference. Similarly, any one who cheats in weighing, counting or the like, deserves the severe torture in the Hereafter.

It is unlawful (_haram_) to lend money to the buyer with the condition to sell one cotton, for example, at a higher price for the sake of the loan. It

is unlawful (*haram*) to lend money to the weaver or any other hired person with the condition to hire that person for less than the going rate for the sake of that loan. It is unlawful (*haram*) to lend money to the farmers with the condition that the farmers sell the loaners their harvest at a slightly lower price.

Explanation: All of the aforementioned matters are examples of the rule explained previously, when the case of *ribal-qard* was discussed. That is, every loan that generates, by its terms, a benefit to the lender alone or to both the lender and the borrower is an act of *riba* (usurious gain).

Many other dealings of the people of this time are also unlawful (*haram*), i.e., they are Islamically illegal.

Explanation: Many of the dealings conducted by the people nowadays are not in compliance with the rules of the Religion. The one who seeks the reward of *Allah* and His acceptance must avoid these matters. To do that, one needs to learn enough of the religious rules of dealings before getting involved in any contract.

Hence, the one who seeks the reward from *Allah*, *subhanah*, and one's safety in the Hereafter and in this life must learn what is lawful (*halal*) and what is unlawful (*haram*) from a knowledgeable person who is pious, sincere, and caring for one's Religion. Seeking the lawful (*halal*) is obligatory upon every Muslim.

Explanation: One must acquire the Obligatory Knowledge of the Religion from a trustworthy knowledgeable person, by which one can know what is *halal* and what is *haram*. Hence, it is unlawful to ask a knowledgeable person who is *fasiq* (enormous sinner) as well as an ignorant one for answers to religious questions. The great *Imam Muhammad Ibn Sirin*, who was among the students of the Companions said, "This knowledge is the Religion. Therefore, watch carefully from whom you take your knowledge."

The author's statement: "Seeking the lawful is obligatory upon every Muslim", means that one is not allowed to earn an unlawful income. It does not mean that one is not allowed to remain jobless. If a person has no financial obligation of supporting dependants, and despite being insolvent, he does not work, then he is not sinful. This holds provided he does not beg or cheat people to take their money.

At-Tirmidhiyy narrated that a person complained to the Prophet ﷺ about his brother by saying: "My brother stays at the mosque all the time. He does not work, and I am the one who supports him." The Prophet ﷺ answered that person by saying:

$$\text{«لَعَلَّكَ تُرْزَقُ بِهِ»}$$

It means: "Perhaps you receive the sustenance because of him." The point of proof in this *hadith* is that the Prophet ﷺ did not dispraise the brother for not working. This *hadith* is classified as *sahih*.

Chapter 38
Supporting Dependents, Including One's Wife

The one who is solvent is obligated to support one's poor parents and grandparents, even if they were able to earn their living. One is also obligated to support one's descendants, i.e., one's children and grandchildren, who are poor and cannot earn their living, because they are non-pubescent or have some ailment.

Explanation: The solvent person has to support one's poor parents. If they do not have enough for their basic needs, one is not allowed to force them to seek employment to support themselves. Rather, one is obligated to fulfill their basic needs. However, if one is poor, then one is not sinful for not supporting one's poor parents. However, if one can find a lawful job that covers one's needs and those of one's parents, then one has to seek it. The same judgment is applicable to the poor grandparents, if their children were dead, or if their children were poor.

It is an obligation on one to pay for the marriage of one's own father when the latter needs it.

The father is also obligated to support his poor non-pubescent children. Similarly, he is obligated to support his poor pubescent children who are not able physically to earn their living because they are paralyzed, blind, insane, or the like. As for his pubescent children, males and females, who are able physically to earn their living, the father is not obligated to support them.

The husband is obligated to support his wife and pay her marriage payment (*mahr*). If the marriage is breached without a reason from her, he must give her a compensation (*mut˄ah*).

Explanation: As long as the wife is not running away from her husband's house, and as long as she does not prevent him from having sexual intercourse with her (without an excuse), then she is entitled to her husband's support. This includes the shelter, food, clothing, and the like. It does not include the complementary matters like the car, television, refrigerator, extra clothes, etc.

The husband is also obligated to pay his wife her marriage payment (*mahr*). If it was not postponed, he has to pay it whenever she asks for it. If it was postponed, he is obligated to pay it at the due time.

Moreover, if the two spouses neither mention the marriage payment (*mahr*) within the marriage contract nor do they agree to it afterwards, and later before having their first sexual intercourse, their marriage is breached not as a result of the wife's act, then she is entitled to a compensatory payment, called in Arabic *mutˆah*. That is, the husband is obligated to pay her that payment. For example, when a non-*Kitabiyy*[53] man embraces *Islam* before his non-*Kitabiyy* wife, the marriage is terminated if the wife's *ˆiddah*[54] expires before her embracing *Islam*. Moreover, since the marriage has terminated as a result of his (not her) act, he must pay her a *mutˆah*.[55]

In the case when she embraces *Islam* before him, the marriage is terminated if the wife's *ˆiddah* expires without him embracing *Islam*. However, since her act led to the marriage termination, she deserves no *mutˆah*.

It is recommended (*sunnah*) that such payment be at least 30 *dirhams* (about 90 grams of silver), without reaching half of the *mahr* given usually to her paternal female relatives who are similar to her in beauty, knowledge, and social status.

The owner of slaves and animals must support them, must not charge them with more work than they can bear, and must not beat them unjustly.

Explanation: The owner of the slaves has to support them in a moderate way with clothes, shelter, food, and the like. The Prophet ﷺ said:

«إِخْوانُكم خَوَلُكُمْ، جَعَلَهُمُ اللَّهُ تَحْتَ أَيْدِيكُم . فَمَنْ كانَ أَخُوهُ
تحتَ يَدِهِ فَلْيُطعِمْهُ مِمَّا يَأْكُلُ، وَلْيُلْبِسْهُ مِمَّا يَلبَسُ . ولا تُكَلِّفُوهُمْ
مَا يَغْلِبُهُم . فإِنْ كَلَّفْتُمُوهُم فَأَعِينُوهُمْ» .

---

[53] A *Kitabiyy* is a Christian or a Jew.

[54] *ˆIddah* is the waiting period a woman observes after being divorced (3 non-menstrual intervals) or widowed (4 lunar months and 10 days). The *ˆiddah* of the pregnant woman ends by delivery.

[55] Note that if two non-Muslim (*Kitabiyy* or not) spouses embrace *Islam* simultaneously, their marriage remains valid. In all the above cases, if the non-Muslim spouse embraces *Islam* before the expiration of the wife's *ˆiddah*, the marriage remains valid. If a *Kitabiyy* man embraces *Islam* before his *Kitabiyy* wife, the marriage remains valid whether or not the wife embraces *Islam*.

This _hadith_ narrated by _al-Bukhariyy_ means: «The (Muslim) slaves that you own are your fellows. _Allah_ willed that you own them. (Had _Allah_ willed the opposite, you would have been under their control.) Thus, let anyone who has his fellow under his control feed him from what he eats and clothe him from what he wears. Do not assign them chores that are beyond their ability. If you do that, then help them (to carry out their chores).»

Similarly, one is obligated to support the animals that one owns. It is _haram_ for one to starve them intentionally.

One must not charge one's slave or animal with work that the slave or the animal cannot bear. Moreover, one is not entitled to beat them unrightfully. Even when one lawfully beats one's animal (for the purpose of discipline) there is a limit for it. For example, one is not allowed to break its arm, break its leg, or hit its face.

Chapter 39
Obligations of the Wife

The wife is obligated to obey her husband in allowing him to enjoy her body, except in what is not lawful. Without her husband's permission, she must not fast the optional fasting or leave his house.

Explanation: The wife has to fulfill the husband's rights in what pertains to the sexual relation. She is not allowed to prevent him from having sexual intercourse with her without a valid excuse, such as having her menstrual or postpartum bleeding, or being harmed by sexual intercourse. If he asks her to wear makeup for him, she must do it when he provides the materials.

She is not allowed to perform optional fasting without his permission, unless he is out of town.

If her husband does not accept for someone to enter his house, she is not allowed to receive him or her in that house, even if it was her parent or her sibling.

Moreover, she may not leave his house without his permission, except for a valid excuse. An example for a valid excuse is going out to learn the Personal Obligatory Knowledge, if there is no other way to do it. Another example is when she fears for her safety at the house, such as the collapse of the house on her.

She must avoid whatever disturbs his sexual enjoyment of her, such as having a bad odor that bothers him, whether from eating garlic, or smoking, or the like.

OBLIGATIONS
AND SINS

Chapter 40
Obligations of the Heart

Among the obligations of the heart are:

Explanation: There are obligations that pertain to the heart, just as there are sins pertaining to the heart. Since the inclinations in the heart change very quickly, each must observe one's heart very closely. The purpose of monitoring the heart is to help one remain obedient to *Allah*. This matter is stated by the Prophet ﷺ in the *hadith* narrated by al-*Bukhariyy* and *Muslim*:

«أَلَا وَإِنَّ فِى الجَسَدِ مُضْغَةً إِذَا صَلَحَتْ صَلَحَ الجَسَدُ كُلُّهُ وَإِذَا فَسَدَتْ فَسَدَ الجَسَدُ كُلُّهُ. أَلَا وَهِيَ القَلْبُ».

It means: «Verily, in the body there is a small piece, which when healthy, the whole body will be healthy; and when diseased, then the whole body will be diseased. Indeed, it is the heart.»

1. To have the belief in *Allah* and what He revealed;

Explanation: Among the obligations of the heart is to believe in *Allah* and the Prophet, *sallallahu ^alayhi wa sallam*. This is the foundation for all the obligations. Believing in *Allah* means to believe firmly, without any doubt in the Existence and Oneness of *Allah*. It entails believing that *Allah* exists without being similar to any of the other existing things. Thus, one believes that *Allah* exists without having dimensions, and without being a quantity, a body composed of parts, or in a place.

2. To have the belief in the Messenger of *Allah* and what he conveyed;

Explanation: Believing in *Allah*'s Messenger means to firmly believe that Prophet *Muhammad*, *sallallahu ^alayhi wa sallam*, was sent by *Allah* to all the human beings and the *jinn* to convey the message from *Allah*. This entails that one has to believe in all what *Allah* revealed and in all what the Prophet conveyed from Him, without excluding even one matter. Thus, one has to believe in the truthfulness of the *Qur'an* and the sayings of the Prophet ﷺ.

3. To have the sincerity (ikhlas), which is to do the good deeds for the sake of Allah only;

Explanation: Having sincerity while doing a good deed is among the obligations of the heart. This means that one must do the good deed without seeking by that the praise of the people. This does not mean that one is sinful for feeling delighted upon the praise of people for his doing a good deed, because this is the nature of the human being. The issue is that one is in danger if one does the good deed in the first place for the sake of people (i.e., seeking their praise and their respect). In such a case, one is committing an enormous sin.

This sin is so enormous to a point that the Prophet ﷺ drew similarity between it and associating a partner with Allah (as related by Ibn Hibban):

$$\text{«اتَّقُوا الرِّيَاءَ فَإِنَّهُ الشِّرْكُ الأَصْغَرُ»}$$

4. To regret sinning;

Explanation: Among the obligations of the heart is to repent of all sins committed, whether they are enormous or small. The greatest integral among the integrals of repentance is to regret sinning. This is why it was mentioned in the hadith of the Prophet ﷺ:

$$\text{«النَّدَمُ تَوْبَةٌ»}$$

This means: «The major part or integral of repentance is to regret the sin.» This hadith is narrated by Ibn Majah and Ahmad. This regret is valid only if it is done because one disobeyed Allah, and not because one is worried about a scandal among the people or the like. Regretting a sin just because one became exposed before the people is not a valid integral of repentance.

5. To rely on Allah;

Explanation: Among the obligations of the heart is to rely on Allah. Reliance on Allah means to believe firmly that Allah is the One Who creates both the benefit and the harm; no one can benefit you with anything that Allah did not will for you to get, and no one can make any harm to you if Allah did not will for that to happen. As a result of this firm belief, one relies on Allah to get one's own

250

sustenance, any other benefit, to be safe from illnesses, to be safe from harm, and to be relieved from the different calamities.

6. To fear *Allah* so as to perform one's obligations and refrain from the unlawful matters;

Explanation: It is an obligation to fear *Allah* in the heart. The correct fear is a fear that prevents the person from neglecting the obligations and committing the sins. This is why once the person becomes accountable (*mukallaf*), one must intend in the heart to refrain from all sins and to perform all the obligations (i.e., to have the aforementioned fear). What helps the person to reach this state is to remember always, in all the different situations that *Allah* knows about one, and that *Allah* sees one.

7. To subjugate oneself to *Allah* and refrain from objecting to Him;

Explanation: Among the obligations of the heart is to subjugate oneself to *Allah*, that is, not to object to *Allah*, neither in one's heart nor with one's tongue. One has to be in this state whether *Allah* willed for one to be in a difficult situation or in an easy one, and whether *Allah* willed for one to be happy or sad, rich or poor, and/or in pain or in relief. In all the different situations, one is not entitled to object to *Allah*, nor is one entitled to question the Destining of *Allah*.

This does not mean that one does not hate the bad things which, of course, occur by the Will of *Allah*. One has to hate the sins. Rather, it means for one not to hate, or question the Will of *Allah*.

8. To exalt the rites of *Allah*;

Explanation: It is an obligation that one exalts the rites of the Religion. These rites are the matters that are famous to be among the matters of the Religion of *Islam*, like the *Adhan, Hajj*, presence at ^*Arafat*, the mosques, and their similars. It is prohibited to degrade any of these rites.

9. To be thankful to *Allah* for His endowments by not using them in disobedience;

Explanation: Thanking *Allah* for His endowments is of two types. One is an obligation and the other is recommended (*sunnah*). The obligatory thanking is to refrain from using the endowments of *Allah* in disobeying Him. It is not simply to say with the tongue, "I thank

Allah", or "Praise be to Allah". Whoever says that 10,000 times every day, while using one's hands, feet, and tongue in disobedience, is not fulfilling the obligatory thanking of Allah. Rather, the obligatory thanking is to use the endowments of Allah only in what is permissible, and not to use them to disobey God.

As to the recommended thanking, an example of it is when one makes du^a' for a person who did one a favor. Another example is to thank Allah with the tongue 100 times every day after the Dawn Prayer.

10. To be patient in performing the obligations;

11. To be patient in refraining from the sins;

12. To be patient with what Allah afflicted one;

Explanation: Among the obligations of the heart is to be patient. There are three types of patience.

One type is to be patient in performing the obligations, whenever performing them entails difficulty. An example of this patience is when the person needs to perform *wudu'* with cold water in the early cold morning.

The second type is to be patient while preventing oneself from committing sins, even when one has a strong inclination inside towards the sin. An example is if a person is financially in a hard situation, and one knows that there is an unlawful way to get a big sum of money, one has to be patient and prevent oneself from taking the unlawful (*haram*) money despite all one's bad inclinations.

The third type is to be patient with calamities. One must be patient and not let calamities that befall one draw one to sinning. For example, if someone is inflicted with a severe sickness, one needs to be patient with that and not let one's situation lead one to object to Allah. Some people, if they are faced with calamities, might blaspheme. This outcome is due to their lack of patience.

13. To hate the Devil;

Explanation: It is an obligation on every accountable person to hate the Devil, because Allah said in *Surat Fatir*, verse 6,

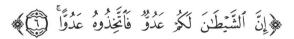

﴿إِنَّ ٱلشَّيْطَٰنَ لَكُمْ عَدُوٌّ فَٱتَّخِذُوهُ عَدُوًّا ۞﴾

252

This verse means: [Certainly, the Devil is your enemy. Hence, take him as an enemy.] All the blasphemous *jinn* are devils. The great grandfather of all the *jinn* is *Iblis*. He is also the head of the devils.

14. To hate sins;

Explanation: Among the obligations of the heart is to hate sins. Even if the person oneself commits a sin, one has to hate it. Similarly, if one knows about a sin committed by someone else, whether in one's presence or not, one must hate that sin as well.

15. To love *Allah*, His *Qur'an*, His Messenger, the Companions, the *Al* (Muslim relatives and wives) of the Prophet, and the righteous Muslims.

Explanation: It is an obligation on the accountable person to love *Allah*. This means that one must exalt *Allah* in the proper way, i.e., the way that befits *Allah*.

Also, it is an obligation to love the revealed Book of *Allah*, the *Qur'an*. One must believe in it and exalt it in the proper way.

Additionally, it is an obligation to love Prophet *Muhammad* ﷺ . This means that one must believe in the Prophet ﷺ and exalt him in the proper way, without going beyond the proper boundaries of the Religion, i.e., without exaggeration. Some people exaggerated in this matter to a point that they claimed that the Prophet knew all what *Allah* knows. This is blasphemy (*kufr*).

Moreover, one has to love the sayings of the Prophet ﷺ. This is a result of loving the Prophet. Similarly, it is an obligation to love the Companions of the Prophet. A Companion, by definition, is one who met the Prophet ﷺ , in the ordinary way while believing in him, and died as a believer. Hence, the prophets who met with our Prophet *Muhammad* ﷺ and prayed behind him during the night of *Isra'* are not considered among his Companions, because their meeting with the Prophet ﷺ was not in a usual way.

It is an obligation to love the Companions because they are the people who supported the Religion of *Allah*. This is especially true concerning the first batches among the Companions who immigrated from *Makkah* to *Madinah* (al-Muhajirun), and the first batches among the believers of *Madinah* (al-Ansar).

253

Finally, it is an obligation to love the _Al_ of the Prophet. The term "_Al_ of the Prophet", in Arabic can bear more than one meaning. The word "_Al_" can bear the meaning "the pious followers". It is an obligation to love the pious followers of Prophet _Muhammad_ ﷺ because _Allah, ta^ala_, ordered us with that love. We do say during the prayer:

«السَّلامُ عَلَينا وَعَلَى عِبادِ الله الصَّالِحِينَ»

Here, we are asking _Allah_ to give good things to the righteous slaves and us. This is a clear sign that we have to exalt the pious followers of the Prophet and love them.

The word "_Al_" can also mean "the relatives of the Prophet". In the religious texts, we are ordered to love these relatives, that is, the believers among them. In this context, the word "_Al_" also includes the Prophet's wives.

Imam Ahmad narrated that the Prophet ﷺ said:

«إِنَّى قَدْ تَرَكْتُ فِيكُم ما إِنْ أَخَذْتُم بِه لَن تَضِلُّوا بَعْدِى الثَّقَلَينِ أَحَدُهما أَكْبَرُ مِنَ الآخَرِ : كِتابُ الله حَبلٌ ممدُودٌ مِنَ السَّماءِ إِلَى الأَرْضِ وَعِتْرَتِى أَهْلُ بَيْتِى».

This _hadith_ contains the meaning: «There are two matters, which if you adhere to, you will never go astray after my death, the Book of _Allah_, and my _Al_.»

This means that the scholars among the _Al_ of the Prophet adhere to the methodology of the Prophet ﷺ. If one adheres to and follows them, one will be safe.

Chapter 41
Sins of the Heart

Among the sins of the heart are:

1. **The insincerity in performing the good deeds (*riya'*), i.e., to do the good deeds for the sake of the people-to be praised by them-and this nullifies their reward. It is an enormous sin;**

Explanation: Being insincere while doing a good deed is an enormous sin. This sin takes place when one performs the good deed seeking the praise of the people and not the reward from *Allah*. Hence, if a person does a good deed (like praying, fasting, paying *Zakah*, teaching Islamic knowledge, paying money in charity, or the like) seeking the praise of the people, one does not get any reward for this deed. Likewise, if one does the good deed seeking both, the reward from *Allah* and the people's praise, one does not acquire any reward. In both cases, one gets no reward and one is committing an enormous sin.

Added to that, if one does these good deeds to delude people into believing that one is a pious person, seeking their gifts, then one's situation becomes worse. Moreover, it is <u>haram</u> for one to take these gifts.

2. **Priding oneself for obeying *Allah* (ˆ*ujb*), deeming one's worship was by one's own ability and forgetting the grace of *Allah*;**

Explanation: After performing one or more types of obedience, some people feel proud. Out of that, they consider themselves as having a high status for doing this or those deeds, while forgetting that *Allah* is the One Who created and enabled them to do whatever they did.

Performing the good deeds, while remembering that they are endowments from *Allah*, helps one to be sincere.

3. **Doubt about *Allah*;**

Explanation: Among the sins of the heart is to have doubt in *Allah*.This is blasphemy, even if this doubt did not last for a long period of time. However, this does not include the bad thoughts that come across one's mind without one's intention and without affecting one's belief, while one rejects them. One must reject such thoughts without allowing one's self to doubt about *Allah*. Such involuntary thoughts do not make the person a blasphemer. Rather, if the person rejects such thoughts, one is safe because one did not sin. In fact, one is rewarded for one's rejection.

These thoughts make the person a blasphemer only if one hesitates, as a consequence, in believing in the Existence of *Allah*, the Oneness of *Allah*, the Knowledge of *Allah*, the truthfulness of the Prophet, or the like. As well, one blasphemes if one flatly denies any of that.

4. **Feeling safe from the punishment of *Allah*;**

5. **Despairing of *Allah*'s mercy;**

Explanation: Among the sins of the heart is for the person to commit sins consistently, relying on a conviction in one's heart that *Allah* will not punish one, and that rather *Allah* will forgive one those sins. This is an enormous sin.

On the other hand, to despair of *Allah*'s mercy is an enormous sin also. This is having the conviction that *Allah* will definitely not forgive one, because of the enormous sins that one committed, without repenting of them. (*Allah* will forgive some great sinners, even though they did not repent, as long as they died as Muslim).

The *Hanafiyys* interpreted being safe from the punishment of *Allah* as for one to believe that *Allah* does not at all punish the sinners for their sins after being confirmed to be believers, and interpreted despairing of *Allah*'s mercy as that *Allah* does not forgive the sins of the sinners. Indeed, both meanings are blasphemous.

For one to be safe, one has to be between these two extreme positions. One must be fearful of the punishment of *Allah*, and at the same time hopeful for the mercy of *Allah*. For the believer, these two feelings are like the two wings for the bird. The bird cannot fly with one wing; it needs both. The believer needs to have these two feelings in one's heart to be safe.

6. **Having arrogance (*kibr*) towards the slaves of *Allah*, which is to reject the truth said by someone and/or to look down on the people;**

Explanation: Among the sins of the heart is to be arrogant.

Arrogance (*Kibr*) is divided into two types, as mentioned in the *hadith* of the Prophet ﷺ, narrated by *Muslim*:

$$\text{«الكِبْرُ بَطَرُ الحَقّ وَغَمْطُ النَّاسِ»}$$

1. The first type is to reject the truth. This occurs when one knows that another person is saying the truth, and despite that, one rejects the truth from him because the other person is poor, has less power, is of the opposite gender, or the like.

2. The second type is for the person to look highly to oneself and look down on others, because *Allah* gave one a lot of money, power, or other advantages.

Arrogance (*Kibr*) is an enormous sin. On the Day of Judgment, the arrogant people will have their human shape made as small as little ants. Other people will step on them, without them dying. Their punishment on that day will be fitting to their sin.

7. **Having enmity in the heart for a Muslim, if one acts in accordance with this and does not hate it;**

Explanation: Among the sins of the heart is to have enmity for a Muslim (*hiqd*). This enmity is to take a Muslim as an enemy without a religious reason. If, as a result, one causes harm to one's fellow Muslim or is firm to do that, then one is sinful. On the other hand, if one rejects such a feeling and does not try to harm, even with the tongue, other Muslims out of it, then one is not sinful.

8. **Envy, i.e., to hate and feel bitter about the endowment on a Muslim, and act in accordance with this feeling;**

Explanation: Envy (*hasad*) is among the sins of the heart. It means for one to feel disturbed that another Muslim has a certain endowment, such as money, to a point that one acts trying to make this Muslim lose this endowment. One may feel this about religious endowments as well as worldly endowments. If one does this, one is committing the sin of envy.

If one only wishes to have something similar to what another Muslim has without trying to make that other Muslim lose this endowment, i.e., neither by sayings or actions, then one is not sinful.

Also, if a thought of envy crosses a person's mind without one being firm about pursuing it, rather one abstains from acting accordingly, then one is not sinful for that.

Of course, if a person makes a firm intention to commit a sin, then that intention itself is sinful. If one does not reach the point of having a firm determination to commit a sin (^azm), then one is not sinful for that. However, in the case of the person who hesitates whether or not to commit blasphemy, immediately, one becomes a blasphemer.

9. **Mentioning the charity given to one with the purpose of breaking one's heart, like to say to the receiver of the charity: "Did I not give you a so-and-so on such and such a day?" This nullifies the reward;**

Explanation: Al-Mannu bis-sadaqah is among the sins of the heart. It consists of one reminding another person about an act of charity that one did for him, with the purpose of breaking the other's heart. An example is for one to address another person in front of people by saying, "Do you remember when you were in deep need for money and I gave you what you needed," with the intention of breaking his heart and humiliating him. Such an action is considered a sin and nullifies the reward of the aforementioned charity.

On the other hand, if one reminds another person of a good act that one had done to him not to break his heart, but for another legitimate intention, then one is not sinful. An example of that is when someone addresses one's brother or friend by saying, "You never helped me when I needed help." In response to that the brother or the friend says, "Don't you remember when I gave you such and such" just to remind one and not to break one's heart. In this case the brother / friend is not sinful for such a saying.

Allah said (al-Baqarah 264):

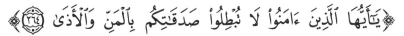

This verse means: [Do not nullify your acts of charity by falling into 'al-mann', i.e., by reminding the person whom you helped about what you did with the purpose of breaking one's heart.]

10. Persisting with sinning;

Explanation: Among the sins of the heart is for one to have the determination to sin in a way that one keeps committing sins until the number of one's sins becomes more than the number of one's good deeds. At the moment the number of the person's sins exceeds the number of one's good deeds, this person falls into the sin of "persisting on sinning", which is an enormous sin.

This matter is contingent upon the number of the sins exceeding the number of good deeds. Still, this sin was cited with the sins of the heart, because the origin of committing those sins is one's heart.

11. Believing that *Allah* shall not grant forgiveness to oneself;

Explanation: Among the sins of the heart is for a person to believe that definitely *Allah* will not forgive one because one committed one or more enormous sins from which one did not repent. This case was explained previously. In Arabic, this sin is called *su'udh-dhanni-billah*.

12. Thinking ill of Muslims;

Explanation: Among the sins of the heart is for one to think ill about one or more Muslims, without relying on any valid evidence. An example is if money is stolen from someone and without relying on any valid evidence, the robbed person believes in one's heart that a specific Muslim is the one who took the money.

On the other hand, if one relies on valid evidence, then one is not sinful. An example is when one knows about a person being a thief, and this person was in the place where the theft happened. Then if someone thinks it is most likely that the thief took the money, then one is not sinful.

However, many people commit this sin of thinking ill about other Muslims when they hate them. They find it easy to attribute bad traits to them. If they see the person whom they dislike doing something that can be interpreted in two ways, one good and one bad, they immediately interpret it in the bad way.

13. Denying the *Qadar* (Destining);

Explanation: Among the sins of the heart is to deny the *Qadar*.

259

This is blasphemy. The *Qadar*, which is the attribute of *Allah*, is making things happen in accordance with the eternal Knowledge and Will of *Allah, ta^ala*. If anyone belies the *Qadar*, that is, one believes that one or more things occur without the Destining of *Allah*, then one blasphemes. The Prophet ﷺ, his Companions, their followers, and the four *Imams*, among others, explicitly mentioned this judgment.

14. Feeling happy about a sin done by oneself or others;

Explanation: As it was explained, it is a sin for one to feel happy about the occurrence of a sin, whether this sin of which one knows occurs now or it occurred in the past, and whether it is committed by oneself or by others, in one's presence or absence.

15. Betraying someone, even a blasphemer, such as to kill one after promising one safety;

Explanation: The Prophet ﷺ told us that betrayal is prohibited. Hence, it is unlawful to betray another person, even if this person is a blasphemer. This is so even if a blasphemer fights the Muslims, but, one Muslim tells him, "Come to us, come to our land, and spend some time, and you are safe." If, because of this guarantee, this blasphemer comes to the Muslim side, and then that Muslim (or any other Muslim who knows about the safety guarantee) kills him, this Muslim committed betrayal, and thus committed a sin.

Betraying another includes the case when one cheats someone else in monetary dealings like buying, selling, and hiring, even if the betrayed person is a blasphemer. It is prohibited.

16. Harming a Muslim deceptively;

Explanation: To harm the Muslim deceptively (*makr* and *khadi^ah*) is among the sins of the heart. This is to make harm to a Muslim in a concealed manner. *At-Tabaraniyy* narrated from the Prophet ﷺ that he said:

$$\text{«المَكْرُ وَالخِدَاعُ فِى النَّارِ»}$$

This means: «The one who harms a Muslim deceptively did an act for which he deserves the torture in Hellfire.»

17. Hating the Companions, the *Al* of the Prophet, and the righteous

260

Muslims;

Explanation: Among the sins of the heart is to hate the Companions of the Prophet. If one hates all of them, one blasphemes. The Companions include those who committed blasphemy after the Prophet died, then they returned to *Islam*. No one of them would lie in conveying from the Prophet ﷺ, whether or not one of them spent a long time with the Prophet ﷺ.

Also, among the sins of the heart is to hate the wives of the Prophet, his relatives (i.e., the *Al* of the Prophet ﷺ), or the righteous Muslims. All of this was explained previously.

Hating *Abu Bakr, ^Umar, ^Uthman, ^Aliyy,* or any Companion among the first batches of the *Muhajirun* and the *Ansar* is an enormous sin. If the person hates even one among the Ten, to whom the Prophet gave the good news of Paradise, one will be an enormous sinner.

18. Abstaining from paying some of what *Allah* made obligatory (*bukhl*);

19. Abstaining from paying a lot or all of what *Allah* made obligatory (*shuhh*);

20. Having a strong desire to be rich in a bad, sinful manner (*hirs*);

Explanation: Being very attached to money is what leads some people to commit those three sins.

The first one among these sins is *bukhl*. In this context, it means to be a miser in paying what *Allah* made obligatory on one. Examples of these obligations are the obligatory support of the wife and the little children, and paying *Zakah*.

If this bad attribute becomes stronger, then it is called *shuhh*. If a person does not support his non-pubescent children only, he is attributed with *bukhl*. However, if he abstains from supporting them and his wife, and from paying *Zakah*, then he is attributed with *shuhh*.

If a person has a strong desire to gather money, because of which one does that even through *haram* ways, then such a bad attribute is called *hirs*.

As you can see, the origin of these three sins is a strong

attachment of the heart to gather money, in a way that is not accepted by *Allah*. This is one of the reasons why the pious people train themselves to be detached from the worldly matters. By doing this, they become stronger against taking *haram* money.

As for the person who gathers money from *halal* sources to spend it in *halal* rewardable ways, like to spend it to fulfill the obligation of supporting one's family, to help one's needy relatives, or to satisfy one's needs in a way that prevents one from falling into sins, one is rewarded by *Allah*. The money that one gathers is praiseworthy money. This is the money which the Prophet, *sallallahu ^alayhi wa sallam*, praised. *Ahmad* narrated from the Prophet ﷺ that he said:

«نِعْمَ المَالُ الصَّالِحُ لِلرَّجُلِ الصَّالِحِ»

This means: «How praised is the good money for the good person (i.e., the pious person).» This *hadith* refers to the lawful money which the person spends in what benefits one in the Hereafter.

21. **Breaching the rules of glorification regarding what *Allah* made glorified (*istihanah*);**

22. **Belittling what *Allah* rendered great, in status and consequence, be it obedience, disobedience, the *Qur'an*, Islamic knowledge, Paradise, or torture of Hellfire.**

Explanation: Among the sins of the heart is for one to breach the rules of glorification for what *Allah* glorified, or to belittle what is considered religiously great.

An example of that is for a person to carry the Book of *Qur'an* without being in the state of purification. This is a sin that results from a lack of the proper glorification in the heart. This does not mean that one does not glorify the *Qur'an* in one's heart at all. If one does not, this is blasphemy. It means that one is deficient in that matter.

An example of belittlement that is blasphemous is what some false Sufis say about Paradise. They say that Paradise is like a toy for the little children. What they mean by that is that they reached (according to their claim) a high level, to a point that their hearts are so full with the love of *Allah* that Paradise does not mean anything to them. They claim that only childlike people will have an interest in or glorify Paradise. This is a blasphemous statement. It belittles Paradise and belies the *Qur'an*. *Allah* praised in the *Qur'an* the righteous people by saying,

$$﴾وَيَدْعُونَنَا رَغَبًا وَرَهَبًا ۝﴿$$

This verse 90 of *Suratul-Ambiya'* means: [They supplicate Us (*Allah*) while hopeful of getting Our reward and fearing Our punishment.] The saying of these false Sufis belies this verse. This is why their statement is blasphemous.

Likewise, blasphemes the one who considers the torture of Hellfire easy, because one is belying several verses of the *Qur'an*. Verse 7 of *al-Baqarah* is:

$$﴾وَلَهُمْ عَذَابٌ عَظِيمٌ ۝﴿$$

It means: [They are going to receive a severe torture in the Hereafter.]

Chapter 42
Sins of the Abdomen

Among the sins of the abdomen are:

1. **To consume the money of usurious gain (*riba*);**

2. **To consume the money of taxes on trade (*maks*);**

3. **To consume the money of others taken from them unjustly (*ghasb*);**

4. **To consume the money of stealing (*sariqah*);**

5. **To consume anything taken through a deal unlawful by the Islamic law (*Shar^*);**

Explanation: This chapter pertains to the sins of the abdomen. The abdomen is one of the seven organs, other than the heart, categorized as doing sins. These organs are the tongue, the hand, the foot, the eye, the ear, the abdomen, and the private parts.

Among the sins of the abdomen is for one to consume what *Allah* made forbidden. Consuming is not exclusive to eating. It includes benefiting. We must not consume anything that *Allah* made prohibited for us to consume.

Examples are to consume the money taken unlawfully whether through stealing, force, usurious gains, taxes on trade, or the like. It was narrated from the Prophet ﷺ, that the first part to decompose in the grave is one's abdomen. If this is the state in which the abdomen becomes in the future, then one must not let the desires related to this abdomen lead one to Hellfire. *Al-Bayhaqiyy* and others narrated from the Prophet ﷺ that he said,

$$ «كُلُّ لَحْمٍ نَبَتَ مِنْ سُحْتٍ فَالنَّارُ أَوْلَى بِهِ» $$

This means: «Hellfire is more deserving of any flesh that grows from *haram*.» Taking money from unlawful sources, or spending it in an unlawful manner is an enormous sin.

6. **To consume alcohol. The punishment of the drinker who is free is forty lashes and the slave receives one-half of that. The caliph may add to that as a disciplinary action (*ta^zir*);**

Explanation: The one who consumes alcohol (i.e., an intoxicating drink) whether an intoxicating amount or not, is punished in accordance to the *Shar^* by the Caliph or his appointees. The free person is whipped forty lashes (in a specific way). As for the slave, he is whipped 20 lashes, one-half of the punishment of the free person. *Allah* made this matter easier for the slaves. The Caliph is entitled to add more lashes to the punishment of the one who drinks alcohol, totaling up to eighty (80) lashes. He can do this if he believes that there will be a benefit in the extra punishment. In this case, it is an extra disciplinary punishment.

Such an extra disciplinary punishment first took place at the time of *^Umar*. At the time of *^Umar*, a large number of new lands and people joined the Islamic state. In comparison to the time of the Prophet and *Abu Bakr*, many more Muslims drank alcohol. When *^Umar* noticed this matter, to prevent this sin from becoming widespread, he ordered to lash the one who drinks alcohol eighty lashes.

Prohibited alcohol has a specific definition. *Al-Bukhariyy* narrated that our Master *^Umar*, may *Allah* raise his rank, mentioned this definition by saying:

$$\text{«الخَمْرُ مَا خَامَرَ العَقْلَ»}$$

This means, "Wine is the drink which influences the mind (causing ecstasy)." Every drink that changes the mind, causing intoxication is a prohibited drink. Even if a person does not reach this state except after drinking a big amount of it, it is still prohibited for him to drink one sip of it. This is so due to the *hadith* of the Prophet ﷺ narrated by *Abu Dawud*:

$$\text{«ومَا أَسْكَرَ مِنْهُ الفَرَقُ فَمِلْءُ الكَفّ مِنْهُ حَرَامٌ»}$$

This means: «If the drink does not intoxicate until one consumes a whole *faraq* of it, then drinking even a handful of it is prohibited.»; A *faraq* is a big container which is equal to sixteen (16) *Baghdadiyy ritls* (about 6 liters or 1.6 gallons)

7. **To consume whatever is intoxicating, *najas*-filthy, and revolting;**

Explanation: In addition to what was mentioned earlier, it is not permissible to consume any substance, which renders one's mind dysfunctional, even if it does not cause intoxication. This includes marijuana, opium, cocaine, hallucination pills, and the like.

Consuming a *najas*-filth is among the sins of the abdomen. Examples of *najas*-filth are blood, pig, and *maytah* (improperly killed animal). Also, it is prohibited to eat anything normally considered revolting. The criterion is that if at the time of the Prophet, the Arabs considered something as *khabith*-revolting, then it is prohibited to consume it. Although not *najas*, it is not permissible to consume snails because it is *khabith*-revolting, and saliva after it separates from the mouth, nasal seepage, and *maniyy* because each of them is revolting. Also, it is prohibited to consume anything that harms one's body, like poison except what is little and beneficial without harm, even if it is not *najas*.

8. To consume the money of the orphan [unrightfully];

Explanation: Consuming the money of an orphan is among the sins of the abdomen. The orphan is the one whose father died while non-pubescent. Even if this orphan gives a poor person a charity from his own money, it is not permissible for the poor person to take it. This is because *Allah* said in *Suratun-Nisa'*, verse 10,

$$\text{﴿إِنَّ ٱلَّذِينَ يَأْكُلُونَ أَمْوَٰلَ ٱلْيَتَٰمَىٰ ظُلْمًا إِنَّمَا يَأْكُلُونَ فِي بُطُونِهِمْ نَارًا ۝﴾}$$

It means: [Those who unjustly consume the belongings of orphans are going to consume fire that fills their abdomens]. It must be an enormous sin.

9. To consume the money of the *waqf*s in a way contrary to the condition set by the one who established it;

Explanation: Among the sins of the abdomen is for one to consume the money of the *waqf* in a way that does not comply with the stipulations set by the one who established it.

The *waqf* is something that a person dedicates to be used immediately, or after one's death, in a lawful way, without it being consumed, to produce a continuous benefit. When something is dedicated as a *waqf*, it is no more in the ownership of the one who did this dedication. Its use is exclusively compliant to the stipulations.

An example is for a person to dedicate a building a *waqf* mosque. Immediately, this building goes out of his ownership, and it must be used exclusively as a mosque. Moreover, it is invalid to later change its usage. If a building is dedicated as a *waqf Hanafiiyy* school, it is not permissible for anyone to sell it or to change its usage to become a *Shafi^iyy* school, for example. This ruling stems from the *hadith* of the Prophet ﷺ, narrated by *al-Bukhariyy*:

$$ «المُسْلِمُونَ عِنْدَ شُرُوطِهِمْ» $$

This means: «The Muslims must honor their stipulations.»

On the other hand, (although it is a rewardable act of charity) dedicating a certain amount of food for poor people is not a valid *waqf*, because the poor people cannot benefit from this food except by consuming it. Dedicating a piece of land to be an Islamic cemetery is a valid *waqf*, because the people can benefit from it by burying the dead Muslims in it without consuming the land.

10. To consume what was given out of shyness and not out of one's good will;

Explanation: Intentional embarrassment of others to give one their money unwillingly is prohibited. Receiving this money is sinful. This money remains in the ownership of the embarrassed giver even if the second one has it in his hands. This is stated in the *hadith* of the Prophet ﷺ narrated by *ad-Daraqutniyy, al-Bayhaqiyy,* and *Ahmad*:

$$ «لا يَحِلُّ مَالُ امْرِئٍ مُسْلِمٍ إلا بِطِيبِ نَفْسٍ مِنْهُ» $$

This means: «It is not permissible to take the belongings of a Muslim except with his good will.»

However, embarrasing others to spend their money unwillingly on matters Islamically deemed necessary is not prohibited.

Chapter 43
Sins of the Eye

Among the sins of the eye are:

1. **For men to look at the faces and hands of marriageable women with desire and at other parts of their bodies with or without desire; similarly, for the women to look between the navels and the knees of marriageable men with or without desire, and to look at other parts of their bodies with desire;**

Explanation: Among the sins of the eye is for a man to look, with or without desire, to any part of a marriageable woman's body, excluding her face and hands. In this context, a marriageable woman refers to a woman other than a "*mahram*". A "*mahram*" is a woman that a man is not permitted to marry under any circumstance, like his daughter, sister, aunt, mother, nursing mother, as well as her daughter, granddaughter, mother, and the like.

It is permissible for the man to look at the face and the hands of a woman without desire. Looking at them with desire is prohibited. This rule does not apply to the face and hands of a man's wife and unmarried slave women.

By consensus, the face of the woman is not an unlawful nakedness. No weight should be given to the saying of some later scholars, who claimed that it was *haram* for the woman to uncover her face in the presence of marriageable men. Their saying breaches the consensus. The *Malikiyy* scholar *Qadi ^Iyad* and the *Shafi^iyy* scholar *Ibn Hajar al-Haytamiyy*, among others, copied the consensus on this matter.

It is also prohibited for the woman to look, with or without desire, at what is between the navel and the knees of a man (other than her husband or master). As for the rest of his body, she is allowed to look at it, if this occurs without desire. A later *Shafi^iyy* scholar said that the woman is not allowed to see from the body of the man, except the parts which he is allowed to see from her body, i.e., the face and the hands. This is a very weak saying to which no consideration should be given.

2. **To look at the unlawful nakedness (^awrahs);**

Explanation: Additionally, it is prohibited for a man to look to what is between the navel and the knees of another man. Similarly, it is prohibited for a Muslim woman to look at what is between the navel and the knees of another Muslim woman. Although the navel and the knee themselves are not ^awrah, it becomes an obligation to cover parts of them to insure that the area in between them is covered.

It is not permissible for the Muslim woman to uncover any part of her body in front of a blasphemous woman, except what a Muslim woman usually uncovers when she works inside her house, such as her hair, arms, feet, and neck.

Note: It is forbidden for the woman to uncover her thigh before her mother, her sister, or her daughter (except if the daughter or sister is two years old or the like).

3. **For a man or woman in solitude to needlessly uncover the unlawful nakedness (^awrah). One may look without desire, at other than the area between the navel and knees of the non-marriageable person or the person of the same sex;**

Explanation: While alone, one is not allowed to uncover one's unlawful nakedness (^awrah) without a need. This signifies that it is permissible to uncover them for any proper reason. Such reasons are bathing, changing clothes, or just to cool off from the heat. In solitude, the unlawful nakedness (^awrah) of the woman is the area between the navel and the knees, and for a man is his penis and anus.

Excluding what is between the navel and the knee, it is permissible for the man to look without desire at the body of another man. Similarly, a woman is allowed to look without desire at the body of another woman, except for what is between the navel and the knee. Moreover, it is permissible for the man to look at the body of a non-marriageable woman and for her to look at his body, without desire, except for what is between the navel and the knees. The case of a person with another non-marriageable person is similar to the case of a man with another man, or a woman with another woman. Desirous looking is prohibited in such cases.

4. **To look down on a Muslim;**

Explanation: This case was mentioned before when the sins of the heart were discussed. It is mentioned again in this chapter to draw one's attention to that it is also related to the eye. From one angle it is cited among the sins of the heart, and from another angle it is cited among the sins of the eye.

5. **To look into someone else's house without one's permission or to look at something one kept hidden.**

Explanation: It is prohibited for a person to look inside someone else's house when the latter does not allow it, such as while the man is sitting alone uncovering his thigh (to cool off), or while his wife is uncovered.

Also, if someone hides something, and one is bothered if others look at it (like one's personal notes), then another is sinful to look at them without one's permission.

Chapter 44
Sins of the Tongue

Among the sins of the tongue are:

Explanation: This chapter pertains to mentioning the sins of the tongue. Most of the sins that the person does are sins of the tongue. Our Prophet said:

«أَكْثَرُ خَطَايَا ابْنِ ءَادَمَ مِنْ لِسَانِهِ»

This means: «Most of the sins of Adam's offspring are from their tongues.» This is a *sahih hadith* narrated by *at-Tabaraniyy* from the route of *^Abdullah Ibn Mas^ud* from the Prophet, *sallallahu ^alayhi wa sallam*.

1. **To commit gossip (*ghibah*), i.e., to mention, in the absence of a Muslim, a true matter about one that one hates to be mentioned;**

Explanation: *Ghibah* (Gossip) is among the sins of the tongue. *Ghibah* is to talk about a Muslim in his absence by mentioning things related to him that he does not like to be said about him. This does not include, of course, praising someone who does not like to be praised. Such praise is not gossip and is not sinful.

Examples of prohibited gossip are to say: "so and so is short," or "he doesn't have good manners," or "his son is not polite," or "he does not recognize the merits of others," or "he is controlled by his wife," or "so and so sleeps (or eats) a lot", or "his clothes are dirty," or "his house is messy."

Whether such statements refer to the Muslim's body, house, family, clothes, car, or the like, it is a prohibited gossip. There are cases where some of these statements may be said unsinfully, because they are used in the context of praising the person. An example of this is praising someone's detachment from worldly matters by saying, "his furniture is old."

Sometimes the sin of gossip is an enormous sin, and other times it is considered a small sin. Gossiping about a pious person is an enormous sin. On the other hand, gossiping about an enormous sinner is not an enormous sin. This gossip is a small sin, except if the person who commits the gossip against this sinful Muslim does that frequently. *Abu Dawud* narrated that the Prophet ﷺ said:

«إنَّ مِنْ أَرْبَى الرِّبَا الاسْتِطَالَةَ فى عِرْضِ المُسْلِمِ بِغَيْرِ حَقّ»

This means: «The unjust, frequent dispraising of another Muslim is similar to the most enormous kind of *riba* (usurious gain).»

Mentioning disparaging matters about a Muslim that are fabrications is a worse sin than gossip; it is called 'buhtan.'

As it is forbidden for one to gossip, it is also forbidden to inexcusably remain silent when gossip is committed before one.

Warning against someone who is causing harm to or cheating Muslims is not considered a prohibited gossip. Rather, this warning is an obligation. An example of that is the case of the person who knows that an employee is cheating his employer. The one who knows that is obligated to tell this employer about this case. Another example is warning against a person who is teaching the wrong religious information, out of ignorance, trickery, or otherwise. Warning about him is not a sin. Rather, it is an obligation.

2. **Talebearing among Muslims to stir up trouble among them (namimah);**

Explanation: Talebearing between two Muslims by conveying to each what one says about the other to cause trouble between them is an enormous sin. *Al-Bukhariyy* and others narrated that the Prophet ﷺ said:

«لا يَدْخُلُ الجَنَّةَ قَتَّاتٌ»

This means: «The one who commits talebearing does not enter Paradise.» The talebearer does not enter Paradise with the early Muslims. Rather, he is tortured. Then, he enters Paradise with the later batches. Committing this sin is among the reasons that cause for many people to be tortured in the grave.

3. **Stirring up trouble without passing words among others-even if it is goading animals to fight each other (tahrish);**

Explanation: Among the sins is to stir up trouble between two or more Muslims, even without passing words between them. Similarly, goading animals to fight one another-like to push two roosters, two goats, or two dogs to fight one another-is sinful, even when this does not include gambling.

4. To lie, i.e., to say what is different from the truth;

Explanation: Lying is for one to report something, while knowing that the truth is different from what one is saying. This is the forbidden lying. If one thinks that things had occurred the way one is narrating, while in reality they occurred in a different way, then one is not sinful.

Lying is considered a sin whether the person commits it jokingly or seriously. There are different levels of lying. Some lies are blasphemous. Other lies are enormous sins, and others are small sins. In a few cases, it is permissible to lie. An example is when someone wants unjustly to kill a Muslim who comes inside your house. In such a case, you protect your Muslim fellow, even if you need to say a lie.

5. To commit perjury, i.e., to solemnly swear to a lie;

Explanation: Among the sins of the tongue is to swear to a lie knowingly. This is an enormous sin.

On the other hand, swearing truthfully by *Allah* or His Attributes is not a sin. However, according to *Imam ash-Shafi^yy,* swearing by other than *Allah* or His Attributes, such as the *Ka^bah* or the Prophet, is very disliked. *Imam Ahmad* ruled it sinful.

Swearing by *Allah* to a lie is not blasphemy because it does not reflect the absence of glorification of God. However, it does lack the proper glorification of *Allah.* Hence, it is deemed an enormous sin.

6. To say words which attribute adultery or fornication (*zina*) to a person or to one of one's relatives, either explicitly or implicitly with that intention. The punishment for one who is free is eighty lashes; the slave receives one-half of that;

Explanation: Among the sins of the tongue is *qadhf,* i.e., to attribute *zina* to a Muslim with an explicit statement, or implicitly with that intention. The Caliph applies a specific punishment (*hadd*) to the one who commits the sin of *qadhf.* On the other hand, insinuating fornication or adultery is sinful, but does not warrant the specific punishment of _qadhf_.

The free person who commits the sin of _qadhf_ is whipped eighty (80) lashes. As for the slave, he receives one-half of that, forty (40) lashes.

The one who commits the sin of _qadhf_ against his child is excluded from the aforementioned punishment

Examples of explicit statements are to address a person, "O you fornicator", or "O you, the son of the fornicator", or "O bastard", or "O you sodomizer".

Addressing a person, "You are a disgrace," or "O you enormous sinner," while intending to attribute _zina_ to him, is considered _qadhf_. Without this specific intention, such statements are not considered _qadhf_.

An example of insinuation is to address a Muslim by saying, "Well, I am not a bastard" meaning that the other person is a bastard. Although such a statement is an enormous sin, the one who says it (in the aforementioned sinful meaning) is not whipped. The ruler determines a suitable punishment in this case, contingent upon the state of the accuser. The judge punishes him in a legitimate way that deters him from doing it later.

7. To cuss the Companions;

Explanation: Among the sins of the tongue is to cuss the Companions of the Prophet. If one cusses or degrades all of them, then he is judged as a blasphemer. Since the Companions conveyed the rules of the Religion, such a statement entails discrediting the Religion. The one who says that all of them were not trustworthy is claiming that we cannot be confident in the rules that they conveyed. Hence, he is judged as a blasphemer.

In _Suratut-Tawbah_, verse 100, _Allah_ praised the early Immigrants and _Ansar_, and those who follow those Companions:

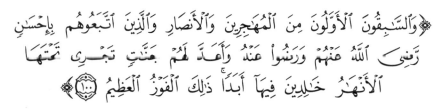

This verse means: [Allah accepts the early Immigrants and Ansar and those who follow their steps. They do not object to Allah's Predestination. Allah prepared for them everlasting enjoyment in Paradise, in very beautiful places with rivers. This is the great success.]

Whoever claims that all the Companions are dispraised belies this verse and is a blasphemer.

The one who slanders one of the pious Companions commits an enormous sin, but not blasphemy. Imam ˆAliyy was a righteous Caliph. It was an obligation on the Muslims to obey him. Consequently whoever disobeyed ˆAliyy and fought him was a sinful person. Hence, no slander is committed against the few Companions who fought Imam ˆAliyy in saying, "Those who fought our master ˆAliyy were unjust".

Muˆawiyah Ibn Abi Sufyan was a Companion, who committed an enormous sin by fighting Imam ˆAliyy. The Prophet ﷺ told about this before it took place by saying:

«وَيْحَ عَمَّارٍ، تَقْتُلُهُ الفِئَةُ البَاغِيَةُ . يَدْعُوهُمْ إِلَى الجَنَّةِ وَيَدْعُونَهُ إِلَى النَّارِ»

This means: «Sympathy to ˆAmmar! The unjust group will kill him. He will call them to Paradise, and they will call him to Hellfire.» This is a sahih hadith narrated by Al-Bukhariyy and many others. It reached the level of tawatur. More than 20 Companions narrated this hadith from the Prophet ﷺ, including Muˆawiyah himself.

ˆAmmar Ibn Yasir was an honorable Companion who embraced Islam very early in Makkah. His parents were tortured and killed for refusing to leave Islam. He was tortured also. The Prophet ﷺ praised him at many occasions. In one situation, the Prophet ﷺ said, «Follow the way of ˆAmmar.» During the caliphate of Imam ˆAliyy, ˆAmmar was killed by the soldiers of Muˆawiyah in the battle of Siffin. This affirms that Muˆawiyah's camp was the unjust group mentioned in the aforementioned hadith. Hence the person who says, "those who fought Imam ˆAliyy were unjust", is only repeating what the Prophet ﷺ said. Certainly, the one who repeats what the Prophet ﷺ said and taught should not be blamed at all.

Although some of the Companions committed enormous sins, in general, they were in a very high situation. The Companions never disagreed about any basic creedal matter. All of them knew and believed that *Allah* does not resemble the creation. They knew that changing is among the attributes of the creation, and this is why they affirmed that *Allah* is free of it. No one among them believed that *Allah* resides in a place, changes His Will, or moves from one place to another. They knew that whatever moves changes and has limits. Those are the attributes of the creation, not the Creator.

Abu Nuˆaym al-Asbahaniyy narrated that *Imam ˆAliyy* said:

$$ \text{«مَنْ زَعَمَ أَنَّ إِلهَنَا مَحْدُودٌ فَقَدْ جَهِلَ الخَالِقَ المَعْبُودَ»} $$

This means: "The one who claims that our Lord has limits is ignorant about God, the One Who deserves to be worshipped." That is, the one who claims that *Allah* is attributed with a form or quantity is a blasphemer. The Companions never disagreed about these basic creeds.

Moreover in exception of few cases, they had good relations with one another, especially the early Immigrants and *Ansar*. Contrary to what some misguided people claim, they had a great love and high respect for each other. One example is that *Imam ˆAliyy* had an intelligent daughter from Lady *Fatimah*. Her name was *Umm Kulthum*. Our master *ˆUmar*, who was in his fifties, wanted to get the blessing of marrying a woman from the *Al* of the Prophet ﷺ. So, he asked our master *ˆAliyy* to give him his daughter, *Umm Kulthum* (the granddaughter of the Prophet), in marriage. She was nine years old then. So, *ˆAliyy* told *ˆUmar*, "She is still young. Look at her. If you like her, I will give her to you in marriage." Then, *Imam ˆAliyy* told *Umm Kulthum*, "Go to *ˆUmar* and ask him, 'Did you like the garment (*hullah*)?' *ˆUmar* said, "Tell your father: 'Yes, I like it' ". She became *ˆUmar*'s wife.

Another example is that *Asma' Bint ˆUmays* was married to *Jaˆfar Ibn Abi Talib* until his death. She bore his child *Muhammad*. Later our master *Abu Bakr* married her and had a son from her named *Muhammad*. After the death of *Abu Bakr*, our master *ˆAliyy* married her. One day, her two sons, *Muhammad*, the son of *Jaˆfar* and

Muḥammad, the son of *Abu Bakr* mentioned boastfully the merits of their fathers. *^Aliyy* told her, "Be the judge between them (having married both *Ja^far*, *^Aliyy's* brother, and *Abu Bakr*)." She said, "I never saw a young man who had better manners than *Ja^far*, and I never saw an erderly who had better manners than *Abu Bakr*." *^Aliyy* laughed and asked her, "What did you leave for me?" meaning, "where do I fit?" *^Aliyy* was not mad at her for praising *Abu Bakr* or *Ja^far*, may *Allah* raise their ranks.

8. To give false testimony;

Explanation: Among the sins of the tongue is to give false testimony. This means to lie while testifying. The sin of giving a false testimony is so enormous, to a point that the Prophet drew a similarity between it and associating a partner with *Allah*. This is only to show the severity of this sin and does not mean at all that it reaches the level of blasphemy.

9. To procrastinate paying one's debt when it is due and one is able;

Explanation: This sin is related to the tongue because the person promises the other of paying back his money. Then he does not keep his promise. Such a person deserves to be punished by the ruler to pay back the debt. It is permissible to warn people against such a person, by saying for example, "Be careful, do not deal with him because he did not give me my money back when it was due, although he was able."

The Prophet ﷺ said in the *ḥadith* narrated by *Abu Dawud, an-Nasa'iyy*, and *Ibn Majah*:

$$ \text{«لَيُّ الوَاجِدِ يُحِلُّ عِرْضَهُ وَعُقُوبَتَهُ»} $$

This means: «It is permissible to warn against the one who procrastinates (paying back his debt) and to punish him.» The ruler may punish him by hitting, or putting him in jail.

10. To cuss, curse, mock, or utter what harms a Muslim;

Explanation: Among the sins of the tongue is to cuss a Muslim (degrading him) without a religious excuse. This is an enormous sin (*fusuq*), as the Prophet ﷺ explicitly mentioned in the *ḥadith* narrated by *Al-Bukhariyy* and *Muslim*. This is true also in the case of damning a Muslim without a valid religious excuse. "Damning" refers to *Allah* withholding His mercy from a person. To emphasize the enormity of this sin, the Prophet ﷺ said in the _hadith_ narrated by _Al-Bukhariyy_ and _Muslim_:

$$\text{«لَعْنُ الْمُؤْمِنِ كَقَتْلِهِ»}$$

This means, «To damn a Muslim is like to kill him.» It does not mean that damning a Muslim is as enormous as killing him. It means it is an enormous sin just as killing is.

It is permissible to damn a Muslim for a religious excuse. If a Muslim is an enormous sinner, then it is permissible to damn him for one of two reasons: To warn against what he is doing, or to put pressure on him to leave the sin that he is doing.

There is an invalid saying that it is not permissible to damn anyone whether a Muslim or a non-Muslim, except those who are known with certainty to die as blasphemers, like _Abu Lahab_ and _Iblis_. The Prophet ﷺ mentioned that the angels damn, until the dawn appears, the woman who does not fulfill her husband's right in what pertains to sexual intercourse. Had it been not permissible to damn except those known for sure will die as blasphemers, then the angels would not have damned such a woman. _Ibn Hibban, al-Bukhariyy_, and _Muslim_ narrated this _hadith_:

$$\text{«إِذَا بَاتَتِ الْمَرْأَةُ هَاجِرَةً فِرَاشَ زَوْجِهَا، لَعَنَتْهَا الْمَلَائِكَةُ حَتَّى تُصْبِحَ»}$$

This is why ^Aliyy Zaynul-^Abidin damned, in the open, a person next to the Ka^bah. Likewise, _Ahmad Ibn Hambal_ was asked if it was permissible to damn Yazid, the son of _Mu^awiyah_;[56] he said "Yes".

Other sins of the tongue are to mock, degrade, or address a Muslim unjustly with any harmful statement. This excludes the cases in which the _Shar^_ permits it.

Also, it is prohibited to do any harmful action to a Muslim, even without uttering words. An example is making a signal that breaks his heart.

---

[56] _Yazid_ was the ruler who ordered the killing of al-_Husayn_, the grandson of the Prophet, _sallallahu ^alayhi wa sallam_.

11. To lie about *Allah* and His Messenger;

Explanation: In general, lying about *Allah* and the Prophet ﷺ is an enormous sin.

In this regard, *al-Bukhariyy* and *Muslim* and many others narrated a *hadith* that reached the level of *tawatur*:

«مَنْ كَذَبَ عَلَيَّ مُتَعَمِّدًا فَلْيَتَبَوَّأْ مَقْعَدَهُ مِنَ النَّارِ»

This means: «Let him who lies about me [Prophet *Muhammad*] on purpose prepare himself to occupy a place prepared for him in Hellfire». This threat should prevent any one among us from lying about the Prophet ﷺ. Even if the person lies about the Prophet ﷺ to urge people to do a good deed, it is still an enormous sin.

Sometimes such sins reach the level of blasphemy, such as claiming that the angels are the daughters of *Allah*, or intentionally attributing blasphemy to the Prophet ﷺ. Similarly, it is blasphemy to attribute to the Prophet ﷺ a statement that contradicts the rules revealed to him, while knowing the fact of the matter.

12. To make a false claim;

Explanation: It is sinful for someone to claim that another person owes him money, or that he has a right on him, while he knows that this is not true. Making such false claims is sinful, whether relying on false testimony, on one's social status, or one's influence.

13. To divorce one's wife while she is menstruating or during a period of purity (*tuhr*) in which one has had sexual intercourse with her (*bid^iyy* divorce);

Explanation: Among the sins of the tongue is the *bid^iyy* divorce. This is to divorce one's wife during her menstruation, postpartum bleeding, or period of purity after having had sexual intercourse with her. This divorce is in effect despite being sinful.

The divorce of one's wife in a period of purity without having sexual intercourse with her during that period is the non-sinful divorce called *Sunniyy* divorce. Calling it a "*Sunniyy* divorce" does not mean that it is necessarily rewardable.

If the wife does not menstruate, then divorcing her is non-sinful regardless of the time.

14. To utter the _dhihar_, like to say to one's wife, "You are to me like my mother," meaning: I now do not copulate with you just as I do not copulate with my mother. If one does not divorce immediately after uttering this, one is obliged to fulfill an expiation (_kaffarah_) which is to free a Muslim slave who has no defects; if unable, to fast two consecutive lunar months; and if unable, to feed sixty poor Muslims sixty _mudd_s;

Explanation: Among the sins of the tongue, is the _dhihar_. _Dhihar_ occurs when a man says to his wife, "You are to me like my mother (sister, etc.)" meaning, "I am now committing myself to not have sexual intercourse with you, just as I am committed to not have it with my mother, sister, or the like." In Arabic, the most common usage of such a statement involves using the term "_dhahr_", which originally means the "back". This is why it is called "_dhihar_". However, it is not a condition that one uses the word "_dhahr_" or its derivatives in Arabic for the aforementioned judgment to take place. The judgment takes place with any statement that gives the explained meaning.

In the Era of Ignorance, such a statement was considered a divorce. In the rules revealed to Prophet _Muhammad_ ﷺ, it is not considered a divorce, except if the one who says it intends by saying it to divorce his wife.

Dhihar is an enormous sin. In the _Qur'an_ (al-Mujadalah, 2),

$$ ﴿ٱلَّذِينَ يُظَٰهِرُونَ مِنكُم مِّن نِّسَآئِهِم مَّا هُنَّ أُمَّهَٰتِهِمْ ۖ إِنْ أُمَّهَٰتُهُمْ إِلَّا ٱلَّٰٓـِٔى وَلَدْنَهُمْ ۚ وَإِنَّهُمْ لَيَقُولُونَ مُنكَرًا مِّنَ ٱلْقَوْلِ وَزُورًا ۚ وَإِنَّ ٱللَّهَ لَعَفُوٌّ غَفُورٌ ﴾ ۞ ٢ ﴿ $$

it is called "_zur_" (fabrication) because it places the man's sexual relationship with his wife at the same footing as his relationship with his mother. Truly, the man does not have the same relationship with the two women.

If the husband divorces his wife immediately after he utters the words of _dhihar_, there is no expiation due on him. If he does not, then an expiation is due. Moreover, it is no more lawful for him to have sexual intercourse with his wife, except after he fulfills this expiation.

The expiation is to free a Muslim slave, who is clear from any defect that reduces his ability to work. If he does not own such a slave, then he buys one and sets him free. It is not a condition that this slave be pubescent or a male.

If he is unable to set a slave free, then he fasts two consecutive lunar months. If unable, then he has to feed sixty (60) poor Muslims by giving every one of them one *mudd* from the most common staple food in the area. It is not valid for him to feed, for example, thirty (30) poor Muslims, by giving each of them two *mudd*s.

15. To commit mistakes when reciting the Qur'an, whether or not those mistakes change the meaning;

Explanation: It is *haram* for a person to commit mistakes while reciting the Qur'an, whether or not these mistakes change the meaning. The ruling is the same when mistakes are committed because of ignorance or carelessness, except for the case of a slip of the tongue. Before one starts reciting by oneself, one must learn reciting the Qur'an from someone who knows the correct recitation. This is the way to be safe.

If one does not know how to pronounce the letters correctly from their exits, or changes the correct pronunciation of the words while reciting Qur'an, then one does not start to recite by oneself, even if one wants to recite to and learn from a qualified teacher. Rather, in this case, the qualified teacher recites first, then one recites after him, so that the teacher can hear the recitation. If the teacher approves one's pronunciation, one knows then that one did it properly and recites in the same way in the future.

If one pronounces the letters correctly from their exits, and does not change the pronunciation of the words, then it is permissible for one to recite to the knowledgeable teacher without the teacher reciting first. In this case, the teacher only needs to listen to one's recitation and affirm that one is reciting in the correct way.

16. To beg while solvent, i.e., while having money or a job;

Explanation: Among the sins of the tongue is for a solvent person to ask other people to give him money, while he has enough to satisfy his needs. It is narrated in al-Bukhariyy and *Muslim*:

«مَا يَزَالُ الرَّجُلُ يَسْأَلُ النَّاسَ حَتَّى يَأْتِىَ يَوْمَ القِيَامَةِ وَلَيْسَ فِى وَجْهِهِ مُزْعَةُ لَحْمٍ»

The _hadith_ means: «The one who keeps begging from people, while it is prohibited for him to do that, will not have any flesh on his face on the Day of Judgment.» In this world, he faced the people, begging of them, with no shyness on his face. Thus, as a punishment on the Day of Judgment, this same face will be deprived of its flesh.

On the other hand, the person who is poor and cannot fulfill his basic needs in a way other than begging is permitted to beg. However it is better for him not to do so, while remaining patient and avoiding unlawful matters.

In the _Qur'an, Allah_ praised the poor people, among the Immigrants of the Companions, who left out begging:

﴿يَحْسَبُهُمُ ٱلْجَاهِلُ أَغْنِيَآءَ مِنَ ٱلتَّعَفُّفِ ۝﴾

This verse means: [They looked and acted as solvent people to the extent that the one who did not know about their case would think that they were solvent.]

17. To utter a vow (_nadhr_) with the purpose of depriving the inheritor;

Explanation: Making a vow (_nadhr_) to give one's possessions to someone, with the mere intention of depriving the inheritors from these possessions, is a sin of the tongue. Such a vow (_nadhr_) is not valid.

An example is when a man makes a vow to give all his possessions to his daughters (because he does not have any son), with the purpose of depriving his brothers from inheriting. This is _haram_ and such a vow is invalid.

18. To neglect leaving a will, which states one's debts to or trusts for others, about which no one other than oneself knows;

Explanation: Among the sins of the tongue is for one to neglect leaving a will that states the debts or the trusts that one owes to others, if no one else knows about them. Debts, in this context, include overdue _Zakah_, and other financial obligations.

For instance, if one owes money to another person, and no one other than the inheritors knows about this debt, then it is obligatory upon this borrower to leave a verbal or a written will that secures the right of the lender.

Similarly, if a person is entrusted with a certain item for safekeeping, and no one else knows about it, then it is incumbent upon the entrusted person to leave a statement that secures the right of the one who owns the entrusted item.

If an upright and trustworthy person, who is not among the inheritors, knows about the debts or trusts, then leaving a will in such a case becomes a recommended matter. For other than the aforementioned matters, it is *sunnah* to write a will, but not an obligation. As mentioned in the *hadith* of the Prophet ﷺ, narrated by *al-Bukhariyy* and *Muslim*:

«مَا حَقُّ امْرِئ مُسْلِم لَهُ شَىءٌ يُوصِى فِيهِ، يَبِيتُ لَيْلَتَيْنِ، إلا وَوَصِيَّتُهُ مَكْتُوبَةٌ عِنْدَهُ»

This means «Every Muslim, who has anything about which a will is to be made, should not wait two consecutive nights without having prepared his written will.» It is recommended (*sunnah*) to write one's will, even if one does not owe any one money or hold trusts.

19. To attribute oneself to other than one's own father or liberator;

Explanation: Among the sins of the tongue, is for one to name as one's father other than the true one. This occurs if one says, "My father is so and so" while one knows that this is false (even if the person that one named adopted one). Likewise, if the owner of a slave sets him free, it is prohibited for the former slave to claim that someone else liberated him. There are certain religious rules associated to the parent-child and the liberator-slave relationship. Denying such relations leads to disregarding the rules associated to them, and to abuse the rights of people.

For example, if an emancipated slave dies without having any heirs among his relatives, then his ex-owner who set him free inherits him. If the ex-slave lies about the one who liberated him, it is clear that the right of inheriting him might be lost.

Another example is the case of the man who owns a slave woman. If he sets her free, and later she wants to get married (without her having a guardian among her relatives to conduct her marriage contract), then her liberator is her *waliyy*. He is the one entitled to perform her marriage. If this emancipated slave woman claims that someone other than her liberator set her free, then her marriage contract conducted by the alleged liberator is invalid.

20. To propose to a woman after she is already engaged to another Muslim;

Explanation: Among the sins of the tongue is for a man to propose to a certain woman whom he knows has been already engaged to another Muslim. Such an action causes harm to the fellow Muslim, and an interruption of relations with him.

However, if one proposes to a woman and, before the approval has been established, another man proposes to her, this is permissible. Likewise, if the second one did not know about the first one's proposal, he is not sinful.

On the other hand, if the first man, who got engaged to a woman, gives the second one permission to propose to her also, it is permissible for the second to do so. That is true, even if by consequence the engagement of the first person gets broken. Of course, if at any moment the fiancé changes his mind, and breaches the engagement, it is lawful for a second person to ask the hand of the woman.

Similarly, if a Christian or Jewish man who is *Dhimmiyy* is engaged to a *Dhimmiyyah* (Christian or Jewish woman), it is prohibited, even for a Muslim man, to propose to this woman.

21. To give an Islamic legal judgment (*fatwa*) without knowledge;

Explanation: Among the sins of the tongue is for one to give an answer (*fatwa*) to an Islamic question, without having the proper knowledge. The one who produces a *fatwa* has to be someone who is at the level of *ijtihad* (like *Shafiˆiyy*, *Abu Hanifah*, *Malik*, and *Ahmad*), or a scholar who is qualified to deduce the judgment of that case from a text of a *mujtahid*, like *al-Bayhaqiyy* and *al-Ghazaliyy*. If the person does not attain any of the aforementioned two levels of *ijtihad*, he is not entitled to produce a *fatwa*. He is only entitled to copy the *fatwa* of a *mujtahid*.

284

A *mujtahid* is a person with specific qualifications. Among those qualifications are to have memorized all the verses of the *Qur'an* that pertain to deducing judgments, the sayings of the Prophet that deal with deducing judgments, and to be sufficiently knowledgeable in the Arabic language. Moreover, he needs to be knowledgeable about the *mutlaq* (not restricted), *muqayyad* (restricted), general, specific, abrogated, abrogating, and unabrogated texts, and to know for every case whether or not consensus has already been established on it. Also, he has to be upright, trustworthy, adhering to the behavior and the ethics of the upright people who belong to his own social rank, and have a sharp mind.

If one is equipped with all the aforementioned qualifications (of a *mujtahid*), then he is entitled to produce a *fatwa* according to his own *ijtihad*. Otherwise (as is the case of most of the Muslims in all the eras), his only proper way is to follow the *fatwa* of a *mujtahid*, or the deductions of the scholars who have the qualification to deduce judgments from the statements of the *mujtahid* (*mujtahids* within a school).

The one who is asked about a particular religious matter, without having knowledge of its judgment, must not neglect saying, "I do not know." It was reported about *Imam Malik*, may *Allah* raise his rank, that once he was asked 48 questions. He answered sixteen (16) of them, and as to the remaining 32, he said, "I do not know."[57]

Also, when our master ^*Aliyy* was asked about a certain matter, he replied:

$$ \text{«وَاَبْرَدَهَا عَلَى الكَبِدِ أَنْ أُسْأَلَ عَنْ شَىْءٍ لَا عِلْمَ لِى بِهِ فَأَقُولَ لَا أَدْرِى»} $$

It means: "It is very soothing for me to say 'I do not know' when I am asked about what I do not know." *Hafidh al-^Asqalaniyy*, in his book *Takhrij Mukhtasar Ibn al-Hajib*, related this incident.

---

[57] Had he chosen to engage his mind into finding the answers for these cases he would have succeeded.

Giving a religious answer without knowledge is an enormous sin. Sometimes it is blasphemy. *Imam ash-Shafi^iyy* narrated from *Imam Malik*, from *Muhammad* the son of *^Ajlan*, that he said:

«إِذَا أَغْفَلَ العَالِمُ لا أَدْرى أُصِيبَتْ مَقَاتِلُهُ»

This means: "If the scholar overlooks saying 'I don't know' then (it is as if) he is hit on his fatal spots." That is, he puts himself into big trouble. This is why there should be no consideration given to the people who say, "Our opinion is this or that" while they did not attain the level of *ijtihad*.

Some people from *Hizb at-Tahrir* said, "Nowadays, it is easy to acquire the six books of *Hadith* and the book of *Qur'an*. This enables one easily to make *ijtihad*." Such people are like the person who says, "I'll buy six of the best horses, and by that I will easily become the best horseman nowadays." Their statement is a result of two matters: ignorance and arrogance. May *Allah* protect us from them.

22. To teach or to seek harmful knowledge without an Islamically valid reason;

Explanation: Among the sins of the tongue is to teach another person any knowledge considered religiously harmful, like sorcery and astrology. Astrology is to consider several issues related to the stars and the planets, and to deduce from that what will happen in the future. This is an enormous sin.

Also among the sins of the tongue is to teach the silly people some cases that are easier, according to some schools, knowing that they will take these judgments as a means to commit sins or to neglect obligations.

23. To judge by other than the Law of *Allah*;

Explanation: Among the sins of the tongue is for the judge to pass an edict against the rules of the Religion. This is an enormous sin, although it is not blasphemy (except if he claims that his judgment is equal to or better than the religious judgment).

Sayyid Qutb claimed that the rulers in all the Islamic countries are blasphemers because they do not implement the religious rules. He added that all the assistants of those leaders are also blasphemers. Moreover, all the subjects are blasphemers because they do not revolt

286

against them. This claim of *Sayyid Qutb* is invalid, has no religious ground, and contradicts the rules revealed to Prophet *Muhammad* ﷺ.

Al-Bukhariyy and *Muslim* related that the Prophet ﷺ prohibited us from revolting against the Caliph, in order to take him out of power, even if the Caliph commits injustice. The Caliph is thrown out of power only if he commits blasphemy, as the Prophet ﷺ mentioned in the *hadith* narrated by *al-Bukhariyy* and *Muslim*.

$$\text{«وَأَنْ لا نُنَازِعَ الأَمْرَ أَهْلَهُ . قَالَ : إِلا أَنْ تَرَوْا كُفْرًا بَوَاحًا عِنْدَكُمْ مِنَ الله فِيهِ بُرْهَانٌ»}$$

In his saying, *Sayyid Qutb* did not follow any *imam* of *Ahlus-Sunnah*. Rather, he followed the saying of a part of the *Khawarij* called *al-Bayhasiyyah*. Only a misguided person accepts to be a follower of these *Khawarij*.

24. To wail and to lament the good attributes of the deceased as if the latter is hearing;

Explanation: "To wail" means to express grief in words uttered loudly in a mournful way mentioning the good attributes of a deceased person, as if talking to him. This is prohibited. Also, it is prohibited-upon the death of a person-to scream, in a way that reflects panic and impatience. Moreover, harming oneself, women uncovering their hair before men due to grief, or tearing one's clothes for the same reason, is also prohibited. However, if one was not sane during that time, then one is not accountable for such actions.

25. To utter words which encourage one to do the unlawful or discourage one from doing the obligatory;

Explanation: All the elements of these rules were explained previously in different parts of the Summary. It is appropriate to reemphasize that encouraging someone to do an unlawful matter is a sin. Also, sinful is to discourage someone from fulfilling an obligation. In many cases, the person commits sins because of one's children or money. When some people know that their children want to do a sin, they do not try to prohibit them from doing it, because they see that their children are very attached to that matter. Instead they help their children to do the sin. This is a sin on their part. If they cannot stop them, these parents are obligated to hate in their hearts what their children are doing, and not help them in it. The one who falls into that sin is included under the _ayahs_ 14-15 of _Suratut-Taghabun:_

$$\text{﴿إِنَّ مِنْ أَزْوَاجِكُمْ وَأَوْلَادِكُمْ عَدُوًّا لَّكُمْ فَاحْذَرُوهُمْ ۝﴾، }$$

$$\text{﴿إِنَّمَا أَمْوَالُكُمْ وَأَوْلَادُكُمْ فِتْنَةٌ ۝﴾ }$$

Together, these two verses mean: [In some cases, your spouses, children, and money are reasons for you to be misguided.] Such a person also falls under the _hadith_ of the Prophet, narrated by _Ibn Majah, Ahmad,_ and _at-Tabaraniyy:_

$$\text{«إِنَّ الوَلَدَ مَبْخَلَةٌ مَجْبَنَةٌ»}$$

This means: «Indeed, the child, in many cases, is a reason for the parent to abstain from fulfilling financial obligations and to act cowardly.» Examples are the one who does not pay _Zakah,_ and the one who does not pay for the necessary needs to spread the proper teachings of _Islam_ and face misguidance, driven by the desire to make more money available for one's children to fulfill their desires. Another example is the person who does not declare a word of truth, when one is obligated to do so, because one wants to secure some worldly issues for one's children. Consequently, one becomes a coward.

26. To utter words which defame _Islam,_ any prophet, the scholars, the Qur'an, or any of the rites of _Allah;_

Explanation: These cases of uttering such blasphemous statements were discussed in details in previous sections of this book.

27. To play the flute;

Explanation: Among the sins of the mouth is to play any type of flute, whether it is the one used in battles, ceremonies, or among the bedouins. All of these types are prohibited. The famous _Malikiyy_ scholar _Al-Qurtubiyy_ said, "I never heard from any reliable scholar that the flute is permissible." Some _Shafi^iyys_ and _Hanafiyys_ said that it was permissible to play flute. These are unreliable sayings because they contradict the _hadiths_ narrated from the Prophet ﷺ about this issue.

28. To refrain from commanding the obligatory (ma^ruf) and from forbidding the unlawful (munkar) without an excuse;

Explanation: Among the sins of the tongue is to refrain from ordering the ma^ruf or from forbidding the munkar without a religious excuse. That is, if one neglects to order fulfilling the obligations or to forbid the unlawful while one is able, and while one is personally obligated to do that, then one is sinful. If one fears that upon doing it one will be killed, dismembered, imprisoned, deprived of one's money, or the like, then in this case, one is excused and not sinful. In the case when ordering the ma^ruf or forbidding the munkar is a collective obligation (fard kifayah) and someone other than oneself fulfills this obligation, then one is not sinful for not doing it.

It is an obligation to forbid the munkar, when the forbidden matter is considered unlawful by consensus. If it is not considered unlawful by consensus, rather some mujtahids said that it was permissible, then we do not object to the person who follows those who judged it as permissible. We can tell him, it is better for you not to do it. However, we do not object to him scornfully or try to force him to leave it out.

On the other hand, if the person who is committing this unlawful matter (which is not judged by consensus as unlawful,) believes that it is unlawful, then we object to him and tell him, "You are sinful. Do not do it."

Leaving out ordering the ma^ruf and forbidding the munkar without an excuse is an enormous sin.

29. To withhold the Obligatory Knowledge from the one who requests it;

Explanation: Among the sins of the tongue is to neglect teaching the person who requests the obligatory knowledge. If one refers this seeker of knowledge to another qualified person who teaches him, then one is not sinful by not oneself doing it.

Ibn Majah, al-Hakim, Ahmad, and *Abu Dawud* narrated from the Prophet ﷺ that he said:

«مَنْ سُئِلَ عَنْ عِلْم فَكَتَمَهُ أُلْجِمَ بِلِجَامٍ مِنْ نَارٍ يَوْمَ القِيَامَةِ»

This means: «The mouth of the one who refrains from teaching the Knowledge, after being asked for it, is going to be blocked by a bridle of fire on the Judgment Day.»

In some cases teaching is a personal obligation. In other cases, it is a collective obligation. It is a personal obligation upon you to teach someone in your town seeking the personal necessary knowledge while there is no one other than you available to teach him. If there are several people in the town who are able to teach him, and whom he can reach easily, then it is a collective obligation on them to teach this person. If one of them does that, it is no more incumbent on the others to teach him.

30. To laugh because a Muslim passed gas, or to laugh at a Muslim to degrade him;

Explanation: Among the sins of the mouth is to laugh voluntarily at a Muslim because of his passing gas. This hurts the Muslim's feelings. If one laughs at him involuntarily, one is not sinful.

Also, if one laughs on purpose in a way that hurts another Muslim, like if one laughs to degrade him, then one is sinful.

31. To withhold testimony;

Explanation: Among the sins of the tongue is to withhold one's testimony, when it is an obligation upon one to testify, i.e., when one is summoned by the judge to testify. If one is not summoned to testify, it is prohibited for one to initiate going to the judge and present one's testimony. The Prophet ﷺ dispraised the people who testify before they are summoned to give their testimony, as narrated by *at-Tirmidhiyy* and others:

$$\text{«ثُمَّ يَنْشَأُ أَقْوَامٌ يَشْهَدُونَ وَلَا يُسْتَشْهَدُونَ»}$$

The exception is the _hisbah_ testimony, in which no human's rights are involved. An example is the case of a person who knows that although a man has divorced his wife three times, they still enjoy each other. In this case, this person presents his testimony to the judge, even if the judge did not know about this matter and no one else complained about it.

32. To neglect the obligatory returning [like saying *wa ˆalaykumus-salam*] of the Islamic salutation [*as-sal_amu ˆalaykum*];

Explanation: Among the sins of the tongue is to refrain from returning the Islamic salutation when returning it is a personal obligation. When an accountable Muslim salutes a specific accountable Muslim by saying *as-salamu ^alaykum* or the like, the latter is obligated to return the salutation.

It is not obligatory to return the Islamic salutation of the non-accountable person, such as an insane or non-pubescent Muslim.

Moreover, when a Muslim, by saying "*as-salamu ^alaykum*", salutes a group of accountable Muslims, then it is a collective obligation on them to say, "*wa ^alaykumus-salam,*" or the like to him. The obligation is fulfilled if at least one of them says it.

The aforementioned details apply to the case of people from the same sex. Other judgments might apply in the case of two different genders. For example, if a young woman addresses a marriageable man with the Islamic salutation, it is not an obligation upon him to say "*wa ^alaykumus-salam,*". It is permissible, but it is not an obligation.

The statement of some later scholars that it is not permissible for the men to address the women by the *salam*, and vise versa, is not a correct saying. It is confirmed that the Prophet ﷺ saluted some women, as narrated by *Abu Dawud* and others:

عن أَسْمَاءَ بِنْتِ يَزِيدَ قَالَتْ : مَرَّ عَلَيْنَا رَسُولُ الله ﷺ فِى نِسْوَةٍ فَسَلَّمَ عَلَيْنَا .

33. **To engage in an arousing kiss intentionally when one is in the state of pilgrimage (*ihram*) for *Hajj* or ^*Umrah*, or is fasting an obligatory fast if one fears ejaculation;**

Explanation: Among the forbidden kisses is for a man, who is involved in *Hajj* or ^*Umrah*, to kiss his wife in an arousing way, whether or not he fears ejaculating. On the other hand, such a man is permitted to give his wife, out of kindness, a non-arousing kiss. However, if a man is fasting an obligatory fast and fears ejaculating by giving an arousing kiss to his wife, then this kiss is prohibited for him.

34. **To kiss those whom one is not allowed to kiss.**

Explanation: To kiss the person whom one is not allowed to kiss is a sin. It is prohibited for a man to kiss a marriageable woman (who is not his wife), and vice versa. Marriageable women are those who are not *mahram*. Hence, it is sinful for a man to kiss other than his wife, mother, sister, daughter, and the like, and for a woman to kiss other than her husband, father, brother, son, and the like.

A group of people nowadays, called *Hizb at-Tahrir*, deviated from the path of the Prophet and claimed that it was permissible for one to kiss a marriageable woman. They said, "Kissing a woman is just moving one's lips in a certain way while touching her skin. Is it prohibited for one to move one's lips?" This is a strange saying. It exists in their publications and it stands against the religious texts.

Note: Some people cited among the sins, "forgetting the parts of the *Qur'an* one has memorized." This is not a true saying. If one forgets verses of the *Qur'an*, one is not sinful for that. The *hadith* narrated by *Abu Dawud* and *at-Tirmidhiyy*, about this case is not a *sahih hadith*. Literally, this *hadith* means: «The sins of my nation were presented to me. I did not find any sin greater than the sin of a person who memorizes a chapter or a verse from the *Qur'an*, then he forgets it.»

Some of the scholars said that the term, 'nasiyaha' «نَسِيَها» which literally means 'to forget it' does not mean that in this *hadith*. Rather, it means to leave out implementing the verse. This interpretation (ta'wil) for this *hadith* was narrated from *Abu Yusuf*, the student of *Abu Hanifah*. According to the Arabic language, this is a valid ta'wil, because in the language, the term *nasiya* can bear the meaning of 'leaving out', as in the saying of *Allah*:

$$﴿فَٱلْيَوْمَ نَنسَىٰهُمْ كَمَا نَسُواْ لِقَآءَ يَوْمِهِمْ هَٰذَا وَمَا كَانُواْ بِـَٔايَٰتِنَا يَجْحَدُونَ ۝﴾$$

This does not mean that *Allah* forgets the blasphemers; rather it means that *Allah* leaves them in Hellfire because they left out holding the proper belief.

In any case, the aforementioned *hadith* did not reach the level of *sahih*. Consequently, even if it is interpreted according to its apparent meaning, it is not a valid proof that it is prohibited for one to just forget one or more verses of the *Qur'an*.

Chapter 45
Sins of the Ear

Among the sins of the ear are:

1. To listen to the private conversation which others meant to hide;

Explanation: It is a sin for one to listen, without excuse, to the conversation of other people, while knowing that they want to hide their conversation from one.

A religious excuse for listening to a conversation without permission is if one knows that those people are conspiring to hurt Muslims. In that case, one may listen to protect the Muslims from their harm.

The Prophet, _sallallahu ^alayhi wa sallam_, said,

$$\text{«ومَنِ اسْتَمَعَ إِلَى حَدِيثِ قَوْم وَهُمْ لَهُ كَارِهُونَ أَوْ يَفِرُّونَ مِنْهُ}$$
$$\text{صُبَّ فِى أُذُنِهِ الآنُكُ يَوْمَ القِيَامَةِ»}$$

This _hadith_ contains the meaning: «On the Day of Judgment, melted lead is poured in the ears of the one who listens to the conversation of others without their permission.» This _hadith_ is related by _Imam al-Bukhariyy_ and refers to the prohibited type of spying.

2. To listen to the flute, _tumbur_, which is an instrument that resembles the lute, and the rest of the unlawful sounds;

Explanation: Among the sins of the ear is for one to listen on purpose to prohibited musical instruments, like the flute and the lute. Every musical instrument that gives enchantment by itself is prohibited.

The tambourine, the drums, the cymbals and the like are not prohibited, as is indicated in several sayings of the Prophet, _sallallahu ^alayhi wa sallam_.

If a person hears prohibited music without listening to it on purpose, like if the sound is coming from one's neighbor's apartment, then one is not sinful for hearing it.

The _duff_ (tambourine) that has small cymbals attached to it is not prohibited, as _Imam al-Juwayniyy_ and _an-Nawawiyy_ mentioned. This is the reliable saying. Some people played the *duff* in the presence of the Prophet ﷺ, and he did not object to it. Playing it is permissible for both males and females. Some people say that using it is only permissible for women and not men. This saying is not correct at all. It is enough for the person to take a trip through the Muslim countries to notice immediately that a great number of men play the tambourine, and to notice also that using it is the habit of the Sufis all around the Islamic world. Thus, it is not originally a practice exclusive to women. Neither the Prophet mentioned it, nor the norm indicates it.

Ibn Majah narrated that the Prophet, *sallallahu ^alayhi wa sallam*, was walking through *al-Madinah*, when he heard some women playing the tambourine (*duff*) while singing a line of poetry:

نَـحْـنُ جَـوَارٍ مِنْ بَـنِـى الـنَّـجَّـارِ   يَـا حَـبَّـذَا مُـحَـمَّـدٌ مِـنْ جَـارٍ

This line said, "We are women from the clan of *Najjar*, and we are so blessed to have Prophet *Muhammad* as our neighbor." The Prophet ﷺ responded:

$$\text{«اللَّهُ يَعْلَمُ إِنِّى لَأُحِبُّكُنَّ»}$$

It means: "*Allah* knows that I certainly love you." This *hadith* clearly proves the permissibility of using the *duff* (tambourine). Moreover, it proves that the voice of the woman is not *^awrah*, (i.e., it is not prohibited for her to let a marriageable man hear it).

The word 'jawari' mentioned in this *hadith* does not mean non-pubescent girls as some people might think. *Jariyah* in the Arabic language (singular of *jawari*) means a woman in general, and does not refer specifically to a non-pubescent female.

3. **To listen to gossip (ghibah), talebearing (namimah), and the like. One is not sinful if one hears this involuntarily and hates it; but if one is able, then one must renounce it.**

Explanation: The one who listens on purpose to gossip or talebearing is sinful, just as the one who utters it is sinful. To be clear of the sin upon witnessing an act of gossip, when able, one must order its committer to stop it.

If one cannot order that person to stop, nor can one force one to stop, then one has to hate this sin in one's heart, leave that session, and not stay there listening to gossip or talebearing. This is the least thing one has to do when unable to stop this sin.

Chapter 46
Sins of the Hands

Among the sins of the hands are:

1. **To give short (cheat) when measuring by volume, weight, or arm length;**

Explanation: When buying, some people take all that they deserve according to the agreement. For example, if they make a contract to buy ten pounds of a matter, they take ten complete pounds. If they make a contract to buy ten gallons of a certain liquid, they take ten complete gallons. On the other hand, when these people sell, they trick the buyer. They make the buyer think that they gave him all that he deserves by that contract, while truly they did not. There are several ways they use to cheat the buyer, but always this is an enormous sin. *Allāh* said, at the beginning of *Suratul-Mutaffifīn,*

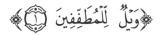

This means: [The people who commit the sin of giving short in measure will suffer a severe torture.]

2. **To steal; if one steals the equivalent of one-quarter of a *Dīnar* from its secured place, one's right hand will be amputated. If one steals again, the left foot will be amputated, then [for the third stealing] one's left hand, then [for the fourth stealing] one's right foot;**

Explanation: Stealing is a sin by consensus. The knowledgeable people and the laymen alike know that stealing is *haram*. "Stealing" here means to take unrightfully the belongings of another in a concealed way. Taking someone else's belonging by force, or openly (relying on running away) is sinful, but this is not the "Stealing" referred to by the author. If someone steals something equivalent at least to one quarter of a golden *dīnar* (about 1 gram) from its secured place, the Caliph punishes one by cutting off one's right hand from the wrist. Of course, when this is done, one must be treated immediately to stop the bleeding to avoid causing one's death. A way to do that is to immediately submerge the cut in hot oil. This stops the bleeding.

A secured place in this context refers to the place where people usually keep items similar to the stolen item. An example is money in a safe. If the aforementioned thief steals again, the left foot will be cut off. Then if one repeats it again, the left hand will be cut off. Then if one does it again, the right foot will be cut off. If one steals after that, the ruler enforces a suitable punishment that does not involve cutting off any part.

Stealing less than what is equivalent to a quarter of a *dinar* is not punished by dismembering the thief. In this case, the ruler inflicts on the thief a suitable punishment.

The same rule applies if a thief steals something from other than its secured place. An example of this is if someone leaves a bag full of money outside, next to his front door. If a thief steals it from there, the punishment of this thief is not to be dismembered. In this case, the ruler punishes him with a suitable punishment that prevents him from committing this bad act again.

The secured place of some items is just to be inside a house. In other cases it is a locked closet, a locked drawer, or a buttoned pocket close to the body. To say that an item is in a secured place depends on the area's circumstances and what kind of item it is.

Some people think cutting off the hand of the thief is a savage thing. Of course, this is a serious punishment, which one will not forget for one's whole life. Yet, once punished, the community is protected, one learns the lesson, and one can go on with one's life. Contrary to this, in the man-made laws, one is put in jail for 5, 10, 20 years or more. In most of the cases one's life is destroyed. Moreover, one's good skills are frozen for all the jail time (if not abolished and replaced by bad ones as a result of the direct contact with other inmates). As it is obvious in the non-Islamic communities nowadays, with the prison system, the community is not protected from violence, robbery, and stealing.

3. **To loot (*nahb*);**

4. **To take the money of others unjustly (*gha<u>s</u>b*);**

5. **To take the traders tax (*maks*);**

6. **To misappropriate the spoils of war (*ghulu<u>l</u>*);**

297

Explanation: Among the sins of the hand is to take money in an unlawful way. This sin occurs by taking a belonging of others unrightfully, relying on running away with it, one's force, or otherwise. It also occurs by taking taxes from traders on their merchandise. This also includes taking a part of the battle spoils in an unlawful way, before they are distributed in the proper, religious manner. The improper taking of spoils is called *ghulul*. *Ghulul* is an enormous sin, even if one takes something with a low value.

A person, who took care of the belongings of the Prophet ﷺ during a battle outside of *al-Madinah*, died in the battlefield. The Prophet said, "He is in Hellfire." The Companions checked to see why the Prophet said that. They found that he had taken a piece of clothing that did not have a big value from the spoils, before they were distributed in the proper way. *Al-Bukhariyy* and others related this *hadith*.

7. **To kill; an expiation (*kaffarah*) is always due for killing; i.e., to free a Muslim slave who has no defects; if unable, one fasts two consecutive lunar months. Deliberate killing is punishable by death, except if the heirs of the killed person forgive the killer for an indemnity (*diyah*) or for free. In the cases of killing by mistake and the accidental killing by assault, the due indemnity (*diyah*) is one-hundred (100) camels for the free, male Muslim victim and half of that for the free, female Muslim victim. The indemnity (*diyah*) varies with the way the killing took place;**

Explanation: Among the sins of the hand is to kill a Muslim unrightfully. This is the most enormous sin after blasphemy. If one kills someone because he is a Muslim, i.e., because he believes in *Islam*, one blasphemes. In this case, if the killer does not return to *Islam*, and dies as a blasphemer, one remains in Hellfire forever.

In verse 93 of *Suratun-Nisa'*, *Allah* said,

$$﴿وَمَن يَقْتُلْ مُؤْمِنًا مُّتَعَمِّدًا فَجَزَآؤُهُ جَهَنَّمُ خَالِدًا فِيهَا ۞﴾$$

This means: «The one who kills a believer on purpose (because he is a believer) is punished in Hellfire forever.»

Killing a Muslim for a worldly matter is a very enormous sin, but does not attain the level of blasphemy.

If one kills a Muslim, whether accidentally or intentionally, one is obligated to fulfill an expiation. This expiation is to free a Muslim slave who does not have any defects that reduce his ability to work. If one is unable to do that, then one fasts two consecutive lunar months. In this kind of expiation, feeding people is not an element (i.e., unlike in the _dhihar_ expiation).

There are three types of killing:

1. To kill in a deliberate way,
2. To kill by mistake,
3. To kill by mistake in a deliberate way.

1. An example of the first type is to hit someone intentionally with something that normally kills. If the hit person dies as a result, then the killer will be punished by execution, except if the heirs of the killed person accept to relieve him from being executed in return for an indemnity (_diyah_) paid to them, or for free. If part or all of the heirs agree, the killer will not be killed. If the heirs do not relieve the killer from being executed, the ruler enables the heirs to kill the killer themselves, according to the proper rules of executing.

2. An example of the second type is when someone is hunting and aims to kill an animal, without noticing the presence of a human being close to the prey. He shoots and, by mistake kills the person. In this case the killer is not executed, but an indemnity is due on him.

3. An example of the third type is to hit someone on purpose with something harmful, but does not usually kill, yet this time the victim dies as a result (like to prick one in the thigh with a needle, and as a result one dies). In this case also the killer is not to be killed, but an indemnity is due on him.

The indemnity is to pay one hundred (100) camels to the heirs if the killed one is a free, male Muslim. If the killed one is a free, female Muslim the indemnity is fifty (50) camels.

Although the numbers of camels do not change, the qualities of the camels change contingent upon the type of killing.

If the person is killed in a deliberate way, the indemnity is thirty (30) female camels that completed three years of age, thirty (30) female camels that completed four years of age, and forty (40) pregnant camels. This *diyah* is an obligation upon the killer himself and has to be paid immediately if he is able.

In the case of killing by mistake in a deliberate way (or killing a *mahram* relative merely by mistake), the camels have the same qualities, but the indemnity is not an obligation upon the killer himself, rather it is an obligation upon the killer's paternal relatives (excluding his ancestors and offspring) to pay it. It does not have to be paid in full immediately, rather it can be paid in payments within three years.

In the case of killing by mistake (other than a *mahram* relative), the indemnity is also paid by the paternal relatives of the killer, in payments within three years.

It is composed of: Twenty (20) female camels that completed one year of age, twenty (20) female camels that completed two years of age, twenty (20) female camels that completed three years of age, twenty (20) female camels that completed four years of age, and twenty (20) male camels that completed two years of age.

If someone, intentionally and unrightfully, cuts off the hand of another Muslim, his finger, his ear or the like, then cutting off the similar organ of the unjust one is the punishment. This takes place by the permission of the ruler and under his supervision to avoid inflicting injustice. However, it is valid for the inflicted person to relieve the unjust one from being punished for free or in exchange of an indemnity.

8. To beat a person unjustly;

Explanation: Among the sins of the hand is to hit a person unjustly. *Abu Dawud* and others narrated in the *sahih hadith* of the Prophet ﷺ that he said:

«إِنَّ اللَّهَ عَزَّ وَجَلَّ يُعَذِّبُ الذِينَ يُعَذِّبُونَ النَّاسَ فِى الدُّنْيَا»

This means: «*Allah* tortures (in the Hereafter) those who torture (unjustly) the people in this life.»

Also, scaring a Muslim unjustly by, for example, pointing a weapon towards him is prohibited.

It is confirmed in the *hadith* narrated by *Ibn Hibban* that the angels damn the one who points a weapon towards his fellow

300

Muslim:

«مَنْ أَشَارَ إِلَى أَخِيهِ بِحَدِيدَةٍ فَإِنَّ الملائِكَةَ تَلْعَنُهُ وَإِنْ كَانَ أَخَاهُ لِأَبِيهِ وَأُمِّهِ»

9. To take and to give a bribe;

Explanation: Among the sins of the hand is to take or give a bribe. The bribe in this context means money that is given to another to establish an unjust case. An example of this is the case of someone who unjustly takes the belongings of another person, and pays the judge money so that he does not force him to return those belongings to their owner. In this case, both the one who gives and the one who takes are sinful. On the other hand, if someone prevents you from getting your right, and you cannot get it unless you pay money to him, then in this case paying money to that person is not sinful on your part. The person who demands and takes this money is sinful, as narrated by *Imam Ahmad*:

«لَعَنَ اللَّهُ الرَّاشِيَ وَالْمُرْتَشِى فِى الْحُكمِ»

10. To burn an animal, unless there was no other way to avoid its harm;

Explanation: Among the sins of the hand is to burn an animal, (that is, a creation that has a soul in it) even if this animal was a harmful one. An exception to that is the case when burning it is the only way to protect oneself from its harm. In such case, it is permissible to do it. The Prophet ﷺ said:

«لا يُعَذّبُ بِالنَّارِ إِلا رَبُّ النَّارِ»

This means: «No one should punish by using fire except the Lord of the fire (i.e., its Creator, *Allah*).»

11. To dismember an animal;

Explanation: Among the sins of the hand is to dismember an animal, i.e., while it is alive, like to cut its nose, its ear, or the like. Likewise, it is *haram* to disfigure an animal.

12. To play with the die and anything that contains gambling, including children's games;

Explanation: Among the sins of the hand is for one to play with the die or any similar game that is contingent on guessing, and not on calculations.

This is so because *Imam Muslim* narrated from the Prophet ﷺ that he said:

$$\text{«مَنْ لَعِبَ بِالنَّرْدَشِيرِ فَكَأَنَّمَا صَبَغَ يَدَهُ فِى لَحْمِ خِنْزِيرٍ وَدَمِهِ»}$$

This means: «The one who plays with die, is as if he immerses his hand in a pig's flesh and blood.» This indicates that he is a sinful person.

Likewise, playing cards is forbidden because such games rely (at least at the beginning) on guessing and not on calculations. These games, as it is witnessed, are reasons to have disputes without any benefit or purpose, and which lead to enmity between friends and relatives. This is why they are, among other reasons, prohibited.

On the other hand, the games that rely on calculation, like chess, checkers and the like, are permissible, although they are disliked.

Enabling small children to play with forbidden games, whether they entail gambling or not, is not permissible. The one who enables or helps them in that is sinful.

13. To play unlawful musical instruments like the _tumbur_, _rabab_, flute, and string instruments;

Explanation: All of this was explained previously in the section pertaining to the sins of the tongue. In a _hadith_ narrated by al-Bukhariyy and others, the Prophet ﷺ dispraised those among his nation who play those instruments, commit *zina*, and wear silk clothes by saying:

$$\text{«لَيَكُونَنَّ مِنْ أُمَّتِى أَقْوَامٌ يَسْتَحِلُّونَ الحِرَ والحَرِيرَ والمَعَازِفَ»}$$

14. To intentionally touch the marriageable woman without a barrier or to touch her lustfully with a barrier even if the person in this case is a non-marriageable kin or of the same sex;

Explanation: Among the sins of the hand is for a man to touch without a barrier, whether with or without desire, the skin of a marriageable woman. "Marriageable" here means the woman whom a man can marry, i.e., other than his sister, daughter, mother, and the like. The same case applies concerning touching other parts of her body, like her hair, her tooth, and her nail. All of that is prohibited.

Imam Muslim narrated the hadith of the Prophet:

$$\text{«وَالْيَدُ زِنَاهَا الْبَطْشُ»}$$

This means: «The zina of the hand is touching (the marriageable person).» This judgment is a case of consensus among all the mujtahids.

If a barrier exists between the skin of the man and the skin of the woman, the judgment is not the same. Hence the shaking of hands between a man and a woman, while one of them at least is wearing a glove, is not prohibited, as long as it takes place without desire. If the same act is done with desire, then it is prohibited.

Moreover, it is prohibited to hug a marriageable woman, even if this action takes place with a barrier (such as clothing).

Two people of the same sex are permitted to shake hands and the like, with or without a barrier, as long as this occurs without desire. The same judgment applies if the man and the woman are mahram (i.e., they are non-marriageable).

15. To depict that which has a soul;

Explanation: Among the sins of the hands is to depict that which has a soul, whether it is a three-dimensional or two-dimensional structure. Both drawing a picture of a human being, or an animal, and making a sculpture of them are prohibited in the Shafi^iyy school. As well, it is prohibited for one to keep such a thing if it has a form with which this human being or animal can live. The same prohibition applies if this picture is drawn on a room's ceiling, wall, or the like.

However, according to the Malikiyy School, it is permissible to draw a picture of an animal or a human being, but it is not permissible to make a sculpture of that. Based on another hadith, they interpreted the prohibition (related by al-Bukhariyy from the Prophet, sallallahu ^alayhi wa sallam,) to mean sculptures and not pictures. They said, "The Prophet meant in the hadith to prohibit making sculptures, and he did not mean to prohibit making pictures of animals and human beings." Imam Ash-Shafi^iyy, Ahmad and Abu Hanifah did not agree with this interpretation.

It is an obligation to alter a picture, or statue of a creature, if it is depicted in a form in which the real object could live. One either

303

totally destroys it or removes some parts of it in a way that, if it was real, this picture or sculpture would not live with that bodily condition.

If the picture already is missing some organs, without which the creature cannot live, then it is permissible to keep it as is. Examples of this are a picture of just a head, or a statue of a person with its head removed.

16. To refrain from paying one's *Zakah* or part of one's *Zakah* after it is due when one is able to pay it, or to pay an invalid *Zakah*, or to give *Zakah* to those who do not deserve it;

Explanation: If *Zakah* is due on a person, then one has to pay it in compliance with *Allah's* orders. One is not allowed to neglect paying it. Also, one is not allowed to delay paying it without a valid excuse. One has to pay it immediately.

Also one has to pay the valid due amount that *Allah* ordered one to pay. If it is an obligation on one to pay a camel, and one pays a sheep instead, it is not valid. Likewise, if one is obligated to pay a sheep, it is invalid for one to pay cash money-even if the amount of money has a value greater than the value of the sheep. One has to do the obligations just as *Allah* ordered one to do them.

Paying *Zakah* to people who do not deserve it is invalid. Consequently, *Zakah* is still due on one. There are eight (8) types whom *Allah* mentioned in the *Qur'an* as being the recipients of *Zakah*. An example of paying *Zakah* to an undeserving party is paying *Zakah* to build a mosque. This is so because paying to build a mosque is not one of the eight types of acceptable *Zakah* payments cited in the *Qur'an*. In this case, the one who paid is sinful, *Zakah* is still due on him, he did not get any reward, and the paid money was paid out of place.

To refrain from paying *Zakah* properly is an enormous sin. To make this issue clear, it is enough to mention that *Ibn Hibban* and *Ahmad* narrated that the one who does not pay *Zakah* is damned by the Prophet, *sallallahu ^alayhi wa sallam*:

عن ابن مسعود أنَّ لاوىَ الصَّدَقَةِ مَلْعُونٌ على لِسانِ مُحَمّدٍ ﷺ

17. To refuse to give an employee his pay;

Explanation: Among the sins of the hands is to prevent one's employee from receiving the salary that he deserves. If an employee does the job agreed upon, and the employer does not give him his salary, then the employer is falling into sin.

Al-Bukhariyy narrated from the Prophet, sallallahu ^alayhi wa sallam:

قَالَ اللَّهُ تعالى : ثَلاثَةٌ أَنَا خَصْمُهُمْ يَوْمَ القِيَامَةِ : رَجُلٌ أَعْطَى بِى ثُمَّ غَدَرَ، وَرَجُلٌ بَاعَ حُرًّا فَأَكَلَ ثَمَنَهُ، وَرَجُلٌ اسْتَأْجَرَ أَجِيرًا فَاسْتَوْفَى مِنْهُ وَلَمْ يُعْطِهِ أَجْرَهُ»

It means: «Three people will be discredited on the Day of Judgment: A man who betrays after making an obligatory oath according to God's laws, a man who sold a free person as a slave and took the price paid to him, and a man who hired a person who fulfilled the job that he was supposed to do without giving him his salary.»

This *hadith* clarifies how ugly is the sin of hiring a person to do a job, then not giving him the salary he deserves.

18. To refuse to give the starving what fulfills one's hunger, and to refrain from saving a drowning person, without an excuse in both cases;

Explanation: Among the sins of the hand is to refuse, without an excuse, to give the starving person what fulfills his hunger. This case is not related only to one's kin. Whether or not the starving person is one's relative, it is still a personal obligation to fulfill his hunger if no one else does it. Similarly, it is an obligation to provide the needy person with sufficient clothes to cover his unlawful nakedness (^awrah), protect him from dying, cold, or the like.

Even if one needs the food for oneself, in the future and not now, then it is an obligation upon one to offer it to the person who is in immediate need of it. One cannot just neglect the case of the needy person and let him suffer or die from hunger, because one believes that one needs this food in the future.

Also among the sins of the hand is not to rescue, without an excuse, a drowning person. An excuse is if one does not know how to swim, and there is no other means to rescue him.

305

19. To write what is prohibited to say;

Explanation: Writing is a way for one to express oneself. Hence, one must avoid, when writing, the same matters which one avoids while speaking. Just as the person must protect one's tongue from committing gossip, one must protect one's pen from committing gossip. Just as one protects one's tongue from uttering a blasphemous saying, one has to protect one's hand from writing a blasphemous saying.

20. To betray, which is opposite of giving sincere advice, and this includes deeds, sayings, and conditions.

Explanation: Betraying is among the sins. Betraying occurs by actions and sayings. If a person gives you money to keep it safe and you accept, it is forbidden to betray him by spending that money. You must not spend this money without his permission, even if you have a firm intention to give him back an equal amount later. What you must do is keep that money in the secured place, where such an item is usually kept.

Likewise, if one hires you to do a job, then you must fulfill the work as agreed upon, and not let the employer think that you are doing the job while you are not.

If a person asks for your advice about something, it is also prohibited for you to betray him, and give him wrong advice on purpose. If a person asks for your opinion about hiring someone for a job, and you know that he is not capable to do this job, then you have to tell him that the person is not capable. Encouraging one to hire an incapable worker is betraying the seeker of your advice.

Another example is for one to act in a certain way, seeking to make others think that one is able to handle a certain position, while one knows about oneself the lack of qualification for it. This can be done even without saying one word about that matter, but just by acting. In such case, one is betraying those people.

Such an attribute is a very mean attribute, to a point that the Prophet ﷺ said (as narrated by *Ahmad* and *Ibn Hibban*):

«لَا إِيمَانَ لِمَنْ لَا أَمَانَةَ لَهُ»

This means: «The one who betrays does not have the perfect belief.» This means that he is an enormous sinner.

Chapter 47
Sins of the Private Parts

Among the sins of the private parts are:

1. **To commit adultery or fornication;**

Explanation: Among the sins of the private parts is to commit *zina*. *Zina* is to insert the glans penis (or more) into the vagina unlawfully. This is the *zina* that is considered among the most enormous sins. If one commits it, one deserves to be punished by the *hadd*, a well-specified punishment mentioned in the religious texts for committing this sin. As for the other actions also called *zina* in the *hadith* (because they are introductions to the real *zina*, like the *zina* of the hand, the *zina* of the eye, etc.), these are sinful actions, the committer of which is not punished by the *hadd*.

2. **To commit sodomy. The penalty for the sodomizer who is free is the same as that of the adulterer and fornicator. However, the penalty for the [one who is willfully] sodomized is one-hundred lashes and one lunar year in exile. The slave receives half of this penalty;**

Explanation: Also among the sins of the private parts is to commit sodomy, that is to insert the glans penis into the anus. This is also an enormous sin for which the *hadd* is due, except upon the person who commits this sin with his wife.

If it is confirmed to the Caliph (according to the rules of the Religion) that someone committed the sin of *zina*, the Caliph (or the person appointed by him) has to punish this enormous sinner by the *hadd*. The punishment differs whether or not one is *muhsan*. The *muhsan* person is the one who had, in accordance with a valid marriage, sexual intercourse with his wife even if it was only once. His punishment differs from the punishment of the one who is not *muhsan*.

The punishment of the *muhsan* person for committing *zina* is to stone him/her with middle-sized stones until he/she dies. *Al-Bukhariyy* narrated that the Prophet ordered, at one time, to stone Maˆiz (a man) and, at another time, to stone a woman from the tribe of *Ghamid*. Both were punished for committing *zina* and both of them were *muhsan*.

Middle-sized stones are those that fill one's palm, i.e., not very small and not very big. It is prohibited to hit the stoned person with a stone that, alone, is enough to kill him.

If a person who is not *muhsan* commits *zina*, he is not stoned. Rather, his punishment is to be whipped 100 lashes and to be exiled for one lunar year. The exile is away from town, at least, to the distance for which it is permissible to shorten the prayer (*qasr* distance).

The punishment of the sodomizer is the same as the punishment of the one who commits *zina*. If the sodomizer is *muhsan*, then he is stoned. If not, he is whipped one hundred (100) lashes and exiled for one year.

According to the reliable saying, the punishment of the sodomized, whether or not *muhsan* is 100 lashes and one-lunar year exile.

The aforementioned details apply for the case of the free, accountable person-whether male or female. As for the slave, his/her punishment is half of that of the free person. Since the punishment of stoning is not divisible in half, the punishment of the slave who commits *zina* or sodomy is in all cases 50 lashes and one-half of a lunar year exile-even if this slave was a *muhsan* slave.

It is better for the person who commits this sin to repent, without telling other people about what he did. Nonetheless, if this person confesses this sin to the ruler, then the ruler has to punish him relying on his confession. This is so whether the sinner does or does not repent of it, except if the sinner revokes his confession.

For this confession and for the testimony about *zina* to be valid, they have to be both explicit and detailed. That is, for example, it is not sufficient for the ruler to punish a person with the *hadd*, when he says, "I committed *zina*," because some people do not know the exact definition of *zina*. They may think that some prohibited acts of touching are the real *zina*. Although these actions are prohibited, the ruler does not punish the one who commits them with the *hadd*. This is why the ruler is not satisfied by someone's saying, "I committed *zina*" to punish him with the *hadd*. Rather, he relies on an explicit and more detailed confession.

The same case applies for the testimony. This means the ruler relies only on an explicit and properly detailed testimony to punish with the _hadd_ (i.e., the witnesses have to testify explicitly that they saw the man inserting his glans penis in the woman's vagina). Testifying that they saw the man and the woman together in bed or under one cover is not enough.

3. **To have sexual intercourse with animals, even if they are one's own;**

4. **To masturbate by the hand of other than one's wife or female slave;**

   Explanation: _Allah_ said in verses 5-7, of _Suratul-Mu'minun_:

   ﴿وَٱلَّذِينَ هُمۡ لِفُرُوجِهِمۡ حَٰفِظُونَ ۝ إِلَّا عَلَىٰٓ أَزۡوَٰجِهِمۡ أَوۡ مَا مَلَكَتۡ أَيۡمَٰنُهُمۡ فَإِنَّهُمۡ غَيۡرُ مَلُومِينَ ۝ فَمَنِ ٱبۡتَغَىٰ وَرَآءَ ذَٰلِكَ فَأُوْلَٰٓئِكَ هُمُ ٱلۡعَادُونَ ۝﴾

   These verses mean: [Praised are the people who do not use their sexual parts with other than their wives and their female slaves. Those who go beyond this boundary are sinful.]

   These verses clearly indicate that having sexual intercourse with animals, and masturbating by one's hand or the hand of other than one's wife or female slave are sinful matters.

5. **To copulate with the woman having menstrual or postpartum bleeding, or to copulate with the woman whose menstruation or postpartum bleeding terminated but she has not performed her purificatory bath (_ghusl_) yet, or it was performed lacking the proper intention, or lacking one of its conditions;**

   Explanation: Among the sins of the private parts is for one to have sexual intercourse with one's wife while she is menstruating or in her postpartum bleeding time. _Allah_ said in the _Qur'an_ (al-Baqarah 222):

   ﴿فَٱعۡتَزِلُواْ ٱلنِّسَآءَ فِى ٱلۡمَحِيضِ ۝﴾

   This verse means: [Do not have sexual intercourse with women when they are menstruating.]

   Except for a new Muslim or the like, whoever claims that it is permissible to have sexual intercourse with one's menstruating wife commits blasphemy. This act is prohibited because it causes harm for the woman. It may also cause illnesses for the man and/or the woman.

After the end of menstruation or postpartum bleeding, it is prohibited to have sexual intercourse (with or without a barrier, such as a condom) with one's wife before the wife takes a valid *ghusl* (purificatory bath) and lifts the state of ritual impurity. If she takes a bath without having the proper intention, he is still prohibited from having sexual intercourse with her, just as if she did not take a bath at all. This is also true if she takes a purificatory bath without fulfilling all the validity conditions.

Besides having sexual intercourse, it is prohibited for the husband to enjoy what is between the navel and the knees of his wife's body as long as she is menstruating, or having postpartum bleeding. Even if the menstruation or postpartum bleeding stopped, he cannot enjoy this area of hers until after she has performed *ghusl*. This judgment applies when this enjoyment takes place without a barrier. So, it is permissible for the husband to enjoy what is between the navel and the knees of his wife from above the clothes, i.e., without his skin touching hers.

6. **To uncover one's unlawful nakedness (^awrah) in front of those who are prohibited to look at it, or to disclose one's unlawful nakedness while alone without a reason;**

Explanation: Just as it is prohibited to look at the unlawful nakedness of others, it is prohibited to disclose one's unlawful nakedness in front of those who are not permitted to look at it. Also, it is prohibited to disclose one's unlawful nakedness while alone for no reason, a matter that was explained previously in chapter 43.

7. **To face the _Qiblah_ or turn one's back to it while urinating or defecating without placing a barrier between one and the _Qiblah_. The barrier must be two-thirds of a cubit or more high and not more than three cubits away. An exception is if the place of urination and defecation was prepared for that purpose;**

Explanation: Except in some cases, when one urinates or defecates, it is prohibited for one to face the _Qiblah_ or to turn one's back to it. A case of exception is if there is, between one and the

310

Qiblah, a barrier which is two-thirds of a cubit high, and 3 cubits or less away from the person.

The second case of exception is if the person urinates or defecates in a designated toilet room. In this case, it is permissible to face the *Qiblah* or turn one's back to it.

8. To defecate on a grave;

Explanation: Among the sins of the private parts is to urinate or defecate on a Muslim's grave. This is so because the Prophet ﷺ said:

$$\text{«لأَنْ يَجْلِسَ أَحَدُكُمْ عَلَى جَمْرَةٍ فَتُحْرِقَ ثِيَابَهُ فَتَخْلُصَ إِلَى جِلْدِهِ}$$
$$\text{خَيْرٌ لَهُ مِنْ أَنْ يَجْلِسَ عَلَى قَبْرٍ»}$$

This means: «It is better for one of you to sit on a burning coal, which burns his clothes and reaches his skin, than to sit (for defecation or urination) on a grave». *Muslim* narrated this *hadith*.

9. To urinate in a mosque-even if it was done in a container-and to urinate on the exalted object;

Explanation: We must glorify the mosques. This glorification implies protecting and clearing them of being places for urinating or defecating. The person, who urinates or defecates inside the mosque, whether he does that on the ground, or in a container, is committing a sin.

Likewise, it is sinful to make the mosque dirty with a disgusting thing (even if it is not *najas*-filthy). Thus, it is prohibited to spit on the mosque's ground.

The same rule applies if one urinates or defecates on a glorified thing. An example is to urinate on a paper that contains religious information. If one does that, while knowing about the content of the paper, one blasphemes. Another example is to urinate or defecate in a narrow place dedicated to perform an act of *Hajj* or ^*Umrah*, like the place of throwing the pebbles. Doing that is prohibited, but is not blasphemy, except if one does it to degrade this religious rite.

311

10. **For the pubescent to neglect having circumcision. This is allowed according to *Imam Malik*, however.**

Explanation: Among the sins of the private parts is to neglect circumcision until after puberty, whether the person is a male or a female. That is, if the person was not circumcised before becoming pubescent, then after becoming pubescent, it is prohibited for one to neglect fulfilling this obligation. It consists of cutting off a well-specified skin from one's genitals.

This is the judgment according to the *Shafi^iyy* school. Prophet *Ibrahim* عليه السلام was ordered with circumcision when he was 80 years old.

However, *Imam Malik*, may *Allah* raise his rank, said that circumcision is an optional, rewardable (*sunnah*) act, and it is not an obligation. The one who follows *Imam Malik*, leaving out circumcision because one does not consider it an obligation, is not blameworthy.

Chapter 48
Sins of the Foot

Among the sins of the foot are:

1. **To walk towards committing a sin, such as walking to incite the ruler to inflict unjust harm on a Muslim, or to walk to kill a Muslim unrightfully;**

Explanation: In the <u>h</u>adith narrated by at-Tirmidhiyy and A<u>h</u>mad, two Jewish men asked the Prophet ﷺ about nine particular enormous sins revealed to Prophet M<u>u</u>s<u>a</u> عليه السلام. The Prophet, <u>s</u>allallahu ^alayhi wa sallam, mentioned that one of those nine sins was taking an innocent person to the ruler to order his killing:

$$\text{«وَلا تَمْشُوا بِبَرِيءٍ إِلَى ذِى سُلْطَانٍ لِيَقْتُلَهُ»}$$

Inciting the ruler to inflict harm on a Muslim unjustly is an enormous sin. Such a sin terrifies the accused, innocent person as well as his family when they know about it. On the other hand, complaining to the ruler rightfully about a person is permissible.

It is also a sin to walk with the purpose of doing another sin, like to walk with the purpose of stealing, fornicating, or committing any prohibited introductions of fornication. Just walking to do that is in itself a sin.

2. **The inexcusable escaping of the slave, the wife, or one who owes a right to others from what is incumbent upon one-be it punishment, debt, obligatory spending, [obligatory] kindness to the parents, or raising the children;**

Explanation: Among the sins of the foot is for the slave, whether male or female, to escape without a valid excuse from his or her owner. Also sinful is the wife who runs away from her husband's house. Both are among the enormous sins, if they are not done for a valid excuse.

Also, it is prohibited for the one who owes a right to another person to run from fulfilling that obligatory right. An example of this is if one runs away from the ruler to escape receiving the religious punishment that one deserves. Another example is for one to run away from paying back debts due on one, or from the obligatory supporting of one's wife or needy parents. *Abu Dawud* and others narrated that running away from supporting those whom one is obligated to support is an enormous sin:

$$\text{«كَفَى بِالمَرْءِ إِثْمًا أَنْ يُضَيِّعَ مَنْ يَقُوتُ»}$$

3. To walk arrogantly with a strutting gait;

Explanation: Among the sins of the foot is to walk arrogantly. A *hadith* narrated by *Al-Bukhariyy* and *Muslim*, which tells about a person who was walking arrogantly and the earth swallowed him, is a clear proof that such an action is a sin.

4. To step over the shoulders of people sitting down, except for the purpose of filling a gap;

Explanation: Among the sins of the foot is for one to step, in a harmful way, over the shoulders of the other people sitting in the mosque. *Abu Dawud* and *Ibn Hibban* narrated that a person did that once when the Prophet was giving the Friday Speech. The Prophet ﷺ addressed him by saying:

$$\text{«اِجْلِسْ فَقَدْ ءَاذَيْتَ»}$$

This means: «Sit down; you have harmed others.» If there is no harm in doing that, then it is disliked. An exception is if the people who were sitting in the mosque left an unoccupied space. Then, it is permissible for one to step over their shoulders to fill the gap, which they fell short in filling. Also, it is not disliked for the *imam* to step over the shoulders of the people to reach the *mihrab* or the platform, if he cannot get there except by this way.

5. To pass in front of the person performing prayer when the conditions of the barrier placed in front of the prayer place (*sutrah*) are fulfilled;

Explanation: If there is something religiously acknowledged as a barrier in front of the person who is praying, then passing between that praying person and the barrier is a sin of the foot. For this barrier to be acknowledged, it should be at least two-thirds of a cubit high and three cubits or less away from the praying person. When such a barrier exists in front of the praying person, it is *sunnah* for one to prevent (by using one's hand for example) anyone who wants to pass between one and this barrier. If such a barrier does not exist, one is not entitled to disturb those who pass in front of one by trying to stop them, even if they pass close to one.

6. **To extend the leg towards the Book of the _Qur'an_ if it is not in a raised location;**

Explanation: Among the sins of the foot is for one to extend one's leg toward the book of the _Qur'an_, if it is close, or toward any close religious book, except if the book was raised or was inside a closet or the like. Also, it is prohibited to write the _Qur'an_ with a *najas*-filth and to touch it with an organ contaminated with *najas*-filth, whether the *najas*-filth is wet or dry. In some _Hanafiyy_ books, it is erroneously mentioned that it is permissible to write the chapter of *Al-Fatihah* with urine, if one knows that this cures an illness. Such a statement is blasphemy, and it contradicts the basis of the _Hanafiyy_ School without any doubt.

7. **Every walking towards committing an unlawful matter;**

8. **Every walking towards abandoning an obligation.**

Explanation: As it is mentioned previously, using the foot to commit any sin, or to walk with the purpose of committing any sin is sinful. Similarly, walking to abandon fulfilling an obligation is a sin, like for a person to walk away to escape paying the due debt that he is able to pay.

Chapter 49
Sins of the Body

Among the sins of the body are:

1. To harm one's parents severely (ˆuquq);

Explanation: This chapter deals with the sins of the body, i.e., the sins that are not restricted to a specific organ. Among those sins is for one to harm severely and unrightfully one or both of one's parents. Similarly, it is sinful to harm one's grand parents, even if one's parents are alive. This sin is an enormous sin. It is confirmed from the Prophet ﷺ that he said:

«ثَلاَثَةٌ لاَ يَدْخُلُونَ الجَنَّةَ : العَاقُّ لِوَالِدَيْهِ، والدَّيُّوثُ، وَرَجُلَةُ النِّسَاءِ»

This means: «Three kinds of people do not enter Paradise (without torture): the one who greatly harms one's parent, the one who facilitates adultery or fornication for the females of his family, and the woman who imitates men.» This is narrated by *Ibn Hibban*.

Severely harming a parent is called in Arabic *ˆuquq*. Scholars defined it as every act or saying that severely harms a parent according to the norm. *Sirajuddin al-Bulqiniyy* explained in one of his *fatwas* (edicts) this definition in a very good way. He said, "If one treats one's parents in a sinful, harmful manner, and had this sin been done to other than the parent it would have been a small sin, then when done to the parent it is judged as the enormous sin of ˆ*uquq*."

2. To flee the battlefield, which is to run away from the battle scene after having entered into it;

Explanation: Among the sins of the body is to flee the battlefield. By consensus, fleeing the battlefield is an enormous sin. If the number of Muslim fighters is half or more compared to the number of blasphemous fighters, then it is prohibited for the Muslims to flee the battlefield, except if they do that as a tactic, or to join other Muslim forces to win the victory. If the number of Muslims in the battle is less than half of the blasphemers, and the Muslims retreat, then they are not sinful. This judgment is clarified in (*Suratul-Anfal* 15 16):

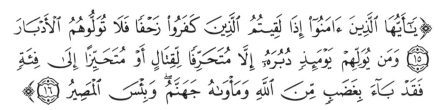

3. To sever the obligatory ties of kinship;

Explanation: Severing the obligatory ties of kinship is an enormous sin by consensus. In the _hadith_, narrated by *Al-Bukhariyy* and *Muslim*, the Prophet ﷺ mentioned that committing this sin causes for one to be tortured in Hellfire.

«لَا يَدْخُلُ الجَنَّةَ قَاطِعٌ»

One commits the aforementioned sin by acting in a way that normally makes the heart of one's kin repel from one, either by not visiting one's kin, or by not supporting them financially when they are in true need. In both cases, the committer is sinful, unless one has an excuse. The kin referred to includes all one's Muslim maternal and paternal relatives.

4. To inflict an apparent harm upon the neighbor, even if the latter was a blasphemer with a granted safety;

Explanation: Harming unrightfully one's neighbor (by doing or saying that which is considered harmful according to the norm) is a sin, even if the neighbor is a blasphemer. Examples of this harm are cursing him, hitting him, and building a structure that harms him (like building a high structure to spy on him and look inside his house). Harming the neighbor with an action or saying is more sinful than harming other than the neighbor with the same action or saying. The Prophet ﷺ said:

«مَا زَالَ جِبْرِيلُ يُوصِينِي بِالجَارِ حَتَّى ظَنَنْتُ أَنَّهُ سَيُوَرِّثُهُ»

This means: «Angel *Jibril* kept drawing my attention to treating the neighbor in a good way to a point that I thought he would tell me that the neighbor could inherit his neighbor.»

5. To dye the hair black;

Explanation: According to the chosen saying in the *Shafi^iyy*

317

school, it is prohibited for both men and women to dye their hair black. *Ibn Majah* and others narrated from the Prophet, *sallallahu ^alayhi wa sallam*, that he said:

$$\text{«يَكُونُ قَوْمٌ فِى ءَاخِرِ الزَّمَانِ يَخْضِبُونَ شُعُورَهُمْ بِالسَّوَادِ لَيْسَ لله بِهِمْ حَاجَةٌ»}$$

This means: «Before the Day of Judgment, a group of people will emerge that dye their hair black. Know that they do not hold any high status».

There are some exemptions to this rule. For example, some *Shafi^iyy* scholars said a wife is permitted to dye her hair black, with the permission of her husband.

6. For men to imitate women or women to imitate men in whatever is specific to the opposite sex, clothing and otherwise;

Explanation: Among the sins of the body is for women to imitate men and men to imitate women in one or more matters that are specific to the opposite gender. This could happen concerning the clothing worn and otherwise. Although both men and women are sinful, the women who commit such a sin are more sinful than the men who commit it. If a type of clothing is known to be originally worn by men only, or by women only, then it is prohibited for members of the opposite sex to wear it. This is so because *Abu Dawud* narrated from *Abu Hurayrah*, may *Allah* raise his rank, that the Prophet ﷺ prohibited men from wearing any clothes specific to women and he prohibited women from wearing any articles specific to men:

$$\text{«لَعَنَ رَسُولُ الله ﷺ الرَّجُلَ يَلْبَسُ لِبْسَةَ الْمَرْأَةِ والمرأَةَ تَلْبَسُ لِبْسَةَ الرَّجُلِ»}$$

7. To wear the dress lower than the anklebones out of vanity;

Explanation: If one wears a garment that goes lower than the anklebones out of vanity, i.e., to show off, one commits an enormous sin. If a man wears the garment lower than the ankles not to show off, i.e., without any prohibited intention, then it is disliked. It is better that his *izar* (waist cloth), or the like, reaches his mid-calf. If it is longer than that, then it is not disliked, as long as it does not pass the ankles.

8. For a man to needlessly dye his hands and feet with henna;

Explanation: Among the sins of the body is for a man, without an excuse, to dye his hands or his feet with henna. Such an act involves imitating women in something that is specific to them. A valid excuse is the need of that dying for treatment.

9. To interrupt the obligatory worship without an excuse;

10. To interrupt the optional _Hajj_ and ^_Umrah_;

Explanation: Once one is involved in performing an obligatory worship, even if one was making one up, then it is prohibited for one to interrupt it without a valid excuse. This judgment applies to the obligatory prayer and other kinds of worship. If one interrupts the obligatory worship for a valid excuse, then one is not sinful. However, just to answer the phone, or open the door are not valid excuses. One is not sinful if one interrupts an optional worship (except the optional _Hajj_ and ^_Umrah_). At-Tirmidhiyy and others narrated from the Prophet ﷺ that he said:

«الصّائِمُ المُتَطَوِّعُ أَمِينُ نَفْسِهِ إِنْ شَاءَ صَامَ وإِنْ شَاءَ أَفْطَرَ»

This means: «The person who is fasting an optional fast has the choice whether to continue one's fast (until sunset) or to interrupt it.» The optional _Hajj_ and ^_Umrah_ are excluded because they have a specific judgment. Once one starts an optional _Hajj_ or ^_Umrah_, it becomes incumbent upon one to continue that worship to the end.

11. To imitate the believer mockingly;

Explanation: If one mockingly imitates a believer, whether in his doings or his sayings, one is sinful. This is so because *Allah* prohibited the believers from mocking one another in *Suratul-Hujurat*, 11:

﴿يَٰٓأَيُّهَا ٱلَّذِينَ ءَامَنُوا۟ لَا يَسْخَرْ قَوْمٌ مِّن قَوْمٍ عَسَىٰٓ أَن يَكُونُوا۟ خَيْرًا مِّنْهُمْ وَلَا نِسَآءٌ مِّن نِّسَآءٍ عَسَىٰٓ أَن يَكُنَّ خَيْرًا مِّنْهُنَّ ۞﴾

It is prohibited to mock a Muslim by laughing at him because he is confused in his speech, he commits mistakes when speaking, or he walks or looks in a certain way.

12. To spy on people, pursuing their defects;

Explanation: One is sinful if one spies on other people, pursuing their defects. *Allah* said in *Suratul-Hujurat*, 12 :

$$ \text{﴿وَلَا تَجَسَّسُوا ﴿١٢﴾﴾} $$

This verse means: [Do not check on people with the purpose of pursuing their defects]. The Prophet ﷺ said:

«فَإِنَّهُ مَنْ تَتَبَّعَ عَوْرَةَ أَخِيهِ المُسْلِمِ تَتَبَّعَ اللَّهُ عَوْرَتَهُ . وَمَنْ تَتَبَّعَ اللَّهُ عَوْرَتَهُ يَفْضَحُهُ وَلَوْ فِى جَوْفِ رَحْلِهِ»

This *hadith* narrated by *at-Tirmidhiyy* means: «*Allah* will expose the one who spies on other Muslims, pursuing their defects, even if one stays inside one's residence.»

13. To tattoo;

Explanation: If one pricks oneself or others with a needle or the like until the blood comes out, then fills those holes with a colorful matter until the place becomes black, blue, red or the like, then one is sinful. This is the prohibited tattooing (*washm*) in the religious rules. *Al-Bukhariyy* and others narrated that the Prophet ﷺ damned the woman who does it and the woman to whom it is done:

«لَعَنَ رَسُولُ الله الوَاصِلَةَ والمُسْتَوْصِلَةَ وَالواشِمَةَ وَالمُسْتَوْشِمَةَ»

Thus, this sin is among the enormous sins. Although the Prophet ﷺ mentioned women, it is sinful if done by men as well.

14. To shun a Muslim for more than three days, without an Islamically valid reason;

Explanation: If one shuns another Muslim for more than three days, to a point that one even leaves out saying *as-salamu ^alaykum* to this Muslim when meeting him, then one is sinful. The Prophet ﷺ said:

«لا يَحِلُّ لِمُسْلِمٍ أَنْ يَهْجُرَ أَخَاهُ المُسْلِمَ فَوقَ ثَلاثِ لَيَالٍ . يَلْتَقِيَانِ فَيُعْرِضُ هذَا ويُعْرِضُ هذا . وَخَيْرُهُما الَّذِى يَبْدَأُ بِالسَّلامِ»

This *hadith* narrated by *Al-Bukhariyy* means: «It is prohibited for a

320

Muslim to shun his fellow Muslim to the point of leaving out addressing him with *salam*, when they meet, for more than three consecutive nights. The best among them is the one who initiates saying *as-salamu ^alaykum* to the other one.» From this *hadith*, it is clear that it is enough for two Muslims to salute one another, when they meet, to avoid committing the sin of shunning the Muslim.

However, the scholars said if one shuns a Muslim for a valid excuse, like to push him to refrain from committing an enormous sin, then one is not sinful. In this case, it is permissible to shun that sinful Muslim until he repents or dies.

15. To sit with an innovator or committer of enormous sins (*fasiq*) to entertain one in one's sinning;

Explanation: Among the sins of the body is to sit, without having a valid excuse, in the same session with a bad innovator (with a creed different from the creed of *Ahlus-Sunnah*) while he is preaching his innovation. One is not sinful if one sits with the purpose of discrediting the sayings of the innovator.

Similarly, it is sinful to sit in the same session with an enormous sinner to entertain him when he is committing an enormous sin. *At-Tirmidhiyy* narrated with a strong chain of narrators that the Prophet ﷺ said:

$$ \text{«مَنْ كَانَ يُؤْمِنُ بِاللَّه وَاليَوْم الآخِر فَلا يَجْلِسْ عَلَى مَائِدَةٍ يُدَارُ عَلَيْهَا الخَمْرُ»} $$

This means: «Let the one who believes in *Allah* and the Day of Judgment not sit at the table of alcohol drinking». This is so unless one has a valid excuse. An example of a valid excuse is for one to have business with one who is drinking alcohol. One enters the session, talks with the specific person about the business, and once done leaves that session. In such a case, one is not sinful.

16. For a man to wear gold, silver, silk, or what is mostly silk-with the exception of a silver ring;

Explanation: It is prohibited for the pubescent male to wear gold (even a golden ring). Also, it is prohibited for him to wear silver, except a silver ring. Likewise, it is prohibited for him to wear silk or an article that is mostly silk in weight. Except for the silver ring, wearing gold, silver, and silk is prohibited for men by consensus. As for the silver ring, it is permissible to wear it because the Prophet ﷺ wore it.

It is permissible for women to wear gold, silver and silk. As for the non-pubescent boy, there are different opinions among the scholars whether or not it is permissible to let him wear gold, silver and/or silk.

17. **For a man to have** *khalwah* **(be alone) with a marriageable woman without the presence of a third person, male or female, who can see them and in front of whom one would be shy to do an indecent act;**

Explanation: It is prohibited for a man to be with a marriageable woman (who is neither his wife nor slave) without a third person, male or female, being with them. The third person has to be trustworthy or a *mahram*. Additionally, it is a condition that this third person not be blind and be old enough so that one usually feels shy to do an indecent act in front of him. If this third person present is only two or three years old, his presence would not be sufficient to prevent them from being considered as if they are alone together (*khalwah*). It is prohibited for the marriageable man and woman to be alone together (*khalwah*) because *at-Tirmidhiyy* narrated from the Prophet ﷺ that he said:

$$\text{«أَلَا لَا يَخْلُوَنَّ رَجُلٌ بِامْرَأَةٍ إِلَّا كَانَ ثَالِثَهُمَا الشَّيْطَانُ»}$$

This means: «Every time a marriageable man and a marriageable woman are alone together, the devil will be the third one with them».

It is not prohibited for a woman to be alone with two men. This is the correct saying, although some *Shafiʿiyy* scholars judged that as prohibited. Their saying is rejected because *Imam Muslim* narrated from the Prophet ﷺ that he said:

$$\text{«لَا يَدْخُلَنَّ رَجُلٌ عَلَى مُغِيبَةٍ إِلَّا وَمَعَهُ رَجُلٌ أَوْ رَجُلَانِ»}$$

This means: «Let no man enter alone the house of a woman, when her husband is away, except if he has with him one or two other men». This *hadith* is classified as *sahih*.

18. For a woman to travel without a non-marriageable male or the like;

Explanation: It is not permissible for a woman to travel without a non-marriageable male or the like accompanying her. Some examples of permissible traveling partners are her father, brother, and pubescent son. This judgment applies for any traveling, whether for the distance of *qasr* or less. It was narrated from the Prophet ﷺ that he prohibited women to travel alone for a half-day distance, for a one-day distance, for a two-day distance, and for a three-day distance.

«لا تُسَافِرِ المرأةُ بَريدًا إلا وَمَعَها ذُو مَحْرَمٍ». (البريد مسيرة نصف يوم) وروايات: «ليلة» و«يومًا وليلة» و«يومين» و«ثلاثًا».

The sum of all those narrations implies that it is prohibited for women to travel for any distance alone, as long as this distance is considered "traveling" according to the norm of the people at the time of the Prophet ﷺ.

On the other hand, if there is a necessity for a woman to travel, and she cannot find any non-marriageable man or the like to accompany her, then it is permissible for her to travel alone.

19. To coerce a free person to do labor;

Explanation: Among the sins of the body is to unjustly enslave a free person, or to coerce him to do a certain job for another, i.e., to force him to do that without his free will.

20. To have enmity with a highly ranked, righteous Muslim (*waliyy*);

Explanation: Among the sins of the body is to have enmity with a *waliyy*. This is an enormous sin. A *waliyy* is a Muslim who fulfills all the obligations, refrains from all the sins and does a lot of optional acts of worship. Having enmity against any *waliyy* is an enormous sin. One is more sinful by having enmity against one of their elite, like the first four Caliphs *Abu Bakr*, ˆ *Umar*, ˆ*Uthman* and ˆ*Aliyy*.

21. To help others to sin;

Explanation: Among the sins of the body is to help anyone to commit a sin. *Allah* said in the second verse of *Suratul-Ma'idah*:

﴿وَلَا تَعَاوَنُوا۟ عَلَى ٱلْإِثْمِ وَٱلْعُدْوَٰنِ ۚ (٢)﴾

This verse means: [Do not help one another to commit sins and unjust acts.] The aforementioned verse is a clear proof that it is prohibited for one to take another person to the blasphemer's place of worship to commit blasphemy. This is so even if that person is one's parent, wife, brother, sister, or child. *Qadi Khan* (a famous *Hanafiyy* scholar), among others, mentioned explicitly this case in his famous *fatawa* (edicts).

22. To circulate counterfeit money;

Explanation: Circulating counterfeit money is cheating; hence it is prohibited in the rules of the Religion.

23. To use and to obtain golden and silver utensils;

Explanation: Among the sins of the body is to use golden and silver utensils for eating, drinking, or any other usage, without a valid excuse. *Imam Muslim* narrated that the Prophet ﷺ said:

$$\text{«إِنَّ الذِى يَأْكُلُ أَوْ يَشْرَبُ فِى ءانِيَةِ الفِضَّةِ وَالذَّهَبِ، فَإِنَّمَا}$$
$$\text{يُجَرْجِرُ فِى بَطْنِهِ نَارًا مِن جَهَنَّم»}$$

This means: «The one that uses silver or golden utensils for eating or drinking is inserting the fire of the Hereafter inside one's stomach». Likewise it is prohibited to have golden or silver utensils, even without using them.

24. To neglect an obligation, to do an obligation leaving out one of its integrals or conditions, or to intentionally commit an invalidator while performing an obligation;

25. To leave out the Friday prayer (*Jumuʿah*) when it is one's obligation, even if one prays _Dhuhr_;

26. For the inhabitants of a place to leave out praying the obligatory prayers in congregation;

Explanation: Among the sins of the body is to leave out doing an obligation, whether it is a prayer or otherwise. Likewise, it is sinful to perform an obligation neglecting any of its integrals, conditions, or with doing one of its invalidators. Also, it is sinful to leave out performing *Jumuʿah* (Friday) prayer, without an excuse, when one is obligated to pray it (even if one prays the _Dhuhr_ prayer instead).

Similarly, if the people of a city, town, or even a small village leave out praying the five obligatory prayers in congregation, they are sinful. Praying those five prayers in congregation is a collective obligation on them (*fard kifayah*) because the Prophet ﷺ said:

«مَا مِنْ ثَلاثَةٍ فِى قَرْيَةٍ وَلا بَدْوٍ لا تُقَامُ فِيهِمُ الصَّلاةُ إلا قَدِ اسْتَحْوَذَ عَلَيْهِمُ الشَّيْطَانُ، فَعَلَيْكَ بِالجَمَاعَةِ، فَإِنَّمَا يَأْكُلُ الذِّئْبُ القَاصِيَةَ»

This *hadith* narrated by *Abu Dawud* and *an-Nasa'iyy* means: «If only three men are in a city or village, and they do not pray in congregation, the devil will control them. Remember that the wolf chooses the sheep distant from the flock to eat it.»

27. To defer one's obligations until the time is over, without an excuse;

Explanation: Among the sins of the body is to inexcusably defer performing the obligation until its time is over. An example of such sinful deferral is to wait without praying the obligatory prayer until its time ends. The one who does that is committing an enormous sin because *Allah* said in *Suratul-Ma^un*, 4-5:

﴿فَوَيْلٌ لِّلْمُصَلِّينَ ۝ ٱلَّذِينَ هُمْ عَن صَلَاتِهِمْ سَاهُونَ ۝﴾

This verse means: [Woe to the people who intentionally delay praying the obligatory prayer until its time is over]. *Abu Dawud* narrated with a *sahih* chain of narrators that ^Umar, may *Allah* raise his rank, said:

«مَنْ جَمَعَ بَيْنَ صَلاتَيْنِ مِنْ غَيْرِ عُذْرٍ فَقَدْ أَتَى بَابًا مِنْ أَبْوَابِ الْكَبَائِرِ»

This means: "The one who joins two prayers without an excuse is committing an enormous sin."

28. To hunt with something that kills the animal by its weight, such as a stone;

Explanation: Among the sins of the body is to hit or to shoot the edible prey with something that kills it by its weight like stones and bullets. This is prohibited because a person asked the Prophet about using an arrow with a big tip (*mi^rad*). The Prophet ﷺ replied by saying:

«مَا أَصَبْتَ بِحَدِّهِ فَكُلْ، وَمَا أَصَبْتَ بِعَرْضِهِ فَهُوَ وَقِيذٌ»

This means: «If the prey is killed by the sharp edges of this arrow then eat it. However, if its blunt force kills it, then it is forbidden to eat it.» At-Tirmidhiyy, Al-Bukhariyy, Muslim, Ibn Majah, An-Nasa'iyy and others narrated this hadith.

29. To use an animal as a shooting target;

Explanation: Among the sins of the body is to use an animal, that is any living creation (with a soul), as a shooting target whether this is done for fun or to learn shooting.

30. For the divorced woman or widow who is observing a post-marital waiting period (mu^taddah) to inexcusably leave her home, and for such a widow to wear perfumes, dress up, and the like;

Explanation: Among the sins of the body is for the woman who is in her post-marital waiting period for the death of her husband or divorce (mu^taddah) to sleep outside of her home without a valid excuse. If she is in the post-marital period (^iddah) because of her husband's death, it is prohibited for her to leave her home with no valid excuse until that ^iddah ends. However, it is permissible for her to go out to her house's yard or garden. It is also permissible for her to visit her neighbor for a period of time, then go back to her house to sleep.

If it is dangerous for her to remain at home, because the house is going to collapse or because of the real fear that some people might break in and harm her, then she is excused to move to somewhere else.

Among the sins of the body is for the widowed woman to wear adornment (in clothing or otherwise) within her post-marital waiting period. Wearing perfume and oiling her hair to beautify it have the same judgment as adornment. It is not prohibited for her to talk with men during that time. Once this period ends, the woman is prohibited from continuing to intend mourning (ihdad) by leaving out adornment and perfume for that purpose.

Observing the rules of ^iddah during the post-marital waiting period gives her a convenient environment to better prepare for the

Hereafter. Women other than wives are prohibited to observe mourning (ihdad) longer than three days, for the death of their mothers, sisters, other relatives, friends or strangers. As for men, it is prohibited categorically for them to intend mourning by leaving out the aforementioned matters. Of course, sadness and grief are not prohibited.

Note: It is not a requirement that the woman wears black clothes for mourning (ihdad). She can wear any kind of clothes of any color with the condition that it is not considered decorative.

31. To stain the mosque with a *najas*-filth or to make it dirty even with a pure (*tahir*) material;

Explanation: It is prohibited to stain the mosque with a *najas*-filth, like urine and blood. Also, it is prohibited to stain the mosque with pure (*tahir*) but filthy materials like spit and mucous. Protecting the mosque from such issues is included in the obligation of glorifying the rites of the Religion. *Al-Bukhariyy* and *Muslim* narrated that the Prophet ﷺ said:

$$«البُزَاقُ فِى المَسْجِدِ خَطِيئَةٌ».$$

This means: «Spitting on the ground of the mosque is a sin.»

32. To delay performing Hajj until death, while able to perform it when alive;

Explanation: Among the sins of the body is to delay performing *Hajj* until one dies, while one is able to perform it when alive. Although according to the School of ash-Shafi^iyy it is permissible for the able person to delay performing *Hajj* for one or more years, if he dies before performing it then he is judged as enormous sinner.

33. To take a loan with the obvious inability to pay it back, without informing the lender;

Explanation: If one is not able to pay back a debt, then one is not permitted to take a loan without informing the lender about one's inability. This is so unless one has a true necessity (like if acquiring the money is one's only means to avoid starvation, and one knows that the lender will not lend if the situation is revealed).

A different case is the following: One may borrow money to

spend it in a *halal* way, and at the time of taking the loan one has a job and other possessions that enable one to pay back the debt. Later unexpectedly one becomes unable to pay the money back, and remains so until death. In this case, the borrower is not sinful and does not deserve any torture in the Hereafter.

34. To refuse to grant more time for the one who is unable to pay one's debt;

Explanation: If someone borrows money and later becomes in a tight situation financially, in a way that he is not able to pay back the due debt (as explained in the previous case), it is an obligation on the lender to grant the borrower more time to pay back the debt. In such a case, it is prohibited for the lender to harm the borrower, verbally or physically. In an attempt to push the borrower to return the debt, the lender must not follow him around harassing, insulting, or putting him in prison.

35. To spend money in disobedience;

Explanation: Among the sins of the body is to spend money in disobeying *Allah*, whether the disobedience is a small sin or an enormous one. Spending money for this purpose is in itself an enormous sin. The Prophet referred to this matter in the *hadith* narrated by *al-Bukhariyy* and others:

«إِنَّ رِجَالاً يَتَخَوَّضُونَ فِى مَالِ اللهِ بِغَيْرِ حَقّ، فَلَهُمُ النَّارُ يَوْمَ القِيَامَةِ»

This means: «Some people manage the money that God created and gave to them in disobeying Him. Their torture on the Day of Judgment is Hellfire.»

36. To belittle the Book of the *Qur'an* (*Mus-haf*) and every Islamic Knowledge, and to enable the child who has reached the age of mental discrimination (*mumayyiz*) to carry the *Qur'an*;

Explanation: Actions denoting a lack of obligatory glorification of the Book of the *Qur'an*, or other religious books are sinful. Examples of that are for one to carry the *Qur'an* while in the state of ritual impurity (i.e., needing to make *wudu'* or *ghusl*), to stretch one's leg towards a book of the *Qur'an, Fiqh, Hadith*, interpretation of *Qur'an* and the like. Also included in that is to enable a child who reached the stage of mental discrimination (*mumayyiz*) to carry the *Qur'an* without having ablution, except if the child needs to carry it to study in it. In this case, it is permissible to enable him to do that and to carry it to the place where he learns. On the other hand, it is not permissible to enable the child who has not yet attained to the mental discrimination to carry the Qur'an. The same judgment applies to the insane person. Thus, it is not permissible for one to ask one's five-year old son to bring the Mus-haf. If the lack of glorification reaches the level of mocking or degrading, then it is blasphemy. An example is when one intentionally steps on, spits on, or degrades the book of the Qur'an in any way.

37. To unjustly change property line markers, i.e., to change the markers between one's own property and that of others;

Explanation: Among the sins of the body is to change unjustly the line border between one's land and the land of one's neighbor, i.e., to append unjustly a piece of the neighbor's property to one's own property. Doing this intentionally is an enormous sin, even if the added piece was only equal to a hand spread. *Imam Muslim* narrated from ˆAliyy that the Prophet ﷺ said:

«لَعَنَ اللَّهُ مَنْ غَيَّرَ مَنَارَ الأَرْضِ»

This saying means: «Damned is the one who unjustly changes the property line markers.»

38. To use the street for that which is unlawful;

Explanation: There are two types of streets. One type is the open road, i.e., both ends of the street are connected to other streets. It is not permissible, in this type of street, to do any thing that harms the passers, like to put one's belongings in it in a way that makes it difficult for the people to pass. The second type of street includes the street with a dead end. In this case, it is not permissible to sit and put the belongings in it without the permission of its residents.

39. To use a borrowed item in other than what one is permitted by its owner, to keep it longer than permitted, or to lend it to someone else;

Explanation: It is not permissible to use a borrowed item in other than what the owner permits. For example, if a person borrows a horse to ride it, i.e., the permission given by the owner to the borrower was restricted to riding it, then it is not permissible for the borrower to use it to pull a cart, or the like. Also, if the owner specifies time for the borrower to return the borrowed item, then it is prohibited for the borrower to keep it for more than the specified time. Likewise, it is not permissible for the borrower to lend the borrowed item to a third party, without the permission of the owner.

40. To prevent others from using what is permissible (unowned), such as preventing others from grazing their animals in an unowned meadow. Similarly, it is sinful to prevent others from collecting firewood from the unowned land, or from extracting salt, gold, silver, and other resources from their unowned origin, or from using drinking water from a self-replenishing source;

Explanation: Among the sins of the body is to appropriate resources that are Islamically judged as being public resources. Examples of this are for one to prevent others from grazing their animals in a land that is unowned or to prevent others from gathering firewood from such a land. It is prohibited to prevent people from taking salt from an unowned mine, or to take gold, silver or any other minerals from an unowned mine. It is prohibited to prevent people from taking their needs of drinking water, or their animals, from a self-replenishing well that was dug in an unowned land. Likewise, it is prohibited to prevent others from benefiting from a burning fire in unowned woods, or to prevent them from benefiting from sea and river shores. *Abu Dawud* and others narrated from the Prophet ﷺ that he said about such cases:

«المسلمون شُرَكَاءُ فِى ثَلاثٍ : فِى الكَلإِ والماءِ والنَّارِ»

This means: «The Muslims are partners in three things: grass, water and fire.»

<u>Beneficial information</u>: If a person takes water in his own container from a river, then this water becomes his. Likewise, if he gathers firewood, grass, or the like from un-owned land, they become his. The same case applies when he lights his wood using a public fire. This new fire on his wood becomes his. In those aforementioned cases, he is entitled to prevent others from using those things. The water, grass and fire mentioned in the aforementioned *hadith* of the Prophet ﷺ refer to un-owned ones.

41. To use the lost-and-found article (*luqatah*) before satisfying the conditions of notification;

Explanation: If one finds an article that is lost by another person in an un-owned place, such as a street, and one does not know its owner, then one has to announce it for a year. It is not permissible for one to use it before announcing it for that period. If one announces in a proper way (with the intention of using it if its owner does not show up) and despite that the owner of this article is not found, only then it is permissible for the finder to consume this article or use it with the intention that if the owner shows up one day, one will return it to him, or pay the owner its value.

42. To sit in a place where disobedience is being committed, without an excuse;

Explanation: If actions of disobedience are done in a certain place, then it is prohibited for one to stay in that session without an excuse. If one is able to prevent the occurrence of that disobedience, whether by oneself or by informing others about it, one is obligated to do so. If one is unable to do that, then one hates this disobedience in one's heart, and leaves that session.

43. To enter into a banquet without permission, or be admitted out of shyness;

Explanation: If one is not invited to attend a banquet, or one knows the invitation was a result of embarrassing the host, it is prohibited for one to attend it. It is not permissible to consume or take others belongings without their consent and good will as is clearly mentioned in the *hadith* narrated by *Ahmad* and *al-Bazzar:*

«لا يَحِلُّ لِمُسْلِمٍ أَنْ يَأْخُذَ عَصَا أَخِيهِ بِغَيْرِ طِيبِ نَفْسٍ»

This means: «It is not permissible for a Muslim to take the staff of his brother without his consent.»

44. To commit inequity among the wives in terms of the obligatory spending and overnight turns. The preference in attraction in the heart to and in the love of one wife over another is not a sin;

Explanation: If a man is married to more than one wife, he has to treat them all with equity in what pertains to obligatory spending and the overnight stays. This means that the husband has to support all of them providing the obligatory support and to give them their proper

331

turns in his overnight stays.

If this husband neglects providing all or part of the obligatory support to one or more wives, then he is sinful. He is also sinful if he neglects fulfilling obligatory support or overnight stays of a wife because, for example, he does not prefer her any more.

On the other hand, he is not sinful for loving one of them more than the others, having sexual intercourse with one more than the others.

45. For a woman to go out with the intention to pass by men to tempt them;

Explanation: For a woman to go out with the intention of tempting men is a sin of the body, whether or not dressed up and perfumed. On the other hand, if she goes out dressed up or wearing perfume while covering all that she is obligated to cover of her body and without having the intention of tempting men, then she is not sinful. In such a case, this action is disliked, because it is better for the woman to leave out wearing perfume, make up, and the like when she goes out in public. *Ibn Hibban* narrated from the Prophet ﷺ that he said:

$$\text{«أَيُّمَا امْرَأَةٍ خَرَجَتْ مُسْتَعْطِرَةً فَمَرَّتْ بِقَوْمٍ لِيَجِدُوا رِيحَهَا}$$
$$\text{فَهِيَ زَانِيَةٌ»}$$

This means: «Any woman that goes out wearing perfume and passes by men to tempt them (with that perfume) is similar to a fornicator.» This is so, because her action is an introduction to *zina*. It is clearly deduced from this *hadith* that if she does not have the intention of tempting the men, then she is not sinful by going out wearing perfume.

46. [To engage in] sorcery;

Explanation: Among the sins of the body is to perform sorcery. Performing any type of sorcery is an enormous sin. Performing sorcery sometimes reaches the level of blasphemy. To perform some types of sorcery, the sorcerer prostrates to the sun, and/or to the devil, which is blasphemy. Other times, one is asked to commit blasphemy to be taught how to do sorcery. *Al-Bukhariyy, Muslim* and others narrated from the Prophet ﷺ several *hadiths* clarifying that sorcery is an enormous sin.

47. **To rebel against the caliph, like those who rebelled against ^Aliyy and fought him. Al-Bayhaqiyy said, "All who fought ^Aliyy were transgressors". Ash-Shafi^iyy said the same, even though some of the best Companions were among those transgressors. It is not impossible for the waliyy to commit a sin, even if it is an enormous sin;**

Explanation: Among the sins of the body is to rebel against the Caliph. *Muslim* narrated from the Prophet ﷺ that he said:

«فَإِنَّهُ لَيْسَ مِنَ النَّاسِ أَحَدٌ خَرَجَ مِنَ السُّلْطَانِ شِبْرًا فَمَاتَ علَيْهِ، إلَّا مَاتَ مِيتَةً جَاهِلِيَّةً»

This means: «Anyone who rebels against the Caliph and breaks the allegiance which he gave to him, then dies without repenting, will have a status similar to the status of those who died in the era of ignorance.» This does not mean that the one who rebels against the Caliph commits blasphemy. Rather, it means that he is an enormous sinner. This is why *Ash-Shafi^iyy* and others mentioned explicitly that each and everyone that fought ^Aliyy was sinful. *Talhah* and *az-Zubayr*, may *Allah* raise their ranks, were sinful by being in the camp of the transgressors against ^Aliyy. Shortly after that, i.e., before they died, they repented of this sin, because *Allah* willed for them a very high status in the Hereafter. They would not die without repenting from such a sin. It is a well-known rule by *Ahlus-Sunnah* that the *waliyy* is not protected against sinning. A *waliyy* may commit an enormous sin. If the *waliyy* does commit an enormous sin, he repents quickly, and surely before dying.

48. **To accept taking care of an orphan or a mosque, or to act as a judge and the like, knowing that one will be unable to perform the task appropriately;**

Explanation: It is sinful for one to accept a position knowing that one will not be able to perform the task in the appropriate way. This includes being a judge, or a teacher, or being in charge of an orphan's money, a *waqf*, a mosque, a religious school, and the like. In such a case, it is prohibited for one to ask to be appointed to such a position, to accept such an appointment, and, more so, to pay money to be appointed.

49. To harbor an unjust person, i.e., to protect one from those who want to obtain their right from one;

Explanation: Among the sins of the body is to protect an unjust person in order to prevent the people who have rights on him from getting their rights. This is an enormous sin because *Muslim* narrated from the route of ^*Aliyy*, may *Allah* raise his rank, that the Prophet ﷺ said:

«لَعَنَ اللَّهُ مَنْ ءَاوَى مُحْدِثًا»

This means: «May *Allah* damn the one who shelters the unjust person [to prevent his punishment or his making him pay the rights that are on him].»

50. To terrorize Muslims;

Explanation: Among the sins of the body is to terrorize a Muslim by pointing a weapon at him. *Ibn Hibban* narrated from the Prophet ﷺ that he said:

«مَنْ أَشَارَ إِلَى أَخِيهِ بِحَدِيدَةٍ فَإِنَّ الملائِكَةَ تَلْعَنُهُ وإِنْ كانَ أَخَاهُ لِأَبِيهِ وأُمِّهِ»

This means: «The angels damn the one who terrorizes his Muslim brother with a weapon, even if the terrorized person is his brother from his father and mother.»

51. To waylay; depending on the committed crime, the waylayer's punishment is either a disciplinary action (ta^zir), or cutting off both the right hand and the left foot, or execution, or execution followed by hanging the body on a pole;

Explanation: Among the enormous sins is to waylay. If the waylayer just scares the passing Muslims, without taking their money or killing any of them, he deserves to be punished with a disciplinary action (ta^zir). The ruler decides the punishment. If the waylayer frightens the people and takes their money, without killing any of them, his punishment is to have his right hand and left foot cut off. If he takes the money and kills the people, then his punishment is to be killed, with his dead body hung on a pole. If he kills without taking any money, then his punishment is to be killed without hanging his dead body. In the case of the waylayer who kills (while waylaying), he is killed despite requests from the relatives of the killed to spare his life. This case differs, concerning punishment, from other types of deliberate killing.

52. To neglect fulfilling the vow (nadhr);

Explanation: If one makes a vow (nadhr) to do a rewardable matter, which is not an obligation, then the vow is valid and one is obligated to fulfill it. The meaning of making a vow is to take upon oneself, as an obligation, to do something that is not normally an obligation. An example of that is for one to make a vow to fast every Monday and Thursday. If one vows it, it becomes an obligation (except for a valid excuse) to fast every Monday and Thursday, until one dies.

If someone makes a vow to do an obligation, a prohibition, a disliked matter, or a permissible but unrewardable matter, then in all these cases the vow is not valid.

53. To continue fasting for two or more days without eating or drinking anything in between;

Explanation: The Prophet ﷺ prohibited us from continuing to fast for two or more days, without eating or drinking anything at night. Anyone who disobeys the Prophet in that is sinful. The Prophet ﷺ is exempted from this judgment. It was permissible for him to fast for two consecutive days without eating or drinking anything in between.

54. To occupy someone else's place in a street or the like, to harmfully crowd one, or to take one's turn.

Explanation: If a person comes first to a spot in the street in which he wants to wait for someone, to display his merchandise, or the like (without hurting the passers), then it is prohibited for someone else to occupy his spot or to harmfully crowd him. Likewise, if someone comes first and sits in the mosque, it is prohibited for someone else to occupy his place without his permission. This judgment applies even after one leaves one's place, as long as one intends to come back soon to it (like if one goes to make *wudu'*). *Muslim* narrated from the Prophet ﷺ that he said:

«مَنْ قَامَ مِنْ مَجْلِسِهِ ثُمَّ رَجَعَ إِلَيْهِ، فَهُوَ أَحَقُّ بِهِ»

335

This means: «The one who leaves his seat and then comes back to it is the most deserving of it.»

On the other hand, if a person leaves his seat without the intention of coming back, then it is permissible for someone else to occupy it.

Also, if a right is established for a group of people to water their plants from a source of water, which is not enough for everyone at the same time, then it is prohibited for any one else to take this group's turn without its permission.

If a group of people choose several adjacent pieces of land in an un-owned area and each one of them cultivates one piece to be planted and plants there, by this action each one of them owns the piece of land that he cultivates. In this case, if they water their lands from a public source of water which is not enough for all of them at once, the one who owned the land first deserves to be the first one to water. Then the second one follows, and then third one, and so on. They must always keep this order in watering their plants for all the coming years. If any of them takes the turn of another without his permission, he is sinful.

The Enormous Sins

The righteous scholars agreed that the sins (excluding blasphemy) are subdivided into two types: enormous sins and small sins. *Allah, ta^ala*, said (*an-Nisa'* 31 ; *an-Najm* 32):

$$﴿إِن تَجْتَنِبُوا۟ كَبَآئِرَ مَا تُنْهَوْنَ عَنْهُ نُكَفِّرْ عَنكُمْ سَيِّـَٔاتِكُمْ وَنُدْخِلْكُم مُّدْخَلًا كَرِيمًا ﴿٣١﴾ ﴾$$

$$﴿ٱلَّذِينَ يَجْتَنِبُونَ كَبَـٰٓئِرَ ٱلْإِثْمِ وَٱلْفَوَٰحِشَ إِلَّا ٱللَّمَمَ إِنَّ رَبَّكَ وَٰسِعُ ٱلْمَغْفِرَةِ ﴿٣٢﴾ ﴾$$

These verses mean that *Allah* forgives those who commit some small sins but avoid committing enormous sins (as long as they do not insist on committing these small sins to the point that their sins exceed their good deeds).

These verses make it clear that sins are of two types. Likewise, *Muslim* narrated from the Prophet ﷺ a *sahih hadith* that clearly subdivides the sins into two types: enormous sins and small sins. The Prophet ﷺ said:

$$«الصَّلَوَاتُ الْخَمْسُ، وَالْجُمُعَةُ إِلَى الْجُمُعَةِ، وَرَمَضَانُ إِلَى رَمَضَانَ، مُكَفِّرَاتٌ مَا بَيْنَهُنَّ إِذَا اجْتَنَبَ الكَبَائِرَ»$$

The aforementioned *hadith* means: «Performing the Five Prayers, praying the Friday Prayer after having prayed the previous Friday Prayer, and fasting *Ramadan* after having fasted the previous *Ramadan* erase the small sins committed in-between them, but not the enormous ones.» No specific number for the enormous sins was ever narrated in any *sahih hadith* from the Prophet ﷺ . ^Abdur-Razzaq narrated in his book of interpretation from Ma^mar from *Ibn Tawus* from his father that *Ibn ^Abbas* was asked, "What is the number of enormous sins? Are they seven?" *Ibn ^Abbas* answered, "They are closer to seventy than to seven".

The scholars defined the enormous sin in several terms. Among the best expressions in defining the enormous sin is: "Every sin is an enormous sin when described in the *Qur'an*, the *hadith* of the

337

Prophet, or by consensus that it is enormous, or that it entails a severe punishment in the Hereafter, or that the one who does it is punished by a specified punishment in the revealed texts (*hadd*), or that the one who does it is very blameworthy."

A difference between the enormous sin and the small sin is that if one commits a small sin, it is erased if afterwards one does a good deed. However, as for the enormous sin, doing a good deed after it does not necessarily erase it. For example, if one commits a small sin and afterwards makes a verbal remembering of God (*dhikr*), then this good deed erases that sin. Sometimes, doing a good deed erases an enormous sin. However, many times it is not erased until one repents of it.

Some of the enormous sins (in the order *As-Suyutiyy* mentioned them) are:

1. Killing.

2. Adultery and fornication (*zina*).

3. Drinking wine or any intoxicating liquid.

4. Sorcery.

5. Accusing unjustly someone with *zina*.

6. Sodomy.

7. Invalidating the obligatory fast.

8. To despair of *Allah*'s mercy.

9. To continue committing sins, feeling safe from the punishment of *Allah*.

10. To take the belongings of others unjustly.

11. Stealing.

12. To give a false testimony.

13. To bribe.

14. To pimp.

15. To withhold paying the due *Zakah*.

16. To facilitate committing *zina* for one's wife or female family members.

17. To run away from the battlefield.

18. To betray in measuring.

19. To address one's wife with the words of <u>dh</u>i<u>h</u>ar.

20. Talebearing.

21. To withhold one's obligatory testimony.

22. To swear by *All<u>a</u>h* when lying.

23. To lie about the Prophet ﷺ.

24. To cuss the Companions of the Prophet ﷺ.

25. To hit a Muslim.

26. To incite the ruler to inflict harm on a Muslim.

27. To harm one's parent severely.

28. To shun the obligatory kinship.

29. Waylaying.

30. To pray before the prayer time is in or to delay the prayer inexcusably until after its time is out.

31. To consume the money of the orphans.

32. To eat pig or *maytah*, i.e., the animal killed improperly.

33. to engage in the usurious gain (*rib<u>a</u>*).

34. To take for oneself a part of the spoils of battle before they are distributed in the proper way (*ghul<u>u</u>l*).

35. To insist on committing small sins until they exceed one's good deeds.

Also, among the enormous sins are:

1. To neglect learning the Personal Obligatory Knowledge of the Religion, even if one is apparently praying, fasting, and the like.

2. For men and women to imitate one another in what is specific to the other gender.

3. For the wife to go out of her husband's house without his permission.

4. For the wife to harm her husband by asking him to divorce her without an excuse.

5. To pluck the eyebrows hair to make them thinner.

6. To tattoo.

7. To connect the human hair with other human hair.

8. To have sexual intercourse with the menstruating woman.

Chapter 50
Repentance

The immediate repentance of sins is obligatory upon every accountable person. It comprises: regretting, quitting, and intending not to return to them. If the sin is leaving out an obligation, one makes it up. If the sin involves a right to a human, one must satisfy it or seek the person's satisfaction.

Explanation: It is an obligation to repent immediately of the enormous and small sins because Allah said (Suratut-Tahrim 8):

$$\text{﴿يَٰٓأَيُّهَا ٱلَّذِينَ ءَامَنُوا۟ تُوبُوٓا۟ إِلَى ٱللَّهِ تَوْبَةً نَّصُوحًا ۝﴾}$$

This verse means: [O believers, repent to Allah a sincere repentance.]

For the repentance to be valid there are requirements that have to be fulfilled. They are:

1. To regret disobeying Allah, out of penitence. If one regrets doing a sin out of a worldly reason, like regretting killing someone unjustly because of the jail sentence that one receives, and not because of disobeying Allah, then this is not a valid repentance. Likewise, if one regrets doing a sin because of one's fear of being exposed before the people, and not because of disobeying Allah, this is not a valid repentance.

Regretting having committed the sin is the most critical element among the integrals of repentance, to a point that Ibn Majah and Ahmad narrated that the Prophet ﷺ said:

$$\text{«النَّدَمُ تَوْبَةٌ»}$$

This literally means: «Repenting is to regret». Truly it means: «The most critical integral among the integrals of repentance is to regret».

2. To immediately stop committing the sin which one regrets doing. Hence, if one regrets committing a sin while one is still doing it, one's regretting is not part of a valid repentance.

3. To have the firm determination in one's heart not to do the same sin again. If this is satisfied, but later one gets weak and repeats the sin, the previous repentance is not invalidated.

The three aforementioned requirements all have to be fulfilled for the validity of the repentance. Moreover, if the committed sin was leaving out an obligation, making-up this obligation is also required. So, if one leaves out an obligatory prayer and later one wants to repent, then one needs to make up that prayer as one of the requirements for the validity of repentance. Likewise, if the sin was leaving out paying the obligatory Zakah or obligatory expiation, then one needs to pay it immediately for one's repentance to be valid. If one is not able, one has to be determined to make it up when one becomes able.

If the sin involves a right of a human being, one must satisfy it, or seek that person's satisfaction. For example, if someone steals the money of another person, one has to give the money back to its owner if the money is still with one. If the stolen item is decomposed or consumed, then one needs to pay the owner or his inheritors (if the real owner dies) the value of the stolen item.

If the owner relieves the thief from paying back what the owner deserves, then the pay back will not be among the integrals of repentance. Al-Bukhariyy and at-Tirmidhiyy narrated with a sahih chain of narrators that the Prophet ﷺ said:

«مَنْ كَانَتْ لَهُ مَظْلِمَةٌ لأَحَدٍ مِنْ عِرْضِهِ أَوْ شَيْءٍ فَلْيَتَحَلَّلْهُ مِنْهُ
اليَوْمَ قَبْلَ أَنْ لا يَكُونَ دِينَارٌ ولا دِرْهَمٌ»

This means: «Let one now satisfy one's Muslim brother, whom one treated unjustly, before the Day of Judgment comes, because on that day one cannot satisfy him either by dirhams or by dinars.»

Hence, if one curses another person unjustly, let one apologize, seeking for the cursed person to relieve oneself in this life before death. Similarly, if one unjustly takes the belongings of another, let one return them, seeking the satisfaction of the robbed one before the Day of Judgment comes. On the Day of Judgment, the satisfaction of the wronged person is not going to be with money. Rather, the wronged person takes from the rewards of the one who wronged him. If the rewards of the unjust are not enough, then some of the victim's sins will be put on the unjust one, who then enters Hellfire (except if *Allah* satisfies the wronged person by His generosity without taking from the rewards of the unjust one).

In the case when one harms another person and it is ordained that the unjust one receives a well specified, religious punishment (*hadd*), one needs to enable the people entitled to punish the unjust one to do so, for one's repentance to be valid. An example of that is killing a Muslim unjustly. In this case, the killer needs to surrender to the heirs of the killed person and tell them, "If you do not relieve me from being killed for free, or for an indemnity (*diyah*), then I am ready to face the proper punishment". If he does not do that, and rather, he runs away from the punishment, his repentance is not valid.

Asking *Allah* for forgiveness by the tongue, although rewardable, is not an integral for the validity of the repentance, as some wrongly think.

Here ends what *Allah* willed of presenting:

A Brief Explanation of
The Summary of ˆ*Abdullah Al-Harariyy*,
Ensuring
the Personal Obligatory Knowledge of the Religion.

Allah knows best. We praise *Allah* and thank Him.

Glossary

The meanings of the words that are mentioned in this Glossary are the ones which closely pertain to the text in the Summary. The words are listed in English alphabetical order (see Transliteration System).

The definite article is added to the Arabic words, wherever proper, to help the reader know the correct way of adding it, in accordance with the rules of the shamsiyy and qamariyy letters: When the definite article «al-» الـ precedes a word starting with a shamsiyy letter, its «l» ل is not pronounced or written (in English) and the shamsiyy letter is doubled. For example, the word «dalil» دَليل becomes «ad-dalil» الدَّليل (not al-dalil) because «d» د is a shamsiyy letter. On the other hand, the word «hilal» هلال becomes «al-hilal» الهلال because the letter «h» هـ is a qamariyy letter. We add the apostrophe ' after «al-» to indicate that the hamzah (followed by a vowel) letter after it is pronounced distinctly, like in the word «al-'imam» الإِمَام. On the other hand, the absence of the apostrophe means that the sound of the hamzah is absent, like in the word «al-ijtihad» الاجْتِهَاد; it is pronounced as «alijtihad» and not «al-'ijtihad» الإجْتِهَاد.

* * * * * * * *

* **A** ء، أ / ^**A** عَ

* **al-'Ad-ha** الأَضْحَى The tenth of *Dhul-Hijjah*; it is a ^*Id* day. It is the day after the standing in the land of ^*Arafah* in *Hajj*. It is forbidden to fast on this day.

* **al-'Ahad** الأَحَد A name of *Allah*, which means 'al-Wahid', and 'the One Who is indivisible'.

* **al-'ajnabiyy** الأَجْنَبِيّ The man who is other than a woman's husband or *mahrams*. A woman's father, uncle, brother, and son are not *ajnabiyys* to her.

* **al-'ajnabiyyah** الأَجْنَبِيَّة The woman who is other than a man's wife or *mahrams*. A man's mother, aunt, sister, and daughter are not *ajnabiyyahs* to him.

* **al-'Al** الآل The family; The *Al* of Prophet *Muhammad* includes his wives, Muslim kin, and the pious Muslims of his nation.

344

* **al-ˆAlim** العَالِم A name of *Allah*', which means 'the One Who knows everything'.

* **Allah** الله The name of the Creator in Arabic, which means 'the One Who deserves to be worshipped' or 'the One attributed with Godhood, the Power to create'.

* **al-ˆamilun ˆalayha** العَامِلونَ عَلَيها Persons hired by the Muslim caliph to collect, take care of, and distribute *Zakah*, but are not given a salary. Instead, they are paid from *Zakah*.

* **Amin** ءَامِين A word which is said at the end of the *Fatihah* or some *duˆa'* and means «O *Allah*, answer our *duˆa'*», or «so be it».

* **ˆArafah** عَرَفَة A plain about 9 miles Southeast of Makkah where Prophet *Muhammad, sallallahu ˆalayhi wa sallam*, gave his 'Farewell Speech'. It is also the place where Muslims performing *Hajj* spend some time between the *Dhuhr* of the ninth of *Dhul-Hijjah* and *Fajr* of the tenth of *Dhul-Hijjah*.

* **al-ˆariyyah** العَارِيَّة Allowing someone to benefit from an Islamically permissible article which is not consumable, such as a cooking pot.

* **al-ˆAsr** العَصْر The obligatory *Salah*, the time of which begins when the length of the shadow of an object becomes equal to the length of the object per se plus the length of its shadow at *Istiwa'*; it continues until *Maghrib* time, i.e., sunset. This *Salah* comprises four *rakˆahs* (cycles).

* **al-ˆAdhab** العَذَاب The suffering that the disobedient people receive on the Day of Judgement, including the torture in Hell.

* **al-ˆawrah** العَوْرَة Unlawful nakedness. For a man and a slave woman, it is the area between the navel and the knees, and for a free woman the whole body except the face and hands. This part of the body must be covered when performing *Salah*. In addition, this ˆawrah must be covered before the ajnabiyy(ah). In the presence of a *mahram* or a Muslim woman, a woman's ˆawrah is the area between her navel and knees.

* **al-'Awwal** الأَوَّل A name of *Allah*, which means 'the First', i.e., 'the One Whose Existence has no beginning'.

* **al-'ayah** الآيَة A sentence (verse) of the *Qur'an*. *Ayat* is the plural of *ayah*. The Qur'an has more than 6000 verses.

* **B** ب

* **al-baligh** البَالِغ Pubescent; a male becomes pubescent when he either

345

attains to 15 lunar years (about 14.5 solar years) or sees his *maniyy*. On the other hand, a female becomes pubescent when she either attains to 15 lunar years, sees her *maniyy*, or starts menstruating. Islamically, a girl may begin menstruating around nine lunar years of age.

* **al-Baṣir** البَصير A name of *Allah* which means: 'the One Who sees what is seeable'.

* **al-Basmalah** البَسْمَلَة Saying «*Bismillah-ir-Rahman-ir-Rahim*» (in the name of *Allah*, ar-Rahman, ar-Rahim), which is the first *ayah* of the *Fatihah*, the first *Surah* of the *Qur'an*.

* **al-Baˆth** البَعْث The Resurrection of the dead on the Day of Judgement.

* **al-Batil** الباطِل The Invalid; the Untrue; this is that which does not comply with the rules of *Islam* and is not accepted by *Allah*.

* **al-bayˆ** البَيع Selling; exchanging or giving goods for a substitute, such as money, in a specific way. The seller would say 'I now sell you this item for so much money'. The buyer would say 'I now buy it for that price'.

* **D ﺩ / D ﺽ**

* **ad-Dafn** الدَّفْن The Burial of the dead; digging a hole in the ground for the dead deep enough to prevent the smell from rising to the surface and to protect the body from animals.

* **ad-Da'im** الدَّائِم A name of *Allah*, which means 'the Everlasting', i.e., 'the One Whose Existence does not end'.

* **ad-daniq** الدَّانِق One-sixth of a dirham, equivalent to about 0.5 grams of silver.

* **ad-Daruriyy** الضَّرُورِيّ The Obligatory; The Essential.

* **ad-Din** الدّين The Religion (of Islam).

* **ad-dinar** الدّينَار A unit of weight measure equivalent to a *mithqal* (about 4 grams of gold).

* **ad-dirham** الدِّرْهَم A unit of weight measure equivalent to about 3 grams of silver.

* **ad-diyah** الدِّيَة Money paid for having, for example, killed a person.

* **ad-duˆa'** الدُّعَاء Supplication; making *duˆa'* is the act of asking *Allah* for things. It is *sunnah* to make *duˆa'* after *Salah*. During sickness,

traveling, and before breaking fast are other times when making *duˆa'* is recommended.

* ## DH ذ / DH ظ

* *adh-dhihar* الظِّهَار Saying to one's wife that her back is forbidden to one as much as the back of one's mother is. People before the Prophethood of *Muhammad, sallallahu ˆalayhi wa sallam*, used to say that to state to their wives their refusal to have sexual intercourse with them. When *dhihar* is uttered without following it with an immediate divorce statement, a *kaffarah* of *dhihar* is inflicted (see *al-kaffarah*).

* *adh-Dhimmiyy* الذِّمِّيّ A non-Muslim, such as a Christian or Jew, who pays *Jizyah* to the Islamic State.

* *adh-dhiraˆ* الذِّرَاع Cubit; the distance from the tip of the fingers to the elbow (hand plus the forearm); two spans, which are equivalent to about 46 centimeters or 18 inches.

* *adh-Dhuhr* الظُّهْر The obligatory *Salah*, the time of which starts with the declination of the sun from its highest apparent position (*Istiwa'* = zenith) towards the west and continues until the length of the shadow of an object becomes equal to that of the object in addition to the shadow cast by the same object when the sun was at *Istiwa'*. It comprises four *rakˆahs*.

* *Dhul-Hijjah* ذُو الحِجَّة The twelveth month of the Islamic (lunar) year.

* *Dhul-Qaˆdah* ذُو القَعْدَة The eleventh month of the Islamic (lunar) year.

* ## F ف

* *al-Fajr* الفَجْر Dawn; The obligatory *Salah*, the time of which starts with the appearance of the horizontal illumination in the eastern horizon, mixed with a slight redness which increases afterwards and continues until sunrise. It comprises 2 *rakˆahs*.

* *al-Fard* الفَرْض The Obligatory; this is what *Allah* has promised its committer with reward and has threatened its avoider with punishment; *rukn*, i.e., an item that is a part of an *ˆibadah* (worship) and without which it would be invalid.

* *al-fasiq* الفَاسِق A person who has committed one or more enormous sins, such as adultery, drinking alcohol, or leaving out the obligatory prayers.

* **al-Fatihah** الفَاتِحَة The first Surah of the Qur'an, consisting of seven verses. It must be read in every rak^ah of Salah.

* **al-fatwa** الفَتْوَى The (Islamic) answer to a problem.

* **al-Fay'** الفَيْء Money taken by the Islamic State from non-Muslims who deserted it without any fight. This money can be used by the caliph in the interest of the Muslims, such as for improving the defenses of the country.

* **al-fidyah** الفِدْيَة For missing days of fasting during Ramadan that require the paying of fidyah, it is giving the poor Muslim(s), a mudd (two average-size cupped handfuls) of wheat, rice, or the like for every day of fasting missed. Concerning Hajj, fidyah comprises slaughtering an animal, fasting several days, or feeding some poor Muslims.

* **al-fi^liyy** الفِعْلِي Pertaining to action, such as in fi^liyy rukn, which means a integral of action, such as sujud.

* **al-Fiqh** الفِقْه In Arabic, comprehension; Islamically, knowing the practical Islamic Rules which were inferred from the detailed proofs. Imam Abu Hanifah said that Fiqh is knowing one's religious rights and obligations.

* **al-Fitr** الفِطْر The first day of the month of Shawwal, after the termination of Ramadan; ^Id-ul-Fitr; Zakat-ul-Fitr.

* **al-fuqara'** الفُقَرَاء In Arabic it means 'the poor'; (Islamically) Muslims who do not have enough to meet half of their basic appropriate needs of lodging, clothing, and food, such as those who need $10 but earn less than $5. Fuqara' is the plural of faqir.

* **GH** غ

* **al-gharimun** الغَارِمُون Muslims who are under debt because, e.g., they borrowed money to spend for their needs, but could not pay it back.

* **al-Ghusl** الغُسْل Purificatory bath; Total washing of the body having the proper intention. It is required after certain things, such as sexual intercourse and the termination of the menses, have occurred; washing the dead.

* **H** ه /**H** ح

* **al-hadath** الحَدَث Ritual impurity. The state of not having wudu' or being required to perform ghusl. The former is called the minor hadath and the latter the major hadath.

* **al-hadith** الحَادِث A creation, i.e., something the existence of which

started at some point in time and it may be annihilated any time later. Paradise and Hellfire, two creations of *Allah*, will never be annihilated because *Allah* has willed that for them.

* ***al-Hadith*** الحَدِيث It refers to what was attributed to the Prophet, *sallallahu ^alayhi wa sallam*, of sayings, deeds, attributes, and acknowledgements. The acknowledgements of the Prophet refer to the matters which occurred during his time that he was told about, or in his presence, but he did not prohibit.

* ***al-hady*** الهَدْى An animal that is slaughtered on the Day of ^Id-ul-'Ad-ha because, e.g., of committing sexual intercourse while performing *Hajj*.

* ***al-Hajj*** الحَجّ Pilgrimage; one of the greatest articles of *Islam*. It is the journey to the *Ka^bah* to perform, at a specific period of the year, certain actions in *Makkah* and its vicinity. The *Hajj* الحَاجّ is the person who performs *Hajj*.

* ***al-Halal*** الحَلال The lawful according to *Islam*; opposite of *Haram*; the person who is not *muhrim*.

* ***al-Halq*** الحَلْق Shaving; in particular, the shaving of all the hair of the head of the male in *Hajj*.

* ***al-Haram*** الحَرَام The forbidden and sinful (opposite of *halal*); this is what *Allah* has threatened its committer with punishment and has promised its avoider with reward.

* ***al-Haramayn*** الحَرَمَيْن *Makkah* and *al-Madinah*, including some area around each of them; *Haraman* is the nominative form of *Haramayn*. Each of them is called *Haram*.

* ***al-hasan*** الحَسَن Good; beautiful; A *Hadith* the relators of which are known for their trustworthiness. It is accepted by the scholars of *Islam*, and is used for inferring Islamic rulings.

* ***al-Hashr*** الحَشْر The Assembling of the people in one place on the Judgement Day.

* ***al-Hawd*** الحَوْض The place where the obedient Muslims will have a drink, after which no thirst is felt. This is before they are admitted to Paradise.

* ***al-hawl*** الحَوْل One lunar year; in the context of *Zakah*, the passage of one lunar year after having had *nisab* of some articles that are subject to *Zakah*.

* **al-hayd** الْحَيْض Menses; the blood that is discharged from the uterus of a female, who has attained to about nine lunar years or more, through her vagina. The minimum time of hayd is twenty-four hours and the maximum time is fifteen days. Al-ha'id الْحَائِض is the menstruating woman.

* **al-Hayy** الْحَيّ A name of Allah which means 'the Alive', i.e., 'the One Who is attributed with an eternal and everlasting Life'.

* **al-Hijaz** الْحِجَاز A region in the West of Arabian Peninsula which includes Makkah and al-Madinah.

* **al-hilal** الهِلال The crescent of the new moon; that which is usually looked for to determine the beginning of a new month, such as the month of Ramadan.

* **al-Hill** الْحِلّ The region which is other than that of the Haram in Makkah. It is the regional Miqat of ^Umrah for those people in Makkah.

* **al-Hisab** الْحِسَاب The displaying of the deeds of the people on the Day of Judgement.

* ع ^I / إ I I

* **al-^Ibadah** الْعِبَادَة Worship, such as Salah (Prayer), Siyam (Fasting), and Hajj (Pilgrimage).

* **Iblis** إِبْلِيس Satan; the Devil, the father of jinn, who refused to make sujud to Adam and blasphemed.

* **ibn-us-sabil** ابْنُ السَّبِيل A person who wants to travel or is traveling but does not have what is enough to help him reach his destination.

* **al-^Id** الْعِيد Islamic celebration (Bairam); this is either ^Id-ul-Fitr or ^Id-ul-'Adha.

* **al-^iddah** الْعِدَّة The length of time a previously married woman must wait before she can marry again. This varies depending on her situation. For a divorced woman, it is three spans of tuhr, i.e., non-menstruating intervals. However, if she is pregnant, the ^iddah ends when she delivers her baby. For a widow, it is four lunar months and ten days, or if she is pregnant, until she delivers the baby.

* **al-'ihdad** الإِحْدَاد Mourning; Leaving out dressing up, including wearing perfume. The period of ihdad for a widow is four months and ten days, during which the woman must avoid dressing up and wearing perfume.

* **al-'Ihram** الإحْرام In _Salah_, it is saying "_Allahu akbar_" to start _Salah_, and in _Hajj_ it is the intention to start _Hajj_.

* **al-'ijarah** الإجَارَة Giving someone the benefit of an Islamically permitted article for a compensation. This contract includes hiring a laborer or leasing a property.

* **al-'Ijma^** الإجْماع One source of Islamic teachings, defined as the unanimous agreement of the _mujtahids_ (top scholars) from among the followers of Prophet _Muhammad, sallallahu ^alayhi wa sallam_, upon a religious matter at a certain time.

* **al-Ijtihad** الاجْتِهاد Exerting effort to find the Islamic answer to a situation relying on the _Qur'an, Sunnah, Ijma^_, and _Qiyas. Ijtihad_ is done only by the qualified _mujtahid_. In the context of _Qiblah_, it is exerting effort to know the direction of _Qiblah_ using Polaris, other stars, the sun, the moon, rivers, and winds.

* **al-'ikhlas** الإخْلاص Sincerity; Doing an obedience for the sake of _Allah_ only.

* **al-^ilm** العِلْم Knowledge; also science. In the Islamic context and texts, it always means Islamic knowledge.

* **al-'imam** الإمَام The leader of _Salah_; the _Khalifah_ (the Muslim Ruler); scholar of _Islam_.

* **al-'Injil** الإنْجيل The Revelation given to Prophet ^_Isa_ (Jesus), _sallallahu ^alayhi wa sallam_. The so-called «the Bible» is not the _Injil_.

* **al-^Iqab** العِقَاب Punishment which is incurred upon the disobedient on the Day of Judgement.

* **al-^Isha'** العِشَاء The obligatory _Salah_, the time of which starts with the disappearance of the twilight and continues until _Fajr_. It comprises four _rak^ahs_.

* **al-'Islam** الإسْلام In Arabic it means submission; it is the Religion of all Prophets of _Allah_ starting with _Adam_ and ending with _Muhammad, sallallahu ^alayhim wa sallam_. It is the belief in and utterance of the _Shahadatayn_, the latter being required of the person who is not already a Muslim.

* **al-istibahah** الاسْتِبَاحَة Recognition of something as allowed.

* **al-Istinja'** الاسْتِنْجَاء The removal of _najas_-filth that exited from the eliminatory outlets. This is done by using water and/or materials such as paper tissues.

351

* **al-Istiwa'** الاسْتِوَاء Zenith; The time when the sun is apparently (high) in the middle of its course through the sky.

* **al-i^tidal** الاعْتِدَال A rukn of Salah which is (resuming) the standing position after having performed ruku^.

* **ج** ل

* **Jahannam** جَهَنَّم Hell-Fire in which some disobedient Muslims will be tortured for some time, and all non-Muslims will suffer forever.

* **al-jam^** الجَمْع Combining Dhuhr and ^Asr or combining Maghrib and ^Isha' while traveling for a qasr distance, for example (compare with qasr).

* **al-Jama^ah** الجَمَاعَة Congregation; Performing Salah by two or more persons with one leading the others; the Muslim group following the Sunnah of Prophet Muhammad, sallallahu ^alayhi wa sallam. The full name is Ahl-us-Sunnah wal-Jama^ah.

* **al-jamarat** الجَمَرَات Places where many pebbles are thrown while performing Hajj. Jamarat is the plural of jamrah.

* **al-janabah** الجَنَابَة The state when one had sexual intercourse or emission of maniyy, whether from a man or a woman, be it from a wet dream, masturbation, sexual intercourse, or fondling.

* **al-Janazah** الجَنَازَة The Funeral; preparing the Muslim dead by washing, wrapping, praying for, and burying him.

* **al-Jannah** الجَنَّة Paradise; the abode that Allah has created and to which only Muslims will be admitted dwelling therein forever.

* **Jibril** جِبْريل The Angel of Revelation (Gabriel); He is the angel who conveyed the orders of Allah to the prophets, sallallahu ^alayhim wa sallam, and is the best of the angels.

* **al-jinn** الجِنّ These are creations of Allah who can change form. They were created from the pure flame of fire. The devils are the non-Muslim jinn, whose chief is Satan (ash-Shaytan).

* **al-Jizyah** الجِزْيَة The compulsory payment of a Dhimmiyy to the Islamic State.

* **al-Jumu^ah** الجُمُعَة Friday; the Salah which is performed on Friday within Dhuhr time, known as Salat-ul-Jumu^ah.

* **al-junub** الجُنُب A person in the state of janabah.

* **K** ك

* ***al-Ka^bah*** الكَعْبَة The cubical-like structure in the Holy Mosque of *Makkah* (*al-Masjid-ul-Haram*) to which Muslims must direct themselves in *Salah*. It was first built by Prophet *Adam*, then rebuilt by Prophets *Ibrahim* (Abraham) and *Isma^il* (Ishmael), *sallallahu ^alayhim wa sallam*.

* ***al-Kafan*** الكَفَن The (three) cloths with which the dead is wrapped, the least of which is one cloth covering the whole body of the dead.

* ***al-kaffarah*** الكَفَّارَة An action that must be done for having committed a certain disobedience. There are different *kaffarah*s which are expounded upon in various books of *Fiqh*.

* ***al-kafil*** الكَافِل Guarantor.

* ***al-kafir*** الكَافِر Blasphemer; any non-Muslim.

* ***al-Kalam*** الكَلام In Arabic it means 'speech'; when it is meant for the attribute of *Allah* then it means 'that attribute by which *Allah* orders, forbids, promises, and threatens', and is not a letter, word, sound, or language.

* ***al-kibr*** الكِبْر Rejecting the truth said by someone and looking down on people.

* ***al-kifayah*** الكِفَايَة In Arabic it means 'sufficient'; *Fard kifayah* (communal obligation) refers to the obligatory actions which if done by some Muslims, the rest of the Muslims are not obligated to do. However, if not done by anyone then every member of the community who is *mukallaf* and was able to do them is sinful for having neglected them.

* ***al-kufr*** الكُفْر Blasphemy; state of being a non-Muslim; any conviction, saying, or action which is blasphemous.

* **KH** خ

* ***al-Khalifah*** الخَلِيفَة Caliph; *Imam*; the Muslim Ruler, who rules according to the Rules of *Islam*. It is obligatory upon Muslims to obey him. There are many requirements which must be satisfied in a man before he is chosen as the *Khalifah* and are mentioned in other books of *al-Fiqh*.

* ***al-Khaliq*** الخَالِق A name of *Allah*, which means 'the Creator', i.e., 'the One Who brings things from non-existence into existence'.

353

* **al-Khawarij** الخَوارِج A deviant group of people that rebelled against and fought *Imam ^Aliyy Ibn Abi Talib*.

* **al-khuff** الخُفَّ A shoe, not necessarily with a hard sole, that covers the foot and the ankle. A pair of *khuffs* are called *khuffan*. *Khuffan* is the nominative form of *khuffayn*.

* **al-khushu^** الخُشُوع Feeling the glorifying fear of *Allah* in one's heart.

* **al-Khutbatayn** الخُطْبَتَيْن The Two Speeches delivered on occasions such as *Jumu^ah* (Friday) and *^Id*. *Khutbatan* is the nominative form of *Khutbatayn*.

* **L** ل

* **al-liwat** اللِّواط Inserting the (glans) penis in the anus of a male or a female. It is a major sin.

* **al-luqatah** اللُّقَطَة The thing that was lost by its owner and was found by somebody else, but its owner is unknown. Lost-and-found item.

* **M** م

* **al-ma^alim** المَعَالِم 'The rites (of Islam)', such as *Salah* and *Hajj*; 'the landmarks' that guide one on the way.

* **al-Madinah** المَدِينَة The City of the Messenger of *Allah, Muhammad, sallallahu ^alayhi wa sallam*, to which he immigrated and where he died and was buried. Its former name was *Yathrib*.

* **al-Maghrib** المَغْرِب Sunset; the obligatory *Salah*, the time of which starts with the total disappearance of the disc of the sun in the western horizon and continues until the disappearance of the twilight. It comprises three *rak^ahs*.

* **al-mahr** المَهْر A benefit that the man gives to the woman for marrying her, including money and teaching her the *Qur'an*.

* **al-mahram** المَحْرَم A person of the opposite sex whom one is forbidden to marry, because of blood relation (brother, mother, uncle, aunt), marriage (father-in law, step-son), or nursing (nursing father or mother, nursing brother or sister).

* **Makkah** مَكَّة The city, in *Hijaz*, in which the *Ka^bah* is located and is the birthplace of Prophet *Muhammad, sallallahu ^alayhi wa sallam*.

* **al-Makruh** المَكْرُوه The Disliked; this is that which if done is not punishable, but if one avoids one is rewarded.

* **al-maks** المَكْس The toll which is taken unjustly by some governors on goods, farms, and the like.

* **al-ma'mum** المَأْمُوم Follower of *imam* in *Salah*.

* **al-Mandub** المَنْدُوب This is that which if done one is rewarded, but one is not punished for neglecting it; also known as *Nafl* and *Sunnah*.

* **al-maniyy** المَنِيّ For a man it is the seminal fluid and for a woman it is the vaginal fluid which is discharged during her orgasm.

* **al-maˆruf** المَعْرُوف Obedience; it includes all that agrees with the teachings of the *Qur'an* and *Sunnah*.

* **al-Marwah** المَرْوَة A hill annexed to *al-Masjid-ul-Haram* where the pilgrim (*Hajj*) performs *Saˆy* starting from *as-Safa* and ending at *al-Marwah*.

* **al-masakin** المَسَاكِين Muslims who have enough money to cover more than half of their basic appropriate needs but not all of them, such as those who need $10 but earn more than $5 but less than $10. *Masakin* is the plural of *miskin*.

* **al-Madhhab** المَذْهَب A framework inferred by a *mujtahid* from the *Qur'an, Sunnah, Ijmaˆ, and Qiyas,* by which he deduces the judgements on the practical matters of *Islam* such as *Taharah, Salah, Zakah, Siyam,* and *Hajj*. The principal *Sunniyy madhhabs* which are in use today are four: the *Hanafiyy Madhhab, Malikiyy Madhhab, Shafiˆiyy Madhhab,* and *Hambaliyy Madhhab*. The respective founders of those *madhhabs* are: *Imam Abu Hanifah* (80-150 A.H.), *Imam Malik* (93-179 A.H.), *Imam ash-Shafiˆiyy* (150-204 A.H.), and *Imam Ibn Hambal* (164-241 A.H.).

* **al-madhiyy** المَذِيّ A clear thin liquid that emerges from the penis of a man or the vagina of a woman upon arousal of sexual desire.

* **al-mawat** المَوَات A land which was never owned. It is not owned except by whoever prepares it for some benefit like plantation or residence.

* **Mina** مِنَى A village, four miles east of *Makkah*, where pilgrims stay for most of the nights of *Tashriq* Days.

* **al-Miqat** المِيقَات The time and place of starting *Hajj* or *ˆUmrah*.

* **al-mithqal** المِثْقَال A unit of measure which is equivalent to the weight of seventy-two average-sized barley grains after their ends are cut without being peeled off (about 4 grams of gold).

* **al-Mizan** الميزان The balance in which the deeds of the people are weighed on the Day of Judgement, good deeds (of Muslims only) being in one pan, while the bad ones (of the disobedient, whether Muslims or non-Muslims) being in the other.

* **al-Muˆadah** المعادة The obligatory *Salah* which one reperforms after having prayed it either alone or in a congregation for the purpose of gaining more reward.

* **al-mu'allafatu qulubuhum** المؤلفة قلوبهم Persons like those who embraced *Islam* but their faith is still weak and if paid their faith will be strengthened, those who are dignified among their people and if paid others like them may be encouraged to become Muslims, and those Muslims who fight non-Muslims who are next to them or fight the ones who refuse to pay *Zakah*.

* **al-Mubah** المباح The Permitted; this is that which, if either done or neglected, neither reward nor punishment is incurred upon one.

* **al-mudd** المد A unit of measure for grains, e.g., which comprises two hands of average size cupped together.

* **al-muhaddith** المحدّث A scholar of *Hadith*.

* **al-muhrim** المحرم Person in the state of *Ihram*, i.e., involved in the actions of *Hajj* or ˆ*Umrah*.

* **al-muhsan** المحصن A person who has had sexual intercourse within a valid marriage. Widows, widowers, divorced men and women, and married people who are free are each considered *muhsan*. The *muhsan* is pelted until death for committing adultery.

* **al-mujtahid** المجتهد A top scholar of *Islam*; A Muslim who is qualified to perform *Ijtihad*, such as the founders of the four *Sunniyy* Schools.

* **al-mukallaf** المكلف Accountable; A person who is pubescent, sane, and, in a language that one understands, has heard of the call of *Islam*, i.e., the *Shahadatayn*.

* **al-Mukhtasar** المختصر Summary.

* **al-Munkar** المنكر Disobedience; this includes all of what disagrees with the teachings of the *Qur'an* and *Sunnah*.

* **al-muqim** المقيم Resident; a person who intends to stay in a place, such as a town, for four days or more, excluding the two days of entry to and exit from that place.

356

* **al-murtadd** الْمُرْتَدّ The apostate; the one who has committed apostasy having previously been a Muslim.

* **al-musafir** الْمُسَافِر Traveler; a person who is traveling for a qasr (shortening) distance, which according to some scholars, is approximately 27 miles (44 kilometers).

* **al-musaqah** الْمُسَاقَاة The agreement between the owner of palm trees or grape vines and a person such that for a specific portion of the product, the latter takes care of them over a specific period of time.

* **al-Mus-haf** الْمُصْحَف The Holy Book of the Muslims, which is also referred to as the _Qur'an_.

* **Muslim** مُسْلِم A believer and follower of _Islam_.

* **al-mustawtin** الْمُسْتَوْطِن A person who lives in a town, leaves it either in the Summer or in the Winter only for some incidental need, and intend to die therein.

* **al-mu^taddah** الْمُعْتَدَّة A (recently) divorced or widowed woman who must observe ^iddah (waiting period).

* **al-mut^ah** الْمُتْعَة Compensatory payment given to a woman if the husband divorced her without any reason from her side.

* **al-mutahhir** الْمُطَهِّر Purifying; _Tahur_; water or soil which effects _Taharah_. A mutahhir water is that which falls from the sky (rain water) and springs out of the ground (spring water, rivers), and sea water; it is also called tahur water. _Tahur_ soil is that which has not been used for Tayammum, and has no najasah mixed with it.

* **al-muwalah** الْمُوَالاة Doing some actions in succession. In _Salah_, it is reading the verses of the _Fatihah_ without stopping between them for longer than what one needs to take a breath.

* **Muzdalifah** مُزْدَلِفَة A place, six miles east of _Makkah_, where those who are performing _Hajj_ stay for at least one moment between the middle of the night and _Fajr_ of _Ad-ha_ Day.

* **N** ن

* **an-nabiyy** النَّبِيّ Prophet; a man who has received _Wahy_ (Revelation) from _Allah_ and conveys it to the people (compare with _rasul_).

* **an-nadb** النَّدْب Mentioning the good qualities of a dead person by raising one's voice.

* **an-Nafl** النَّفْل See _al-Mandub_.

357

* **an-Nahr** النَّحْر Slaughter; Nahr Day is the Day of ^Id-ul-'Ad-ha when some Muslims slaughter some animals.

* **an-najasah** النَّجَاسَة In Arabic, a material which is deemed filthy like feces, urine, vomit, blood, dogs and pigs; Islamically, those filthy things which, if unexempted, prevent the validity of a worship, such as Salah.

* **an-najis** النَّجِس also an-najas النَّجَس Najas-filth; Najasah; something blemished with a najasah.

* **an-namimah** النَّمِيمَة Talebearing; conveying the words of one person to another to cause dissension.

* **an-Nar** النَّار Hellfire; Jahannam.

* **an-nadhr** النَّذْر A vow to Allah by which one commits oneself to do any good deed, such as fasting a certain number of days or paying charity. It is obligatory to fulfill one's nadhr.

* **an-nifas** النِّفَاس Postpartum bleeding; Blood coming out of the vagina of a woman after childbirth. Its minimum time is a moment, its maximum is 60 days, and is most often 40 days.

* **an-nisab** النِّصَاب Quotum; The (minimum) amount of money or number of animals that is subject to Zakah.

* **an-niyahah** النِّيَاحَة Screaming out of impatience upon the death of a person.

* **an-nufasa'** النُّفَسَاء The woman who is in the state of nifas (postpartum bleeding).

* **Q** ق

* **al-qada'** القَضَاء Make-up; refers to missed Salah, Siyam, or any obligation that must be made up.

* **al-Qadar** القَدَر Qadar has two meanings: (1) Taqdir, i.e., Destining, a perfect attribute of Allah: Making things happen according to the Will and Knowledge of Allah; (2) maqdur, destined, i.e., the creation, some of which is good and some of which is evil.

* **al-Qadi** القَاضِى Judge; a title given to an Islamic scholar when acting as a judge.

* **al-Qadim** القَدِيم A name of Allah, which means 'al-'Awwal', i.e., 'the One Whose Existence has no beginning'.

* **al-Qadir** القَادِر A name of Allah, which means 'the Almighty'; 'the One Who has Power with which He affects the creation'.

358

* **al-qasr** القَصْر Shortening; praying exclusively *Dhuhr*, ^*Asr* and ^*Isha'* as two cycles instead of four for traveling a *qasr* distance, which is approximately 27 miles (approximately 44 kilometers) or more. One can also combine the praying of *Dhuhr* and ^*Asr*, or the praying of *Maghrib* and ^*Isha'* in the time of either one of these prayers to be combined. This is called *jam*^. As soon as the *musafir* (traveler) leaves the boundaries of his town place, he can perform *Salah* in the *qasr* and *jam*^ modes, provided his traveling is not sinful. However, if the traveler intends to stay in the destination place for four days or more, other than the two days of entry and exit, then he cannot perform *jam*^ or *qasr* while residing in his destination place.

* **al-qadhf** القَذْف Unjustful, verbal accusation of a person of fornication or adultery.

* **al-Qayyum** القَيُّوم A name of *Allah*, which means 'the Everlasting' and 'the One Who does not need anything'.

* **al-Qiblah** القِبْلَة The direction to which Muslims direct themselves in *Salah*. This is towards the *Ka*^*bah*, the cubical-like structure in the Holy Mosque of *Makkah*.

* **al-qirad** القِرَاض Authorizing a person to invest one's own money for a known percentage of profit.

* **al-qiyam** القِيَام The standing position before *ruku*^ in *Salah*.

* **al-Qiyamah** القِيَامَة The day that starts with the rising of the dead from their graves (Resurrection) on the Judgement Day, until those who earned Paradise are admitted to it and those who earned Hell are admitted therein.

* **al-Qudum** القُدُوم Coming; *Tawaf-ul-Qudum* is the optional *Tawaf* performed by the pilgrim upon entering *Makkah*.

* **al-qullatan** القُلَّتَان A volume measure which is about 190 liters. This comprises the fill of a round hole that measures one *dhira*^ (cubit) in diameter and one *dhira*^ and a half in depth. Alernatively, it is the fill of a cubical hole, the side of which measures one *dhira*^ and a quarter. *Qullatan* is the nominative form of *qullatayn*, the dual form of *qullah*.

* **al-Qur'an** القُرْءان The Holy Book of *Islam*, revealed to Prophet *Muhammad*, *sallallahu* ^*alayhi wa sallam*, throughout the 23 years of his Prophethood. The *Qur'an* comprises 30 juz's (Parts), 114 *Surahs* (Chapters), and more than 6000 *ayahs* (verses).

* **R** ر

* *ar-Rahim* الرَّحِيم A name of *Allah*, which means 'the One Who is very merciful with the Muslims only, on the Day of Judgement'.

* *ar-Rahman* الرَّحْمَن A name of *Allah*, which means 'the One Who is very merciful with the Muslims and non-Muslims in this world (life)'.

* *ar-rahn* الرَّهْن Pledge; giving or holding a certain article as a security to guarantee the payment of a debt from it when the debt cannot be paid.

* *ar-rak^ah* الرَّكْعَة A cycle involving sayings, such as reciting the *Fatihah* and actions, such as *ruku^*, *i^tidal*, and *sujud*.

* *Ramadan* رَمَضَان The ninth month of the Islamic lunar calendar, which is obligatory to fast.

* *ar-rasul* الرَّسُول Messenger of *Allah*; a prophet who comes with canceling some of the laws brought by the previous messenger, or with a new set of laws. The prophet follows the laws of the messenger who came before him. Every messenger is a prophet, but not every prophet is a messenger.

* *ar-Raziq* الرَّازِق A name of *Allah*, which means 'the Provider', i.e., 'the One Who gives the means of sustenance to His creations'.

* *ar-riba* الرِّبَا A contract that contains a specific substitute, the equivalent of which is unknown at the time of conducting the contract, or with deferring either of or both substitutes.

* *ar-riddah* الرِّدَّة Apostasy; becoming non-Muslim after having been Muslim by committing any blasphemous action or saying, or holding a blasphemous conviction.

* *ar-rikaz* الرِّكَاز A treasure which had been buried before the Prophethood of *Muhammad, sallallahu ^alayhi wa sallam*, and was found after that. Only the gold and silver *rikaz* are subject to *Zakah*.

* *ar-riqab* الرِّقَاب (In *Zakah*) Slaves who are owned legally, according to the Islamic rules, and whose masters have agreed to give them their freedom after paying a certain amount of money.

* *ar-riya'* الرِّيَاء Insincerity; doing obedience for the sake of people or for this along with the intention to obey *Allah*.

* *ar-rukn* الرُّكْن Requisite; Integral; *fard*; an obligatory action, utterance, or intention which is a part of a worship, such as *Tawaf* in *Hajj*, and without which it would be invalid.

* **ar-ruku** الرُّكوع Bending one's back forward down enough so that the palms could reach the knees, without inexcusably bending the knees. Placing the hands on the knees is *sunnah*, i.e., optional and rewardable.

* **S س / S ص**

* **as-sa** الصَّاع A measure which comprises four *mudd*s. *Asu*ˆ is the plural of *sa*ˆ.

* **as-Safa** الصَّفا One of the two hills now annexed to *al-Masjid-ul-Haram* where *Hajj* (the pilgrim) performs *Sa*ˆy. It is the place where one begins *Sa*ˆy proceeding to *al-Marwah*. One goes from one hill to the other, seven times.

* **as-Sahih** الصَّحيح The True; the Valid; this is that which agrees with the rules of *Islam* and hence is accepted by *Allah*.

* **as-sajdah** السَّجْدَة *Sujud*; prostration; a requisite of *Salah* done by putting part of one's forehead, knees, toes, and hands on the ground.

* **as-Salah** الصَّلاة The Prayer: a series of sayings and actions usually commenced with saying *Allahu akbar* (*Allah* is the Greatest) and terminated with saying *as-salamu* ˆ*alaykum* (peace be upon you), with certain conditions to be satisfied.

* **as-salam** السَّلام Peace; saying «*as-salamu* ˆ*alaykum*», i.e., peace be upon you, said as a salutation. It is also the last requisite performed in *Salah*.

* **as-Sami** السَّميع A name of *Allah*, which means: 'the One Who hears what is hearable'.

* **as-Sawm** الصَّوْم *As-Siyam*; one of the greatest articles of *Islam*. It is (in general) fasting the month of *Ramadan*. *Siyam* or *Sawm* (Fasting) is abstaining from inserting any object with a volume from an open inlet, such as the mouth and the eliminatory outlets, into the head, intestines, etc. during the daytime having had at night the intention, in the heart, to fast the following day.

* **as-Sa**ˆ**y** السَّعْى Plying the distance between *as-Safa* and *al-Marwah*, seven times, starting at *as-Safa* and ending at *al-Marwah* during *Hajj* or ˆ*Umrah*.

* **as-siddiq** الصِّدّيق A very righteous Muslim, who believed in *Allah* and His messengers, such as the best companions of Prophet *Muhammad*, *sallallahu* ˆ*alayhi wa sallam*.

* **as-Siqt** السِّقْط A child born early before the completion of the months of pregnancy. If the *siqt* were born alive, such as it screamed at birth and died afterwards, then washing, shrouding, *Salat-ul-Janazah*, and burial would be obligatory to perform for it. However, if it were born dead and had the features of a human being, then only the washing, shrouding, and burial would be obligatory. It is *haram* to perform *Salat-ul-Janazah* for it. However, if the born *siqt* had no human features, then, although it is not obligatory to shroud or bury it, it is recommended to do so.

* **as-Sirat** الصِّراط Path; the Bridge extending over Hell which all people, on the Day of Judgement, will cross at different speeds. All non-Muslims and some Muslim sinners will slip off it into Hell.

* **as-siwak** السِّوَاك A stick or the like, used as a tooth cleaner. It is a very rewardable *sunnah* to use *siwak*. The best *siwak* is that which is obtained from the *Arak* tree.

* **as-Siyam** الصِّيَام See *as-Sawm*.

* **as-Subh** الصُّبْح *Al-Fajr*; the obligatory *Salah* the time of which starts after ˆIshaˆ time and continues until sunrise; the morning.

* **subhan** سُبْحان Praising *Allah*, such as in the statement 'subhanallah'; see *subhanahu*.

* **Subhanah(u)** سُبْحانَهُ This means that 'He (*Allah*) is clear of any imperfection', or it means 'praise to Him'. It is usually mentioned after the name of *Allah* and followed sometimes by the word 'taˆala' which means that 'He (*Allah*) is above any imperfection'.

* **as-sujud** السُّجُود Performing a *sajdah; sajdah*.

* **as-sukun** السُّكُون Literally 'no motion'. It is the opposite of *harakah*; it indicates the absence of a vowel such as the sound of the letter 's' in the word street or 'f' in the word fruit.

* **as-Sunnah** السُّنَّة In general, the word *Sunnah* refers to what was attributed to the Prophet, *sallallahu ˆalayhi wa sallam*, of sayings, deeds, attributes, and acknowledgements. The acknowledgements of the Prophet refer to the matters which occurred during his time that he was told about, or in his presence, but he did not prohibit; *al-Mandub; an-Nafl*.

* **Surah** سُورة A chapter of the *Qur'an*. The *Qur'an* has 114 *Surahs*. *Suwar* is the plural of *Surah*.

362

* **as-sutrah** السُّتْرَة An object placed in front of the person performing Salah, which is two-thirds of a cubit high and within three cubits from the person who is performing Salah.

* **SH** ش

* **Sha^ban** شَعْبَان The eighth month of the Islamic (lunar) year.

* **ash-Shafa^ah** الشَّفَاعَة The Intercession of the prophets, angels, martyrs, some devout scholars, and others on the Day of Judgement for some Muslims who committed enormous sins and died without repenting of them.

* **ash-Shahadah** الشَّهَادَة Martyrdom; dying while and as a result of fighting non-Muslims; the Shahadatayn, or one of them.

* **ash-Shahadatan** الشَّهَادَتَان The Two Professions or Testimonies; the greatest article of Islam; the creedal statement which means 'I profess that no one is God but Allah, and (I profess) that Muhammad is the Messenger of Allah'. Shahadatan is the nominative form of Shahadatayn and the dual form of Shahadah.

* **ash-shahid** الشَّهِيد Martyr; the Muslim who died while or as a result of fighting non-Muslims.

* **ash-Shar^** الشَّرْع The Religion of Islam; this term is used whenever rules are mentioned.

* **ash-Shari^ah** الشَّرِيعَة The Law of Islam, interchangeable with Shar^.

* **ash-Sharif** الشَّرِيف A Muslim descendent of Prophet Muhammad, sallallahu ^alayhi wa sallam.

* **ash-sharikah** الشَّرِكَة Partnership; a contract which ascertains the right of two or more persons to dispose of their merged monies.

* **Shawwal** شَوَّال The tenth month of the Islamic (lunar) year.

* **ash-Shaykh** الشَّيْخ The title of an Islamic teacher.

* **ash-Shuruq** الشُّرُوق Sunrise; the appearance of the upper part of the disc of the sun in the eastern horizon.

* **ash-shurut** الشُّرُوط Prerequisites; items that are not part of an act of worship, such as Taharah in Salah, but upon which, the validity of the worship is dependent. Shurut is the plural of shart.

* **T** ت / **T** ط

* **ta^ala** تَعَالَى It means that 'Allah is above any imperfection' (see subhanahu).

363

* **at-Tafsir** التَّفْسِير The Science of explaining the _Qur'an_.

* **at-Tahajjud** التَّهَجُّد The optional _Salah_ done after waking up at night. Its obligation upon Muslims was abolished in the _Qur'an_.

* **at-Taharah** الطَّهَارَة Doing what renders _Salah_ permissible. This includes the action of removing _najasah_ by, for instance, performing _Istinja'_, or lifting off _hadath_ by performing _Wudu'_, or _Ghusl_.

* **at-taharrum** التَّحَرُّم Starting _Salah_ usually by saying 'Allahu akbar'; see _al-'Ihram_.

* **at-tahir** الطَّاهِر Anything which is in the state of _Taharah_; clear of _hadath_ and _najasah_.

* **at-tahur** الطَّهُور See _mutahhir_.

* **at-takbirah** التَّكْبِيرَة The statement 'Allahu akbar'.

* **at-ta'min** التَّأْمِين Saying '_Amin_' after finishing the _Fatihah_ or saying a _du^a'_.

* **at-tamyiz** التَّمْيِيز The age at which a child is able to answer when asked and understand when addressed. Some scholars explained it as the ability of the child, if taught, to eat, drink, and perform _Istinja'_ independently.

* **at-Taqsir** التَّقْصِير Trimming the hair as a _rukn_ of _Hajj_ or _^Umrah_.

* **at-taqwa** التَّقْوَى Fearing _Allah_; obeying _Allah_ by performing the obligatory and refraining from the forbidden.

* **at-tashahhud** التَّشَهُّد A statement which must be said while in the last sitting of _Salah_ and includes the _Shahadatayn_, the creedal statement of _Islam_.

* **at-tashdidat** التَّشْدِيدَات Stresses, each of which, in Arabic, comprises two similar letters assimilated together. The first letter is unvoweled (has a _sukun_) and the second is voweled (has a _harakah_).

* **at-Tashriq** التَّشْرِيق It refers to the three days after _Ad-ha_ (the eleventh, twelfth, and thirteenth of _Dhul-Hijjah_).

* **at-Tawaf** الطَّوَاف Going, counterclockwise, around the _Ka^bah_ in the Holy Mosque of _Makkah_ during _Hajj_, _^Umrah_, or other occasions as well.

* **at-Tawrah** التَّوْرَاة The Revelation given to Prophet _Musa_ (Moses), _sallallahu ^alayhi wa sallam_. The so-called 'the Old Testament' and 'the Torah' are not the _Tawrah_.

* ***at-Tayammum*** التَّيَمُّم A substitute, under certain conditions, of *Wudu'* or *Ghusl* in which soil is used on the face, hands and forearms, including the elbows.

* ***at-ta`zir*** التَّعْزِير Disciplining; Punishment which is less than those for *zina*, killing, and the like. Examples are imprisonment and beating.

* ***at-tuhr*** الطُّهْر The time interval between two menstruating intervals. The minimum time of *tuhr* is fifteen days and there is no maximum time because, though rare, a woman may menstruate once in her lifetime.

* ***at-tuma'ninah*** الطُّمَأْنِينَة Having all the organs settled at once in *ruku^*, *i^tidal*, *sujud*, and the sitting between the two *sujud*s for as long as saying *'subhanallah'* takes.

* **TH** ث

* ***ath-Thawab*** الثَّوَاب The reward that Muslims will enjoy on the Day of Judgement.

* **U** أ **/ ^U** عُ

* ***al-'Ummah*** الأُمَّة Nation; it refers to the Muslim Nation; the *Ummah* of Prophet *Muhmmad* includes those who believed in him (Muslims) and those whom he was sent to, but did not believe in him and remained *kafir*, i.e., non-Muslim. The first group is called *Ummat-ul-'Ijabah* (the *Ummah* of acceptance) and the second *Ummat-ud-Da^wah* (the *Ummah* of Call).

* ***al-^Umrah*** العُمْرَة An act of worship which is done in *Makkah* at any time of the year. It is obligatory upon one once in a lifetime and is similar to *Hajj* in many ways.

* ***al-^uquq*** العُقُوق It includes any deed that harms one or both parents immensely.

* **W** و

* ***al-Wada^*** الوَدَاع Farewell; *Tawaf-ul-Wada^* is the last *Tawaf* to be performed before leaving *Makkah*.

* ***al-wadi^ah*** الوَدِيعَة Consignment; entrusting another with something to protect it.

* ***al-Wahid*** الوَاحِد A name of *Allah*, which means 'the One Who has no partners in His Godhood'.

* ***al-Wahy*** الوَحْى Revelation; information from *Allah* passed, through or without an angel, to whomever He chose from among His slaves for Prophethood.

* **al-wajib** الوَاجِب *Fard* (Obligatory); in the context of *Hajj*, it is an action the leaving out of which is *haram* but does not invalidate *Hajj*. However, a *fidyah* is due.

* **al-wakalah** الوَكالَة Proxy; authorizing a person to act for oneself with whatever is valid to deputize others.

* **al-waliyy** الوَلِّي Righteous Muslim; Muslim who performs the obligations, avoids the prohibitions, and performs a lot of *nafl*; guardian.

* **al-waqf** الوَقْف Property dedicated to be used in a specific manner, such as dedicating a building to be a mosque or dedicating some water for drinking only.

* **al-wasq** الوَسْق A dry volume measure, equivalent to sixty *sa*^s.

* **al-wird** الوِرْد Sayings or acts of worship, such as fasting Mondays and/or Thursdays, which are rewardable to do.

* **al-Wudu'** الوُضُوء Washing parts of the body as a prerequisite to several things, one of which is *Salah*.

* **al-Wuquf** الوُقُوف Standing or being present in the land of ^*Arafah*, during *Hajj*, for at least a moment between *Dhuhr* time of the ninth of *Dhul-Hijjah* and *Fajr* of the tenth of *Dhul-Hijjah*.

* **Y** ى

* **al-yamin** اليَمِين The right (side); oath.

* **Z** ز

* **az-Zakah** الزَّكاة In Arabic it means purification and edification; one of the greatest articles of *Islam*. Paying a certain portion of one's money or animals to specific types of people with certain conditions.

* **az-Zawal** الزَّوال The beginning of *Dhuhr* time; the time when the sun has declined westward from its *Istiwa'* (zenith) position.

* **az-zina** الزِّنى The sexual intercourse with a person of the opposite sex other than one's spouse or female slave. It includes both adultery and fornication.

Unit Conversion Factors

LENGTH

1 inch	= 3 barleycorns
1 palm	= 3 inches
1 hand	= 4 inches
1 span	= 9 inches
1 cubit	= 18 inches
1 pace	= 3 feet
1 digit	= 3/4 inch

dhira^	= 1 cubit
	≈ 46 centimeters*
	≈ (18 inches)
mil (Hashimiyy)	= 2000 dhira^s
	≈ 920 meters
	(≈ 1000 yards)
farsakh	= 3 mils
	= 6000 dhira^s
	≈ 2760 meters
	(≈ 3018 yards)
ghawth distance	≈ 300 dhira^s
	≈ 138 meters (≈ 543 feet)
qurb distance	≈ 1/2 farsakh = 1.5 mils
	= 3000 dhira^s
	≈ 1380 meters (≈ 5430 feet)
qasr distance	= 16 farsakhs = 48 mils
	≈ 44 kilometers
	(≈ 27 customary miles)

MASS (WEIGHT)

daniq	= 1/6 dirham
	≈ 0.5 grams of silver.
dinar	= 1 mithqal
	≈ 4.24 grams of gold
dirham	≈ 2.97 grams of silver.
mithqal	= 1 3/7 dirham
	≈ 4.24 grams of gold
Zakah Nisab	
gold	
	= 20 mithqals of gold
	≈ 84.875 grams
	≈ 3 oz (24 karats)
	≈ 97 grams (21 karats)
	≈ 113.17 grams
	(18 karats)
silver	
	= 200 dirhams of silver
	= 140 mithqals
	≈ 594.125 grams
	≈ 21 oz

VOLUME

mudd	= two hands of average size cupped together
sa^	= 4 mudds
gullatan	≈ 190 liters
wasq	= 60 sa^s

TIME

day	= Fajr to Maghrib (dawn to sunset)
night	= Maghrib to Fajr (sunset to dawn)
hawl	= 1 lunar year ≈ 354 days

*The sign ≈ means approximately equal.

Transliteration System

Français	English	بالعربية		Français	English	بالعربية
‘	‘	الهمزة (ء)		<u>T</u>	<u>T</u>	ط
B	B	ب		<u>Dh</u>	<u>Dh</u>	ظ
T	T	ت		^	^	ع
Th	Th	ث		Gh	Gh	غ
<u>J</u>	J	ج		F	F	ف
<u>H</u>	<u>H</u>	ح		<u>Q</u>	<u>Q</u>	ق
Kh	Kh	خ		K	K	ك
D	D	د		L	L	ل
Dh	Dh	ذ		M	M	م
R	R	ر		N	N	ن
Z	Z	ز		H	H	هـ
Ç ou S	S	س		W	W	و
Ch	Sh	ش		Y	Y	ى
<u>S</u>	<u>S</u>	ص		A	A	أَ
<u>D</u>	<u>D</u>	ض		<u>A</u>	<u>A</u>	اء

‘a’ après la lettre	‘a’ after the letter	الفتحة
‘ou’ après la lettre	‘u’ after the letter	الضمة
‘i’ après la lettre	‘i’ after the letter	الكسرة
‘<u>a</u>’ après la lettre	‘<u>a</u>’ after the letter	المد بالألف
‘<u>ou</u>’ après la lettre	‘<u>u</u>’ after the letter	المد بالواو
‘<u>i</u>’ après la lettre	‘<u>i</u>’ after the letter	المد بالياء
La lettre est doublé	The letter is doubled	الحرف المشدَّد